PRACTICE
MAKES
PERFECT

French Verb Tenses

Trudie Maria Booth

Mc
Graw
Hill

New York   Chicago   San Francisco   Lisbon   London   Madrid   Mexico City
Milan   New Delhi   San Juan   Seoul   Singapore   Sydney   Toronto

1 2 3 4 5 6 7 8 9 10 11 12 13 14 15 16 17 18 19 20   QPD/QPD   0 9 8 7

ISBN   978-0-07-147894-6
MHID   0-07-147894-9
Library of Congress Control Number: 2006931859

Interior design by Village Typographers, Inc.

McGraw-Hill books are available at special quantity discounts to use as premiums and sales promotions, or for use in corporate training programs. For more information, please write to the Director of Special Sales, Professional Publishing, McGraw-Hill, Two Penn Plaza, New York, NY 10121-2298. Or contact your local bookstore.

This book is printed on acid-free paper.

Contents

 THE PRESENT TENSE

II THE PAST TENSES

III THE FUTURE TENSES, THE CONDITIONAL, AND THE SUBJUNCTIVE

IV ▸ THE INFINITIVE, THE IMPERATIVE, THE PRESENT PARTICIPLE AND GERUND, AND THE PASSIVE VOICE

Introduction

The verb is the most important part of the sentence. It expresses an action or state of the subject and indicates the time and mood of an occurrence. In order to be able to communicate in a language, you must know how its verb tenses and moods are formed and how they are used.

Practice Makes Perfect: French Verb Tenses is a manual and workbook which offers the learner a clear and comprehensive explanation of the French verb system, as well as the opportunity to practice the newly acquired skills in numerous exercises that follow each section. Differences between French and English usage are pointed out throughout the book, and idiomatic expressions are presented where literal translations would be incorrect. The vocabulary in the examples and exercises is taken from current usage and is useful for daily communication. Vocabulary presentations make translations easier, and a glossary is provided so that the student can look up new words or words that he/she may have forgotten. Finally, an answer key allows the user to correct the completed work.

Many years of teaching experience at American universities have taught me where the difficulties of the French language lie for native English speakers when choosing a tense or mood, and when inserting a verb in the sentence. The choice of the correct past tense (imperfect or *passé composé*, for example) and the addition of direct and indirect objects can be quite a challenge for the student. *French Verb Tenses* is designed to help the learner overcome these difficulties and to master an important aspect of French grammar. The book can be used for additional practice in beginning, intermediate, and advanced language classes; it is ideal for self-study and review, and can also serve as a reliable reference tool for students and teachers of French.

All French grammar books have sections on verbs, but cannot devote as much space as necessary to this subject. Most French verb books on today's market focus on conjugations and give little, if any, information about the usage of verbs and idioms. What sets *French Verb Tenses* apart from other books on the same subject is its goal to offer not only a thorough description of all contemporary verb forms and moods, but also to show how they are used in a given context. Clear definitions of grammatical terms in the introduction and throughout the manual facilitate comprehension. In addition, cultural information about France has been included in the exercises so that the learner, while refining his/her written and oral communication skills, also gets an insight into aspects of French culture.

We hope that this book will help the student acquire a good understanding of the French verb system as well as enable him/her to use the structures presented with competence and confidence.

Useful grammatical terminology for verbs

Infinitive

The *infinitive* is the basic, unconjugated form of the verb. In English, all infinitives are preceded by *to*. In French, infinitives end in -**er, -ir,** or -**re** (**donn***er* [*to give*], **chois***ir* [*to choose*], **vend***re* [*to sell*]).

Subject

The *subject* of a sentence is the person or thing that performs the action. The subject determines the form of the verb: *I* go. *You* sing. *David* asks. *We* dance. *The students* work. The subject can be a noun (*David, the students*) or a pronoun (*I, you, he,* etc.)

Conjugation

When one lists the six existing verb forms in a particular tense by adapting the verb to each of the subject pronouns, one *conjugates* the verb. Contrary to English, most French verb forms change from one person to another during the conjugation.

Compare the following two present tense conjugations:

> French: **je parle, tu parles, il/elle/on parle, nous parlons, vous parlez, ils/elles parlent.** (Only two forms are alike.)

> English: *I speak, you speak, he/she/one speaks, we speak, you speak, they speak.* (All forms are the same except one.)

Stem

The *stem* is what is left of the verb after dropping the infinitive ending -**er, -ir,** or -**re**. Thus, the stem of **parler** is **parl**-, the stem of **réussir** is **réuss**- and the stem of **attendre** is **attend**-.

Verb ending

A verb *ending* is what is added to the stem during the conjugation. Regular -**er** verbs, for example, have the endings -**e, -es, -e, -ons, -ez, -ent** in the present indicative. The verb ending indicates the subject, tense, and mood, i.e., it shows who or what performs the action, when this action occurs, and how it is perceived.

Tense

The *tense* of a verb indicates when the action takes place, in the present, past, or future. The verb can be in a *simple tense,* which consists of one word only (such as the present tense), or in a *compound tense,* which consists of two words, the auxiliary and the past participle (such as the **passé composé**).

Mood

Grammatical *mood* means "manner." It shows how the speaker perceives what he or she is saying. There are four personal and two impersonal moods in French.

The indicative, subjunctive, imperative, and conditional are *personal* moods. The infinitive and the participle (present and past) are *impersonal* moods. Impersonal moods do not show who performs the action.

Elision

A vowel is *elided* when it is dropped and replaced by an apostrophe (**je danse**, but **j'adore**).

Subject pronouns

The following set of *subject pronouns* are used when conjugating a verb in French:

	SINGULAR		PLURAL	
first person	**je**	*I*	**nous**	*we*
second person	**tu**	*you*	**vous**	*you*
third person	**il**	*he, it*	**ils**	*they*
	elle	*she, it*	**elles**	*they*
	on	*one*		

The French subject pronouns differ from their English counterparts in the following way:

- ◆ There are two ways to say *you,* depending on whom one addresses (see Note).
- ◆ There are two ways to say *they,* due to gender (see Note).
- ◆ There is no specific word for *it.* French refers instead to a masculine thing with **il** (*he*), and to a feminine thing with **elle** (*she*).

Note: The **e** in **je** is elided (i.e., dropped) and **je** becomes **j'** before a verb that starts with a vowel or mute **h: j'aime, j'habite.**

The pronouns **il** and **elle** can be used for persons, animals, and things.

The pronoun **il** expresses

- ◆ *he* (replacing a masculine person)
- ◆ *it* (replacing a masculine thing—or an animal—and used as a subject in impersonal expressions)

The pronoun **elle** expresses

- ◆ *she* (replacing a feminine person)
- ◆ *it* (replacing a feminine thing or animal)

The indefinite pronoun **on** expresses *one, they, people.*

Comment dit-**on** « chair » en français?	*How does **one** say "chair" in French?*
On parle français en Belgique.	***People** (= They) speak French in Belgium.*

Note that in informal French, **on** is frequently used instead of **nous**.

On s'aime.   *We love each other.*

There are two ways to express *you* in French.

1. The pronoun **tu** is familiar singular and is used to address one person whom one would call by his/her first name in France, i.e., a family member, a good friend or colleague, a fellow student, or a child. **Tu** is also used when praying to God and when talking to a pet.

2. The pronoun **vous** is both singular and plural formal and addresses one adult or a number of adults whom one doesn't know very well (strangers, service personnel, professional contacts, acquaintances, etc.). It is also the plural of **tu**, i.e., used when speaking to more than one family member, close friend, fellow student, or child.

In the exercises in this book, *fam.* (= familiar) indicates that **tu** should be used, *pol.* (= polite) indicates that **vous** should be used to translate *you*.
There are two ways to express *they* in French.

1. The pronoun **ils** replaces masculine beings or things, or masculine *and* feminine beings or things combined.

2. The pronoun **elles** replaces feminine beings or things only.

Verb categories

- **Regular verbs.** The conjugation of these verbs follows a fixed pattern. Once you learn this pattern, you can conjugate each verb within one group (**-er**, **-ir**, or **-re** verbs). With regular verbs, the stem of the infinitive remains intact during the conjugation, and all verbs within one group have the same endings.
- **Irregular verbs.** The conjugation of each of these verbs does not follow a fixed pattern and therefore must be memorized.
- **Auxiliaries.** These verbs (**avoir** and **être** in French) are also called *helping verbs* because they help to build a compound tense.
- **Transitive verbs.** These are verbs which can take a (direct or indirect) object. An object is a person who (or a thing which) receives the action of the subject. In the sentence **je visite le musée** (*I visit the museum*), **le musée** is the object. The verb **visiter** is *transitive*.

  In dictionaries, transitive verbs are often indicated by the abbreviation *v.tr.* (**verbe transitif**). You will find a more detailed explanation of the different kinds of objects in the section *Verbs and their objects*, pages 25–32.
- **Intransitive verbs.** Intransitive verbs, such as **aller** (*to go*), **venir** (*to come*), and **rester** (*to stay*), cannot take an object. You cannot *go, come,* or *stay* "someone" or "something." In dictionaries, intransitive verbs are usually indicated by the abbreviation *v.i.* (**verbe intransitif**).
- **Reflexive verbs.** The infinitive of these verbs is preceded by the reflexive pronoun **se** (or **s'**). The verbs **se coucher** (*to go to bed*) and **s'amuser** (*to have a good time*) are reflexive verbs.
- **Impersonal verbs.** These are verbs which are only used in the third-person singular (= **il**) form. Many impersonal verbs describe the weather: *Il pleut.* (*It is raining.*)

A few remarks about French pronunciation

Beginning students of French usually have no difficulty writing the words they have learned, but find it hard to pronounce them. In French, numerous letters are silent and some represent sounds that do not exist in English. Depending on its environment within the word, one letter may have several different pronunciations, and one sound may have several different spellings. Although French uses the same alphabet as English, the rules of English pronunciation do not apply. The sounds that the letters of the alphabet produce in French are frequently quite different from those they produce in English.

To indicate how a letter or combination of letters is pronounced, the symbols of the International Phonetic Alphabet are often used, i.e., the letters are transcribed phonetically. Phonetic transcriptions are always placed in square brackets. The word **temps** for example is transcribed [tã], the word **homme** [ɔm]. Note that silent letters (**m, p, s** in the first example, **h** and **e** in the second example) do not appear in phonetic transcriptions.

There are thirty-six phonetic symbols that represent the thirty-six sounds of the French language. If you learn these extremely useful symbols, and if you know which sounds they describe, you will be able to understand the transcriptions given in this book, and look up the pronunciation of French words in many dictionaries.

Consonants

Most of the symbols representing the consonants and half-consonants (or semi-vowels) are derived from the Latin alphabet that we use to write French and English.

SYMBOL	FRENCH WORDS THAT CONTAIN THIS SOUND	ENGLISH WORDS THAT CONTAIN A SIMILAR SOUND
[b]	**barbe**	**boy**
[d]	ma**d**ame	**day**
[f]	**f**enêtre	**f**ox
[g]	**g**arçon	**g**arage
[k]	**c**œur (Contrary to English, the sound [k] is *never* aspirated, i.e., *never* articulated with air.)	s**k**i
[l]	**l**ivre (Contrary to English, [l] is always pronounced with the tongue pressing against the upper front teeth.)	**l**ate

(continued)

SYMBOL	FRENCH WORDS THAT CONTAIN THIS SOUND	ENGLISH WORDS THAT CONTAIN A SIMILAR SOUND
[m]	**m**onsieur	**m**an
[n]	ba**n**a**n**e	ba**n**a**n**a
[p]	**p**lage (Contrary to English, the sound [p] is never aspirated.)	s**p**ouse
[ʀ]	**r**ouge (Contrary to English the sound [ʀ] is produced between the back of the tongue and the upper part of the back of the mouth.)	no equivalent in English
[s]	mer**c**i	**s**un
[t]	**t**able (Contrary to English, the sound [t] is never aspirated.)	s**t**op
[v]	**v**oilà	**v**an
[j]	b**i**en	**y**es
[w]	**ou**i	**w**est
[z]	chai**s**e	**z**ebra

The following phonetic symbols are *not* taken from the Latin alphabet:

SYMBOL	FRENCH WORDS THAT CONTAIN THIS SOUND	ENGLISH WORDS THAT CONTAIN A SIMILAR SOUND
[ʃ]	**ch**ocolat	**sh**oe
[ʒ]	**j**eu	plea**s**ure
[ɲ]	monta**gn**e	o**ni**on
[ŋ]	smoki**ng**	smoki**ng**
[ɥ]	n**u**it	no equivalent in English

Vowels

Note that French vowel sounds are much tenser than the English ones.

SYMBOL	FRENCH WORDS THAT CONTAIN THIS SOUND	ENGLISH WORDS THAT CONTAIN A SIMILAR SOUND
[a]	**pa**pa	c**a**r
[e]	**é**t**é** (To produce the [e] sound, extend your lips as if you were smiling; no equivalent in English.)	
[ɛ]	tr**è**s (To produce the [ɛ] sound, open the jaw.)	b**a**d
[i]	m**i**di	f**i**t
[o]	styl**o**	no equivalent in English
[ɔ]	p**o**rte	n**o**t
[ø]	d**eu**x (To produce the [ø] sound, project your lips forward to form a circle.)	no equivalent in English
[œ]	b**eu**rre	f**u**r
[u]	v**ou**s	sh**oe**
[y]	s**u**r (To produce the [y] sound, place the tip of the tongue behind the lower front teeth and project	no equivalent in English

	your lips forward as far as possible as if to whistle.)
[ə]	je (The sound [ə] is similar to the [ø] sound, but weaker. The lips are projected less far forward; no equivalent in English.)

Nasal vowels

Note that these vowels are transcribed with a tilde [~] above them and that the sounds they represent resonate in the nose.

SYMBOL	FRENCH WORDS THAT CONTAIN THIS SOUND	ENGLISH WORDS THAT CONTAIN A SIMILAR SOUND
[ã]	comm**ent**	no equivalent in English
[ɛ̃]	v**in**	no equivalent in English
[ɔ̃]	b**on**	no equivalent in English
[œ̃]	l**un**di	no equivalent in English

Abbreviations

The following abbreviations are used in this book:

adj.	adjective
e.g.	for example
fam.	familiar (you [*fam.*] = **tu**)
f. or fem.	feminine
f.pl.	feminine plural
i.e.	that is, that is to say
inf.	infinitive
lit.	literally (indicating a literal translation of a French expression or sentence)
m. or masc.	masculine
m.pl.	masculine plural
p.	page
pl. or plur.	plural
pol.	polite (you [*pol.*] = **vous**)
qch	**quelque chose** (*something*)
qn	**quelqu'un** (*someone*)
sing.	singular
sb	somebody
sth	something

THE PRESENT TENSE

The present tense of regular verbs

In English as in French, the present tense is used to express what happens and what is true at the present time.

> He *lives* in Paris.
> I *like* chocolate.

Note, however, that whereas English has three present tense forms, the *simple present* (*she sings*), the *continuous present* (also called *present progressive*) which consists of the present tense of *to be* and the verb ending in *-ing* (she *is* sing*ing*), and the *emphatic present* (she does sing), French has only the *simple present* (**elle chante**) which translates all three English forms.

This chapter will treat the present tense in the indicative mood which states facts objectively.

There are three groups of regular verbs in French

◆ verbs ending in **-er**, for example **fumer** (*to smoke*)
◆ verbs ending in **-ir**, for example **finir** (*to finish*)
◆ verbs ending in **-re**, for example **entendre** (*to hear*)

The conjugation of regular *-er* verbs

Formation

The present tense of regular verbs ending in **-er** consists of the *stem* of the verb and certain *endings*. The stem of the verb (which is the same for all persons) is found by dropping the **-er** ending of the infinitive. The personal endings which are added to the stem of all regular **-er** verbs are: **-e, -es, -e, -ons, -ez, -ent**.

The following is the present tense conjugation of the verb **demander**. It can serve as a model for all regular **-er** ending verbs in the present tense.

demander *to ask*	
je demand**e**	*I ask, I am asking, I do ask*
tu demand**es**	*you (familiar singular) ask, you are asking, you do ask*
il demand**e**	*he asks, he is asking, he does ask*
elle demand**e**	*she asks, she is asking, she does ask*
on demand**e**	*one asks, one is asking, one does ask*
nous demand**ons**	*we ask, we are asking, we do ask*
vous demand**ez**	*you (formal singular and plural, familiar plural) ask, you are asking, you do ask*
ils demand**ent**	*they ask, they are asking, they do ask*
elles demand**ent**	*they ask, they are asking, they do ask*

Note:

- Since the verb endings of the first-, second-, and third-person singular, as well as of the third-person plural (**demande, demandes, demande, demandent**) are silent, these four verb forms are pronounced alike [dəmãd].
- Since the final -**s** in **ils** and **elles** is silent, **il demande** and **ils demandent** are pronounced alike [ildəmãd], and **elle demande** is pronounced the same way as **elles demandent** [ɛldəmãd].
- If however the verb begins with a vowel or a mute **h**, the final **s** of **ils** and **elles** is audible in the *liaison*, and the pronunciation of the third-person singular and plural is *not* identical. *Compare:*

  | il aime [ilɛm] *he/it likes* | → | ils aiment [ilzɛm] *they like* |
  | elle habite [ɛlabit] *she/it lives* | → | elles habitent [ɛlzabit] *they live* |

- If the stem of the verb ends in **r**, this **r** must of course be pronounced: j'entre, tu rencontres, il montre, elle rentre, etc.
- If the stem of the verb ends in a vowel, this vowel must be pronounced (except in verbs ending in -**guer**).

j'étudie [ʒetydi]	*I study*
tu oublies [tyudli]	*you forget*
il remercie [ilʀəmɛʀsi]	*he thanks*

- Remember that if the verb begins with a vowel or a mute **h**, the **e** of **je** is dropped.

  | j'adore | *I adore* |
  | j'hésite | *I hesitate* |

- Note also that the expression **tout le monde** (*everybody*) takes the third-person *singular* verb form.

  | Tout le monde **demande**. | *Everybody is asking.* |

Listed here are some commonly used regular -**er** verbs.

admirer *to admire*
adorer *to adore*
aider *to help*
aimer *to like, love*
apporter *to bring*
arriver *to arrive*
chanter *to sing*
chercher *to look for*
coûter *to cost*
danser *to dance*
déjeuner *to have/eat lunch*
demander (à) *to ask*
dépenser *to spend (money)*
détester *to detest, hate*
dîner *to have/eat dinner*
donner *to give*
écouter *to listen (to)*
embrasser *to hug, kiss*

enseigner *to teach*
entrer (dans) *to enter, come in*
étudier *to study*
fermer *to close*
fumer *to smoke*
gagner *to win, earn*
habiter *to live (reside)*
jouer *to play*
laver *to wash*
marcher *to walk*
monter *to go up*
montrer *to show*
oublier *to forget*
parler *to speak, talk*
passer *to go / pass / come by, spend (time), take (a test)*
penser *to think*
pleurer *to cry*
porter *to wear, carry*
quitter *to leave (a person or place)*
raconter *to tell (a story)*
regarder *to look at, watch*
remercier *to thank*
rencontrer *to meet*
rentrer *to return (home)*
rester *to stay*
retourner *to return*
sonner *to ring (bell, telephone, alarm clock, etc.)*
téléphoner (à) *to call on the telephone*
tomber *to fall*
tourner *to turn*
travailler *to work*
traverser *to cross*
trouver *to find*
visiter *to visit (places)*

EXERCICE

1·1

Complétez les phrases suivantes avec la forme correcte du verbe entre parenthèses. (Fill in the blanks with the correct form of the verb in parentheses.)

1. (habiter) Marie _____ à Cannes.

2. (travailler) Je _____ dans une usine.

3. (coûter) Le livre _____ vingt euros.

4. (jouer) Les enfants _____ dans le jardin.

5. (sonner) Le téléphone _____ souvent.

6. (écouter) Nous _____ la radio.

7. (tourner) Tu _____ à gauche.

8. (danser) Vous _____ très bien.

9. (adorer) Elle _____ le chocolat.

10. (aimer) Tout le monde _____ les vacances.

EXERCICE

1·2

Traduisez les mots entre parenthèses. (Translate the words in parentheses.)

1. (*We visit*) _____ la France.

2. (*She teaches*) _____ le latin.

3. (*You [pol.] sing*) _____ la chanson.

4. (*I think*) _____ que oui.

5. (*We go up*) _____ l'escalier.

6. (*We show*) _____ la photo.

7. (*He hugs*) _____ l'enfant.

8. (*They [masc.] find*) _____ la solution.

9. (*They [masc.] kiss*) _____ le bébé.

10. (*I fall*) _____ dans le piège.

11. (*He tells*) _____ une histoire (a story).

12. (*She watches*) _____ la télévision.

13. (*We eat dinner*) _____ à sept heures.

14. (*They [masc.] eat lunch*) _____ à midi.

15. (*He cries*) _____ tout le temps.

16. (*You [fam.] play*) _____ au tennis.

17. (*I stay*) _____ à la maison.

18. (*They [fem.] study*) _____ le français.

19. (*He lives*) _____ à Rouen.

20. (*You [fam.] close*) _____ la porte.

21. (*I forget*) _____ tout.

22. (*They [masc.] help*) _____ le vieil homme.

23. (*You [pol.] bring*) _____ une bouteille de vin.

24. (*You [fam.] give*) _____ de l'argent aux pauvres.

25. (*I like*) _____ les animaux.

26. (*They [masc.] win*) _____ le match.

27. (*We thank*) _____ nos parents.

28. (*They [masc.] cross*) _____ la rue.

29. (*She is wearing*) _____ une jolie robe blanche.

30. (*He works*) _____ dans un bureau.

Est-ce vrai ou faux? (Write V [*Vrai*] in the blank if the statement is true, write F [*Faux*] if it is false.)

_____ 1. Je chante mal.

_____ 2. J'étudie le français à l'université.

_____ 3. Ma mère joue du piano.

_____ 4. Je regarde la télévision chaque jour.

_____ 5. Mes amis aiment danser.

_____ 6. Je déjeune à midi.

_____ 7. Mon ami(e) porte souvent un jean.

_____ 8. J'habite à Paris.

_____ 9. Je danse très bien.

_____ 10. Je dépense beaucoup d'argent.

Remplissez les tirets avec la forme correcte des verbes suivants. (Fill in each blank with the correct form of a verb that fits best in the context. Use each verb from the following list only once.)

regarder, écouter, jouer, chanter, pleurer, danser, aimer, habiter, enseigner, parler

1. Nous _____ la télévision.

2. Les professeurs _____ .

3. À la discothèque, on _____ .

4. J'_____ les bonbons.

5. À l'opéra, on _____ .

6. Les bébés (*babies*) _____ souvent.

7. Vous _____ au golf.

8. Les Américains _____ anglais.

9. Tu _____ la radio.

10. David _____ à San Francisco.

The negative form

To make a statement negative, one places **ne** (**n'** before a vowel or mute **h**) before the verb and **pas** after it.

Je **ne** pense **pas**.	*I don't think (so).*
Il **ne** parle **pas** allemand.	*He doesn't speak German.*
Vous **n'**écoutez **pas**.	*You don't listen.*
Ils **n'**habitent **pas** aux États-Unis.	*They don't live in the United States.*

EXERCICE

1·5

Est-ce vrai (V) ou faux (F) (true or false)?

_____ 1. Le président français n'habite pas à New York.

_____ 2. Les Français n'aiment pas le vin.

_____ 3. Les Américains ne fument pas.

_____ 4. Tiger Woods ne joue pas au golf.

_____ 5. Céline Dion ne chante pas bien.

_____ 6. Les chômeurs (*The unemployed*) ne trouvent pas de travail.

_____ 7. L'équipe de basket-ball de ma ville ne gagne pas souvent.

_____ 8. Les étudiants ne restent pas à la maison tout le temps.

EXERCICE

1·6

Écrivez les phrases suivantes à la forme négative. (Make the following statements negative.)

1. Je tombe souvent malade. _____

2. J'aime les chats. _____

3. Il travaille dur. _____

4. Nous parlons chinois. _____

5. Les Français dînent à cinq heures. _____

6. Le livre coûte cher. _____

7. Vous habitez ici. _____

EXERCICE
1·7

Répondez négativement aux questions suivantes.

1. Vous détestez le lait? _____

2. Tu arrives demain? _____

3. Il admire son frère? _____

4. J'étudie trop? _____

5. Je parle mal? _____

The conjugation of -*er* verbs with spelling changes

There are a number of -**er** ending verbs that, although being otherwise regular, show slight spelling changes (which almost always affect the pronunciation) in some of their present tense forms. Whether these verbs add an **accent grave** (è), change an **accent aigu** (é) to an **accent grave**, double a consonant, or turn a **y** into an **i**, these changes always occur in all singular persons as well as in the third-person plural, i.e., in those persons where the verb ending is silent. The **nous** and **vous** forms, the endings of which are pronounced, will conserve the spelling of the infinitive, since its ending is audible as well.

And here is another way to remember where the spelling changes occur. If one conjugates these verbs by writing the singular (**je, tu, il**) forms in one column and the plural (**nous, vous, ils**) forms in another, and if one draws a line around the affected verb forms, one gets the shape of a boot. All forms inside the boot will show the change, **nous** and **vous** will not.

The verb **appeler** (*to call*) for example doubles its **l** inside the boot.

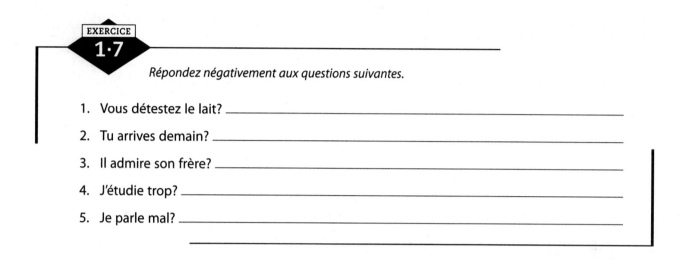

j'appelle	nous appelons
tu appelles	vous appelez
il/elle/on appelle	ils/elles appellent

The following spelling changes occur:

A. Verbs that have -**e**- in the next to last syllable of the infinitive.

1. Some of these verbs double the last consonant of the stem in all persons except **nous** and **vous**.

jeter *to throw*	
je jette [ʒəʒɛt]	nous jetons [nuʒətɔ̃]
tu jettes [tyʒɛt]	vous jetez [vuʒəte]
il/elle/on jette [ilʒɛt]	ils/elles jettent [ilʒɛt]

Other such verbs are:

appeler *to call*
épeler *to spell*
projeter *to plan*
rappeler *to call back, remind*

2. Some change the **e** into **è** in all persons except **nous** and **vous**.

acheter *to buy*

j'achète [ʒaʃɛt]   nous achetons [nuzaʃtɔ̃]
tu achètes [tyaʃɛt]   vous achetez [vuzaʃte]
il/elle/on achète [ilaʃɛt]   ils/elles achètent [ilzaʃɛt]

Other such verbs are:

achever *to finish (complete a task)*
amener *to bring (a person)*
élever *to raise, bring up (children)*
emmener *to take (a person)*
enlever *to take off, kidnap*
geler *to freeze*
lever *to lift, raise*
mener *to lead*
peser *to weigh*
promener *to take for a walk*

EXERCICE
1·8

Écrivez (Write) la forme correcte du verbe entre parenthèses.

1. (appeler) Ils _____ le médecin.

2. (promener) Elle _____ son chien.

3. (peser) Tu _____ soixante kilos.

4. (emmener) Nous _____ les enfants au cinéma.

5. (enlever) J' _____ mon manteau.

6. (épeler) Vous _____ votre nom.

7. (geler) On _____ ici.

8. (mener) Tous les chemins (*All roads*) _____ à Rome.

9. (acheter) Elles _____ un magnétoscope (*VCR*).

Traduisez (Translate) en français les mots entre parenthèses.

1. (*She buys*) _____ tout en solde (*on sale*).

2. (*They [fem.] throw*) _____ l'argent par la fenêtre.

3. (*We throw*) _____ les livres par terre.

4. (*I call*) _____ mes parents.

5. (*He brings*) _____ son frère.

6. (*We raise*) _____ trois enfants.

7. (*She raises*) _____ la main.

8. (*You [pol.] call back*) _____ ce soir.

B. Verbs that have an **é** in the next to last syllable of the infinitive change **é** to **è** in all persons except **nous** and **vous**.

espérer *to hope*	
j'espère [ʒɛspɛʀ]	nous espérons [nuzɛspeʀɔ̃]
tu espères [tyɛspɛʀ]	vous espérez [vuzɛspere]
il/elle/on espère [ilɛspɛʀ]	ils/elles espèrent [ilzɛspɛʀ]

Other such verbs are:

céder *to yield*
célébrer *to celebrate*
considérer *to consider*
exagérer *to exaggerate*
posséder *to own*
préférer *to prefer*
protéger *to protect*
répéter *to repeat*

Écrivez la forme correcte du verbe entre parenthèses.

1. (protéger) Ils _____ la nature.

2. (exagérer) Vous _____ tout le temps!

3. (considérer) Je _____ cette possibilité.

4. (céder) Elle _____ rarement.

5. (préférer) Nous _____ attendre.

6. (répéter) Tout le monde _____ la question.

Traduisez (Translate) en français les mots entre parenthèses.

1. (*I hope*) _____ bien.

2. (*You [fam.] prefer*) _____ le chocolat noir.

3. (*They [masc.] don't repeat*) _____ la phrase.

4. (*We celebrate*) _____ une grande victoire.

5. (*He owns*) _____ un restaurant.

6. (*She exaggerates*) _____ toujours.

C. Verbs ending in -**yer**

1. Verbs ending in -**ayer** *can* change the **y** into an **i** in all persons except **nous** and **vous**. They can also keep the **y** throughout the conjugation.

payer *to pay (for)*	
je paie (je paye)	nous payons
tu paies (tu payes)	vous payez
il/elle/on paie (il paye)	ils/elles paient (ils payent)

Other such verbs are:

balayer *to sweep*
essayer *to try, try on*

2. Verbs ending in -**oyer** or in -**uyer** *must* change the **y** into an **i** in all persons except **nous** and **vous**.

nettoyer *to clean*	
je nettoie	nous nettoyons
tu nettoies	vous nettoyez
il/elle/on nettoie	ils/elles nettoient

ennuyer *to bore, bother, annoy*	
j'ennuie	nous ennuyons
tu ennuies	vous ennuyez
il/elle/on ennuie	ils/elles ennuient

Other such verbs are:

appuyer *to press, lean*
employer *to use, employ*
envoyer *to send*
essuyer *to wipe*

D. Verbs ending in **-ger** and **-cer** show spelling changes only in the **nous** form for phonetic reasons.

1. Verbs ending in **-ger** add **e** after the letter **g** in the **nous** form of the present tense in order to make the *g* sound [ʒ] and thereby conserve the [ʒ] sound of the infinitive throughout the conjugation. Without the inserted **e**, the letter **g** would be pronounced [g] since **g** followed by a "dark" vowel (**a**, **o**, **u**) = [g].

manger *to eat*	
je mange	nous mangeons [numãʒɔ̃]
tu manges	vous mangez
il/elle/on mange	ils/elles mangent

Other such verbs are:

changer *to change*
corriger *to correct*
déranger *to disturb, bother*
engager *to hire*
envisager *to plan*
exiger *to demand*
interroger *to interrogate*
mélanger *to mix*
nager *to swim*
obliger *to oblige, force*
partager *to share*
plonger *to dive*
protéger *to protect*
ranger *to tidy up, put away*
télécharger *to download*
voyager *to travel*

2. Verbs ending in **-cer** add a **cédille** to the **c** in the **nous** form of the present tense in order to make the **c** sound [s] and thereby conserve the [s] sound of the infinitive throughout the conjugation. Without the **cédille**, the **c** would be pronounced [k] since **c** followed by a "dark" vowel (**a**, **o**, **u**) = [k].

commencer *to begin, start*	
je commence	nous commençons [nukɔmãsɔ̃]
tu commences	vous commencez
il/elle/on commence	ils/elles commencent

Other such verbs are:

annoncer *to announce*
effacer *to erase*
forcer *to force*
menacer *to threaten*
placer *to place, put*
prononcer *to pronounce*

Écrivez la forme correcte du verbe entre parenthèses.

1. (payer) Elle _____ la facture.

2. (essayer) Nous _____ les vêtements.

3. (appuyer) J' _____ sur le bouton.

4. (envoyer) Ils _____ un courriel.

5. (ranger) Nous _____ nos affaires.

6. (effacer) Nous _____ le tableau.

7. (télécharger) Nous _____ des jeux.

8. (employer) Il _____ la force.

Traduisez en français les mots entre parenthèses.

1. (*We pronounce*) _____ les mots correctement.

2. (*We share*) _____ une chambre.

3. (*He travels*) _____ en Italie.

4. (*We are eating*) _____ des cuisses de grenouille (*frogs' legs*).

5. (*Vegetarians* [**Les végétariens**] *don't eat*) _____ de viande.

6. (*I try*) _____ de faire de mon mieux.

7. (*She sends*) _____ un cadeau à son petit ami.

8. (*We send*) _____ une carte postale.

9. (*You [fam.] clean*) _____ la maison.

10. (*We begin*) _____ le travail.

11. (*We swim*) _____ dans la piscine.

12. (*We don't disturb*) _____ nos voisins.

13. (*They [masc.] sweep*) _____ le garage.

14. (*You [pol.] download*) _____ des logiciels gratuits.

15. (*I pay*) _____ en espèces (*cash*).

The conjugation of regular -ir verbs
Formation

The present tense of regular verbs ending in -ir consists of the *stem* of the verb and the following *endings*: -is, -is, -it, -issons, -issez, -issent. Here is a model conjugation:

finir *to finish*	
je finis	nous finissons
tu finis	vous finissez
il/elle/on finit	ils/elles finissent

Other such verbs are:

applaudir *to applaud*
bâtir *to build*
choisir *to choose*
(dés)obéir (à) *to (dis)obey*
grandir *to grow up*
grossir *to get fat, put on weight*
guérir *to heal, cure, get well*
maigrir *to lose weight*
punir *to punish*
ralentir *to slow down*
rougir *to blush, turn red*
réfléchir (à) *to think, reflect (on)*
remplir *to fill, fill in*
réussir (à) *to succeed, be successful*
vieillir *to grow old*

EXERCICE
1·14

Écrivez la forme correcte du verbe entre parenthèses.

1. (remplir) Vous _____ le verre.

2. (réussir) Tu _____ à l'examen.

3. (choisir) Je _____ un bon dessert.

4. (guérir) Le médecin _____ le malade.

5. (rougir) Nous _____ quelquefois.

6. (obéir) Ils _____ à leurs parents.

7. (vieillir) Tout le monde _____.

8. (grossir) Ils _____ toujours pendant les vacances.

Traduisez en français les mots entre parenthèses.

1. (*We choose*) _____ la meilleure solution.

2. (*They [masc.] grow up*) _____ vite.

3. (*One doesn't put on weight*) _____ quand on mange des légumes.

4. (*They [masc.] reflect*) _____ avant de prendre une décision.

5. (*We applaud*) _____ le gagnant.

6. (*You [pol.] build*) _____ des châteaux en Espagne.

7. (*She doesn't punish*) _____ l'enfant.

8. (*I blush*) _____ rarement.

9. (*You [fam.] slow down*) _____ au carrefour.

10. (*She doesn't lose weight*) _____ facilement.

The conjugation of regular *-re* verbs

Formation

The present tense of regular verbs ending in **-re** consists of the *stem* of the verb and the following *endings*: **-s, -s, —** (no ending), **-ons, -ez, -ent**. Here is a model conjugation:

attendre to wait (for)	
j'attend**s**	nous attend**ons**
tu attend**s**	vous attend**ez**
il/elle/on attend	ils/elles attend**ent**

Other such verbs are:

descendre *to go down*
entendre *to hear*
perdre *to lose*
rendre *to give back*
répondre [à] *to answer*
vendre *to sell*

Note:

◆ The verbs **rompre** (*to break*) and **interrompre** (*to interrupt*) add **-t** to the third person singular: il romp**t**, il interromp**t**.
◆ The verb **rendre** is used in the expression **rendre visite à** (*to visit [a person]*).
◆ If the verb **rendre** is used with an adjective, it means *to make* (*sb angry, sad, etc.*).

Il **rend** sa femme **heureuse**.   *He makes his wife happy.*
Elle **rend** son père fou.   *She drives her father crazy. (lit.: She makes her father crazy.)*

EXERCICE

1·16

Écrivez la forme correcte du verbe entre parenthèses.

1. (descendre) Je _____ l'escalier.

2. (interrompre) Il _____ la réunion.

3. (entendre) Nous _____ un bruit.

4. (rendre) Tu _____ les livres.

5. (perdre) On _____ son argent à Las Vegas.

6. (vendre) Ils _____ leur voiture.

7. (rendre) Ça (*That*) _____ les gens tristes.

EXERCICE

1·17

Traduisez en français les mots entre parenthèses.

1. (*We don't sell*) _____ les meubles.

2. (*I give back*) _____ l'argent.

3. (*You [pol.] go down*) _____ à la cave.

4. (*She loses*) _____ la tête (*her mind*).

5. (*You [fam.] hear*) _____ mal.

6. (*I am not waiting*) _____ patiemment.

7. (*He doesn't answer*) _____ correctement.

8. (*They [masc.] lose*) _____ toujours leurs clés.

9. (*We visit*) _____ nos parents.

EXERCICE

1·18

Est-ce vrai (V) ou faux (F)?

_____ 1. J'achète tous mes vêtements en solde (*on sale*).

_____ 2. De nos jours (*Nowadays*), beaucoup de gens tombent malade du SIDA (*AIDS*).

The present tense of regular verbs   **17**

_____ 3. En France, on dîne plus tôt (*earlier*) qu'aux États-Unis.

_____ 4. Les Français célèbrent leur fête nationale le 14 juillet.

_____ 5. Je nettoie ma chambre tous les matins (*every morning*).

_____ 6. Mes parents possèdent un hôtel.

_____ 7. Je pèse soixante kilos (≈ *130 pounds*).

_____ 8. Je perds mes cheveux.

_____ 9. Les médecins guérissent les malades.

_____ 10. Dans un ascenseur en France, on appuie sur le bouton 0 (ou RC) pour arriver au rez-de-chaussée.

EXERCICE 1·19

Traduisez en français.

My aunt Élodie lives in Lyon. She works in a middle school where she teaches Spanish. She doesn't earn a lot of money but she likes her job a lot. Every morning, she leaves the house early, and she arrives at school at seven-thirty. She goes up to the second floor where her students are waiting. While she speaks, the students listen. Sometimes, they sing a song that (**que**) their teacher chooses. Élodie's classes finish at three P.M. Usually, she stays at school 'til four o'clock and helps the students. Some of them think that she gives too much homework. When she hears the bell, Élodie closes her office door and goes home.

Élodie's husband, Marc, works in the shoe department of a department store which (**qui**) employs more than five hundred people. He always wears a suit and a tie. His customers try on sandals, boots, tennis shoes, and flip-flops, but they don't buy anything if they don't find the color and the style which (**qu'**) they are looking for. Occasionally, Marc loses patience. Nevertheless, he sells at least one hundred pairs of shoes every day.

VOCABULAIRE			
at least	**au moins**	to leave	**quitter**
bell	**la cloche**	middle school	**le collège**
boots	**des bottes** *(f.pl.)*	nevertheless	**néanmoins**
customer	**le client, la cliente**	occasionally	**de temps en temps**
department (*of a store*)	**le rayon**	a pair	**une paire**
		sandals	**des sandales** *(f.pl.)*
department store	**le grand magasin**	the second floor	**le premier étage**
early	**de bonne heure**	some of them	**certains d'entre eux**
every morning	**tous les matins**	teacher	**la maîtresse**
flip-flops	**des tongs** [tɔ̃g] *(f.pl.)*	tennis shoes	**des tennis** *(f.pl.)*
her office door	**la porte de son bureau**	till	**jusqu'à**
		too much	**trop (de)**
job	**le travail**	while	**pendant que**

_____

_____

_____

_____

_____

_____

_____

_____

_____

_____

Asking questions

In French as in English, there are two types of questions.

1. Questions that expect *yes* (**oui**) or *no* (**non**) for an answer.

2. Questions that ask for specific information.

Note that whereas English uses a form of *to do* to form most questions, **faire** (*to do*) is not used in French to ask a question.

Questions asking for a *yes* or *no* answer

There are three ways to form this type of question in French.

1. By placing **est-ce que** (**est-ce qu'** before a vowel sound) at the beginning of the declarative sentence without changing its word order. **Est-ce que** is invariable. A question formed with **est-ce que** can be used both in formal and informal style, in speaking as well as in writing.

Est-ce que je parle trop vite?	*Do I speak too fast?*
Est-ce que tu fumes?	*Do you smoke?*
Est-ce qu'elle travaille?	*Does she work? Is she working?*
Est-ce que l'étudiant répond?	*Does the student answer?*

2. By using *inversion*. Questions using inversion generally belong to the formal use of the language. There are two types of inversion depending on whether the subject of the sentence is a noun or a personal pronoun.

  1. Simple inversion. *Simple inversion* is used when the subject is a *personal pronoun*. The pronoun (except **je** which is used in an inverted question only with a few irregular verbs) is placed after the verb and linked to it by a hyphen.

Travailles-tu?	*Do you work? Are you working?*
Écoutent-ils? [ekutətil]	*Do they listen? Are they listening?*
Parlez-vous français?	*Do you speak French?*
Finit-il la leçon? [finitil]	*Does he finish the lesson?*

  When the third person singular (**il, elle, on**) verb form ends in a *vowel*, the letter **t** must be inserted surrounded by two hyphens between the verb and the pronoun. This is the case with all regular -**er** ending verbs.

The present tense of regular verbs **19**

Habite-**t**-il en France?	*Does he live in France?*
Dépense-**t**-elle beaucoup d'argent?	*Does she spend a lot of money?*
Parle-**t**-on français ici?	*Does one speak French here? (Is French spoken here?)*

2. Complex inversion. When the subject is a *noun*, simply inverting subject and verb is not possible in French. In this case, *complex inversion* is used. The noun is placed at the beginning of the sentence, followed by the verb and the corresponding subject pronoun (i.e., **il** for any masculine singular noun, **elle** for every feminine singular noun, etc.). There is a hyphen (or a hyphen+ **t** + hyphen if the verb ends in a vowel) between the verb and the subject pronoun. Questions using complex inversion are used in formal written French.

Marie étudie-t-**elle** le français?	*Does Marie study French?*
Les étudiants travaillent-**ils**?	*Do the students work?*
[tʀavajtil]	

3. By *intonation* (i.e., by raising the pitch of one's voice at the end of a statement). This type of question is of course restricted to the spoken language. It is very common on an informal level.

Tu aimes le français?	*Do you like French?*
Vous trouvez?	*Do you think so?*

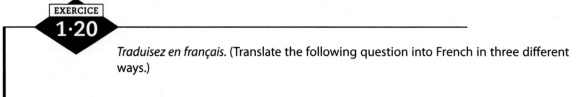

EXERCICE 1·20

Traduisez en français. (Translate the following question into French in three different ways.)

Do you (*fam.*) like hamburgers (**les hamburgers**)?

_____

_____

_____

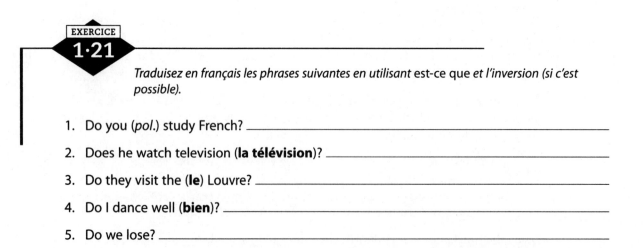

EXERCICE 1·21

Traduisez en français les phrases suivantes en utilisant est-ce que *et* l'inversion *(si c'est possible).*

1. Do you (*pol.*) study French? _____

2. Does he watch television (**la télévision**)? _____

3. Do they visit the (**le**) Louvre? _____

4. Do I dance well (**bien**)? _____

5. Do we lose? _____

6. Do you (*fam.*) live in Mexico (**au Mexique**)? _____

7. Do I eat too much (**trop**)? _____

8. Are you (*fam.*) staying at home (**à la maison**)? _____

9. Does the teacher earn a lot of money? _____

10. Do the volunteers (**les bénévoles [m.pl.]**) help? _____

Note: If the question expects an answer that confirms what has been asked, **n'est-ce pas** (which is invariable) can be added at the end of the declarative statement without changing its word order. Depending on the sentence, **n'est-ce pas** has various equivalents in English: *right?, isn't it?, doesn't he?, haven't you?, don't you?, do you?,* etc.

Tu enseignes l'anglais, **n'est-ce pas?**   *You teach English, don't you?*

David n'aime pas la pizza, **n'est-ce pas?**   *David doesn't like pizza, right?*

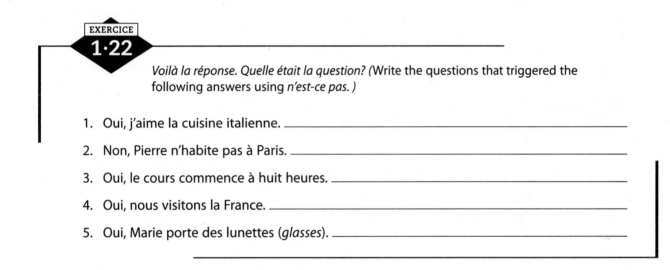

EXERCICE
1·22

Voilà la réponse. Quelle était la question? (Write the questions that triggered the following answers using n'est-ce pas.)

1. Oui, j'aime la cuisine italienne. _____

2. Non, Pierre n'habite pas à Paris. _____

3. Oui, le cours commence à huit heures. _____

4. Oui, nous visitons la France. _____

5. Oui, Marie porte des lunettes (*glasses*). _____

Questions asking for specific information

Such questions begin with interrogative expressions (interrogative adverbs, interrogative pronouns, or interrogative adjectives).

A. Interrogative adverbs

où	*where*
quand	*when*
comment	*how*
combien (de)*	*how much, how many*
pourquoi	*why*

*Note that the noun following **combien** is always preceded by **de**. If **combien** is not followed by a noun, **de** is not used.

Combien dépenses-tu?   *How much do you spend?*

Combien d'argent dépenses-tu?   *How much money do you spend?*

1. If the subject is a *pronoun*, the interrogative adverbs are followed either (except with **je**) by *simple inversion* (= verb + hyphen + pronoun) or by **est-ce que** and regular word order.

> **Où** habites-tu?   *Where do you live?*
> (or: **Où** *est-ce que* tu habites?)
> **Quand** arrivons-nous?   *When do we arrive?*
> (or: **Quand** *est-ce que* nous arrivons?)
> **Comment** trouvez-vous le vin français?   *How do you like French wine?*
> (or: **Comment** *est-ce que* vous trouvez le vin français?)
> **Combien de** langues parle-t-il?   *How many languages does he speak?*
> (or: **Combien de** langues *est-ce qu*'il parle?)
> **Pourquoi** détestez-vous les chats?   *Why do you hate cats?*
> (or: **Pourquoi** *est-ce que* vous détestez les chats?)

2. If the subject is a *noun*, the interrogative adverbs are followed either by *complex inversion* (= noun + verb + corresponding pronoun) or by **est-ce que** and regular word order.

> **Quand** *est-ce que* le professeur arrive   *When does the teacher arrive at school?*
>   à l'école?
> (or: **Quand** le professeur **arrive-t-il** à l'école?)

Note: After **où, comment, quand,** and **combien** simple inversion can be used with a noun subject in short sentences consisting only of a question word, a verb (in a simple tense) and a subject (which comes at the end of the question).

> **Où travaille** votre père?   *Where does your father work?*
> **Quand commence** le film?   *When does the movie start?*
> **Combien coûte** le CD?   *How much does the CD cost?*

But: After **pourquoi,** simple inversion is *never* used if the subject is a noun.

> **Pourquoi** votre mère **travaille-t-elle**?   *Why does your mother work?*
> (or: **Pourquoi est-ce que** votre mère travaille?)

EXERCICE
1·23

*Traduisez en français les phrases suivantes. (Use both *est-ce que* and inversion [if possible] with each question.)*

1. Where do you (*fam.*) work? _____

2. When do we return? _____

3. How does he travel? _____

4. How many houses do they (*masc.*) own? _____

5. Why do you (*pol.*) ask? _____

6. Where does your sister (**votre sœur**) live? _____

7. When do I arrive? _____

8. Why is the boy (**le garçon**) crying? _____

B. Interrogative pronouns

qui (subject or object of the sentence)   *who(m)*
que (**qu'** before vowel) (object of the sentence)   *what*
(or: **qu'est-ce que** [**qu'est-ce qu'** before a vowel sound])
quoi (used after a preposition such as **de, à, avec**, etc.)   *what*

Qui étudie le français?   *Who studies French?*
Qui invitez-vous?   *Whom do you invite?*
Que pensez-vous?   *What do you think?*
(or: **Qu'est-ce que** vous pensez?)
De quoi parlez-vous?   *What are you talking about?*
                                              (lit.: Of what do you speak?)

EXERCICE
1·24

Traduisez en français les phrases suivantes.

1. What do they (masc.) buy? _____

2. What does he study? _____

3. What do we like? _____

4. Who succeeds? _____

5. Who(m) do you (*fam.*) love? _____

6. What are you (*pol.*) waiting for? _____

7. What are you looking (*pol.*) for? _____

8. What are you (*fam.*) talking about? _____

C. The interrogative adjective *quel*

The interrogative adjective **quel** (*which, what*) precedes the noun with which it agrees in gender and number. Its four forms are:

	SINGULAR	PLURAL
masculine	**quel**	**quels**
feminine	**quelle**	**quelles**

Quel(le)(s) is used to express *what* (instead of **que** or **qu'est-ce que**) when a noun (or a form of the verb **être** [*to be*] + *noun*) follows immediately. The verb **être** is irregular and will be presented later on. Its third-person singular form is **est** (*is*); its third-person plural form is **sont** (*are*).

Quel sport pratiques-tu?   *What sport do you play?*
Dans **quel pays** habite-t-elle?   *In what country does she live?*
À **quelle heure** déjeunez-vous?   *At what time do you eat lunch?*
Quelles lunettes achètes-tu?   *Which (eye)glasses do you buy?*
Quels ciseaux utilisez-vous?   *Which scissors do you use?*
Quel est votre nom?   *What is your name?*

Quelle est la différence entre *bon* et *bien*?	***What*** *is the difference between "bon" and "bien"?*
Quelle est votre nationalité?	***What*** *is your nationality?*
Quelles sont vos coordonnées?	***What*** *is your address and phone number?*

EXERCICE
1·25

Traduisez en français les phrases suivantes.

1. Which newspapers do they sell? _____

2. At what time do you (*fam.*) eat dinner? _____

3. In which city do you (*fam.*) live? _____

4. What is your (*votre*) phone number (**numéro [m.] de téléphone**)? _____

   _____

5. Which dessert do you (*pol.*) choose? _____

6. What is the date of your (*ton*) birthday? _____

7. What are your (*vos*) favorite leisure time activities (**loisirs [m.pl.]**)? _____

   _____

8. What is your (*votre*) size (**taille [f.]**)? _____

EXERCICE
1·26

Répondez aux questions avec des phrases complètes.

Exemple: Question: Aimez-vous le vin?

Réponse: *Non, je n'aime pas le vin.* or: *Oui, j'aime le vin.*

1. Habitez-vous à Paris? _____

2. Qu'est-ce que vous cherchez? _____

3. Parlez-vous italien? _____

4. Est-ce que vous réussissez toujours aux examens? _____

5. À quelle heure déjeunez-vous en général (*usually*)? (à midi? à une heure?) ____

6. Quand est-ce que vous dînez d'habitude? (à six heures?) _____

7. Qu'est-ce que vous étudiez? _____

8. Mangez-vous beaucoup? _____

9. Qui attendez-vous? _____

10. Pourquoi étudiez-vous le français? _____

Voilà la réponse. Quelle était la question? (What was the question that triggered the following answers? Ask about the highlighted words using interrogative expressions.)

Exemple: Réponse: J'achète **deux livres**.

Question: Combien de livres achètes-tu?

1. J'habite **à Paris**. _____

2. J'attends **mon ami**. _____

3. Elle voyage **en avion** (*by plane*). _____

4. J'étudie le français **parce que j'aime le français**. _____

5. Nous détestons **la pluie** (*the rain*). _____

6. Je suis **américain(e)**. _____

7. Ils dînent **à sept heures**. _____

8. La voiture coûte **vingt mille dollars**. _____

9. Il invite **trois personnes**. _____

10. Elle arrive **demain**. _____

Verbs and their objects

An *object* is a noun or pronoun towards which the action of the subject is directed. In the sentence, "*Peter closes the door*," for example, *Peter* is the subject and *the door* is the object.

There are three kinds of objects: direct objects, indirect objects, and objects of a preposition. In French, a *direct noun object* follows the verb without the presence of a preposition; an *indirect noun object* is always preceded by **à** (*to*); and a *noun object of a preposition* is separated from the verb by a preposition other than **à**, such as **de** (*of*), **pour** (*for*), **avec** (*with*), **dans** (*in*), etc.

- In the sentence **j'aime ma mère** (*I like/love my mother*), **ma mère** is a direct object because it is not preceded by a preposition.
- In the sentence **je parle *à* ma mère** (*I speak **to** my mother*), **ma mère** is an indirect object because it is separated from the verb by **à**.
- In the sentence **j'habite *avec* ma mère** (*I live **with** my mother*), **ma mère** is the object of the preposition **avec**.

Most French verbs add on an object in the same manner as their English equivalents, that is, when English doesn't use a preposition, French doesn't either: **il oublie le livre** (*he forgets the book*), **j'entends la musique** (*I hear the music*). When English requires a certain preposition, French often uses the corresponding one, for example, **j'envoie la lettre *à* mon fils** (*I send the letter **to** my son*), **il travaille *pour* son père** (*he works **for** his father*). There are however some French verbs which add on an object differently from English and therefore require special attention. We will review the most important ones.

A. Verbs taking a direct object in French, but a preposition (*for, at, to*) in English

attendre qn/qch *to wait for sb/sth*
chercher qn/qch *to look for sb/sth*
écouter qn/qch *to listen to sb/sth*
payer qch *to pay for sth*
regarder qn/qch *to look at sb/sth*

Elle **attend** votre réponse.	*She is waiting for your answer.*
Je **cherche** mes clés.	*I am looking for my keys.*
Nous **écoutons** le CD.	*We listen to the CD.*
Tu **paies** les billets.	*You pay for the tickets.*
Ils **regardent** le tableau.	*They look at the painting.*

EXERCICE
1·28

Traduisez en français.

1. We look at the pictures. _____

2. They (*masc.*) listen to the radio. _____

3. I pay for the meal. _____

4. He is waiting for the bus. _____

5. She is looking for her (*son*) dog. _____

6. You (*pol.*) pay for the drinks. _____

Note: If the object of these verbs is a pronoun (*him, her, them,* etc.) rather than a noun (*the bus, the radio,* etc.), direct object pronouns are used, preceding the verb.

Here are the forms of the direct object pronouns before a word beginning with a consonant and before a word beginning with a vowel sound: **me/m'** (*me*), **te/t'** (*you*), **le/l'** (*him, it*), **la/l'** (*her, it*), **nous** (*us*), **vous** (*you*), **les** (*them*).

Note that the direct object pronoun comes *before* the verb in French, while in English, it follows.

Cherches-tu le savon? —Oui, je **le** cherche.
Are you looking for the soap? —Yes, I am looking for it.
Attendez-vous le plombier? —Non, je ne **l'**attends pas.
Are you waiting for the plumber? —No, I am not waiting for him.

B. Verbs taking an indirect object in French, but a direct object in English

assister à qch *to attend sth (an event, lecture, etc.)*
demander à qn *to ask sb*
obéir à qn/qch *to obey sb/sth*
répondre à qn/qch *to answer sb/sth*
rendre visite à qn *to visit sb*
ressembler à qn/qch *to resemble sb/sth*
réussir à (un examen) *to pass (an exam)*
téléphoner à qn *to call sb (on the phone)*

Note: When the preposition **à** is followed by the masculine singular definite article **le** (*the*), it contracts to **au**; if it is followed by the plural definite article **les** (*the*), it contracts to **aux**. The singular articles **la** and **l'** (used before a noun starting with a vowel or mute **h**) do not contract with the preposition **à**.

J'assiste **au** concert.	*I attend the concert.*
Nous demandons **au** professeur.	*We ask the teacher.*
Ils obéissent **aux** lois.	*They obey the laws.*
Réponds-tu **à** la question?	*Do you answer the question?*
Est-ce que vous rendez visite **à** votre sœur?	*Do you visit your sister?*
Il ressemble **à** sa mère.	*He resembles his mother.*
Elle téléphone **à** l'homme.	*She calls the man.*
Soixante-quinze pour cent des élèves français réussissent au bac*.	*Seventy-five percent of French students pass the baccalaureate exam.*

C. The verb **entrer.** Whereas *to enter* takes a direct object in English (*He enters the building.*), **entrer** requires the preposition **dans** (*in*) before the object.

J'entre **dans** la classe.	*I enter the classroom.*

EXERCICE
1·29

Traduisez en français.

1. Do you (*fam.*) obey your father? _____

2. The children obey the parents. _____

3. We answer the letter. _____

4. He answers Marie. _____

5. We ask the boy. _____

6. She calls her (**son**) boyfriend. _____

7. They enter the house. _____

8. I visit my (**ma**) aunt. _____

9. She resembles her (*son*) brother. _____

10. We attend the wedding. _____

11. They (*masc.*) always pass the exam. _____

Note: If the object of the verbs taking **à** before a noun is a pronoun, the *indirect object pronouns* are used. Here are their forms before a word beginning with a consonant, and before a word beginning with a vowel: **me/m'** (*to me*), **te/t'** (*to you*), **lui** (*to him*), **lui** (*to her*), **nous** (*to us*), **vous** (*to you*), **leur** (*to them*).

Like the direct object pronouns, the indirect object pronouns are placed before the verb in French.

*The **baccalauréat** exam (also called **le bac**) is an exam French students must pass at the end of high school in order to be able to go to college.

Téléphones-tu **au** médecin? —Oui, je **lui** téléphone.
Do you call (Are you calling) the doctor? —Yes, I call (I'm calling) him/her.
Demandez-vous **aux** enfants? —Non, je ne **leur** demande pas.
Do you ask the children? —No, I don't ask them.

D. **Jouer à** and **jouer de**

When a *game* or *sport* is played, the verb **jouer** is followed by the preposition **à**. Here are some games and sports one can play:

jouer au billard *to play billiards, pool*
jouer au bridge *to play bridge*
jouer au poker *to play poker*
jouer aux cartes *to play cards*
jouer aux dames *to play checkers*
jouer aux échecs *to play chess*
jouer à un jeu *to play a game*
jouer au base-ball *to play baseball*
jouer au basket-ball *to play basketball*
jouer au football *to play soccer*
jouer au football américain *to play football*
jouer au golf *to play golf*
jouer au hockey *to play hockey*
jouer au tennis *to play tennis*
jouer au volley-ball *to play volleyball*

EXERCICE
1·30

Traduisez en français les phrases suivantes.

1. Denise plays cards. _____

2. They (*masc.*) don't play chess. _____

3. We play pool. _____

4. Do you (*fam.*) play golf? _____

5. Do you (*pol.*) play volleyball? _____

6. They are playing a game. _____

7. The children are playing soccer. _____

8. Our team plays basketball very well. _____

À quoi jouent les personnes suivantes?

Exemple: Pélé *Il joue au football.*

1. Tiger Woods _____

2. David Beckham et Zinédine Zidane _____

3. Babe Ruth _____

4. Michael Jordan _____

5. Bobby Fisher et Boris Spasky _____

6. Chris Evert et Andre Agassi _____

7. Joe Namath _____

When a *musical instrument* is played, the verb **jouer** is followed by the preposition **de**.

When the preposition **de** is followed by the masculine singular definite article **le** (*the*), it contracts to **du**. The singular articles **la** and **l'** (used before a noun starting with a vowel or mute **h**) do not contract with the preposition **de**.

Here are some instruments one can play:

jouer de la batterie *to play drums*
jouer de l'accordéon *to play the accordion*
jouer de la flûte *to play the flute*
jouer de la guitare *to play the guitar*
jouer de la harpe *to play the harp*
jouer de la trompette *to play the trumpet*
jouer de l'orgue *to play the organ*
jouer du piano *to play the piano*
jouer du violon *to play the violin*

Comment dit-on en français?

1. Who plays the guitar? _____

2. My brother plays the piano and the flute. _____

3. Do you (*fam.*) play the violin? _____

4. I don't play the trumpet. _____

5. Antoine plays the organ. _____

6. They [*masc.*] don't play the harp. _____

Formez des phrases avec les éléments donnés. Ajoutez (Add) une préposition si c'est nécessaire.

Exemple: les étudiants / obéir / le professeur

*Les étudiants obéissent **au** professeur.*

1. les étudiants / demander / les professeurs _____

2. Anne / répondre / le téléphone _____

3. nous / attendre / le train _____

4. je / écouter / la musique _____

5. David / téléphoner / ses copains _____

6. vous / entrer / la chambre _____

7. tu / jouer / le piano _____

8. Sébastien / jouer / le tennis _____

9. les enfants / chercher / les jouets _____

E. **Manquer** and **manquer à** (to miss)

The verb **manquer** takes a direct object (like its English equivalent) when one misses something by not arriving on time or by not being present.

Mon frère **manque** souvent la classe.	*My brother often misses class.*
Je **manque** quelquefois l'avion.	*I sometimes miss the plane.*

The verb **manquer** takes an *indirect* object when the absence of someone or something is regretted. If the object is a noun, it is preceded by **à**, if it is a pronoun, one of the *indirect object pronouns* is used. Remember that these pronouns precede the verb.

   To translate sentences with *to miss* in this context correctly, one must know that while in English one says "somebody misses someone or something," in French, one says "someone or something *lacks **to*** somebody."

My parents miss me.	Je manque **à** mes parents. (*literally: I lack to my parents.*)
They miss me.	Je **leur** manque. (*literally: I lack to them.*)

Note that the object of the English sentence (*me* in the English examples above) becomes the subject of the French sentence (**je**), and the subject of the English sentence (*my parents* and *they* in the examples above) becomes the *indirect* object (**à mes parents** and **leur**) of the French sentence.

He misses the children.	Les enfants **lui** manquent.
I miss him.	Il **me** manque.
He misses me.	Je **lui** manque.
I miss you a lot.	Tu **me** manques beaucoup.
They miss us.	Nous **leur** manquons.

We miss them.   Ils **nous** manquent.
*Do **you** miss France?*   Est-ce que la France **te** (**vous**) manque?
*Do **you** miss me?*   Est-ce que je **te** (**vous**) manque?
He doesn't miss us.   Nous ne **lui** manquons pas.

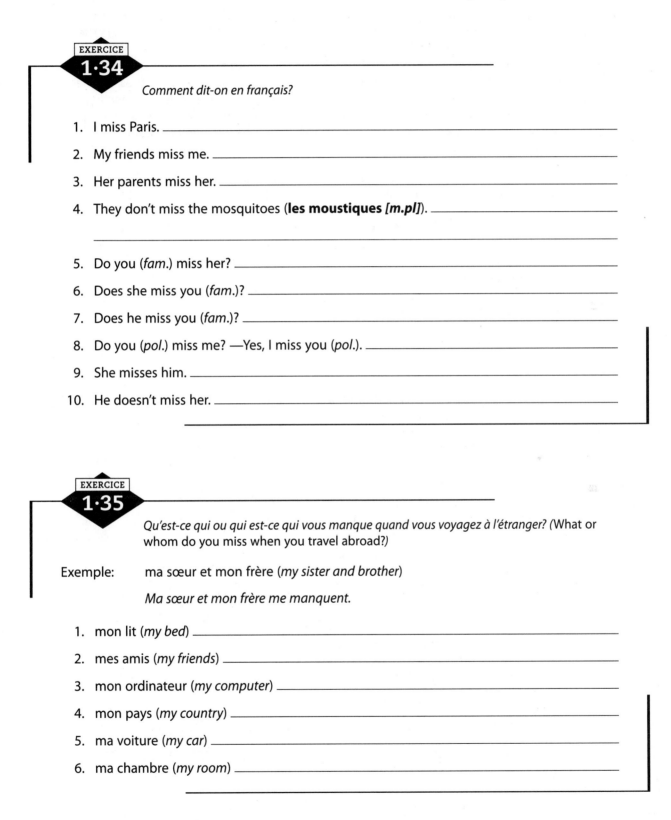

Comment dit-on en français?

1. I miss Paris. _____

2. My friends miss me. _____

3. Her parents miss her. _____

4. They don't miss the mosquitoes (**les moustiques [m.pl]**). _____

_____

5. Do you (*fam.*) miss her? _____

6. Does she miss you (*fam.*)? _____

7. Does he miss you (*fam.*)? _____

8. Do you (*pol.*) miss me? —Yes, I miss you (*pol.*). _____

9. She misses him. _____

10. He doesn't miss her. _____

Qu'est-ce qui ou qui est-ce qui vous manque quand vous voyagez à l'étranger? (What or whom do you miss when you travel abroad?)

Exemple: ma sœur et mon frère (*my sister and brother*)

Ma sœur et mon frère me manquent.

1. mon lit (*my bed*) _____

2. mes amis (*my friends*) _____

3. mon ordinateur (*my computer*) _____

4. mon pays (*my country*) _____

5. ma voiture (*my car*) _____

6. ma chambre (*my room*) _____

The present tense of regular verbs   **31**

Traduisez en français.

Anne, Mary, Bill, and Tom study French at a private high school in Oregon. They adore that language and they never miss class. Every day, their French teacher, Miss Dutronc, enters the building at eight o'clock sharp. While she is waiting for the elevator, she is looking for her office key. Sometimes, she calls her parents in Belgium. She misses them a lot. Luckily, her father pays for these calls, because they are expensive. Miss Dutronc's students always obey their teacher and most of the time, they answer her questions correctly. They often ask Miss Dutronc to play the piano, and they listen attentively to the music. Once a month, they look at slides that (**que**) their teacher brings to class. On Fridays, in order to reward her (*ses*) students, Miss Dutronc plays games with them (**eux**).

VOCABULAIRE			
to be expensive	**coûter cher**	most of the time	**la plupart du temps**
building	**le bâtiment**	never	**ne... jamais**
(phone) call	**l'appel (téléphonique) (*m.*)**	once a month	**une fois par mois**
		private	**privé(e)**
every day	**chaque jour, tous les jours**	to reward	**récompenser**
		(at eight o'clock)	**(à huit heures)**
high school	**le lycée**	sharp	**précises**
in order to	**pour**	slide (*photo*)	**la diapositive**
language	**la langue**		

The present tense of irregular verbs

The conjugation of irregular verbs

The following is a list of the most commonly used irregular verbs and their present tense conjugations. You will have to memorize them.

aller *to go*

je vais	nous allons
tu vas	vous allez
il/elle/on va	ils/elles **vont**

avoir *to have*

j'ai	nous avons
tu as	vous avez
il/elle/on a	ils/elles **ont**

battre *to beat*

je bats	nous battons
tu bats	vous battez
il/elle/on bat	ils/elles battent

boire *to drink*

je bois	nous buvons
tu bois	vous buvez
il/elle/on boit	ils/elles boivent

conduire *to drive*

je conduis	nous conduisons
tu conduis	vous conduisez
il/elle/on conduit	ils/elles conduisent

Construire (*to build*), **détruire** (*to destroy*), **produire** (*to produce*), and **traduire** (*to translate*) are conjugated like **conduire**.

connaître *to know*

je connais	nous connaissons
tu connais	vous connaissez
il/elle/on connaît	ils/elles connaissent

Apparaître (*to appear*), **disparaître** (*to disappear*), **paraître** (*to seem*), and **reconnaître** (*to recognize*) are conjugated like **connaître**.

courir *to run*	
je cours	nous courons
tu cours	vous courez
il/elle/on court	ils/elles courent

craindre *to fear*	
je crains	nous craignons
tu crains	vous craignez
il/elle/on craint	ils/elles craignent

Contraindre (*to compel, force*), **éteindre** (*to extinguish, turn off*), **feindre** (*to pretend*), **peindre** (*to paint*), **plaindre** (*to pity, feel sorry for*), and **rejoindre** (*to join*) are conjugated like **craindre**.

croire *to believe*	
je crois	nous croyons
tu crois	vous croyez
il/elle/on croit	ils/elles croient

devoir *to have to, to owe*	
je dois	nous devons
tu dois	vous devez
il/elle/on doit	ils/elles doivent

dire *to say, tell*	
je dis	nous disons
tu dis	vous **dites**
il/elle/on dit	ils/elles disent

EXERCICE
2·1

Traduisez en français les mots entre parenthèses.

1. (*I go*) _____ aux toilettes.

2. (*They [masc.] go*) _____ à la plage.

3. (*They [masc.] have*) _____ des animaux domestiques (*pets*).

4. (*She goes*) _____ à l'hôpital.

5. (*I have*) _____ les yeux marron.

6. (*We have*) _____ des cartes de crédit.

7. (*We are going*) _____ au zoo.

8. (*He has*) _____ les cheveux roux.

9. (*We're drinking*) _____ de la bière.

10. (*Do you [fam.] drink*) _____ du thé?

11. (*They [masc.] don't drink*) _____ de café.

12. (*Do I drive*) _____ bien?

13. (*He drives*) _____ lentement.

14. (*I know*) _____ cette ville.

15. (*They [masc.] know*) _____ mon père.

16. (*Does he run*) _____ vite?

17. (*We must*) _____ travailler.

18. (*They fear*) _____ la solitude.

19. (*I fear*) _____ le pire (*the worst*).

20. (*Do you [fam.] believe*) _____ cette histoire?

EXERCICE

2·2

Répondez en français aux questions suivantes.

1. Allez-vous souvent au cinéma? _____

2. Qu'est-ce que vous buvez au petit déjeuner? (du café? du jus d'orange? du chocolat chaud? du thé?) _____

3. Courez-vous vite? _____

4. Dites-vous toujours la vérité? _____

5. Croyez-vous aux horoscopes? _____

6. Connaissez-vous Paris? _____

7. Qu'est-ce que tu dois faire (*do*) aujourd'hui? _____

8. Conduis-tu prudemment (*carefully*)? _____

9. Éteignez-vous la lumière quand vous quittez la chambre? _____

10. Avez-vous des* frères et sœurs? (*brothers and sisters?*) _____

---

*Note that the indefinite articles **un**, **une**, and **des** become **de** in a *negative* sentence (except after **être**):

As-tu **une** voiture?	Do you have a car?
—Oui, j'ai **une** voiture	—Yes, I have a car.
—Non, je n'ai pas **de** voiture.	—No, I don't have a car.

The definite articles (**le, la, l', les**) do *not* change in a negative sentence.

Aimes-tu **les** chats?	Do you like cats?
—Oui, j'aime **les** chats.	—Yes, I like cats.
—Non, je n'aime pas **les** chats.	—No, I don't like cats.

dormir *to sleep*

je dors	nous dormons
tu dors	vous dormez
il/elle/on dort	ils/elles dorment

Mentir (*to tell a lie*), **partir** (*to leave*), **sentir** (*to feel, smell*), **servir** (*to serve*), and **sortir** (*to go out*) are conjugated like **dormir**.

écrire *to write*

j'écris	nous écrivons
tu écris	vous écrivez
il/elle/on écrit	ils/elles écrivent

Décrire (*to describe*) is conjugated like **écrire**.

être *to be*

je suis	nous sommes
tu es	vous **êtes**
il/elle/on est	ils/elles **sont**

faire *to do, make*

je fais	nous faisons
tu fais	vous **faites**
il/elle/on fait	ils/elles **font**

falloir *to be necessary*

il faut

lire *to read*

je lis	nous lisons
tu lis	vous lisez
il/elle/on lit	ils/elles lisent

mettre *to put, put on*

je mets	nous mettons
tu mets	vous mettez
il/elle/on met	ils/elles mettent

Admettre (*to admit*), **permettre** (*to allow*), and **promettre** (*to promise*) are conjugated like **mettre**.

mourir *to die*

je meurs	nous mourons
tu meurs	vous mourez
il/elle/on meurt	ils/elles meurent

ouvrir *to open*

j'ouvre	nous ouvrons
tu ouvres	vous ouvrez
il/elle/on ouvre	ils/elles ouvrent

Couvrir (*to cover*), **découvrir** (*to discover*), **offrir** (*to offer*), and **souffrir** (*to suffer*) are conjugated like **ouvrir**.

plaire to *please*	
je plais	nous plaisons
tu plais	vous plaisez
il/elle/on plaît	ils/elles plaisent

pleuvoir to *rain*	
il pleut	

Note that **pleuvoir** and **falloir** are impersonal verbs, i.e., they only exist in the third-person singular (= **il**) form.

pouvoir to *be able to, can*	
je peux (puis)	nous pouvons
tu peux	vous pouvez
il/elle/on peut	ils/elles peuvent

Note that **pouvoir** has two forms in the first-person singular. The form **puis** (and *not* **peux**) is used in the inverted question form (**Puis-je?**).

Puis-je aller aux toilettes?	*Can I / May I go to the bathroom?*
Que **puis-je** pour vous?	*What can I do for you?*

prendre to *take*	
je prends	nous prenons
tu prends	vous prenez
il/elle/on prend	ils/elles prennent

Apprendre (*to learn*), **comprendre** (*to understand*), and **surprendre** (*to surprise*) are conjugated like **prendre**.

EXERCICE
2·3

Traduisez en français les mots entre parenthèses.

1. (*She is sleeping*) _____ sur le canapé.

2. (*They [masc.] sleep*) _____ bien.

3. (*We go out*) _____ souvent.

4. (*I am leaving*) _____ ce soir (*tonight*).

5. (*They [fem.] don't leave*) _____ avant demain.

6. (*That [**Ça**] smells*) _____ bon.

7. (*I am writing*) _____ une lettre.

8. (*They [masc.] write*) _____ un poème.

9. (*Are you [pol.]*) _____ fatigué?

10. (*I am*) _____ malade.

11. (*He is*) _____ pressé (*in a hurry*).

12. (*They [masc.] are*) _____ tristes.

13. (*I make*) _____ beaucoup de fautes.

14. (*Does he make*) _____ son lit?

15. (*We make*) _____ un gâteau.

16. (*They [fem.] do*) _____ leurs devoirs.

17. (*What are you [pol.] doing*) _____ cet après-midi?

18. (*I read*) _____ une revue.

19. (*We read*) _____ le journal.

20. (*They [masc.] don't understand*) _____ le jeu.

21. (*She puts*) _____ le vase sur la table.

22. (*I am dying*) _____ de faim.

23. (*Do you [fam.] promise*) _____ de le faire?

24. (*They [fem.] put on*) _____ des gants.

25. (*I open*) _____ la fenêtre.

26. (*Do you [pol.] take*) _____ des photos?

27. (*It is raining*) _____ à seaux (*buckets*).

28. (*They [masc.] cannot*) _____ attendre.

29. (*Can you [pol.]*) _____ rester jusqu'à demain?

30. (*Can I*) _____ vous poser une question?

Répondez aux questions suivantes avec des phrases complètes.

1. Dormez-vous bien ou mal? _____

2. Écris-tu beaucoup de courriels (*e-mails*) à tes amis? _____

3. Êtes-vous optimiste ou pessimiste? _____

4. Qu'est-ce que vous faites en ce moment? _____

5. Combien de livres lisez-vous par an (*per year*)? _____

6. Mettez-vous un pull-over en hiver (*in winter*)? _____

7. Quelle langue étrangère apprenez-vous? _____

8. À quelle heure est-ce que les magasins ouvrent? _____

9. Pleut-il souvent dans la région où vous habitez? _____

10. Pouvez-vous sortir ce soir? _____

recevoir to receive	
je reçois	nous recevons
tu reçois	vous recevez
il/elle/on reçoit	ils/elles reçoivent

Apercevoir (*to perceive, see*) and **décevoir** (*to disappoint*) are conjugated like **recevoir**.

rire to laugh	
je ris	nous rions
tu ris	vous riez
il/elle/on rit	ils/elles rient

Sourire (*to smile*) is conjugated like **rire**.

savoir to know	
je sais	nous savons
tu sais	vous savez
il/elle/on sait	ils/elles savent

suivre to follow, take (a class)	
je suis	nous suivons
tu suis	vous suivez
il/elle/on suit	ils/elles suivent

tenir to hold	
je tiens	nous tenons
tu tiens	vous tenez
il/elle/on tient	ils/elles tiennent

Appartenir (*to belong*) and **obtenir** (*to get, obtain*) are conjugated like **tenir**.

valoir to be worth, cost	
je vaux	nous valons
tu vaux	vous valez
il/elle/on vaut	ils/elles valent

venir to come	
je viens	nous venons
tu viens	vous venez
il/elle/on vient	ils/elles viennent

Devenir (*to become*), **intervenir** (*to intervene*), **parvenir** (*to succeed*), **prévenir** (*to warn, inform*), and **revenir** (*to come back*) are conjugated like **venir**.

vivre to live	
je vis	nous vivons
tu vis	vous vivez
il/elle/on vit	ils/elles vivent

Survivre (*to survive*) is conjugated like **vivre**.

voir to see	
je vois	nous voyons
tu vois	vous voyez
il/elle/on voit	ils/elles voient

Prévoir (*to foresee, anticipate*), **revoir** (*to see again*) are conjugated like **voir**.

vouloir to want	
je veux	nous voulons
tu veux	vous voulez
il/elle/on veut	ils/elles veulent

Note:

◆ The first-person plural of irregular verbs ends in **-ons** except: **nous** *sommes*.
◆ The second-person plural ends in **-ez** except: **vous** *dites*, **vous** *êtes*, **vous** *faites*.
◆ The third-person plural ends in **-ent** except: **ils/elles** *font*, **ils/elles** *ont*, **ils/elles** *sont*, **ils/elles** *vont*.
◆ Verbs which end in a vowel in the third-person singular add **-t-** before the pronoun in the inverted question form.

A-**t**-il une voiture?	*Does he have a car?*
Va-**t**-elle à l'église?	*Does she go to church?*

EXERCICE
2·5

Traduisez en français les mots entre parenthèses.

1. (*I receive*) _____ une lettre.

2. (*Do you [pol.] receive*) _____ un cadeau?

3. (*We don't laugh*) _____ assez (*enough*).

4. (*Why do you [pol.] laugh*) _____ tout le temps?

5. (*She doesn't know*) _____ son adresse.

6. (*Do you [pol.] know*) _____ la réponse?

7. (*They [masc.] follow*) _____ son conseil.

8. (*The house is worth*) _____ un million d'euros.

9. (*I come*) _____ de Paris.

10. (*Do they come*) _____ du Maroc?

11. (*She lives*) _____ au-dessus de ses moyens (*above her means*).

12. (*People live*) _____ de plus en plus vieux.

13. (*What do you [fam.] want*) _____ boire.

14. (*Do you [pol.] see*) _____ les étoiles?

15. (*One sees*) _____ avec les yeux.

EXERCICE
2·6

Est-ce vrai ou faux?

_____ 1. Je reçois beaucoup de e-mails.

_____ 2. Je ris rarement.

_____ 3. Mon ami(e) ne sait pas où j'habite.

_____ 4. Mon livre de français vaut quarante dollars.

_____ 5. Je viens de New York.

_____ 6. Je vis aux États-Unis.

_____ 7. Les femmes vivent plus longtemps que les hommes.

_____ 8. Je vois mes amis tous les jours (*every day*).

_____ 9. Je suis un cours de français.

_____ 10. Je suis souvent malade.

EXERCICE
2·7

Remplissez les tirets (Fill in the blanks) avec la forme correcte du verbe entre parenthèses.

1. (aller) Nous _____ à la maison.

2. (avoir) Nous _____ faim.

3. (aller) Ils _____ à l'aéroport.

4. (boire) Il _____ du vin.

5. (conduire) Les Français _____ bien.

6. (courir) Je _____ cinq kilomètres tous les matins (*every morning*).

7. (connaître) Elle _____ bien cette ville.

8. (croire) Nous _____ aux miracles.

9. (croire) Ils _____ en Dieu.

10. (devoir) Vous _____ partir maintenant.

11. (dire) On _____ « A vos (tes) souhaits » quand quelqu'un éternue.

12. (dire) Qu'est-ce que vous _____?

13. (dormir) Frère Jacques, _____-vous?

14. (partir) Quand _____-tu?

15. (voir) Elles ne _____ rien.

16. (voir) Qu'est-ce que vous _____?

17. (voir) Nous _____ un arc-en-ciel (*a rainbow*).

18. (venir) Elle _____ des États-Unis.

19. (venir) D'où _____-vous?

20. (écrire) Vous _____ un poème.

21. (être) Nous _____ heureux.

22. (être) Vous _____ chanceux.

23. (être) Ils _____ en retard.

24. (faire) Il _____ ses études à Paris.

25. (faire) Mes amis _____ des progrès.

26. (faire) Qu'est-ce que vous _____ dans la vie?

27. (falloir) Il _____ agir vite.

28. (lire) _____ tu un roman policier (*detective novel*)?

29. (mettre) Je _____ les achats dans un chariot (*shopping cart*).

30. (permettre) Vous _____? (*May I?*)

31. (ouvrir) La bibliothèque _____ à dix heures.

32. (offrir) J'_____ un bouquet de fleurs à ma mère.

33. (pouvoir) _____-je vous être utile? (*May I help you?*)

34. (pouvoir) Ils _____ vous aider.

35. (pouvoir) _____-vous me dire où est la gare?

36. (pouvoir) On _____ toujours espérer.

37. (pouvoir) Si tu as beaucoup de contraventions, tu _____ dire « au revoir » à ton permis de conduire (*you can kiss your driver's license good-bye*).

38. (prendre) Je _____ une douche.

39. (prendre) Nous _____ un taxi.

40. (prendre) Les Parisiens _____ le métro pour aller au travail.

41. (recevoir) Elles _____ un colis.

42. (recevoir) Elle _____ beaucoup de cadeaux à Noël.

43. (rire) _____-tu quelquefois?

44. (valoir) Cette ville _____ bien une visite.

45. (valoir) Vous le _____ bien! (*You are worth it!*)

46. (vouloir) Nous _____ rester ici.

47. (vouloir) Il _____ rendre le monde meilleur.

48. (savoir) Ils _____ son nom.

49. (savoir) Je _____ que je peux faire beaucoup mieux.

50. (pleuvoir) Il _____ à verse.

51. (vivre) Je _____ seul(e).

52. (vivre) Vous _____ en Suisse, n'est-ce pas?

Traduisez en français.

Today is Wednesday and I have a day off. The children don't go to school either. They are delighted because they can do what (**ce que**) they want. Usually on Wednesdays, we sleep until ten o'clock. Then we eat breakfast. We eat waffles or toast with butter and jam, and we drink hot chocolate or coffee with milk. Later, we often go to the museum or to the library. Sometimes, we go for a walk in the forest. There, we see squirrels, bears, does, and pretty butterflies. Occasionally, my nephews come with us. Our favorite place is a small picturesque lake surrounded by high mountains. One can take a boat and fish for trout. If one has a good catch, one is, as the saying goes, "happy as a fish in the water." When we come back in the evening, we are tired. I say "good night" to my sons because I have to be at the office at eight A.M. on Thursdays.

VOCABULAIRE			
as the saying goes	**comme le dit le dicton**	in the evening	**le soir**
		lake	**le lac**
bear	**l'ours** *(m.)*	later	**plus tard**
(small) boat	**la barque**	mountain	**la montagne**
butterfly	**le papillon**	not either	**ne... pas non plus**
coffee with milk	**du café au lait**	on Wednesdays	**le mercredi**
a day off	**un jour de congé**	picturesque	**pittoresque**
doe	**la biche**	squirrel	**l'écureuil** *(m.)*
favorite	**préféré(e)**	surrounded by	**entouré(e) de**
to fish	**pêcher**	then	**ensuite**
to go for a walk	**faire une promenade**	toast	**du pain grillé**
a good catch (*fish*)	**une belle pêche**	trout	**la truite**
good night	**bonne nuit**	until	**jusqu'à**
high	**haut(e)**	waffle(s)	**la gaufre (des gaufres)**
hot chocolate	**du chocolat chaud**		

The uses of the present tense

As in English, the present tense is used in the following cases:

1. to express actions or situations occurring at the time of speaking. It is often accompanied by adverbs of time such as **aujourd'hui** (*today*), **actuellement** (*presently, at the present time*), **à présent** (*presently*), **maintenant** (*now*), **en ce moment** (*at the moment*), etc.

Qu'est-ce que vous **faites** en ce moment?	*What are you doing* at the moment?*
J'**écris** une lettre.	*I am writing a letter.**

   *Remember that French does not have a present progressive form (as English does with the -*ing* form). The simple present is used instead.

   Vous faites means both *you do* and *you are doing*. **J'écris** expresses both *I write* and *I am writing*, etc.

   To emphasize that an action is in progress, French uses the expression **être en train de** (+ *infinitive*) *to be in the process of (doing sth)*.

   Je **suis en train de** réviser pour l'examen.   *I am (in the process of) reviewing for the exam.*

   To emphasize the momentary aspect of an action, French uses the expression **être sur le point de** (+ *infinitive*) *to be about to (do sth)*.

   Il **est sur le point de** partir.   *He is about to leave.*

EXERCICE
2·9

Comment dit-on en français?

1. Is he coming? _____

2. She is reading a novel. _____

3. Now I understand. _____

4. At the present time (**Actuellement**), the French president is in the United States. _____

   _____

5. Today, I have to write a paper. _____

6. We are in the process of cleaning the house. _____

7. They (*masc.*) are about to begin. _____

---

2. to express a general truth (proverbs and facts)

Tout **est** bien qui **finit** bien.	*All's well that ends well.*
La terre **est** ronde.	*The earth is round.*

3. to express repeated or habitual actions, often accompanied by expressions such as: **d'habitude** (*usually*), **en général** (*generally*), **tous les jours** (*every day*), **tous les matins** (*every morning*), **le vendredi** (*on Fridays*), **toujours** (*always*), etc.

Chaque jour il **lit** le journal. *Every day he reads the newspaper.*
En général, je **prends** le petit déjeuner *Usually, I eat breakfast at eight o'clock.*
    à huit heures.

4. to express actions in the future which will soon or surely take place

Le train **arrive** dans une heure. *The train arrives in an hour.*
Il **vient** cet après-midi. *He is coming this afternoon.*

EXERCICE
2·10

Comment dit-on en français?

1. France is a beautiful country. _____

2. Bill Gates has a lot of money. _____

3. She goes to church on Sundays. _____

4. He always tells the truth. _____

5. They (*masc.*) are going to the movies tonight. _____

6. I am leaving tomorrow. _____

7. They (*fem.*) are coming next week. _____

Unlike in English, the *present tense* is used in French with **depuis** (*for, since*) for actions or situations which started in the past, but continue to go on in the present. In English, the present perfect (*have/has + past participle*) or the present perfect continuous (*have / has been . . . -ing*) is used for such actions or situations.

Note that **depuis** means *for* when it is followed by a time period (such as: *two hours, a week, three months, four years*, etc.). **Depuis** means *since* if it is followed by a time point (such as: *yesterday, July, the first of August, Monday, Christmas*, etc.)

Depuis combien de temps **étudiez**-vous *(For) how long **have** you **studied** / **have** you*
    le français? ***been studying** French?*
J'**étudie** le français *depuis* deux ans. *I **have studied** / **have been studying** French for*
    two years.

Depuis quand **travaillez**-vous ici? *Since when **have** you **worked** / **have** you **been***
    ***working** here?*
Je **travaille** ici *depuis* Noël. *I **have worked** / **have been working** here since*
    Christmas.

Note that **ça fait... que, il y a... que** or **voilà... que** (not used in a question) can replace **depuis** when it means *for*. With these expressions, the verb is in the present tense as well.

Ça fait / Il y a combien de temps *que* *(For) how long **have** you **studied** / **have** you*
    vous **étudiez** le français? ***been studying** French?*
Ça fait / Il y a / Voilà deux ans *que* *I **have studied** / **have been studying** French*
    j'**étudie** le français. *for two years.*

Comment dit-on en français?

1. For how long have you (*pol.*) lived here? (*Give three possible translations.*)

   a. _____

   b. _____

   c. _____

2. I have lived here for five years. (*Give four possible translations.*)

   a. _____

   b. _____

   c. _____

   d. _____

3. We have been dating (**sortir ensemble**) since August. _____

4. I have known her husband since January. _____

5. Have you (*pol.*) been waiting for a long time? _____

Répondez aux questions suivantes. (Invent an answer if the question doesn't apply.)

1. Depuis combien de temps avez-vous le permis de conduire (*driver's license*)? _____

2. Ça fait combien de temps que vous travaillez? _____

3. Il y a combien de temps que vous étudiez le français? _____

4. Depuis combien de temps êtes-vous malade (*ill*)? _____

5. Ça fait combien de temps que vous habitez dans cette ville (*in this city*)? _____

6. Il y a combien de temps que vous jouez du piano? _____

Voilà la réponse. Quelle était la question? What was the question that triggered the following answers? Use the French equivalents of "since when" (asking for a time point) or "for how long" (asking for a time period) in your questions.

1. Je suis marié(e) (*married*) depuis six semaines. _____

2. Il joue du violon depuis dix ans. _____

3. Ça fait neuf mois (*months*) qu'ils cherchent du travail. _____

4. Je connais son père depuis longtemps. _____

5. Ça fait trois ans que nous sortons ensemble. _____

6. Elle est malade depuis hier (*yesterday*). _____

7. Je travaille depuis sept heures du matin. _____

8. Nous attendons la lettre depuis le vingt février. _____

9. J'apprends l'italien depuis Pâques (*Easter*). _____

10. Il est au chômage (*unemployed*) depuis le premier mars. _____

EXERCICE 2·14

Anne, qui n'habite plus chez ses parents, parle d'une journée typique dans la vie de sa famille. Traduisez en français ce qu'elle dit.

My parents have a big house near Tours. They have lived there for more than thirty years. My dad says that he doesn't want to move because he prefers the country to the city. In his opinion, life is much more pleasant in a little village. During the week, my father gets in his car at seven-fifteen A.M. and goes to work. He usually takes the freeway because he can drive faster. In the meantime, my mom drives her daughters (my younger sisters) to school. When she comes back at about eight o'clock, she cleans the kitchen and the bathroom. Afterwards, she goes out to buy meat and bread. She comes (=is) back an hour later and cooks lunch. At noon, my sisters take the bus. When they arrive at home, they are starved. My dad cannot have lunch with them (**eux**) because he doesn't have enough time. That is the reason why he doesn't see his family until six P.M. In the afternoon, my mom reads her e-mail and writes to her friends. I believe (that) she is always very busy because she knows a lot of people. In the evening, my father sets the table and my mother serves dinner. During the meal, they laugh a lot. If the weather allows it, they eat on the balcony, but when it is raining, they stay in the dining room. Later on, my sisters do their homework and my parents read the newspaper or watch television. At midnight, everyone is in bed and sleeps until the next morning.

VOCABULAIRE			
afterwards	**après**	later on	**plus tard**
at about (+ clock time)	**vers (+ clock time)**	a lot of people	**beaucoup de monde**
		meat	**de la viande**
at midnight	**à minuit**	my younger sisters	**mes sœurs cadettes**
at noon	**à midi**	near	**près de**
to be back	**être de retour**	the next morning	**le lendemain matin**
to cook lunch	**préparer le déjeuner**	not until	**pas avant**
country	**la campagne**	to set the table	**mettre la table**
dining room	**la salle à manger**	starved	**affamé(e)**
during the week	**en semaine**	that is the reason why	**c'est la raison pour laquelle**
enough time	**assez de temps**		
freeway	**l'autoroute (f.)**	there	**y**
in his opinion	**à son avis**	traffic jam	**l'embouteillage (m.)**
in the afternoon	**l'après-midi (m.)**	until	**jusqu'à**
in the meantime	**pendant ce temps**		

_____

_____

_____

_____

_____

_____

_____

_____

_____

Special uses of *aller* and *venir*

The close future (present tense of *aller* + infinitive)

When one uses the verb **aller** (*to go*) in the present tense, one can express a future action by adding a verb in the infinitive to the conjugated form of **aller**. This construction corresponds to English *am/is/are going to* + *infinitive*.

Elle **va avoir** un bébé.	*She is going to have a baby.*
Ils ne **vont** pas **venir**.	*They are not going to come.*
Qu'est-ce que tu **vas faire**?	*What are you going to do?*
Je **vais** vous **laisser**.	*I am going to leave you.*

Comment dit-on en français?

1. I am going to try. _____

2. Is it going to rain next week? _____

3. You (*fam.*) are going to get (**avoir**) a traffic ticket. _____

4. Are they (*masc.*) going to go to the movies? _____

5. What are we going to do tomorrow? _____

6. They (*fem.*) are not going to wait. _____

7. Who is going to win? _____

8. That (**Ça**) is not going to work. _____

9. It is going to snow tonight. _____

10. Where are you (*fam.*) going to eat? _____

The recent past (present tense of *venir* + *de* + infinitive)

When one uses the verb **venir** (*to come*) in the present tense, one can express an action or situation in the *recent past* by adding the preposition **de** (**d'** before vowel or mute **h**) + *infinitive* to the conjugated form of **venir**. This construction corresponds to English *have/has just* + *past participle* or *just* + *simple past* of the verb in question.

Il **vient de partir**.	He (has) just left.
Nous **venons d'arriver**.	We (have) just arrived.
Ils **viennent de téléphoner**.	They (masc.) (have) just called.
Je **viens de manger**.	I just ate.

EXERCICE 2·16

Comment dit-on en français?

1. They (*masc.*) just bought a recreational vehicle. _____

2. We just received a fax. _____

3. That's what (**C'est ce que**) I just said. _____

4. I have just read the article. _____

5. He just wrote a composition. _____

6. The investigation (**L'enquête [f.]**) has just started. _____

7. Did you (*pol.*) just move? _____

8. Do you (*fam.*) know what (**ce qui**) just happened? _____

9. He just spent a week in the mountains. _____

10. She just got (**avoir**) her driver's license. _____

EXERCICE 2·17

Répondez aux questions suivantes.

1. Qu'est-ce que vous allez faire cet après-midi? _____

2. Où vas-tu aller l'été prochain? _____

3. À quelle heure (*At what time*) allez-vous dîner ce soir? _____

4. Quand allez-vous déjeuner demain? _____

5. Vas-tu sortir le week-end prochain? _____

6. Allez-vous étudier l'allemand l'année prochaine? _____

7. Qu'est-ce que vous venez de faire? _____

Savoir and connaître

Since both **savoir** and **connaître** mean *to know*, the uses of these verbs need clarification.

Savoir means to know information, to have thorough knowledge of something, to know how to (do sth), and to know whether (when, where, why, how, that, etc.) something is happening.

Connaître means to be familiar with a place or thing, and to know a person.

Savoir

Savoir is used with a following *noun* (which cannot be a place or a person)

1. when one knows a fact, such as a name, address, phone number, the time of day, a date or an age, and when one knows the truth or the answer.

Je **sais** son adresse.	*I know his/her address.*
Nous ne **savons** pas votre numéro de téléphone.	*We don't know your phone number.*
Savez-vous la réponse?	*Do you know the answer?*

2. when one knows something very well from studying or memorizing.

Sais-tu ta grammaire?	*Do you know your grammar?*
Elle **sait** sa leçon.	*She knows her lesson.*
Je **sais** le poème par cœur.	*I know the poem by heart.*

EXERCICE
2·18

Comment dit-on en français?

1. I don't know his name. _____

2. Do you (*fam.*) know the date of the French Revolution (**la Révolution française**)? _____

_____

3. We don't know his age. _____

4. Do you (*pol.*) know the time (**l'heure**)? _____

5. Does he know the poem by heart? _____

6. Who knows the answer to this question? _____

7. Do they (*masc.*) know the truth? _____

Savoir is used with a following *infinitive* to express *to know how to (do something)*. Note that the infinitive follows **savoir** immediately. *How* is not expressed in French.

Sais-tu **faire** la cuisine?	*Do you know how to cook?*
Elle **sait jouer** du piano.	*She knows how to play the piano.*
Nous **savons patiner**.	*We know how to ice-skate.*

Comment dit-on en français?

1. They (*fem.*) know how to read and write. _____

2. I don't know how to swim. _____

3. Do you (*fam.*) know how to ski? _____

4. He doesn't know how to drive. _____

5. We know how to fly (**piloter**) an airplane. _____

6. Do you (*pol.*) know how to prepare this dish? _____

Savoir is used in the main clause (at the beginning of the sentence) when a *subordinate clause* follows. Subordinate clauses are introduced by words such as **quand** (*when*), **où** (*where*), **si** (*whether*), **pourquoi** (*why*), **qui** (*who*), **comment** (*how*), **combien** (*how much, how many*), **que** (*that*), **quel, quelle** (*which, what*), etc.

Je ne **sais** pas **pourquoi** il est fâché.	*I don't know why he is angry.*
Sais-tu **comment** il va?	*Do you know how he is (doing)?*
Il **sait que*** c'est vrai.	*He knows (that) this is true.*

Note: In English, one can either say "I know **that** this is true," or "I know this is true." In French, the conjunction **que** (*that*) cannot be omitted after **savoir**.

Je **sais que** tu as raison.	*I know (that) you are right.*
Sais-tu **qu'**elle est enceinte?	*Do you know (that) she is pregnant?*

Comment dit-on en français?

1. We don't know where he works. _____

2. They (*masc.*) know (that) you (*pol.*) are demanding (**exigeant[e]**). _____

3. I don't know whether he is coming to the party. _____

4. Do you (*fam.*) know when the movie begins? _____

5. He knows who is responsible. _____

6. She doesn't know why the baby cries. _____

7. Do you (*pol.*) know how much he earns? _____

8. Does she know how long (**combien de temps**) he is going to stay? _____

Savoir is used *alone*, i.e., without a following object.

Je (le) **sais**.	*I know (it).*
Je ne **sais** pas.	*I don't know.*
Qui **sait**?	*Who knows?*
On ne **sait** jamais.	*One never knows.*
Tu **sais** quoi?	*You know what?*
Je ne **sais** pas quoi faire.	*I don't know what to do.*
Comment tu le **sais**?	*How do you know?*
Je ne **sais** pas pourquoi.	*I don't know why.*

EXERCICE
2·21

Comment dit-on en français?

1. Where are my keys? —I don't know. _____

2. That is true, you (*fam.*) know. _____

3. Is it going to rain tomorrow? —Who knows? _____

4. They (*fem.*) don't know what to say. _____

5. You (*fam.*) know what? He just called. _____

6. We don't know anything. (= We know nothing.) _____

Connaître

Connaître is used

1. when one knows a *person.*

Connais-tu ce monsieur?	*Do you know this man?*
Oui, je le **connais**.	*Yes, I know him.*
Je **connais** Pierre depuis longtemps.	*I have known Pierre for a long time.*
Connaissez-vous quelqu'un?	*Do you know anyone?*
Je ne **connais** personne.	*I don't know anyone.*
Ils **connaissent** les Duval.	*They know the Duvals.*

2. when one knows a *place* (a country, a city, a street, a restaurant, a building, etc.)

Je **connais** bien la France.	*I know France well.*
Connais-tu ce musée?	*Do you know this museum?*
Il ne **connaît** pas ce restaurant.	*He doesn't know this restaurant.*

Connaître is used when one is *familiar* with something that one read, saw, heard or experienced (a book, a play, a movie, a song, literature, paintings, etc.)

Je **connais** les tableaux de Picasso.	*I know the paintings of Picasso.*
Connais-tu ce film?	*Do you know this movie?*
Il ne **connaît** pas cette chanson.	*He doesn't know this song.*
Je **connais** le poème.	*I know the poem. (= I have read it.)*

Note: However, one uses **savoir** with **par cœur** (*by heart*) because it implies a thorough knowledge after learning:

Je **sais** le poème **par cœur**.   *I know the poem by heart.*

Comment dit-on en français?

1. Do you (*fam.*) know your (*tes*) neighbors? —Yes, I know them very well. _____

    _____

2. I don't know this place (**cet endroit**). _____

3. He doesn't know this woman, but I know her. _____

4. Do you (*pol.*) know this hotel? _____

5. We know this street well. _____

6. She knows this city like the back of her hand (**comme sa poche**). _____

    _____

7. The students know the play *Huis clos*. _____

8. My sister knows classical music (**la musique classique**). _____

9. I know someone in England. _____

10. Have you (*fam.*) been to (=Do you know) Japan? _____

11. We don't know you (*pol.*). _____

12. Do I know you (*pol.*)? _____

Note:

◆ Only **savoir** can be used with a following *infinitive*, with a *subordinate clause*, and without an *object*.

◆ Only **connaître** can be used when the object is a *person* or *place*. **Connaître** must have an *object* (noun or pronoun); it cannot be used alone.

◆ With a language, either **connaître** or **savoir** can be used.

Sais-tu (Connais-tu) le latin?   *Do you know Latin?*

◆ **Savoir** is generally used when a thorough knowledge is implied.

Il **sait** l'italien; c'est sa langue maternelle.   *He knows Italian; it's his mother tongue.*
Je **sais** l'allemand. Je le parle couramment.   *I know German. I speak it fluently.*

◆ **Connaître** is used when the knowledge is considered incomplete.

Elle **connaît** plusieurs langues étrangères.   *She knows several foreign languages.*
Nous **connaissons** un peu de russe.   *We know a little Russian.*

Exercices de révision

Remplissez les tirets avec la forme correcte de savoir *ou* connaître.

1. _____-vous ce roman?

2. Tu _____ les nouvelles de Maupassant, n'est-ce pas?

3. Il ne _____ pas quel âge elle a.

4. Je _____ cette femme de vue (*by sight*), mais je ne _____ pas
   son adresse ni son numéro de téléphone.

5. Elle _____ parler couramment le français et elle _____ un peu
   d'espagnol.

6. Beaucoup d'Européens _____ au moins une langue étrangère.

7. Je ne _____ plus mes conjugaisons (*conjugations*).

8. Les analphabètes (*The illiterate*) ne _____ ni lire ni écrire.

9. Est-ce qu'il va neiger cette année? —Qui _____?

10. Mes amis _____ très bien ce pays.

11. Pourquoi rit-elle? —Je ne _____ pas.

12. Prends un parapluie. On ne _____ jamais.

13. Nous _____ ce poème mais nous ne le _____ pas par cœur.

14. _____-tu ce monsieur? —Oui, je le _____.

15. Ils sont très impolis (*rude*). —Je le _____!

16. _____-tu qu'elle a des animaux domestiques?

17. Vous _____ bien jouer de la guitare.

18. _____-tu comment elle s'appelle? —Non, je ne _____ pas son
    nom.

19. _____-vous quand il va revenir?

20. Les gens ne _____ pas où j'habite.

Traduisez en français.

I have known my friend Sandrine for several years. She knows how to cook but (and I don't know why) she doesn't know French cuisine. That is why I am going to take Sandrine to a French restaurant which (**que**) I know very well. I know the owner but I don't know whether he is French. I know (that) my friend is going to like the food of this restaurant because she knows culinary art. And who knows, perhaps she is going to speak French some day. One never knows.

VOCABULAIRE	culinary art	**l'art culinaire** *(m.)*	several years	**plusieurs années**
	food	**la cuisine**	to take (a person)	**emmener**
	owner	**le/la propriétaire**	that is why	**c'est pour ça que**

_____

_____

_____

_____

_____

_____

_____

Idioms with *avoir, faire, être, aller, vouloir,* and *prendre*

Idioms are expressions which cannot be translated literally from one language to another. While in English someone *is hungry* or *thirsty*, in French someone *has hunger* or *thirst*. Whereas in English, a person or thing *is* a certain number of years *old*, in French, this person or thing *has* a certain number of *years,* and so on. You will find the most common of these idiomatic expressions listed below. Note that they can be used in any tense.

Idioms with *avoir*

avoir (très) faim *to be (very) hungry*

   J'ai très faim.   *I am very hungry.*

avoir (très) soif *to be (very) thirsty*
avoir chaud* *to be hot*
avoir froid* *to be cold*
avoir raison* *to be right*
avoir tort* *to be wrong*

   *Note that these expressions are used only if someone, a *person* (*not* something) is hot, cold, right, or wrong.

avoir sommeil *to be sleepy*
avoir (très) peur (de) *to be (very) afraid (of)*

Il **a** (très) **peur des** examens.	*He is (very) afraid of the exams.*

avoir... ans *to be . . . years old*

Quel âge **as**-tu? —J'**ai** dix ans.*	*How old are you? —I am ten (years old).**
Ce château **a** cent ans.*	*This castle is one hundred years old.*

*Note that contrary to English, the word **an(s)** cannot be omitted in French when indicating an age.

avoir l'air (+ adjectif) *to look (+ adjective)*

Elle **a l'air** malade.	*She looks ill.*

avoir l'air de (+ inf.) *to look as if, seem to*

Vous **avez l'air d'**avoir faim.	*You look as if you are hungry.*
Tu n'**as** pas **l'air de** comprendre.	*You don't seem to understand.*

avoir l'air de (+ un(e) + nom) *to look like*

Il **a l'air d'**un mendiant.	*He looks like a beggar.*

avoir de la chance *to be lucky*
avoir besoin de qn/qch *to need sb/sth*

De quoi **as**-tu **besoin?**	*What do you need?*
J'**ai besoin d'**argent / **d'**un aspirateur.	*I need money / a vacuum cleaner.*

avoir besoin de (+ inf.) *to need (to do)*

Tu n'**as** pas **besoin de** venir.	*You don't need to come.*

avoir envie de qch *to feel like sth, want sth*

J'**ai** (très) **envie d'**un verre de vin.	*I want a glass of wine (badly).*

avoir envie de (+ inf.) *to feel like (doing)*

Je n'**ai** pas **envie de** sortir.	*I don't feel like going out.*

avoir lieu *to take place*

Le concert **a lieu** ce soir.	*The concert takes place tonight.*

avoir mal à (+ part of body) *to have a(n) . . . ache*
avoir mal à la gorge *to have a sore throat*
avoir mal à la tête *to have a headache*
avoir mal à l'estomac *to have a stomachache*
avoir mal au dos *to have a backache*
avoir mal aux dents *to have a toothache*
avoir mal aux cheveux *to have a hangover*
avoir hâte de (+ inf.) *to be anxious to, look forward to*

J'**ai hâte de** te revoir.	*I can't wait to see you again.*

avoir l'habitude de (+ inf.) *to be used to, be accustomed to*
avoir l'intention de (+ inf.) *to intend to*

Je n'**ai** pas **l'intention d'**accepter votre offre.	*I don't intend to accept your offer.*

Comment dit-on en français?

1. I have a headache. _____

2. Are you (*pol.*) hungry? —No, but I am very thirsty. _____

3. She is cold. _____

4. He is right and you (*fam.*) are wrong. _____

5. She is not sleepy. _____

6. I am very afraid. _____

7. How old are you (*pol.*)? —I am thirty (years old)._____

8. How old is your (**ton**) boss? —He is forty (years old). _____

9. I need a stapler (**une agrafeuse**). _____

10. We need a vacation. _____

11. He needs to study. _____

12. They (*masc.*) don't feel like traveling. _____

13. You (*fam.*) look tired. _____

14. I look forward to opening my presents. _____

15. You (*pol.*) are lucky! _____

Mettez l'expression avec avoir qui convient dans les phrases suivantes.

1. Quand on veut acheter quelque chose, on _____ _____
   _____ argent.

2. Je dois manger quelque chose, j'_____ _____.

3. Si tu ne bois rien, tu _____ _____.

4. Quand on ne porte pas de manteau en hiver, on _____ _____.

5. En été, nous _____ _____.

6. Tu fumes? Tu _____ _____, c'est mauvais pour la santé.

7. Si vous dites que le français est la plus belle langue du monde,
   vous _____ _____.

8. Sa fille est jeune. Elle _____ treize _____.

9. Mon ami vient de gagner un million d'euros. Il _____ _____
   _____ _____!

10. Quand le cours de français est ennuyeux, les étudiants _____ _____ _____ partir.

11. Je dois aller chez le dentiste. J'_____ _____ _____ dents.

12. Quand je vois un monstre, j'_____ _____.

13. Elle est pâle et maigre. Elle _____ _____ _____ malade.

14. Quel âge as-tu? —J'_____ _____ _____.

15. Si on mange trop, on _____ _____ _____ l'estomac.

Idioms with *faire*

faire attention (à) *to pay attention (to)*
faire semblant (de) (+ inf.) *to pretend (to)*

Il **fait semblant de** dormir. *He pretends to sleep.*

faire peur (à qn) *to frighten (sb)*

Vous me **faites peur.** *You frighten me.*

faire (qch) exprès *to do (sth) on purpose*

Je le **fais exprès.** *I am doing it on purpose.*

faire la cuisine *to cook, do the cooking*
faire la connaissance de qn *to meet sb (for the first time), make the acquaintance of sb*

Tu vas **faire sa connaissance** ce soir. *You are going to meet him/her tonight.*

faire la fête *to celebrate, party*
faire la grasse matinée *to sleep late (in the morning), sleep in*
faire (la) grève *to be on strike, go on strike*
faire la lessive *to do the laundry*
faire la queue *to stand in line, line up*
faire la sieste *to take a nap*
faire la vaisselle *to do the dishes*
faire l'école buissonnière *to play hooky*
faire le ménage *to do the housework*
faire le pont *to extend a holiday through the weekend*
faire les provisions *to go grocery shopping, buy groceries*

EXERCICE
2·27

Est-ce vrai ou faux?

_____ 1. En classe, les bons étudiants font attention au professeur.

_____ 2. Les Français ne font jamais la grève.

_____ 3. D'abord on fait la cuisine, ensuite on fait la vaisselle.

_____ 4. Beaucoup d'Européens détestent faire la queue.

_____ 5. Tout le monde aime faire la fête.

EXERCICE
2·28

Remplissez les tirets avec une expression qui contient faire.

1. Demain, nous allons dormir jusqu'à midi. Nous allons _____.

2. Les ouvriers (*The workers*) refusent de travailler. Ils _____.

3. Je dors souvent après le déjeuner. Je _____ souvent _____.

4. Quand une fête tombe (*falls on*) un jeudi, les Français _____, c'est-à-dire ils
   ne travaillent pas vendredi non plus.

5. Ce garçon n'aime pas aller à l'école. Il _____ quelquefois _____.

6. Quand on fait quelque chose intentionnellement (*intentionally*), on le
   (*it*) _____.

EXERCICE
2·29

Comment dit-on en français?

1. He pretends to be rich. _____

2. I do the cooking and the children do the dishes. _____

3. Who does the laundry at your house (**chez vous**)? _____

4. My husband does the housework and I do the grocery shopping. _____

5. He is playing hooky today. _____

6. Do you (*pol.*) often take a nap? _____

7. One stands in line at the post office (**à la poste**) and at the bank (**à la banque**). _____
   _____

Here are more idioms with **faire:**

> **faire de l'auto-stop** *to hitchhike*
> **faire du baby-sitting** *to baby-sit*
> **faire du lèche-vitrines** *to window-shop, go window-shopping*
> **faire du shopping / des achats / des emplettes** *to go shopping*
> **faire du tourisme** *to go sightseeing, sightsee*

The present tense of irregular verbs   **59**

faire des courses *to go shopping, run errands*
faire des économies *to save (money)*
faire des progrès *to make progress*
faire un rêve / un cauchemar *to have a dream / a nightmare*
faire un stage *to do an internship*
faire un tour (dans le parc) *to take a stroll in, walk around (the park)*
faire un voyage *to go on a trip, take a trip*
faire une pause *to take a break*
faire une promenade *to go for a walk*
faire une promenade (à vélo, en voiture, etc.) *to go for a (bike, car, etc.) ride*
faire de son mieux *to do one's best*
faire ses études *to study*
faire/défaire ses valises *to pack/unpack (one's suitcase)*

EXERCICE
2·30

Comment dit-on en français?

1. They (*masc.*) rarely hitchhike. _____

2. I window-shop all the time. _____

3. When do we go shopping? _____

4. I am going to save money. _____

5. You (*pol.*) are making progress. _____

6. Next month, we're going on a trip. _____

7. Are you (*fam.*) going for a walk? _____

8. They (*fem.*) take a break at noon. _____

9. I always do my best. _____

10. He packs (his suitcases). _____

11. She's doing an internship this summer. _____

12. When do you (*fam.*) baby-sit? _____

The verb **faire** is also present in numerous expressions indicating sports activities.

faire de l'alpinisme *to go mountain climbing*
faire du camping *to go camping*
faire du cheval *to go horseback riding*
faire de l'escalade *to go rock climbing*
faire du footing / du jogging *to go jogging*
faire de la gymnastique *to exercise, do gymnastics*
faire de la natation *to swim, go swimming*
faire du ski (alpin) *to go (downhill) skiing*
faire du ski de fond *to go cross-country skiing*
faire du ski nautique *to go waterskiing*

faire du snowboard *to go snowboarding*
faire du sport *to play sports, exercise*
faire du vélo *to go bicycle riding*

The following are common phrases with **faire:**

Ça ne **fait** rien.	*It doesn't matter. It's all right. That's OK.*
Ça **fait** combien?	*How much is it? How much does it cost?*
Qu'est-ce que vous **faites** dans la vie?	*What do you do for a living?*
C'est bien **fait** pour toi (vous).	*It serves you right.*
Si cela ne vous **fait** rien.	*If you don't mind.*
L'argent ne **fait** pas le bonheur. (*proverb*)	*Money doesn't buy happiness.*

EXERCICE
2·31

Comment dit-on en français?

1. He goes mountain climbing. _____

2. She goes swimming. _____

3. They (*masc.*) exercise every day. _____

4. Where do they (*fem.*) ski? _____

5. On Sunday, we go bicycle riding. _____

6. From time to time, I go horseback riding. _____

7. She goes jogging every morning. _____

8. That doesn't matter. _____

9. How much is it? _____

10. What do you (*fam.*) do for a living? _____

For expressions with **faire** in weather-related expressions see *A few impersonal verbs,* pages 67–72. For **faire** + *infinitive,* see *Infinitive.*

Other verbal idioms

Idioms with *être*

être à qn *to belong to sb*

À qui est ce sac? —Il **est à** moi.*	*Whose bag is this? —It belongs to me.*
Le vélo **est à** ma sœur.	*The bike belongs to my sister.*
Ces crayons **sont au** professeur.	*These pencils belong to the teacher.*

être d'accord (avec qn) *to agree (with sb)*

Je **suis d'accord avec** toi.*	*I agree with you.*

*Note that *stressed pronouns* are used after **être à** and after **être d'accord avec**. The stressed pronouns are: **moi** (*me*), **toi** (*you, fam.*), **lui** (*him*), **elle** (*her*), **nous** (*us*), **vous** (*you, pol.*), **eux** (*them, masc.*), **elles** (*them, fem.*)

être à l'heure *to be on time*
être en retard *to be late (= not on time)*
être en avance *to be early (= ahead of time)*
être au chômage *to be unemployed*
être au courant (de qch) *to be informed (about sth), be up to date (on sth)*
être au régime *to be on a diet*
être de bonne/mauvaise humeur *to be in a good/bad mood*
être (originaire) de *to be (originally) from*

Elle **est (originaire)** d'Afrique.   *She is (originally) from Africa.*

être en colère *to be angry*
être en vie *to be alive*
être en train de (+ inf.) *to be in the process of (doing)*
être sur le point de (+ inf.) *to be about to (do)*
être égal à qn *to be all the same to sb*

Ça **m'est égal**.   *It's all the same to me. I don't care.*

être enrhumé(e) *to have a cold*
être pressé(e) *to be in a hurry*

EXERCICE
2·32

Comment dit-on en français?

1. The watch belongs to her. _____

2. The dog belongs to them. _____

3. The umbrella belongs to Véronique. _____

4. These notebooks belong to the students. _____

5. The computer doesn't belong to me. _____

6. I don't agree with him. _____

7. I am sometimes late. _____

8. She is always on time. _____

9. They are unemployed. _____

10. Why are you (*fam.*) angry?. _____

11. She is on a diet. _____

12. Are you (*pol.*) in a bad mood? _____

13. We are originally from Vancouver. _____

14. I am in a hurry. _____

15. The hostages are still alive. _____

Répondez aux questions suivantes.

1. D'où êtes-vous originaire? _____

2. Quand es-tu très en colère? _____

3. Qu'est-ce que vous êtes en train de faire? _____

4. Que faites-vous quand vous êtes enrhumé(e)? _____

5. Qu'est-ce que vous faites quand vous êtes pressé(e)? _____

Complétez avec une expression qui contient être.

Exemple: Le cours commence à neuf heures. J'arrive à neuf heures vingt.

*Je **suis** en retard.*

1. Elle mange seulement du céleri et des carottes parce qu'elle _____ .

2. Ils ne trouvent pas de travail, ils _____ .

3. Voulez-vous de la limonade (*lemon soda*) ou du citron pressé (*lemonade*)?
   —Ça _____ .

4. Elle _____ de ce qui se passe (*of what happens*) dans le monde parce qu'elle lit le journal chaque jour.

5. La conférence commence à huit heures. Nous arrivons à huit heures moins le quart.
   Nous _____ .

Idioms with *aller*

Comment **allez**-vous?	*How are you?*
—Je **vais** bien, merci.	*—I'm fine, thank you.*
Comment **va** votre père?	*How is your father?*
—Il **va** (beaucoup) mieux.	*—He is (much) better.*
Comment **vont** vos parents?	*How are your parents?*
Ça **va**? (*informal*)	*How is it going?*

Traduisez en français les phrases suivantes.

1. How are you *(fam.)*? _____

2. How is your (votre) sister? _____

3. She is not well; she has the flu. _____

4. We are (feeling) better. _____

5. How are you doing? *(fam.)* _____

Idioms with *vouloir*

vouloir dire *to mean*
Que **voulez**-vous **dire**?   *What do you mean?*
(or: Qu'est-ce que vous **voulez dire**?)
Que **veut dire** «flag» en français?   *What does "flag" mean in French?*
«Flag» **veut dire** «drapeau» en français.   *"Flag" is translated "drapeau" in French.*
Ça ne **veut** rien **dire**.   *That doesn't mean anything.*

Idioms with *prendre*

prendre une décision *to make a decision*
prendre froid *to catch a cold*
prendre rendez-vous *to make an appointment*
prendre sa retraite *to retire, go into retirement*
prendre un verre *to have a drink*
prendre le petit déjeuner *to eat/have breakfast*
prendre le déjeuner (= **déjeuner**) *to eat/have lunch*
prendre le dîner (= **dîner**) *to eat/have dinner*
prendre qch/qn au sérieux *to take sth/sb seriously*

Comment dit-on en français?

1. What do you *(fam.)* mean? _____

2. Do you *(pol.)* know what (**ce que**) I mean? _____

3. What does "porte" mean in English? _____

4. Who makes the decision? _____

5. When do we eat breakfast? _____

6. The French have dinner at eight P.M. _____

7. We are having a drink at the bar (**au bar**). _____

8. He is going to retire in May. _____

9. You are (*fam.*) going to catch a cold. _____

10. We don't take Pierre seriously. _____

EXERCICE
2·37

Traduisez en français.

Happy birthday, Anne! Today is my sister Anne's birthday. She is sixteen years old. Anne is anxious to eat the cake. She just blew out the candles and she looks happy. The gifts are on the table and she must open the boxes. Anne is lucky because there are many gifts and cards. Tonight, we are going to celebrate. Mom is going to do the cooking and I am going to do the dishes.

   I hope that Anne is not going to have a stomachache because she always eats too much. Luckily, she is not on a diet. Tomorrow, Anne is going to play hooky and she is going to sleep late. The teacher is going to be angry, but that doesn't matter. The day after tomorrow, we do not need to go to school because it is Saturday.

VOCABULAIRE			
because	**parce que**	happy	**heureux, heureuse**
birthday	**l'anniversaire (m.)**	happy birthday	**bon anniversaire**
to blow out	**souffler**	luckily	**heureusement**
box	**la boîte**	too much	**trop**
candle	**la bougie**		
the day after tomorrow	**après-demain**		

_____

_____

_____

_____

_____

_____

_____

Plaire (à)

The verb **plaire** (*to please*) is frequently used instead of **aimer** to express *to like*. In order to use **plaire** correctly, one must know that while in English one says "somebody likes someone (or something)," in French one literally says "someone (or something) *pleases to* somebody." Consider the following example:

Teenagers like this motorcycle. *(literally: This motorcycle pleases to the teenagers.)*	Cette motocyclette **plaît aux** adolescents.

Note that, as with **manquer** *à* (*to miss*), the object of the English sentence (*this motorcycle* in the example above) becomes the subject of the French sentence (**cette motocyclette**), and the subject of the English sentence (*teenagers* in the example above) becomes the *indirect* object (introduced by **à** when it is a noun: *aux* **adolescents**) of the French sentence.

When the *subject* of the English sentence is a pronoun, it becomes an indirect object pronoun in French. Remember that the French indirect object pronouns (which precede the verb) are: **me** (*to me*), **te** (*to you*), **lui** (*to him, to her*) **nous** (*to us*), **vous** (*to you*), **leur** (*to them*).

He likes the movie.	Le film **lui** plaît.
They like these clothes.	Ces vêtements **leur** plaisent.
We like these shoes a lot.	Ces chaussures **nous** plaisent beaucoup.

EXERCICE
2·38

Traduisez en français les phrases suivantes.

1. Do you (pol.) like the musical? _____

2. Women like him. _____

3. Do they like that (**ça**)? _____

4. She likes these (eye)glasses. _____

5. I like your (**votre**) house a lot. _____

6. We don't like this dish. _____

7. I like my new job. _____

8. I don't like you with short hair. _____

9. Do you (*fam.*) like this kind of (**ce genre de**) music? _____

A few impersonal verbs

Verbs that do not have a personal subject (such as *I, you, we, they, Mary, the students,* etc.) are called impersonal verbs. In French, the subject of these verbs is the impersonal pronoun **il,** corresponding to *it* in English.

Some verbs (such as **falloir** and **pleuvoir**) only exist in the impersonal form (**il faut, il pleut**), while others (such as **faire, être,** and **avoir**) are used impersonally in certain expressions (**il fait froid, il est midi, il y a**).

Here are some common impersonal verbs and their most frequent uses.

Weather verbs

Most verbs indicating *weather* are impersonal or used impersonally.

The verb **faire**

Quel temps **fait-il**?	*What is the weather like? How is the weather?*
il fait beau	*the weather is good, it is nice out*
il fait mauvais	*the weather is bad*
il fait chaud	*it is hot*
il fait froid	*it is cold*
il fait frais	*it is cool*
il fait doux	*it is mild*
il fait (du) soleil	*it is sunny*
il fait du vent	*it is windy*
il fait du brouillard	*it is foggy*

Other weather verbs

il pleut   *it is raining*
il neige   *it is snowing*

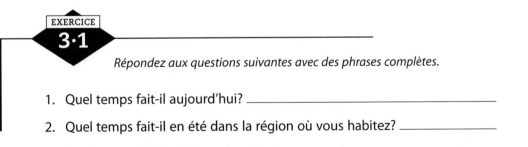

EXERCICE

3·1

Répondez aux questions suivantes avec des phrases complètes.

1. Quel temps fait-il aujourd'hui? _____

2. Quel temps fait-il en été dans la région où vous habitez? _____

3. Quel temps fait-il en hiver dans les montagnes? _____

4. En quel mois fait-il d'habitude du soleil? _____

5. En quel mois fait-il d'ordinaire du vent? _____

6. Quel temps fait-il en général le jour de votre anniversaire? _____

7. Quel temps fait-il au printemps dans votre ville natale? _____

8. Est-ce qu'il fait froid en août? _____

9. Est-ce qu'il fait souvent du brouillard à San Francisco? _____

The impersonal use of *être*

The verb **être** is used impersonally:
  When *telling time*

Quelle heure **est-il**?	*What time is it?*
Il est midi/minuit.	*It is noon/midnight.*
Il est deux heures et demie du matin.	*It is 2:30 A.M.*
Il est trois heures et quart de l'après-midi.	*It is 3:15 P.M.*
Il est neuf heures moins le quart du soir.	*It is 8:45 P.M.*
Il est dix heures vingt.	*It is 10:20.*
Il est onze heures moins cinq.	*It is 10:55.*
Il est tôt/tard.	*It is early/late.*

When followed by an adjective in numerous expressions which we will learn in the infinitive and subjunctive chapters respectively.

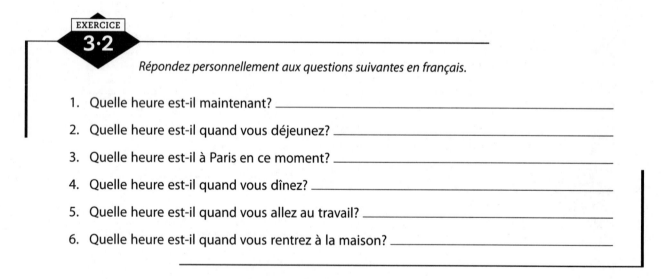

EXERCICE
3·2

Répondez personnellement aux questions suivantes en français.

1. Quelle heure est-il maintenant? _____

2. Quelle heure est-il quand vous déjeunez? _____

3. Quelle heure est-il à Paris en ce moment? _____

4. Quelle heure est-il quand vous dînez? _____

5. Quelle heure est-il quand vous allez au travail? _____

6. Quelle heure est-il quand vous rentrez à la maison? _____

The impersonal use of *avoir*

The verb **avoir** is used impersonally in the expression **il y a** (*there is, there are*).

Il y a une clôture autour de la maison,	*There is a fence around the house.*
Il y a quelqu'un?	*Is anyone there? (Is there anyone?)*
Il y a trois voitures dans le garage.	*There are three cars in the garage.*
Heureusement, **il** n'**y a** que trois blessés.	*Fortunately, there are only three injured people.*

Note that **il y a** is always in the singular

Il y a des cuillers sur la table.   *There are spoons on the table.*

The interrogative form of **il y a** is **est-ce qu'il y a** or **y a-t-il**? (*is/are there?*)

Est-ce qu'il y a (y a-t-il) des fourchettes dans le tiroir?   *Are there any forks in the drawer?*

The negative form of **il y a** is **il n'y a pas** (*there is/are not*) (+ **de** + *noun*)

Il n'y a pas de couteaux dans le lave-vaisselle.   *There aren't any knives in the dishwasher.*

Traduisez en français les phrases suivantes.

1. There is a cat in the kitchen. _____

2. There aren't any napkins on the table. _____

3. Is there a computer in the classroom? _____

4. How many universities are there in France? _____

5. Is there a restroom on this floor (**à cet étage**)? _____

6. There are clouds in the sky. _____

7. Is there a lost and found (**un bureau des objets trouvés**) here? _____

8. There is a satellite dish (**une parabole**) on the roof. _____

9. There is no money in my wallet. _____

10. There is no freedom of speech (**liberté [f.] d'expression**) in this country. _____

Qu'est-ce qu'il y a dans votre maison ou votre appartement? Describe (using *il y a*) what there is in each room of your house or apartment. Mention also what is not there.

Exemple: Dans ma maison, il y a huit pièces, la cuisine, etc.

Dans le salon, il y a un canapé, etc. Sur le plancher, il y a un tapis, etc.

VOCABULAIRE			
armchair	**le fauteuil**	desk	**le bureau**
bathroom	**la salle de bains**	dining room	**la salle à manger**
bathtub	**la baignoire**	dishwasher	**le lave-vaisselle**
bed	**le lit**	door	**la porte**
bedroom	**la chambre à coucher**	fireplace	**la cheminée**
chair	**la chaise**	floor (of a room)	**le plancher**
chest of drawers	**la commode**	hallway	**le couloir**
closet	**l'armoire (f.)**	kitchen	**la cuisine**
curtains	**les rideaux (m.pl.)**	lamp	**la lampe**

A few impersonal verbs   **69**

living room	**le salon**	sink (*bathroom*)	**le lavabo**
microwave	**le micro-ondes**	sink (*kitchen*)	**l'évier (*m.*)**
mirror	**le miroir**	sofa	**le canapé**
refrigerator	**le réfrigérateur**	table	**la table**
rug	**le tapis**	wall	**le mur**
shower	**la douche**	window	**la fenêtre**

Il y a can also mean *ago*. Note that unlike its English equivalent, **il y a** precedes the time period.

il y a huit jours	*eight days ago (= a week ago)*
il y a un mois	*a month ago*
il y a trois ans	*three years ago*

EXERCICE
3·5

Traduisez en français les expressions suivantes.

1. five weeks ago _____

2. four hours ago _____

3. two centuries ago _____

4. a decade ago _____

5. a long time ago _____

Other impersonal expressions

il faut	*it is necessary, one must*

Il faut faire attention en classe.	*One must pay attention in class.*
Il ne faut pas fumer dans des endroits publics.	*One must not smoke in public places.*

il vaut mieux	*it is better*

Il vaut mieux rester ici.	*It is better to stay here.*

Comment dit-on en français?

1. One must be polite. _____

2. One must not do that (**ça**). _____

3. One must study pedagogy in order to (**pour**) become a teacher. _____

   _____

4. One must have patience. _____

5. It is better to leave. _____

6. It is better to tell the truth. _____

EXERCICE

3·7

Est-ce vrai ou faux?

_____ 1. Il y a plus de 300 variétés de fromage en France.

_____ 2. Quand il est minuit à Los Angeles, il est neuf heures du matin à Paris.

_____ 3. Il n'y a pas de limitation de vitesse (*speed limit*) sur les autoroutes françaises.

_____ 4. Il fait toujours froid en Californie.

_____ 5. En France, il faut payer la TVA (*value added tax*) sur tout ce qu'on achète.

_____ 6. Il n'y a pas de lait sur la carte d'un restaurant français.

_____ 7. Si on va au théâtre en France, il vaut mieux ne pas donner de pourboire à l'ouvreuse (*usher*).

_____ 8. Quand on dîne chez des Français, il vaut mieux ne pas mettre le pain sur la nappe (*tablecloth*).

EXERCICE

3·8

Traduisez en français.

In Provence, the weather is almost always good. It rains only very rarely and it almost never snows. But it is often windy. One calls this strong wind which (**qui**) blows from the north "le Mistral." In this region, there are a lot of olive trees and lavender fields just about everywhere. In June, July, and August, it is very hot. In September, October, and November, it is cool. In December, January, and February, it is rather cold. And in March, April, and May, it is mild. The inhabitants of Provence all have a good suntan because it is sunny most of the time.

When it is noon, many merchants close their shops to go to lunch. When they come back, it is two pm.

In the summer, there are a lot of tourists in Provence. When they go to the beach, they put on suntan lotion because they know that one must protect the skin from sunburns. It is better to be careful.

VOCABULAIRE

to blow	**souffler**	merchant	**le commerçant, la commerçante**
to have a good suntan	**être bien bronzé(e)**	most of the time	**la plupart du temps**
the inhabitants of Provence	**les Provençaux (m.pl.)**	olive tree	**l'olivier** *(m.)*
just about everywhere	**un peu partout**	only	**ne... que**
		rather	**assez**
		sunburn	**le coup de soleil**
lavender fields	**des champs** *(m.pl.)* **de lavande**	suntan lotion	**la crème solaire**

Reflexive verbs

A verb is reflexive when it expresses an action that the subject performs on him/her/itself. The verb in the sentence *he washes the car*, for example, is not reflexive because it expresses an action that is performed by the subject (*he*) and received by an object (*the car*). If the verb is reflexive, the action remains within the subject, or, if you wish, is "reflected" back to the subject. Therefore, the verb in the sentence *he washes himself* is reflexive. As these examples show, the same verb can exist both in a reflexive and in a non-reflexive form.

There are reflexive verbs in English, such as *to burn oneself, to hurt oneself, to cut oneself, to control oneself,* and so on, but there are many more in French. In English, reflexive verbs are followed by a pronoun ending in *-self* (*-selves*). In French, these verbs are preceded by the reflexive pronoun **se** (**s'** before vowel or mute **h**) when listed in their infinitive form, such as **se présenter** (*to introduce oneself*), **s'accuser** (*to accuse oneself*), etc. During the conjugation, this pronoun changes with each person and agrees with the subject in the following way:

SUBJECT PRONOUN	CORRESPONDING REFLEXIVE PRONOUN
je	**me (m')**
tu	**te (t')**
il/elle/on	**se (s')**
nous	**nous**
vous	**vous**
ils/elles	**se (s')**

Note that **il/elle/on** and **ils/elles** have the same reflexive pronoun.

The present tense of reflexive verbs

To conjugate a reflexive verb in the present tense, follow the model given below.

se présenter *to introduce oneself*	
je **me** présente	*I introduce myself*
tu **te** présentes	*you introduce yourself*
il **se** présente	*he introduces himself*
elle **se** présente	*she introduces herself*
on **se** présente	*one introduces oneself*
nous **nous** présentons	*we introduce ourselves*
vous **vous** présentez (*yourselves*)	*you introduce yourself*
ils **se** présentent	*they introduce themselves*
elles **se** présentent	*they introduce themselves*

In the *negative form*, **ne** precedes the reflexive pronoun, **pas** follows the verb.

je **ne** me présente **pas** (*I don't introduce myself*)	nous **ne** nous présentons **pas**
tu **ne** te présentes **pas**	vous **ne** vous présentez **pas**
il/elle/on **ne** se présente **pas**	ils/elles **ne** se présentent **pas**

In the *interrogative form* with **est-ce que**, the positive word order is retained as with all other verbs.

Est-ce que je me présente? (*Do I introduce myself?*)	Est-ce que nous nous présentons?
Est-ce que tu te présentes?	Est-ce que vous vous présentez?
Est-ce qu'il se présente?	Est-ce qu'ils se présentent?
Est-ce qu'elle se présente?	Est-ce qu'elles se présentent?

In the *inverted interrogative form*, the reflexive pronoun stays before the verb.

(does not exist)	**nous** présentons-nous?
te présentes-tu? (*Do you introduce yourself?*)	**vous** présentez-vous?
se présente-t-il?	**se** présentent-ils?
se présente-t-elle?	**se** présentent-elles?

Note:

- The reflexive pronouns **me, te, se, nous, vous, se** are placed immediately before the conjugated verb.
- If the verb starts with a vowel or mute **h, me, te,** and **se** become **m', t',** and **s':**

    je **m'**applique (*I apply myself*).   tu **t'**habilles (*you get dressed*).

- The pronouns **me, te, se,** etc., correspond to *myself, yourself, himself, herself,* etc., only if the French reflexive verb has an English equivalent which is reflexive as well, as with **ils *se* blessent** (*they injure **themselves***). But since most of the French reflexive verbs are not reflexive in English, the French reflexive pronouns rarely have an equivalent in English: **je *me* lève** (*I get up*), **il *s'*amuse** (*he has a good time*), **nous *nous* douchons** (*we take a shower*).

Common French reflexive verbs and their use

Regular verbs

s'amuser *to have a good time, enjoy oneself*
s'appeler *to be named (literally: to call oneself)*
s'arrêter *to stop*
se cacher *to hide*
se coucher *to go to bed, set (sun)*
se demander *to wonder*
se dépêcher *to hurry*
se déshabiller *to get undressed*
se disputer *to argue, quarrel, have an argument*
s'ennuyer *to get/be bored*
se fâcher *to get angry*
s'habiller *to get dressed*
s'inquiéter *to get/be worried*

se lever *to get up, to rise (sun)*
se marier (avec) *to get married (to), marry*
se moquer de *to make fun of*
se passer *to happen*
se peigner *to comb one's hair*
se promener *to go for a walk*
se rappeler *to remember*
se raser *to shave*
se reposer *to rest*
se réveiller *to wake up*
se tromper *to be mistaken*
se trouver *to be (located)*

Note: The following verbs have spelling changes during the present tense conjugation:

◆ **S'appeler** and **se rappeler** are conjugated like **appeler**, i.e., they double the **l** in all persons except **nous** and **vous**.

Comment t'appelles-tu?	*What is your name (fam.)?*
Je m'appelle Brice.	*My name is Brice.*
Comment vous appelez-vous?	*What is your name (pol.)?*
Comment s'appelle-t-elle?	*What is her name?*
Elle s'appelle Marie.	*Her name is Marie.*
Comment s'appellent-ils?	*What are their names?*
Est-ce que tu te rappelles?	*Do you remember?*
Ils ne se rappellent pas.	*They don't remember.*

◆ **S'ennuyer** changes the **y** into **i** in all persons except **nous** and **vous**: je m'ennuie, tu t'ennuies, il/elle/on s'ennuie, etc.

◆ **S'inquiéter** (like **espérer**) changes the **accent aigu** into an **accent grave** in all persons except **nous** and **vous**: je m'inquiète, tu t'inquiètes, il/elle/on s'inquiète, etc.

◆ **Se lever** and **se promener** are conjugated like **acheter**, i.e., they change -e- into -è- in all persons except **nous** and **vous**: je me lève, tu te lèves, il/elle/on se lève, etc., je me promène, tu te promènes, il/elle/on se promène, etc.

EXERCICE
4·1

Traduisez les phrases suivantes en français. (Use reflexive verbs throughout.)

1. I always have a good time. _____

2. They (*fem.*) are not having a good time. _____

3. What is your name (*pol.*)? _____

4. What is your name (*fam.*)? _____

5. My name is Romain. _____

6. What is his name? _____

7. His name is Jean. _____

8. The TGV (= **le train à grande vitesse**) doesn't stop often. _____

9. I go to bed late. _____

10. You (*pol.*) hurry. _____

11. They (*masc.*) get undressed at night. _____

12. Do you (*pol.*) argue often with your parents? _____

13. I am bored. _____

14. He never gets angry. _____

15. We get dressed. _____

16. They worry about (**pour**) their (**leur**) son. _____

17. Do you (*pol.*) get up early? _____

18. At what time do you (*fam.*) usually get up? _____

19. Damien marries my daughter next month. _____

20. They (*masc.*) make fun of the teacher. _____

21. What (**Qu'est-ce qui**) is happening? _____

22. The story happens in Canada (**au Canada**). _____

23. I comb my hair. _____

24. They (*fem.*) go for a walk every day. _____

25. Do you remember (*pol.*)? _____

26. I don't remember any more. _____

27. Where is the train station please? _____

28. When do you (*fam.*) rest? _____

29. I wake up when the alarm (**le réveil**) rings. _____

30. You (*pol.*) are mistaken. _____

More regular reflexive verbs

s'attendre à *to expect*
se baigner *to go swimming, take a bath*
se comporter *to behave*
se débrouiller *to get by, manage*
se détendre *to relax*
se doucher *to take a shower*
s'entendre (avec) *to get along (with)*
s'excuser *to apologize*
se fiancer *to get engaged*
s'habituer à *to get used to*
s'intéresser à *to be interested in*
se maquiller *to put on make-up*
se noyer *to drown*

s'occuper de qn/qch *to take care of sb/sth*
se perdre *to get lost*
se rendre compte (de) *to realize*
se spécialiser en *to major in*
se terminer *to come to an end*

Note: **Se fiancer** is conjugated like **commencer**, i.e., it gets a **cédille** in the **nous** form of the present tense (**nous nous fiançons**).

EXERCICE
4·2

Comment dit-on en français?

1. They (*fem.*) expect the worst (**le pire**). _____

2. She goes swimming once a week. _____

3. They (*masc.*) behave badly. _____

4. I am getting by in French. _____

5. She doesn't relax. _____

6. I apologize. _____

7. We are getting engaged this summer. _____

8. One gets used to everything. _____

9. Are you (*fam.*) interested in politics? _____

10. He is majoring in political science. _____

Irregular reflexive verbs

> **s'apercevoir (de)** *to notice*
> **s'asseoir** *to sit down*
> **se conduire** *to behave*
> **s'en aller** *to go away*
> **s'endormir** *to fall asleep*
> **se mettre à** (+ inf.) *to begin to* (+ *infinitive*)
> **se plaindre** *to complain*
> **se sentir** *to feel (physically or emotionally)*
> **se servir de** *to use*
> **se souvenir (de)** *to remember*
> **se taire** *to be quiet*

Note:

- **S'apercevoir** is conjugated like **recevoir**: je m'aperçois, nous nous apercevons, etc.
- **S'asseoir** has two possible conjugations in the present tense.

je m'assieds	nous nous asseyons
tu t'assieds	vous vous asseyez
il/elle/on s'assied	ils/elles s'asseyent

or:

je m'assois	nous nous assoyons
tu t'assieds	vous vous asseyez
il/elle/on s'assoit	ils/elles s'assoient

or:

tu t'assois	vous vous assoyez
il/elle/on s'assied	ils/elles s'asseyent

- ◆ **S'en aller** is conjugated like **aller**, with **en** preceding the verb: je m'en vais, tu t'en vas, il/elle/on s'en va, nous nous en allons, vous vous en allez, ils/elles s'en vont.
- ◆ **Se conduire** is conjugated like **conduire**.
- ◆ **S'endormir, se sentir,** and **se servir** are conjugated like **dormir**: je m'endors, nous nous endormons, etc.; je me sens, nous nous sentons, etc.; je me sers, nous nous servons, etc.
- ◆ **Se mettre** is conjugated like **mettre**.
- ◆ **Se plaindre** is conjugated like **craindre**: je me plains, tu te plains, il/elle/on se plaint, nous nous plaignons, vous vous plaignez, ils/elles se plaignent.
- ◆ **Se souvenir** is conjugated like **venir**: je me souviens, tu te souviens, etc. If the sentence with **se souvenir** has an object, **de** precedes it.

    Nous **nous souvenons de** nos vacances.   *We remember our vacation.*

- ◆ **Se taire** is conjugated like **plaire** but has no circumflex accent in the third-person singular: je me tais, tu te tais, il/elle/on se tait, nous nous taisons, vous vous taisez, ils/elles se taisent.

EXERCICE
4·3

Traduisez en français les phrases suivantes.

1. They (*fem.*) never notice their errors (**erreurs [f.pl.]**). _____

2. I sit down. _____

3. We sit down. _____

4. Do they (*masc.*) sit down? _____

5. They (*fem.*) are not going away. _____

6. Are you (*fam.*) going away? _____

7. We fall asleep. _____

8. I don't fall asleep. _____

9. He begins to cry. _____

10. They (*masc.*) complain all the time. _____

11. I don't feel well today. _____

12. We feel safe. _____

13. You (*fam.*) behave well. _____

14. I don't remember this man. _____

15. He doesn't remember anything. _____

16. Do you (*fam.*) remember me? _____

17. They (*fem.*) still remember their (**leur**) childhood. _____

18. My grandmother always remembers my birthday. _____

    _____

19. The Chinese use chopsticks (**baguettes *[f.pl.]***) to eat. _____

    _____

20. They (*masc.*) are never quiet. _____

The use of reflexive verbs with parts of the body

Contrary to English, French tends to avoid the use of possessive adjectives, such as **mon** (*my*), **ton** (*your*), **son** (*his/her*), etc., when someone does something to a part of his or her own body. Instead, the body part is preceded by the definite article (**le, la, les**), and the verb used *reflexively*. Hence, "I brush **my** teeth," is expressed in French by "I brush **myself** *the* teeth," and "she washes **her** hands" by "she washes **herself** *the* hands."

se **brosser *les* dents** *to brush one's teeth*

    Je **me** brosse **les** dents.   *I brush **my** teeth.*

se **laver *la* tête** / *les* **cheveux** *to wash one's hair*

    Elle **se** lave **la** tête.   *She washes **her** hair.*

Also:

    se **brosser *les* cheveux** *to brush one's hair*
    se **sécher *les* cheveux** *to dry one's hair*
    se **casser *la* jambe** *to break one's leg*
    se **raser *les* jambes** *to shave one's legs*
    se **laver *les* mains** *to wash one's hands*
    se **laver *la* figure** *to wash one's face*
    *s'***essuyer *les* pieds** *to wipe one's feet*
    se **limer** / *se* **couper *les* ongles** *to file/cut one's nails*

EXERCICE
4·4

Comment dit-on en français?

1. Do you (*fam.*) brush your teeth often? _____

2. I wash my hair. _____

3. She shaves her legs. _____

4. You (*pol.*) brush your hair. _____

5. We wash our hands. _____

6. They (*masc.*) don't wipe their feet. _____

7. You (*pol.*) cut your nails. _____

The infinitive of reflexive verbs

Normally, the infinitive of a reflexive verb is preceded by **se** (**s'**), for example *se lever* (*to get up*). When however the infinitive follows a conjugated verb in a sentence, the reflexive pronoun (which precedes the infinitive) agrees with the subject.

Je vais **me coucher**.	*I am going to go to bed.*
Il va **se fâcher**.	*He is going to get angry.*
Tu as l'air de **t'ennuyer**.	*You seem to be bored.*
Je viens de **me réveiller**.	*I just woke up.*
Nous détestons **nous lever** tôt.	*We hate to get up early.*
Vous devez **vous reposer**.	*You have to rest.*

EXERCICE
4·5

Traduisez en français.

1. I would like (**Je voudrais**) to introduce myself. _____

2. You (*fam.*) have to hurry. _____

3. We are going to get dressed. _____

4. She doesn't want to go to bed late. _____

5. Do you (*pol.*) like to get up early? _____

6. We just got married. _____

7. I cannot remember. _____

8. I want to go swimming. _____

9. You (*fam.*) are going to manage. _____

Exercices de révision

EXERCICE
4·6

Est-ce vrai ou faux?

_____ 1. En général, je me couche tard.

_____ 2. Je me lave les cheveux tous les jours.

_____ 3. Je ne m'intéresse pas à la politique.

_____ 4. Je me trompe rarement.

_____ 5. Je ne me plains jamais.

_____ 6. Je m'inquiète pour l'avenir.

_____ 7. Je me brosse les dents deux fois par jour.

_____ 8. Je me fâche souvent.

_____ 9. Je me souviens très bien de mon enfance.

_____ 10. Je m'appelle François.

EXERCICE
4·7

Répondez en français aux questions suivantes.

1. À quelle heure est-ce que le soleil se couche en été? _____

2. Combien de fois par jour vous lavez-vous les mains? _____

_____

3. Quand est-ce que vous vous ennuyez? _____

4. Est-ce que vous vous trompez quelquefois? _____

5. Comment s'appellent vos parents? _____

6. Dans quel pays se trouvent les chutes *(falls)* du Niagara? _____

_____

7. Quand est-ce que vous vous plaignez? _____

Remplissez les tirets (Fill in the blanks) avec la forme correcte du verbe convenable tirée de la liste suivante. Utilisez chaque verbe une fois seulement.

se reposer, s'ennuyer, s'asseoir, s'arrêter, se dépêcher, se moquer de

1. Quand le professeur est ridicule, les étudiants _____ lui.

2. Nous _____ quand la classe n'est pas intéressante.

3. Si on est en retard, on _____.

4. Quand le métro _____, les gens descendent.

5. Je suis fatigué(e). Je vais _____ un peu.

6. Cette place est libre. Vous pouvez _____ si vous voulez.

Remplissez les tirets (Fill in the blanks) avec la forme correcte du verbe convenable de la liste suivante. Utilisez chaque verbe une fois seulement.

se souvenir, se rappeler, s'inquiéter, se coucher, s'endormir, se lever, se plaindre

1. Les élèves _____ avant un examen.

2. Samedi soir, les jeunes gens _____ tard. Ils sont si fatigués qu'ils _____ tout de suite.

3. Le dimanche matin, je fais la grasse matinée, c'est-à-dire je ne _____ pas avant midi.

4. Qu'est-ce que vous avez fait le jour de votre troisième anniversaire? —Je ne _____ pas!

5. J'ai une mauvaise mémoire. Je ne _____ de rien.

6. Quand le professeur donne trop de devoirs, les étudiants _____.

Traduisez en français.

My name is Anne and I am twenty years old. Every morning, I wake up at seven o'clock, but I don't get up right away. I stay in bed for thirty minutes. Then, I brush my teeth and take a shower. I put on my make-up and get dressed. Then, I eat breakfast. Afterwards, I go to work. When it is late, I hurry because I don't want to be late. At noon, I eat a ham sandwich and a piece of apple pie. In the afternoon, I go for a walk or I take a rest. At five P.M., I go home. In the evening, I sit down in front of the television and I relax.

I am rarely worried and I am never bored. Sometimes, I go out to a nightclub with my friends and I have a good time. At midnight, I get undressed and I go to bed. I usually fall asleep quickly.

VOCABULAIRE	afterwards	**après**	never	**ne... jamais**
	apple pie	**tarte (f.) aux pommes**	a piece of	**un morceau de**
	every morning	**tous les matins**	right away	**tout de suite**
	to go to a nightclub	**sortir en boîte**	to stay in bed	**rester au lit**
	a ham sandwich	**un sandwich au jambon**		

_____

_____

_____

_____

_____

_____

_____

_____

_____

Reflexive and non-reflexive use

While some French reflexive verbs, such as **se souvenir** (*to remember*), **se moquer de** (*to make fun of*), **s'en aller** (*to go away*), only occur in the reflexive form, most also exist in a non-reflexive form.

Of these verbs, many have the same meaning both in their reflexive and non-reflexive forms. *Compare:*

NON-REFLEXIVE USE	REFLEXIVE USE
améliorer *to improve (sb or sth)*	**s'améliorer** *to improve*
Cela va **améliorer** le résultat. *This is going to improve the result.*	La situation **s'améliore**. *The situation is improving.*
arrêter *to stop (sb or sth)*	**s'arrêter** *to stop*
Elle **arrête** l'autobus. *She stops the bus.*	L'autobus **s'arrête**. *The bus stops.*

(continued)

NON-REFLEXIVE USE	REFLEXIVE USE
cacher *to hide (sb or sth)*	*se* **cacher** *to hide*
Nous **cachons** nos bijoux. *We hide our jewelry.*	Nous **nous cachons** dans la cave. *We hide in the cellar.*
casser *to break (sth)*	*se* **casser** *to break*
Il **casse** la tasse. *He breaks the cup.*	La tasse **se casse**. *The cup breaks.*
couper *to cut (sth)*	*se* **couper** *to cut oneself*
Ils **coupent** le gâteau. *They cut the cake.*	Ils **se coupent**. *They cut themselves.*
inquiéter *to worry (sb)*	*s'***inquiéter** (de) *to worry (about)*
J'**inquiète** mes parents. *I worry my parents.*	Je **m'inquiète**. *I worry.*
réveiller *to wake up (sb)*	*se* **réveiller** *to wake up*
Il **réveille** le bébé. *He wakes up the baby.*	Il **se réveille**. *He wakes up.*
tuer *to kill (sb or sth)*	*se* **tuer** *to kill oneself*
Il **tue** l'ours. *He kills the bear.*	Il **se tue**. *He kills himself.*

EXERCICE 4·11

Reflexive or not? Choose the verb that fits in the sentence. Then write the correct form of this verb in the present tense. Remember that when the verb is reflexive, the action is performed and received by the subject.

1. Nous (arrêter / s'arrêter) _____ au feu rouge.

2. Nous (arrêter / s'arrêter) _____ le taxi.

3. Ils (cacher / se cacher) _____ leur argent sous le lit.

4. Ils (cacher / se cacher) _____ derrière l'arbre.

5. Je (réveiller / se réveiller) _____ tôt tous les jours.

6. Je (réveiller / se réveiller) _____ les enfants à six heures.

7. Les chasseurs (tuer / se tuer) _____ les biches.

8. Certains jeunes gens (tuer / se tuer) _____ par désespoir.

9. Tu (inquiéter / s'inquiéter) _____ de ton avenir.

10. Tu (inquiéter / s'inquiéter) _____ tes amis.

Some verbs however have a different meaning in their reflexive and non-reflexive forms. *Compare:*

NON-REFLEXIVE USE	REFLEXIVE USE
amuser *to amuse, entertain*	**s'amuser** *to have a good time*
Le clown **amuse** les enfants. *The clown amuses the children.*	Les enfants **s'amusent** au cirque. *The children have a good time at the circus.*
appeler *to call*	**s'appeler** *to be named*
J'**appelle** la police. *I call the police.*	Je **m'appelle** Fred. *My name is Fred.*
rappeler *to call back*	*se* **rappeler** *to remember*
Je **rappelle** mes amis. *I call my friends back.*	Je **me rappelle**. *I remember.*
attendre *to wait for*	**s'attendre** (à) *to expect*
Il **attend** le train. *He waits for the train.*	Il **s'attend au** pire. *He expects the worst.*
conduire *to drive*	*se* **conduire** *to behave*
Elle **conduit** une Peugeot. *She drives a Peugeot.*	Elle **se conduit** mal. *She behaves badly.*
coucher *to put to bed, lay down*	*se* **coucher** *to go to bed*
La petite fille **couche** sa poupée. *The little girl puts her doll to bed.*	Elle **se couche**. *She goes to bed.*
demander *to ask*	*se* **demander** *to wonder*
Tu **demandes** à l'homme. *You ask the man.*	Tu **te demandes**. *You wonder.*
douter (de) *to doubt*	*se* **douter** (de/que) *to suspect (sth/that)*
Elle **doute de** sa sincérité. *She has doubts about his sincerity.*	Elle **se doute de** quelque chose. *She suspects something.*
entendre *to hear*	**s'entendre** (avec) *to get along (with)*
Ils **entendent** une voix. *They hear a voice.*	Ils **s'entendent** bien. *They get along well.*
excuser *to excuse*	**s'excuser** *to apologize*
Il **excuse** mon absence. *He excuses my absence.*	Il **s'excuse**. *He apologizes.*
lever *to raise*	*se* **lever** *to get up*
Nous **levons** la main. *We raise our hands.*	Nous **nous levons**. *We get up.*
mettre *to put, put on*	*se* **mettre à** (+ inf.) *to begin*
Il **met** ses chaussettes. *He puts on his socks.*	Il **se met à** travailler. *He begins to work.*

(continued)

Reflexive verbs **85**

NON-REFLEXIVE USE	REFLEXIVE USE
passer *to pass/go by*	*se* **passer** *to happen*
Je vais **passer** à la confiserie.	Qu'est-ce qui **se passe**?
I'll go by the candy store.	*What is happening?*
plaindre *to pity*	*se* **plaindre** *to complain*
Elle le **plaint**.	Elle **se plaint**.
She pities him.	*She complains.*
promener *to take for a walk, walk (an animal)*	*se* **promener** *to go for a walk*
Elle **promène** son chien.	Elle **se promène** dans le parc.
She walks her dog.	*She goes for a walk in the park.*
servir *to serve*	*se* **servir (de)** *to use*
Le serveur **sert** le repas.	Je **me sers d**'un stylo bille.
The waiter serves the meal.	*I use a ballpoint pen.*
tromper *to deceive, be unfaithful to*	*se* **tromper** *to be mistaken*
Elle **trompe** son mari.	Elle **se trompe**.
She cheats on her husband.	*She is mistaken.*
trouver *to find*	*se* **trouver** *to be (situated)*
Vous **trouvez** la clé.	La clé **se trouve** sur la commode.
You find the key.	*The key is on the chest of drawers.*

EXERCICE
4·12

Reflexive or not? Choose the verb that fits in the sentence. Then write the correct form of this verb in the present tense.

1. Les comiques (amuser / s'amuser) _____ les gens.

2. Les adolescents (amuser / s'amuser) _____ bien aux boums.

3. Elle (appeler / s'appeler) _____ Suzanne.

4. Le professeur (appeler / s'appeler) _____ l'étudiant.

5. Je te (rappeler / se rappeler) _____ ce soir.

6. Je ne (rappeler / se rappeler) _____ pas son nom.

7. Est-ce que vous (attendre / s'attendre) _____ le facteur?

8. À quoi est-ce que vous (attendre / s'attendre) _____?

9. Si on insulte les gens, on ne (conduire / se conduire) _____ pas bien.

10. Si on a beaucoup d'accidents de voiture, on (conduire / se conduire) _____ probablement mal.

11. La mère (coucher / se coucher) _____ les enfants à sept heures.

12. Ma mère (coucher / se coucher) _____ toujours tard.

13. Je (demander / se demander) _____ à mes parents de m'accompagner.

14. Il n'est pas venu. Je (demander / se demander) _____ pourquoi.

15. Il (excuser / s'excuser) _____ d'être en retard.

16. Il (excuser / s'excuser) _____ mon retard.

17. Nous (mettre / se mettre) _____ les fleurs dans le vase.

18. Nous (mettre / se mettre) _____ à rire.

19. Cette histoire (passer / se passer) _____ en Russie.

20. Elle (passer / se passer) _____ à la douane.

21. Je (promener / se promener) _____ tous les dimanches.

22. Je (promener / se promener) _____ mon caniche tous les soirs.

23. Ce monsieur n'a pas raison, il (tromper / se tromper) _____ .

24. Ce monsieur (tromper / se tromper) _____ sa femme depuis longtemps.

25. Ils ne (trouver / se trouver) _____ pas la sortie.

26. Ces châteaux (trouver / se trouver) _____ dans le Val de Loire.

27. Où (trouver / se trouver) _____ la bibliothèque?

The use of the reflexive pronoun to indicate reciprocal action

When two or more people do something to one another, French uses the plural reflexive pronouns (**nous, vous, se**) to express *each other*.

Nous **nous** aidons.	*We help **each other**.*
Vous **vous** connaissez?	*Do you know **each other**?*
Ils **s'**aiment bien.	*They like **each other**.*
Elles **s'**écrivent souvent.	*They often write **to each other**.*
Nous **nous** téléphonons.	*We call **each other**.*
Les Français **se** disent « bon appétit » avant de commencer à manger.	*The French say "have a nice meal" to **each other** before they begin to eat.*

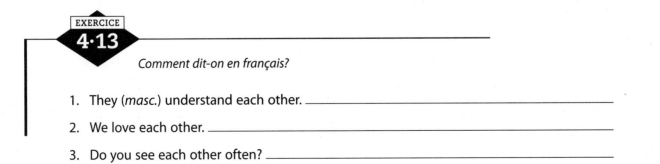

EXERCICE
4·13

Comment dit-on en français?

1. They (*masc.*) understand each other. _____

2. We love each other. _____

3. Do you see each other often? _____

4. They (*fem.*) hate each other. _____

5. You help each other. _____

6. They (*masc.*) hug each other. _____

7. They (*fem.*) don't speak to each other any more. _____

8. Have you known each other for a long time? _____

9. My daughter and I telephone each other every other day (**tous les deux jours**). _____

_____

10. We say "hello" to each other. _____

Reflexive constructions with a passive meaning

French transitive verbs, that is, verbs that take an *object*, are sometimes used with the reflexive pronoun **se** (**s'**) in the third-person singular or plural to replace the *passive voice* (English: *is/are + past participle*) or a construction with **on** (*one*). The subject of these sentences is always a thing, frequently the pronoun **cela** (*that*), or its abbreviated form **ça**. Usually, a habit or general truth is expressed in this manner.

Le mot français « mariage » **s'écrit** avec un seul « r ».	The French word "mariage" **is written** with one "r" only.
Cela (or: Ça) ne **se dit** pas.	**One doesn't say** that.
Les homonymes sont des mots qui **se prononcent** de la même façon.	Homonyms are words that **are pronounced** the same way.
Les verbes pronominaux **se conjuguent** avec « être » aux temps composés.	Reflexive verbs **are conjugated** with être in the compound tenses.

EXERCICE
4·14

Remplacez le sujet on *par la forme pronominale* (se + verbe). (*Rewrite the following sentences using a reflexive construction with a passive meaning.*)

Exemple: On boit le vin rouge chambré (*at room temperature*).   Le vin rouge **se boit** chambré.

1. On ouvre les portes du magasin à neuf heures. _____

2. On écrit le mot « adresse » avec un seul « d ». _____

3. On lave ce costume à la main. _____

4. On ne fait pas ça en France. _____

5. On ne dit pas « visiter quelqu'un ». _____

6. On joue la pièce à la Comédie-Française. _____

7. On emploie souvent cette expression. _____

8. On voit la tour Eiffel de loin. _____

9. Comment dit-on « singe » en anglais? _____

10. On n'apprend pas le français en un jour. _____

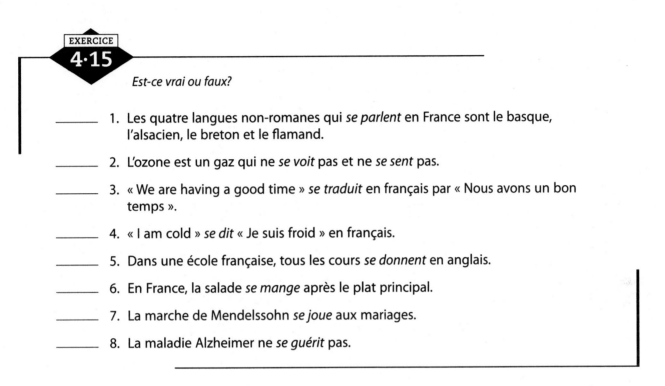

Est-ce vrai ou faux?

_____ 1. Les quatre langues non-romanes qui *se parlent* en France sont le basque, l'alsacien, le breton et le flamand.

_____ 2. L'ozone est un gaz qui ne *se voit* pas et ne *se sent* pas.

_____ 3. « We are having a good time » *se traduit* en français par « Nous avons un bon temps ».

_____ 4. « I am cold » *se dit* « Je suis froid » en français.

_____ 5. Dans une école française, tous les cours *se donnent* en anglais.

_____ 6. En France, la salade *se mange* après le plat principal.

_____ 7. La marche de Mendelssohn *se joue* aux mariages.

_____ 8. La maladie Alzheimer ne *se guérit* pas.

THE PAST TENSES

The *passé composé*

The **passé composé** is one of the past tenses used in French. It is generally translated into English by the simple past (*I lived, she wrote*), but can also be translated by the present perfect (*I have lived, she has written*), and by the emphatic past (*I did live, she did write*).

Do not assume however, that every simple past corresponds to the **passé composé**. If an action was habitual or repeated an unspecified number of times, the imperfect tense, which will be discussed in the next chapter, translates the simple past.

If you know how long a past action lasted (*I worked for forty years*), how many times it occurred (*we visited her four times*), or at what precise moment it happened (*I called you last night; she met him yesterday*), you will use the **passé composé**. A more detailed description of the use of the **passé composé** will follow the review of its formation.

The formation of the *passé composé*

Like the English present perfect, the **passé composé** is a compound tense, i.e., it consists of two words, a helping verb (also called *auxiliary*) and the *past participle* of the verb in question. In English, the auxiliary is always the verb *to have* (*I **have** lived, he **has** stayed*); in French, it can be either **avoir** or **être** (*j'**ai** habité, il **est** resté*). Most French (regular and irregular) verbs use **avoir** to build the **passé composé**. Several intransitive verbs, as well as all reflexive verbs, use **être**. The second element of the **passé composé** is the *past participle*. To form the past participle of *regular verbs*, do the following:

With -**er** verbs, drop the -**er** ending and
replace it with -**é**:   parler → parlé
With -**ir** verbs, drop the -**ir** ending and
replace it with -**i**:   finir → fini
With -**re** verbs drop the -**re** ending and
replace it with -**u**:   répondre → répondu

The past participles of irregular verbs cannot be derived from the infinitive. Their forms will be presented later.

The *passé composé* of verbs conjugated with *avoir*

The **passé composé** of these verbs is formed by combining the present tense of **avoir** with the *past participle* of the verb in question.

Regular verbs

parler *to speak*

j'ai parlé   *I spoke, I have spoken, I did speak*
tu as parlé
il/elle/on a parlé
nous avons parlé
vous avez parlé
ils/elles ont parlé

finir *to finish*

j'ai fini   *I finished, I have/am finished, I did finish*
tu as fini
il/elle/on a fini
nous avons fini
vous avez fini
ils/elles ont fini

répondre *to answer*

j'ai répondu   *I answered, I have answered, I did answer*
tu as répondu
il/elle/on a répondu
nous avons répondu
vous avez répondu
ils/elles ont répondu

The negative and interrogative forms

In the negative form, **ne** precedes the auxiliary, **pas** follows it.

je **n'**ai **pas** parlé   *I didn't speak, I haven't spoken*
tu **n'**as **pas** parlé
il/elle/on **n'**a **pas** parlé
nous **n'**avons **pas** parlé
vous **n'**avez **pas** parlé
ils/elles **n'**ont **pas** parlé

The interrogative form can either use **est-ce que** or *inversion*.

est-ce que j'ai parlé?   *Did I speak? Have I spoken?*
est-ce que tu as parlé?
est-ce qu'il/elle/on a parlé?
est-ce que nous avons parlé?
est-ce que vous avez parlé?
est-ce qu'ils/elles ont parlé?

In the inverted question, the subject pronoun is placed after the auxiliary and linked to it by a hyphen. In the third-person singular (**il, elle, on**), the letter -**t**- is inserted between the auxiliary and the subject pronoun. With **je**, it is preferable to use **est-ce que**.

as-tu parlé?
a-t-il/elle/on parlé?
avons-nous parlé?
avez-vous parlé?
ont-ils/elles parlé?

Did you speak? Have you spoken?

EXERCICE
5·1

Traduisez en français les phrases suivantes.

1. I forgot. _____

2. She worked. _____

3. We didn't listen. _____

4. They (*masc.*) cried. _____

5. How much money did you (*fam.*) spend? _____

6. I didn't ask. _____

7. He bought a blanket. _____

8. They (*fem.*) played cards. _____

9. You (*pol.*) brought pastries. _____

10. She lost control (**le contrôle**) of her (**sa**) car. _____

11. They (*masc.*) studied. _____

12. I heard the noise. _____

13. We tried. _____

14. I didn't wait. _____

15. Did you (*pol.*) answer? _____

16. Are you (*fam.*) finished? (= Did you finish?) —Yes, I (have) finished. _____

17. She obeyed her father. _____

18. We didn't succeed. _____

19. They (*fem.*) applauded. _____

20. She reflected a long time. _____

Irregular verbs

Irregular verbs have irregular past participles which must be memorized. The past participles listed below use **avoir** to build the **passé composé**. Note the verb groups below, listed under their "model" verb in bold, which have the same past participle endings.

INFINITIVE	ENGLISH MEANING	PAST PARTICIPLE
avoir	*to have*	**eu**
boire	*to drink*	**bu**
conduire	*to drive*	**conduit**
construire	*to build*	construit
détruire	*to destroy*	détruit
produire	*to produce*	produit
traduire	*to translate*	traduit
connaître	*to know*	**connu**
disparaître	*to disappear*	disparu
paraître	*to seem*	paru
reconnaître	*to recognize*	reconnu
courir	*to run*	**couru**
croire	*to believe*	**cru**
devoir	*to have to, owe*	**dû**
dire	*to say*	**dit**
dormir	*to sleep*	**dormi**
écrire	*to write*	**écrit**
être	*to be*	**été**
faire	*to make, do*	**fait**
falloir	*to be necessary*	**fallu**
lire	*to read*	**lu**
mettre	*to put, put on*	**mis**
permettre	*to allow, permit*	permis
promettre	*to promise*	promis
ouvrir	*to open*	**ouvert**
découvrir	*to discover, find out*	découvert
offrir	*to offer*	offert
souffrir	*to suffer*	souffert
plaire	*to please*	**plu**
pleuvoir	*to rain*	**plu**
pouvoir	*to be able to*	**pu**
prendre	*to take*	**pris**
apprendre	*to learn*	appris
comprendre	*to understand*	compris
recevoir	*to receive*	**reçu**
rire	*to laugh*	**ri**
sourire	*to smile*	souri
savoir	*to know*	**su**
suivre	*to follow*	**suivi**
valoir	*to be worth*	**valu**
vivre	*to live*	**vécu**
voir	*to see*	**vu**
vouloir	*to want*	**voulu**

Below you will find the conjugations of two irregular verbs conjugated with **avoir** in the **passé composé**.

faire *to do, make*		
j'ai fait	*I did, I have done, I did do*	nous avons fait
tu as fait		vous avez fait
il/elle/on a fait		ils/elles ont fait

être _to be_		
j'ai été	_I was, I have been_	nous avons été
tu as été		vous avez été
il/elle/on a été		ils/elles ont été

Comment dit-on en français?

1. I drank a glass of water. _____

2. She didn't have the time. _____

3. He ran. _____

4. We believed this story. _____

5. She had to laugh. _____

6. What did you (_fam._) say? _____

7. We didn't understand anything. (= We understood nothing.) _____

8. Did you (_pol._) sleep well? _____

9. I didn't write the poem. _____

10. Have you (_pol._) ever (**déjà**) been to Denmark (**au Danemark**)? _____

11. Did you (_fam._) receive my gift? _____

12. What did you (_fam._) do? _____

13. He made a mistake. _____

14. Did you (_pol._) read the newspaper? _____

15. Where did she put the calculator? _____

16. The wine steward (**le sommelier**) opened the bottle. _____

17. Did you (_fam._) see the show? _____

18. It rained. _____

19. I liked the performance a lot. (_Use_ **plaire.**) _____

20. I took the elevator. _____

Verbs with a special meaning in the _passé composé_

Of the irregular verbs conjugated with **avoir**, **savoir** (_to know_), **connaître** (_to know_ [_sb_]), **pouvoir** (_to be able to_), and **vouloir** (_to want_) can change their meaning in the **passé composé**.

When used in this tense, these verbs often mean the following:

savoir *to find out, to learn*

Elle ne l'**a su** que ce matin.   *She only **found out** (about that) this morning.*

connaître *to meet (for the first time), make the acquaintance of*

J'**ai connu** mon mari en France.   *I **met** my husband in France.*

pouvoir *could (and did)*

Grâce à sa tante, il **a pu** faire ses études   *Thanks to his aunt, he **could** study in France.*
en France.

ne pas pouvoir *could not (failed to [but tried])*

Je n'**ai** pas **pu** le joindre.   *I **could not** reach him (by phone).*

vouloir *to try to, decide to*

Il **a voulu** y aller.   *He **tried to** go there.*

ne pas vouloir *to refuse to*

Ils n'**ont** pas **voulu** partir.   *They **refused to** (would not) leave.*

EXERCICE
5·3

Comment dit-on en français?

1. When did you (*fam.*) find out the truth? _____

2. My dad met my mom at a party (**dans une soirée**). _____

3. He could go to college. _____

4. I couldn't (= failed to) do it. _____

5. They tried to get up. _____

6. She refused to say her (**son**) name. _____

The agreement of past participles combined with *avoir*

As we have seen above, the past participle of verbs using **avoir** to form the **passé composé** remains unchanged during the conjugation. If used in a sentence however, the past participle can change under certain circumstances. When this happens, one says that it *agrees* with another word, that is, assumes the same gender (masculine or feminine) and number (singular or plural) as this word. Here is the rule:

The past participle of verbs using **avoir** as auxiliary to form the **passé composé** agrees in gender and number with a *preceding direct* object. If this object is feminine singular, **-e** is added to the past participle; if it is masculine plural, **-s** is added (except when the past participle ends in **-s**); if it is feminine plural, **-es** is added.

The preceding direct object can be

- A direct object pronoun (**la [l'], nous, les**...).

    Il **nous** a reconnu**s**.   He recognized us.
    As-tu vu **la pièce**? —Oui, je l'ai vu**e**.   Did you see the play? —Yes, I saw it.

- The relative pronoun **que** and a (feminine or plural) noun which precedes it.

    La lettre que j'ai écrit**e** est longue.   The letter (that) I wrote is long.

- The interrogative adjectives **quelle, quels, quelles** (+ *noun* and the interrogative pronouns **laquelle, lesquels, lesquelles.**

    Quels livres avez-vous lu**s**?   Which books did you read?
    Lesquels avez-vous lu**s**?   Which ones did you read?
    Quelle imprimante ont-ils acheté**e**?   Which printer did they buy?

- A noun introduced by the exclamatory adjective **quelle**... ! (**quels**... !, **quelles**... !).

    Quelle chance elle a eu**e**!   How lucky she was!

- A noun introduced by **combien de.**

    Combien de photos avez-vous pri**ses**?   How many pictures did you take?

Note:

- Remember that agreement of the past participle of verbs conjugated with **avoir** only occurs when the object is *direct* and if it *comes before* the past participle. The past participle of these verbs remains unchanged if there is no preceding direct object, if the direct object *follows* the past participle, or if the preceding object is *indirect.*

    Elle a **vu_** la générale.   She saw the dress rehearsal.

    There is a direct object (**la générale**), but since it *follows* the past participle, no agreement occurs.

    Ils **leur** ont **répondu_**.   They answered them.

    There is a preceding object (**leur**), but since it is *indirect*, no agreement occurs.
- Most past participle agreements are not audible in spoken French. The pronunciation will only differ when the past participle ends in a consonant and receives a feminine ending. *Compare:*

    J'ai mis [mi] les tasses dans le   I put the cups in the dishwasher.
        lave-vaisselle.
    Je **les** ai mi**ses** [miz] dans le   I put them in the dishwasher.
        lave-vaisselle.

EXERCICE
5·4

Écrivez le participe passé du verbe entre parenthèses et faites l'accord si c'est nécessaire.

1. Ils ont (vendre) _____ l'immeuble.

2. J'ai acheté des fleurs et je les ai (mettre) _____ dans un vase.

3. Quels magazines avez-vous (lire) _____?

4. Où sont les photos (*fem.*) que tu m'as (montrer) _____ .

5. Nous avons (fermer) _____ les portes.

6. As-tu (recevoir) _____ toutes les lettres que je t'ai

   (envoyer) _____ ?

7. Tous les peuples ont (souffrir) _____ de cette guerre.

8. Sa sœur a (croire) _____ toutes les histoires qu'on lui a

   (raconter) _____ .

9. La bière que nous avons (boire) _____ était excellente.

10. La pièce que nous avons (voir) _____ nous a beaucoup

    (plaire) _____ .

The *passé composé* of verbs conjugated with *être*

The auxiliary **être** is used to form the **passé composé** with the following *intransitive verbs* (most of which express movement or a change of state).

In the list below, when possible, verbs are grouped by opposites for easier memorization, and irregular past participles are indicated in parentheses.

> **aller** *to go*
> **venir (venu)** *to come*
> **arriver** *to arrive (also: to happen, succeed)*
> **partir** *to leave*
> **sortir** *to go out*
> **entrer** *to enter, come in*
> **monter** *to go up, get on (a train, bus, plane), get in (a car)*
> **descendre** *to go down, get off (a train, bus, plane), get out of (a car)*
> **naître (né)** *to be born*
> **mourir (mort)** *to die*
> **passer** *to pass by, come by, go past, pass through, be (on TV)*
> **rester** *to stay*
> **retourner** *to go back, return (to a place)*
> **tomber** *to fall*

Also conjugated with **être** are compounds of the verbs above, such as **rentrer** (*to go/return home*), **devenir** (*to become*), and **revenir** (*to come back*).

Here is a model conjugation:

aller *to go*			
je **suis** allé(e)	*I went, I have gone, I did go*	nous **sommes** allé(e)s	*we went*
tu **es** allé(e)	*you went*	vous **êtes** allé(e)(s)	*you went*
il/on **est** allé	*he/it/one went*	ils **sont** allés	*they went*
elle **est** allée	*she/it went*	elles **sont** allées	*they went*

The agreement of past participles combined with *être*

The past participle of verbs conjugated with **être** agrees in gender and number with the *subject*. If the subject is feminine singular, **-e** is added to the past participle, if the subject is masculine plural, **-s** is added, and if the subject is feminine plural, **-es** is added. When a woman writes about herself, for example, she will write **je suis allée** (for a man, the correct form is **je suis allé**). If a group of female persons is addressed, one writes **vous êtes all*ées***.

EXERCICE 5·5

Comment dit-on en français?

1. Where did you (*fam. masc.*) go? _____

2. He came alone. _____

3. What became of her (= What did she become)? _____

4. You (*pol. fem.*) came back. _____

5. When did they (*fem.*) arrive? _____

6. We (*masc.*) left at noon. _____

7. Who came in? _____

8. Did you (*fam. fem.*) go out last night? _____

9. They (*masc.*) got off the train in Lyon. _____

10. They (*fem.*) went up to the third floor (**au deuxième étage**).* _____

11. Where were you (*fam. fem.*) born? _____

12. My grandmother died last year. _____

13. How long did you stay (*fam. fem.*) in France? _____

14. She returned to her country. _____

15. I (*fem.*) fell in the trap. _____

_____

*Note that "le premier étage" is the second floor in the United States, "le deuxième étage" is the third floor, etc. The American first floor corresponds to "le rez-de-chaussée" in France.

EXERCICE 5·6

Complétez avec l'antonyme (the opposite) du verbe souligné (au passé composé).

1. Mes amis <u>sont</u> d'abord <u>venus</u> chez moi, ensuite, ils _____ au cinéma.

2. L'avion <u>est arrivé</u> à Chicago à midi, et il _____ pour San Francisco à treize heures.

3. Ma grand-mère est née en 1920, et elle _____ en 1996.

4. Les étudiants sont entrés dans le musée à neuf heures, ils _____ à quinze heures.

5. Les touristes sont montés à la tour Eiffel par l'ascenseur, ils _____ à pied.

Verbs that can be conjugated with *être* or *avoir*

Six of the intransitive verbs which are normally conjugated with **être** (**monter, descendre, sortir, rentrer, retourner, passer**) can be used transitively, i.e., with a direct object. In this case, they are conjugated with **avoir**.

When followed by a direct object (i.e., a noun that is *not* preceded by a preposition),

- ◆ **monter** and **descendre** keep their meaning (*to go up, to go down*) in some contexts (when followed by a place such as *stairs, street,* etc., that someone goes up or down), and have a different meaning (*to take sth up, to take sth down*) in other contexts (when followed by an object that is being transported up or down).
- ◆ **sortir, rentrer, retourner** change their meaning to *to take sth out, to take sth inside, to turn sth over.*
- ◆ **passer** means *to spend (time), to take (an exam), to hand (sth to sb),* and *to have (a good day, a good vacation, etc.).*

Compare:

INTRANSITIVE USE (CONJUGATED WITH **ÊTRE**)	TRANSITIVE USE (CONJUGATED WITH **AVOIR**)
Je **suis** monté au premier étage.	J'**ai** monté l'escalier.
I went up to the second floor.	*I went up the stairs.*
Il **est** monté dans le taxi.	Il **a** monté la valise au grenier.
He got in the taxi.	*He took the suitcase up to the attic.*
Ils **sont** descendus au sous-sol.	Ils **ont** descendu la rue.
They went down to the basement.	*They went down the street.*
Elle **est** descendue de l'autobus.	Elle **a** descendu le vin à la cave.
She got off the bus.	*She took the wine down to the cellar.*
Elle **est** sortie de la salle.	Elle **a** sorti la poubelle.
She went out of the room.	*She took out the garbage can.*
Je **suis** rentré tard hier soir.	J'**ai** rentré les chaises.
I came home late last night.	*I took the chairs inside.*
Elle **est** retournée dans son pays.	Elle **a** retourné les crêpes.
She returned to her country.	*She turned over the crêpes.*
Le facteur **est** déjà passé.	Il **a** passé trois jours à Barcelone.
The mailman already came by.	*He spent three days in Barcelona.*
Je **suis** passé à l'orange.	Elle **a** passé l'examen hier.
I passed through a yellow light.	*She took the exam yesterday.*

Est-ce avoir *ou* être? *Mettez les verbes entre parenthèses au passé composé.*

1. (rentrer) À quelle heure _____-elle _____ hier soir?

2. (rentrer) Est-ce que tu _____ la voiture au garage?

3. (retourner) Elle _____ en train.

4. (retourner) Le vent _____ le bateau.

5. (monter) Nous _____ le courrier (*the mail*).

6. (monter) Est-ce que tous les passagers _____ dans l'avion?

7. (descendre) Nous _____ la colline (*the hill*).

8. (descendre) Ils _____ au rez-de-chaussée.

9. (sortir) Est-ce que vous _____ le champagne du réfrigérateur?

10. (sortir) Le livre _____ en novembre.

11. (sortir) Elle _____ un livre en novembre.

12. (passer) Ils _____ à la télé. (*They were on TV.*)

13. (passer) Nous _____ devant la mairie (*town hall*).

14. (passer) Je _____ une nuit blanche (*a sleepless night*).

15. (passer) Quand est-ce que tu _____ l'examen?

16. (passer) _____-vous _____ de bonnes vacances?

17. (passer) Elle _____ l'aspirateur. (*She vacuumed.*)

The *passé composé* of reflexive verbs

The auxiliary **être** is also used to form the **passé composé** of all *reflexive verbs*. Here is a model conjugation.

s'amuser *to enjoy oneself*	
je me suis amusé(e)	*I enjoyed myself*
tu t'es amusé(e)	*you enjoyed yourself*
il/on s'est amusé	*he/one enjoyed himself/oneself*
elle s'est amusée	*she enjoyed herself*
nous nous sommes amusé(e)s	*we enjoyed ourselves*
vous vous êtes amusé(e)(s)	*you enjoyed yourself(ves)*
ils se sont amusés	*they enjoyed themselves*
elles se sont amusées	*they enjoyed themselves*

Negative form

je **ne** me suis **pas** amusé(e)	*I didn't enjoy myself*
tu ne t'es pas amusé(e)	

il/on ne s'est pas amusé
elle ne s'est pas amusée
nous ne nous sommes pas amusé(e)s
vous ne vous êtes pas amusé(e)(s)
ils ne se sont pas amusés
elles ne se sont pas amusées

Interrogative forms with *est-ce que*

est-ce que je me suis amusé(e)?   *did I enjoy myself?*
est-ce que tu t'es amusé(e)?
est-ce qu'il/on s'est amusé?
est-ce qu'elle s'est amusée?
est-ce que nous nous sommes amusé(e)s?
est-ce que vous vous êtes amusé(e)(s)?
est-ce qu'ils se sont amusés?
est-ce qu'elles se sont amusées?

Inverted interrogative form

As with most verbs, there is no inverted interrogative form in the first-person singular (**je**).

t'es-tu amusé(e)?   *did you enjoy yourself?*
s'est-il/on amusé?
s'est-elle amusée?
nous sommes-nous amusé(e)s?
vous êtes-vous amusé(e)(s)?
se sont-ils amusés?
se sont-elles amusées?

Irregular reflexive verbs

INFINITIVE	PAST PARTICIPLE	*PASSÉ COMPOSÉ*
s'apercevoir	**aperçu**	**je me suis aperçu(e)**
s'asseoir	**assis**	**je me suis assis(e)**
se conduire	**conduit**	**je me suis conduit(e)**
s'endormir	**endormi**	**je me suis endormi(e)**
se mettre à	**mis**	**je me suis mis(e)**
se plaindre	**plaint**	**je me suis plaint(e)**
se sentir	**senti**	**je me suis senti(e)**
se servir	**servi**	**je me suis servi(e)**
se souvenir	**souvenu**	**je me suis souvenu(e)**
se taire	**tu**	**je me suis tu(e)**

The **passé composé** of the verb **s'en aller** is as follows:

je m'en suis allé(e)
tu t'en es allé(e)
il/on s'en est allé
elle s'en est allée
nous nous en sommes allé(e)s
vous vous en êtes allé(e)(s)
ils s'en sont allés
elles s'en sont allées

The agreement of the past participle of reflexive verbs

Although reflexive verbs are conjugated with **être**, their past participle does not agree with the subject, but rather with the preceding direct object.

With many verbs, the reflexive pronoun (with the same gender and number as the subject) *is* this *direct object*.

Elle **s'**est souven**ue**.	*She remembered.*
Ils **s'**en sont all**és**.	*They (masc.) went away*
Elle **s'**est plain**te**.	*She complained.*
Ils **se** sont serv**is** d'un ordinateur.	*They (masc.) used a computer.*
Elles **se** sont tromp**ées**.	*They (fem.) were mistaken.*
Je **me** suis dépêch**ée**.	*I (fem.) hurried.*
Nous **nous** sommes ennuy**és**.	*We (masc.) got bored.*
Elle **s'**est regard**ée** dans la glace.	*She looked at herself in the mirror.*
Elles **se** sont assi**ses**.	*They (fem.) sat down.*
Ils **se** sont cach**és**.	*They (masc.) hid.*
Elles **se** sont compri**ses**.	*They (fem.) understood each other.*

The reflexive pronoun is an *indirect object* (with which *no* agreement is made)

◆ when a direct object follows the past participle. *Compare:*

Elle **s'**est lav**ée**.	*She washed herself.*

In the sentence above, no direct object follows the verb. The reflexive pronoun **se** is a *direct object*. Thus, there is agreement of the past participle with **se**.

Elle **s'**est lavé_ **les cheveux**.	*She washed her hair.*

In this sentence, a direct object, **les cheveux**, follows the verb. The reflexive pronoun **se** is now an *indirect object*. Thus, there is *no* agreement of the past participle with **se**.

◆ with verbs (such as **téléphoner à, parler à**) which, when used non-reflexively, take an *indirect object* (preceded by **à**).

Ils **se** sont téléphoné_.	*They called each other.*	(Je téléphone **à** mon père.)
Elle **s'**est demandé_.	*She wondered.*	(Je demande **à** ma mère.)

EXERCICE

5·8

Comment dit-on en français?

1. We (*masc.*) had a good time. _____

2. When did you (*pol. masc.*) go to bed? _____

3. At what time did you (*fam. fem.*) wake up? _____

4. She hurried. _____

5. My boss (*masc.*) got angry. _____

6. Did you get (*fam. fem.*) bored? _____

7. They (*fem.*) went for a walk. _____

8. I (*fem.*) didn't remember. (*Use two different verbs.*) _____

9. The clock stopped. _____

10. His wife was mistaken. _____

11. She apologized. _____

12. They (*fem.*) got lost. _____

13. We (*masc.*) relaxed. _____

14. The children were silent. _____

15. They got engaged. _____

16. She sat down. _____

17. They (*fem.*) went away. _____

18. The baby fell asleep. _____

19. I (*fem.*) broke my leg. _____

20. What (**Qu'est-ce qui**) happened? (*Use* **se passer**) _____

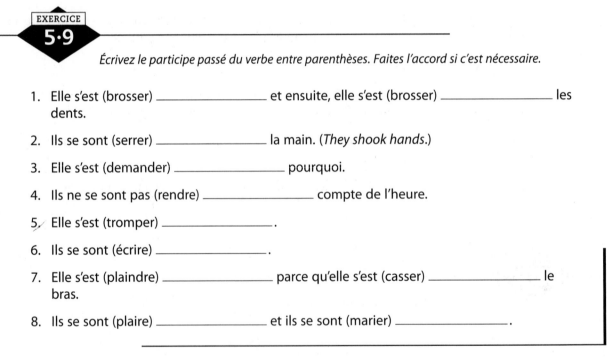

Écrivez le participe passé du verbe entre parenthèses. Faites l'accord si c'est nécessaire.

1. Elle s'est (brosser) _____ et ensuite, elle s'est (brosser) _____ les
dents.

2. Ils se sont (serrer) _____ la main. (*They shook hands.*)

3. Elle s'est (demander) _____ pourquoi.

4. Ils ne se sont pas (rendre) _____ compte de l'heure.

5. Elle s'est (tromper) _____ .

6. Ils se sont (écrire) _____ .

7. Elle s'est (plaindre) _____ parce qu'elle s'est (casser) _____ le
bras.

8. Ils se sont (plaire) _____ et ils se sont (marier) _____ .

Exercices de révision

EXERCICE
5·10

Mettez les verbes entre parenthèses au passé composé.

1. Elle (va) _____ en Écosse.

2. Ils (viennent) _____ malgré le mauvais temps.

3. Je (ne peux pas) _____ fermer l'œil de la nuit.

4. Vous (faites) _____ attention.

5. Je (suis) _____ son conseil.

6. Je (suis) _____ déçu(e).

7. Elles (font) _____ un voyage en Inde.

8. Je (dois) _____ ralentir.

9. Il y (a) _____ beaucoup de neige.

10. Il (faut) _____ une bonne heure pour y arriver.

11. Ils (reçoivent) _____ une bourse (*a scholarship*).

12. Tu (veux) _____ le faire.

13. Il (découvrir) _____ un trésor.

14. Elles (conduisent) _____ les enfants à l'école.

15. Nous (voyons) _____ l'accident de la circulation.

EXERCICE
5·11

Écrivez le participe passé du verbe entre parenthèses et faites l'accord si c'est nécessaire.

1. Les souris (*fem.*) sont (sortir) _____ de leur trou.

2. Tous mes amis sont (venir) _____ à la réunion.

3. Beaucoup de soldats sont (mourir) _____ sur le champ de bataille.

4. Ses projets sont (tomber) _____ à l'eau.

5. Ma sœur est (naître) _____ en janvier.

6. Ils ont (boire) _____ du jus de pamplemousse.

7. Mon frère a (pleurer) _____ parce qu'il a (pleuvoir) _____ .

8. Est-ce que le film vous a (plaire) _____ ?

9. Avez -vous (être) _____ surpris?

Donnez le passé composé des verbes entre parenthèses. Faites l'élision si c'est nécessaire.

1. La jeune fille (tomber) _____ dans les pommes (*fainted*).

2. Il (deviner = *to guess*) _____ ce que son amie (devenir) _____ .

3. Hier, je (recevoir) _____ une mauvaise nouvelle.

4. (finir) _____ -tu _____ ? —Oui, je _____ !

5. (ne pas comprendre) Je _____ ce qu'il (dire) _____ .

6. (montrer) Quand je lui _____ la photo, il (rire) _____ .

7. (monter) _____ -tu _____ à pied?

8. (devoir) Qu'est-ce que vous _____ faire pour réussir?

9. (ouvrir) Quand il _____ la porte, il (voir) _____ que sa maison avait été cambriolée.

10. (mettre) Elle _____ son imperméable et elle (partir) _____ .

11. (dormir) _____ -vous bien _____ ?

12. (ne pas prendre) Je _____ la décision. Je (perdre) _____ courage.

The uses of the *passé composé*

The **passé composé** is used in the following situations:

A. To express a past action which was completed at a *precise moment*, i.e., a specific (time of) day, date, month, year, etc., or within a *limited period of time*, frequently after expressions such as:

ce matin	*this morning*
hier	*yesterday*
hier soir	*last night (evening hours)*
la nuit dernière (= cette nuit)	*last night (night time hours)*
hier matin	*yesterday morning*
hier après-midi	*yesterday afternoon*
avant-hier	*the day before yesterday*
l'autre jour	*the other day*

lundi/mardi, etc. dernier	*last Monday/Tuesday, etc.*
le week-end dernier	*last weekend*
la semaine dernière	*last week*
le mois dernier	*last month*
l'année dernière	*last year*
l'été dernier	*last summer*
l'hiver dernier	*last winter*
il y a huit jours	*eight days ago (= a week ago)*
il y a six semaines	*six weeks ago*
il y a deux mois/ans	*two months/years ago*
tout à l'heure	*a little while ago*
le... février/mars, etc.	*on the . . . of February/March, etc.*
à... heures	*at . . . o'clock*
quand...	*when . . .*
pendant (+ *time period*)	*for (+ time period [which is finished]*

Elle **est arrivée** *il y a quinze jours*.	*She arrived two weeks ago.*
Le réveil **a sonné** *à sept heures*.	*The alarm clock rang at seven o'clock.*
Nous **sommes allés** au Japon *l'année dernière*.	*We went to Japan last year.*
Cette guerre **a duré** *trente ans*.	*This war lasted thirty years.*
J'**ai vécu** *cinq mois* à Madrid.	*I lived in Madrid for five months.*
Dimanche, il **a plu** toute la journée et il **a fait** un froid de canard.	*On Sunday, it rained all day and it was freezing cold.*

B. To indicate an action that *happened* only *once*, especially with verbs that express events which are generally not repeated, such as **mourir** (*to die*), **naître** (*to be born*), **se marier** (*to get married*), **avoir... ans** (*to turn a specific age*), etc.

Elle **est morte** des suites d'un cancer.	*She died of cancer.*
Il **est né** à l'hôpital.	*He was born in the hospital.*
Mes parents **ont divorcé**.	*My parents divorced.*
Ils **se sont mariés** à l'église.	*They got married in the church.*
Mon fils **a eu** quinze ans hier.	*My son turned fifteen yesterday.*
Ce jeune homme **s'est suicidé**.	*That young man committed suicide.*

C. To express an action which was *repeated* a *specified* (precise or approximate) *number of times* (usually within a limited period of time).

Elle **est allée** trois fois chez le dentiste la semaine dernière.
She went to the dentist three times last week.
J'**ai essayé** plusieurs fois de vous avertir.
I tried several times to warn you.

D. To indicate an action of *short duration*, or a *sudden occurrence* or *change* of such an action. The suddenness is often indicated by expressions such as:

soudain	*suddenly*	**immédiatement**	*immediately*
tout à coup	*suddenly*	**tout de suite**	*right away*

Elle **a ouvert** la porte.	*She opened the door.*
J'**ai rencontré** un ami en ville.	*I met a friend downtown.*
Soudain, j'**ai eu** peur.	*Suddenly, I got scared.*
Nous **avons** *tout de suite* **prévenu** la police.	*We immediately notified the police.*

E. To express a series of actions which took place *successively*, the previous one being *completed* when the new one starts. Words like **d'abord, puis, ensuite, après, alors,** or **enfin** may be present to make it clear that one action follows the other.

> D'abord, je me **suis levé(e)**, ensuite j'**ai pris** le petit déjeuner, puis je me **suis habillé(e)** et enfin j'**ai quitté** la maison.
> *First I got up, then I had breakfast, then I got dressed, and finally I left the house.*

F. With **depuis** and **ça fait… que** in *negative* sentences to indicate an action or situation which has *not* taken place for a period of time up to the present.

> Je *ne* l'**ai** *pas* **vu** *depuis* une éternité.   *I haven't seen him for ages.*
> or: **Ça fait** une éternité *que* je *ne* l'**ai** *pas* **vu**.

EXERCICE
5·13

Traduisez en français. Then justify the use of the *passé composé* by adding: "precise moment," "limited time," "specified number of times," etc., to your answer.

1. I received the message yesterday afternoon. _____

2. We lived in Ireland between 2002 and 2004. _____

3. The other day, she moved. _____

4. He had an accident last week. _____

5. I went to the movies last night. _____

6. I had a nightmare last night. _____

7. Her son took an exam the day before yesterday. _____

8. The first time she came to Europe, she stayed for five days. _____

9. They (*masc.*) left three years ago. _____

10. We visited the museum two times last year. _____

11. When he saw me, he laughed. _____

12. Sleeping Beauty (**La Belle au bois dormant**) slept for one hundred years. _____

_____

EXERCICE
5·14

Traduisez en français. Then justify the use of the *passé composé* by adding: "precise moment," "limited time," "specified number of times," etc., to your answer.

1. Did it rain last weekend? _____

2. Suddenly, the weather changed. _____

3. We sold our house last month. _____

4. I immediately felt comfortable (**à l'aise**). _____

5. He took the mouse and clicked on the link. _____

6. Last Sunday, we saw a detective movie (**un film policier**). _____

7. She died in a car accident. _____

8. The firefighters came right away. _____

9. We learned the news this morning. _____

10. She got married in June. _____

11. Yesterday, I got up at five o'clock. _____

12. First, she ran to the doctor, and then she went to the pharmacy. _____

Répondez personnellement aux questions suivantes avec des phrases complètes.

1. Quand et où êtes-vous né(e)? _____

2. Où êtes-vous allé(e) l'été dernier? _____

3. Qu'est-ce que vous avez fait hier soir? _____

4. Êtes-vous sorti(e) avec quelqu'un le week-end dernier? _____

5. À quelle heure êtes-vous rentré(e) à la maison dimanche soir? _____

6. Qu'est-ce que vous avez pris comme boisson (*drink*) au petit déjeuner ce matin? _____

7. Qu'est-ce que vous avez mangé hier à midi? _____

8. Est-ce que vous vous êtes ennuyé(e) samedi soir? _____

9. Avez-vous appris le français l'année dernière? _____

10. Quels vêtements avez-vous mis aujourd'hui? _____

Describe (using the passé composé*) what you did yesterday. Use many regular and irregular verbs (even if not everything you say is true!) as well as the following reflexive verbs in chronological order. When appropriate, add where, when, and why you did (or didn't do) those things.*

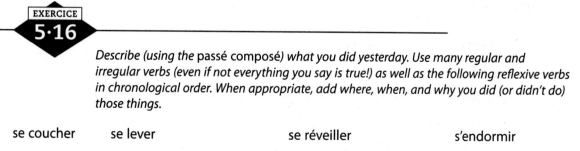

| se coucher | se lever | se réveiller | s'endormir |
| se doucher | se détendre | se brosser les dents | s'habiller |

se déshabiller   s'amuser   se dépêcher   se peigner

se maquiller (or: se raser)   s'asseoir (sur le canapé?)   se laver les mains

_____

_____

_____

_____

EXERCICE

5·17

Traduisez en anglais les mots soulignés.

1. J'ai suivi un cours de français. *I* _____ *a French class.*

2. J'ai fait des courses. *I* _____ *errands.*

3. Il a fallu ouvrir une autre classe. *They* _____ *open another class.*

4. Ils ont disparu il y a six mois. *They* _____ *six months ago.*

5. Nous avons passé un bon moment. *We* _____ .

6. A-t-il plu hier soir? _____ *last night?*

7. Est-ce que ce plat vous a plu? _____ *this dish?*

8. Les élèves se sont tus. *The students* _____ .

9. Je n'ai pas pu dormir la nuit dernière. *I* _____ *sleep last night.*

10. L'entreprise a dû fermer. *The company* _____ *close.*

11. J'ai eu un PV de stationnement hier. *I* _____ *a parking ticket yesterday.*

12. Il a pris le taureau par les cornes. *He* _____ *the bull by the horns.*

EXERCICE

5·18

Est-ce vrai ou faux?

_____ 1. Lance Armstrong a perdu le dernier Tour de France.

_____ 2. Napoléon I est né à Ajaccio en Corse.

_____ 3. Gutenberg a inventé l'imprimerie (*the printing press*).

_____ 4. La France a gagné la Coupe du monde en 1998.

_____ 5. Le mur de Berlin est tombé en 2000.

_____ 6. John F. Kennedy est mort à New York.

_____ 7. Victor Hugo a écrit *Les Misérables*.

_____ 8. Louis Pasteur a découvert la pénicilline.

EXERCICE
5·19

L'année dernière, Mireille a étudié en France. Traduisez en français ce qu'elle raconte. Use the *passé composé* throughout.

I left for France on September 1, and I arrived in Marseille the next day at four o'clock in the afternoon. My host family picked me up at the airport. I gave them gifts and I received a bouquet of flowers. When we arrived at the house of Monsieur and Madame Rivière, I immediately went up to my room to change. I put on my pretty pink dress and went downstairs for dinner. We spent three hours at the table and the Rivières asked me many questions. Madame Rivière served goose liver pâté as an appetizer, snails as a first course, and scallops as a main course. After the salad, we ate cheese and for dessert, we had yogurt. And of course we drank wine with (= to accompany) our meal.

My classes started on October 15th. On that day, every student had to take a placement test. On New Year's Day, my parents visited me, and we traveled to Italy and Austria. Everywhere, we saw extraordinary landscapes and works of art. We even took the French bullet train. In July, I returned to the United States with a lot of good memories. I must say that I liked my stay in France a lot (*use* **plaire**).

VOCABULAIRE			
as	**comme**	the next day	**le lendemain**
to ask a question	**poser une question**	to pick up sb	**venir chercher qn**
to change (clothes)	**se changer**	pink	**rose**
even	**même**	placement test	**le test d'orientation**
every	**chaque**	scallops	**des coquilles *(f.pl.)***
first course	**entrée *(f.)***		**Saint-Jacques**
the French bullet train	**le TGV (train à grande vitesse)**	that day	**ce jour-là**
		to travel (*to a destination*)	**aller**
goose liver pâté	**du foie gras**		
host family	**la famille d'accueil**	work of art	**l'œuvre *(f.)* d'art**
main course	**le plat principal**	yogurt	**du yaourt**
New Year's Day	**le Jour de l'An**		

_____

_____

_____

_____

_____

_____

The imperfect tense

Like the **passé composé**, the imperfect (**l'imparfait**) is a past tense. But unlike the **passé composé**, which denotes actions of limited (short or long) duration, the imperfect expresses actions and situations that lasted an indeterminate amount of time (*he had a lot of money*), occurred an unspecified number of times (*she went to church every Sunday*), or were in progress, often when something else happened (*it was raining [when they arrived]*). The main characteristic of the imperfect is the unlimited aspect. If you do not know at what specific time the action you are describing took place, or how long it lasted, you will generally use the imperfect.

The imperfect tense is translated into English by the past progressive form (*I was playing*), indicating an action that was going on, by *used to* + infinitive (*I used to play*) and *would* + infinitive (*I would play*), expressing a habitual past action, and by the simple past (*I played*), but only if the action was repeated, ongoing, or of unlimited duration.

A more detailed description of the use of the imperfect will follow the review of its formation.

The formation of the imperfect tense

The stem of the imperfect tense of all verbs (except **être**) is found by dropping the **-ons** ending from the **nous** form of the present tense. The imperfect endings are: **-ais, -ais, -ait, -ions, -iez, -aient**. These endings are valid for all verbs, regular and irregular.

A. To conjugate a regular -**er**, -**ir**, or -**re** ending verb in the imperfect tense, follow the models given below.

parler *to speak*	
(nous parl**ons**)	
je parl**ais**	*I spoke, I was speaking, I used to speak*
tu parl**ais**	
il/elle/on parl**ait**	
nous parl**ions**	
vous parl**iez**	
ils/elles parl**aient**	

finir *to finish*	
(nous finiss**ons**)	
je finiss**ais**	*I finished, I was finishing, I used to finish*
tu finiss**ais**	
il/elle/on finiss**ait**	

115

nous finiss**ions**
vous finiss**iez**
ils/elles finiss**aient**

entendre *to hear*

(nous entend**ons**)
j'entend**ais**   *I heard, I was hearing, I used to hear*
tu entend**ais**
il/elle/on entend**ait**
nous entend**ions**
vous entend**iez**
ils/elles entend**aientg**

Note:

◆ The endings **-ais**, **-ait**, and **-aient** have the same pronunciation. They are all pronounced [ɛ].
◆ Verbs ending in **-cer** have a **cédille** under the **c** in all persons of the imperfect except in the **nous** and **vous** forms to conserve the sound [s]. In these persons, the **cédille** is not needed under the **c** since the following **i** makes the **c** sound [s].

commencer *to begin*

je commençais	nous commencions
tu commençais	vous commenciez
il/elle/on commençait	ils/elles commençaient

◆ Verbs ending in **-ger**, such as **voyager** (*to travel*), **partager** (*to share*), **déménager** (*to move*), etc., insert an **e** after the **g** in all persons of the imperfect except in the **nous** and **vous** forms to conserve the sound [ʒ]. In these persons, the inserted **e** is not needed since the following **i** makes the **g** sound [ʒ].

nager *to swim*

je nageais	nous nagions
tu nageais	vous nagiez
il/elle/on nageait	ils/elles nageaient

◆ Verbs with stems that end in **-i**, such as **étudier** (*to study*), **remercier** (*to thank*), etc., have a double **i** in the **nous** and **vous** forms.

oublier *to forget*

j'oubliais	nous oubliions
tu oubliais	vous oubliiez
il/elle/on oubliait	ils/elles oubliaient

B. Since the *irregular verbs* also derive their imperfect stem from the first-person plural of the present tense, you will easily find this stem if you know the present tense of these verbs. Once you have found the stem, all you need to do is add the appropriate endings. Here are some examples:

INFINITIVE	*NOUS* FORM OF PRESENT TENSE	IMPERFECT TENSE
aller *to go*	nous all**ons**	j'all**ais**
s'asseoir *to sit down*	nous nous **assey**ons	je m'**assey**ais (or: je m'**assoy**ais)
avoir *to have*	nous **av**ons	j'**av**ais
boire *to drink*	nous **buv**ons	je **buv**ais

INFINITIVE	*NOUS* FORM OF PRESENT TENSE	IMPERFECT TENSE
craindre *to fear*	nous **craign**ons	je **craign**ais
croire *to believe*	nous **croy**ons	je **croy**ais
dire *to say*	nous **dis**ons	je **dis**ais
dormir *to sleep*	nous **dorm**ons	je **dorm**ais
faire *to do*	nous **fais**ons [nufəzɔ̃]	je **fais**ais [ʒəfəzɛ]
pouvoir *to be able to*	nous **pouv**ons	je **pouv**ais
recevoir *to receive*	nous **recev**ons	je **recev**ais
rire *to laugh*	nous **ri**ons	je **ri**ais (nous **ri**ions, vous **ri**iez)
vouloir *to want*	nous **voul**ons	je **voul**ais

C. The verb **être** is the only verb which has an irregular stem (**ét-**) in the imperfect tense. Here is its conjugation:

j'**ét**ais	*I was*	nous **ét**ions	*we were*
tu **ét**ais	*you were*	vous **ét**iez	*you were*
il/elle/on **ét**ait	*he/she/it/one was*	ils/elles **ét**aient	*they were*

D. The imperfect forms of the impersonal verbs **falloir**, **pleuvoir**, and **neiger** (which do not exist in the **nous** form) are as follows:

falloir	*to be necessary*	il **fall**ait	*it was necessary*
pleuvoir	*to rain*	il **pleuv**ait	*it was raining*
neiger	*to snow*	il **neige**ait	*it was snowing*

EXERCICE

6·1

Est-ce vrai ou faux?

Quand j'étais petit(e),…

_____ 1. je jouais avec des poupées.

_____ 2. je regardais rarement des dessins animés.

_____ 3. j'avais peur des araignées (*spiders*).

_____ 4. j'allais souvent au zoo.

_____ 5. je ne pleurais jamais.

_____ 6. j'obéissais toujours à mes parents.

_____ 7. je ne buvais pas de lait.

_____ 8. je mangeais beaucoup de bonbons.

_____ 9. j'étais toujours heureux (heureuse).

_____ 10. je ne riais pas.

Donnez l'imparfait des verbes entre parenthèses.

1. À l'époque, je (travailler) _____ à l'ambassade.

2. Il (jouer) _____ souvent du piano.

3. Stéphanie (perdre) _____ ses clés fréquemment.

4. Nous (remercier) _____ rarement nos parents.

5. Est-ce que tu (partager) _____ tes jouets avec tes frères et sœurs quand tu (être) _____ petit(e)?

6. L'école (commencer) _____ à huit heures tous les matins.

7. Il (falloir) _____ se dépêcher chaque jour.

8. Chaque fois qu'elle (mentir) _____ elle (rougir) _____ .

9. Nous (faire) _____ du ski chaque hiver.

10. Ils (dormir) _____ quand le cambrioleur est entré dans la maison.

11. Pourquoi (rire) _____-vous tout le temps?

12. Nous (croire) _____ que la situation (aller) _____ s'améliorer.

13. Il (pleuvoir) _____ quand elle est partie.

14. Il ne (pleurer) _____ pas.

15. Autrefois, j' (avoir) _____ un chien et un chat.

16. D'habitude, j' (aller) _____ au gymnase avant de rentrer.

17. Il (neiger) _____ quelquefois dans mon pays.

18. Comment (s'appeler) _____ vos amis?

19. À quelle heure (prendre) _____-tu le petit déjeuner le dimanche?

20. Le samedi, nous (se lever) _____ tard.

The uses of the imperfect tense

A. The imperfect is used to describe *habitual* or *repeated actions* in the past. Often, the verb in the imperfect tense is accompanied by an expression of time that indicates or implies repetition, such as:

à l'époque / à cette époque-là	*in those days*
autrefois	*formerly, in the past*
avant	*before*
chaque été/hiver	*every summer/winter*
chaque année	*every year*
chaque fois que	*each time*

chaque jour	*every day*
chaque mois	*every month*
de temps en temps	*from time to time*
d'habitude	*usually*
fréquemment	*frequently*
généralement	*generally*
jamais	*never*
le lundi / le mardi, etc.	*on Mondays / on Tuesdays, etc.*
quand j'étais adolescent(e)	*when I was a teenager*
quand j'étais enfant	*when I was a child*
quand j'étais étudiant(e)	*when I was a student*
quand j'étais jeune	*when I was young*
quand j'étais petit(e)	*when I was little*
quelquefois/parfois	*sometimes*
rarement	*rarely*
souvent	*often*
toujours	*always*
tous les ans	*every year*
tous les jours	*every day*
tous les matins	*every morning*
tous les soirs	*every evening*
tous les lundis, mardis, etc.	*every Monday, Tuesday, etc.*

EXERCICE 6·3

Traduisez en français les phrases suivantes.

1. My grandmother went to church every Sunday. _____

2. They (*masc.*) got up early every morning. _____

3. She frequently went out. _____

4. When I was little, I watched cartoons all the time. _____

5. You (*fam.*) played the guitar every day. _____

6. We ate together from time to time. _____

7. In those days, my parents and I lived in Rome. _____

8. You (*pol.*) always forgot your glasses. _____

9. I rarely saw him. _____

10. Now, I weigh sixty-five kilos; before I weighed fifty-five kilos. _____

11. Each time he had an exam, he slept badly. _____

12. When she was a child, she liked ice cream a lot. _____

When the imperfect describes *repeated* actions in the past, the English expressions *used to* (+ infinitive) and *would* (+ infinitive) can be seen as the equivalent of this tense, because *used to* and *would* indicate that an action or situation occurred an unknown number of times.

EXERCICE
6·4

Traduisez en français les phrases suivantes.

1. They used to travel a lot. _____

2. Where did you (*pol.*) used to live? _____

3. You (*fam.*) used to read a lot of comics. _____

4. My friend used to call me every night. _____

5. I used to go to bed early. _____

6. She used to drink a glass of milk every morning. _____

7. We used to see each other often. _____

8. They used to complain about (**de**) everything. _____

EXERCICE
6·5

Traduisez en français les phrases suivantes.

1. Each time the teacher would enter, all the students would get up. _____

   _____

2. He would always help me. _____

3. When we lived in France, we would drink wine for lunch and dinner. _____

   _____

4. When I was a student, I would eat in the dining commons (**au resto-U**) every day. _____

   _____

5. My mom would visit me once a month (**une fois par mois**). _____

6. Each time, she would bring money, gifts, and treats (**des friandises** *[f.pl.]*). _____

   _____

7. I would never miss class. _____

8. My housemates and I would study in the library every afternoon. _____

9. In the evenings (**le soir**), we would go out together and we would have a good time.

   _____

B. The imperfect is also used for an *action* which was *in progress* for an unknown period of time, or for two actions that were going on *simultaneously*. In English such actions are usually expressed by *was/were . . . -ing.*

*The children **were** playing outside.*	Les enfants **jouaient** dehors.
*Anne **was** driving while her son **was** resting in the back of the car.*	Anne **conduisait pendant que** son fils **se reposait** à l'arrière de la voiture.

EXERCICE

6·6

Traduisez en français. Utilisez l'imparfait.

1. The car wasn't working. _____

2. I was looking for the remote control. _____

3. She was wondering where you (*pol.*) were. _____

4. Everyone was having a good time. _____

5. I was thinking about you (**à toi**) all the time. _____

6. It was raining cats and dogs (**des cordes**). _____

7. The baby was crying. _____

8. Were they (*fem.*) telling the truth? _____

9. What was she doing? _____

10. You (*pol.*) were working hard. _____

11. I was joking (**plaisanter**). _____

12. He was listening to the radio while his wife was getting dressed. _____

_____

The imperfect and the **passé composé** are used in the same sentence when the action in progress serves as *background* for another action, which took place while the first action was still going on. The interrupting action is in the **passé composé.**

*It **was** snowing when we left.*	Il **neigeait** quand nous sommes partis.

EXERCICE

6·7

Traduisez en français les phrases suivantes.

1. I was cleaning the house when the mailman arrived. _____

2. They (*masc.*) were playing soccer when it started to rain. _____

3. Andrée was going to the movies when she met her friends. _____

The imperfect tense   **121**

4. We were sleeping when someone knocked on the door. _____

5. You (*fam.*) were writing a letter when the phone rang. _____

6. I was driving the children to school when the car broke down. _____

_____

7. What were you (*pol.*) saying when I entered the room? _____

C. The imperfect is used to give *descriptions* of people (including the indication of their names and ages) and things (including weather) in the past; that is, it shows what someone or something was like rather than what happened.

> La jeune femme **s'appelait** Anne et elle **avait** vingt ans. Elle **était** petite et jolie.
> *The young woman's name was Anne and she was twenty years old. She was short and pretty.*

EXERCICE

6·8

Traduisez en français les phrases suivantes.

1. She had green eyes and brown hair. _____

2. The bridegroom was wearing a tuxedo. _____

3. The bride was beautiful. _____

4. How old were you (*fam.*) at that time? _____

5. What was the name of your (*fam.*) neighbor? _____

6. What was the weather like? _____

7. It was sunny. _____

8. He was 1 m 90 tall (= he measured 1 m 90) and weighed one hundred kilos. _____

9. The appetizers were delicious. _____

10. The landscape was magnificent. _____

Note:

◆ With *age*, the **passé composé** expresses *to turn* a certain age.

> Elle **a eu** soixante ans lundi dernier.   *Last Monday, she **turned** sixty.*

◆ With *weather*, the **passé composé** is used when a specific or limited time is mentioned.

> Il **a fait** beau pendant une semaine.   *The weather was good for a week.*
> Hier, il **a fait** du vent.   *Yesterday, it was windy.*

D. The imperfect describes *mental, physical, or emotional states* of unlimited duration. The following verbs which indicate such states are therefore often used in the imperfect:

> **adorer** *to adore*
> **aimer** *to like*
> **s'attendre à** *to expect*
> **avoir (faim, peur, mal à la tête, etc.)** *to be (hungry, afraid, etc.), to have (a headache, etc.)*
> **connaître** *to know*
> **croire** *to believe*
> **désirer** *to wish*
> **détester** *to detest*
> **espérer** *to hope*
> **être (malade, fatigué, heureux, etc.)** *to be (ill, tired, happy, etc.)*
> **penser** *to think*
> **pouvoir** *to be able*
> **préférer** *to prefer*
> **regretter** *to regret*
> **savoir** *to know*
> **sembler** *to seem*
> **se sentir** *to feel*
> **souhaiter** *to wish*
> **vouloir** *to want*

EXERCICE 6·9

Traduisez en français les phrases suivantes.

1. She adored children. _____

2. I hoped to be famous some day. _____

3. He didn't expect that (**cela**). _____

4. They (*masc.*) were afraid. _____

5. She didn't want to leave. _____

6. Were you (*fam.*) cold? _____

7. Robert had a fever (**de la fièvre**). _____

8. Did you (*pol.*) know this person? _____

9. Did he believe this story? _____

10. Sophie hated red; she preferred purple. _____

11. They (*masc.*) felt guilty (**coupable**). _____

12. I was disappointed. _____

13. Were they (*masc.*) in a good mood (**de bonne humeur**)? _____

14. I thought (= believed) that you (*fam.*) didn't like that (**ça**). _____

15. They (*fem.*) didn't know that he was ill. _____

But: When the mental, physical or emotional state is momentary, of limited duration, or if it changes or occurs suddenly (as is the case in the following examples), the **passé composé** is used with the verbs listed above.

Ce matin, j'**ai cru** qu'il grêlait.	*This morning, I thought it was hailing.*
Tout à coup, il **a eu** sommeil.	*Suddenly, he was (= became, got) sleepy.*

E. The imperfect is also used to indicate the *time of day*, *the day of the week*, *the date*, *the month*, *the year*, and *seasons* in the past.

Il **était** dix heures quand je me suis réveillé(e).	*It was ten o'clock when I woke up.*
C'**était** l'hiver.	*It was winter.*

EXERCICE
6·10

Traduisez en français les phrases suivantes.

1. What time was it when you (*fam.*) came home? _____

2. It was three o'clock. _____

3. It was noon when we had lunch. _____

4. It was a quarter to five when she called. _____

5. What day was it? —It was Thursday. _____

6. It was the first of January. _____

7. It was too late. _____

F. Other uses of the imperfect tense

The imperfect is also used after **si**

◆ in *exclamations* to express a *wish* (here, **si** is generally followed by **seulement**)

Si seulement j'**étais** riche!	*I wish I were rich! (If only I was rich!)*

◆ in *questions* to express a *suggestion* or a *supposition* made in the present (English: *What if . . . ? How about . . . -ing?*)

Si on allait se baigner?	*What if we went swimming?*
Si on prenait un verre?	*How about having a drink?*

The imperfect is the *only* past tense used when the following expressions are in a past context.

aller + (inf.) *to be going to (do sth)*

J'**allais** sortir.	*I **was going to** go out.*

venir de + (inf.) *to have just (done sth)*

Il **venait de** rentrer.   He **had just** come home.

être en train de + (inf.) *to be in the process of (doing sth)*

Nous **étions en train de** manger.   We **were in the process of** eating.

être sur le point de + (inf.) *to be about to (do sth)*

Ils **étaient sur le point de** partir.   They **were about to** leave.

For the use of the imperfect after **depuis**, see *The uses of the pluperfect tense*, page 136. For the use of the imperfect in conditional sentences, see *The conditional*, page 169.

For the use of the imperfect after **depuis**, see *The uses of the pluperfect tense*, page 136. For the use of the imperfect in conditional sentences, see *The conditional*, page 169.

EXERCICE 6·11

Traduisez en français les phrases suivantes.

1. If only I had more time! _____

2. What if we (**on**) went to the movies tonight? _____

3. I was going to give her a gift but I changed my mind. _____

_____

4. She was going to buy a camera but she didn't have enough money. _____

_____

5. We were going to do the laundry but the washing machine was broken. ____

_____

6. What were you (*fam.*) going to say? _____

7. They believed that the strike was going to stop. _____

8. I knew that this (**ça**) was going to be difficult. _____

9. We had just moved. _____

10. They (*masc.*) had just arrived when I saw them. _____

11. She was in the process of washing the dishes. _____

12. They (*masc.*) were about to lose patience. _____

EXERCICE 6·12

Nicole parle de son enfance. Traduisez en français ce qu'elle raconte.

When I was little, my grandmother always came to visit us at Christmas. It was a long trip for her, because we lived in the United States, and she came from France. Therefore, her arrival was a big event for me, and I always anticipated it with great joy. Every year, my grandma spoiled me with many gifts, and there was always chocolate and a new doll. When I was older, she brought me CDs with French songs which (**que**) I adored, and she would continue to offer me chocolate. During her stay she would cook wonderful dishes and her cookies were a delight. She always made a **bûche de Noël** for us and we celebrated a French Christmas in America.

VOCABULAIRE

to anticipate	**attendre**	a delight	**un délice**
arrival	**l'arrivée (f.)**	in (+ *continent*)	**en**
at Christmas	**à Noël**	joy	**la joie**
CD	**le CD**	my grandma	**ma mamie**
to celebrate	**fêter**	older	**plus âgé(e)**
chocolate	**du chocolat**	to spoil	**gâter**
to cook	**cuisiner**	therefore	**donc**
cookie	**le gâteau**	wonderful	**magnifique**

_____

_____

_____

_____

_____

_____

_____

_____

_____

_____

The uses of the *passé composé* and imperfect tense contrasted

Now that you have learned two past tenses, the **passé composé** and the imperfect, you will have to distinguish between them. Remember that any French verb can be used in either tense. It is the context that determines which tense must be used. The following guidelines which contrast the most frequent uses of the **passé composé** and the imperfect will help you choose the right tense in a given context. Remember the following:

The *imperfect* emphasizes *habit, continuity,* and *unlimited duration*. It describes *repeated, ongoing, non-completed* past actions or states, without indicating their beginning or end. The **passé composé** stresses *limited duration* and *completion*. It presents past actions or states as *finished* at a specific moment or as *completed* within a *limited* period of time.

- The imperfect expresses a *habitual* action or state that was *repeated* an *unspecified number* of times within an *unlimited period of time*. (English: *used to* or *would* + verb).
- The **passé composé** expresses an action or state that occurred only *once* or was *repeated* a *specified number of times* and/or within a *limited period of time*.

IMPERFECT	PASSÉ COMPOSÉ
Il **se promenait** tous les soirs.	Hier soir, il **s'est promené**.
He **used to (would)** go for a walk every evening.	Last night, he went for a walk.
J'**allais** voir mes parents tous les jours.	Entre 1980 et 1995, je **suis allé** voir mes parents tous les jours.
I **used to (would)** visit my parents . every day	Between 1980 and 1995, I visited my parents every day.
Elle le **rencontrait** souvent.	Cette semaine, elle l'**a rencontré** plusieurs fois.
She met him often.	This week, she met him several times.

◆ The imperfect describes an action or state which *was going* on for an *unlimited time* in the past, without indication of a beginning or end.

◆ The **passé composé** describes an action or state that was *completed* either at a *precise moment* or within a *specified period of time*.

IMPERFECT	PASSÉ COMPOSÉ
À l'époque, j'**étudiais** en Suisse.	J'**ai étudié** en Suisse pendant quatre ans.
In those days, I **studied** in Switzerland.	I studied in Switzerland for four years.
Il **faisait** beau.	Il **a fait** beau en septembre.
The weather was beautiful.	The weather was beautiful in September.
Quand j'étais jeune, j'**habitais** en Allemagne.	J'**ai habité** en Allemagne en 1990.
When I was young, I lived in Germany.	I lived in Germany in 1990.

◆ The imperfect describes an *ongoing action* that is the *background* for another action that interrupted it. (English: *was/were . . . -ing.*) The other action is in the **passé composé**.

◆ The **passé composé** describes a *momentary action* that occurred while a continuous action was going on. The ongoing action is in the imperfect.

IMPERFECT	PASSÉ COMPOSÉ
Il **pleuvait** quand l'avion a atterri.	Il pleuvait quand l'avion **a atterri**.
It **was raining** when the plane landed.	It was raining when the plane **landed**.

◆ The imperfect describes two or more actions or states that *were going on at the same time.*

◆ The **passé composé** describes two or more actions or states that *happened consecutively.*

IMPERFECT	PASSÉ COMPOSÉ
Il lisait pendant que j'écrivais.	J'**ai écrit** la lettre, je l'**ai mise** dans une enveloppe et je l'**ai postée**.
He was reading while I was writing.	I wrote the letter, I put it in an envelope, and I mailed it.

EXERCICE
6·13

Passé composé ou imparfait? Remplissez les tirets avec la forme correcte du verbe entre parenthèses.

1. Il (neiger) _____ cette nuit.

2. Est-ce qu'il (neiger) _____ quand tu es sorti(e)?

3. Quel temps (faire) _____-il? —Il (faire) _____ froid.

4. Il (faire) _____ froid pendant presque une semaine.

5. Cette année nous (partir) _____ en vacances en août.

6. Avant, nous (partir) _____ en vacances en juillet.

7. Quand j'étais adolescent(e), je (jouer) _____ toujours au golf.

8. La semaine dernière je (jouer) _____ deux fois au golf.

9. Éloïse (travailler) _____ dans cette usine quand je l'ai connue.

10. Est-ce qu'elle y (travailler) _____ entre 2004 et 2006?

11. Ils (déménager) _____ il y a trois jours.

12. Autrefois, ils (déménager) _____ assez souvent.

13. À l'époque, les jeunes gens (se marier) _____ plus tôt.

14. Ils (se marier) _____ le week-end dernier.

15. Quand elle (venir) _____ à Paris la dernière fois, elle (descendre) _____ dans cet hôtel.

16. Chaque fois qu'elle (venir) _____ à Paris, elle (descendre) _____ dans cet hôtel.

EXERCICE
6·14

Passé composé ou imparfait? Traduisez en français les phrases suivantes.

1. Every winter, we went skiing _____

2. We went skiing last week. _____

3. He went to the flea market (**au marché aux puces**) last Sunday. _____

4. He used to (= would) go to the flea market every Sunday. _____

5. When I was a child, I always had the same dream. _____

6. I had a bad dream last night. _____

7. I would always work from eight A.M. until five P.M. _____

8. Yesterday, I worked from eight A.M. until five P.M. _____

9. We were waiting for the bus. _____

10. We waited for the bus for one hour. _____

11. Last year, they (*masc.*) ate out several times. _____

12. I was cleaning (**ranger**) my room while he was sleeping. _____

- The imperfect describes a *mental*, *physical*, or *emotional* state of *unlimited duration*.
- The **passé composé** describes a *mental*, *physical*, or *emotional* state of *limited duration* or the sudden occurrence or change of such a state.

IMPERFECT	PASSÉ COMPOSÉ
Quand j'**étais** petit, je **croyais** au père Noël.	Quand je me suis réveillé(e), j'**ai cru** que la terre tremblait.
When I was little, I believed in Santa Claus.	*When I woke up, I believed that the earth was shaking.*
Je **pensais** ne jamais avoir d'enfants.	Un moment, j'**ai pensé** ne jamais avoir d'enfants.
I thought I would never have any children.	*For a time, I thought I would never have any children.*
Il **avait** soif.	Tout à coup, il **a eu** soif.
He was thirsty.	*Suddenly, he got thirsty.*
Nous **étions** tristes.	Nous **avons été** tristes à ce moment-là.
We were sad.	*We were sad at that moment.*

- The imperfect is used with **devoir, connaître, savoir, pouvoir,** and **vouloir** to express *was supposed to, knew, could,* and *wanted.*
- The **passé composé** is used with **devoir, connaître, savoir, pouvoir,** and **vouloir** to express *had to, met, found out, managed to, failed to, tried to,* and *refused to.*

IMPERFECT	PASSÉ COMPOSÉ
Il **devait** y aller.	Il **a dû** y aller.
He was supposed to go there.	*He had to go there.*
Je **connaissais** ce monsieur.	J'**ai connu** ce monsieur hier.
I knew this man.	*I met this man yesterday (for the first time).*
Je ne **savais** pas ça.	J'**ai su** plus tard qu'il était divorcé.
I didn't know that.	*I found out later that he was divorced.*
Il **pouvait** se souvenir de tout.	Il **a pu** se souvenir de tout.
*He could remember (**was capable of** remembering) everything.*	*He could (**was able to, managed to**) remember everything.*
Il ne **pouvait** pas tricher.	Il **n'a pas pu** tricher à l'examen.
*He could not cheat (= **was incapable of** cheating).*	*He could not (**was unable to, failed to**) cheat on the exam.*
Elle **voulait** venir avec moi.	Elle **a voulu** ouvrir un restaurant.
She wanted to come with me.	*She tried to open a restaurant.*
Elle **ne voulait pas** sortir avec lui.	Elle **n'a pas voulu** sortir avec lui.
She didn't want to go out with him.	*She refused to go out with him (on a particular occasion).*

- The imperfect is used with **toujours** and **jamais** for actions and situations that occurred repeatedly in the past, but do not reach into the present.
- The **passé composé** is used with **toujours** and **jamais** for actions and situations which occurred on a regular basis in the past, and continue to do so in the present.

IMPERFECT	PASSÉ COMPOSÉ
Je **payais toujours** mes factures à temps.	J'**ai toujours payé** mes factures à temps.
I always used to pay my bills on time (but I no longer do).	*I have always paid my bills on time (and I still do).*

- The imperfect describes what someone or something *was/looked like.*
- The **passé composé** describes what *happened*, what someone did.

IMPERFECT	PASSÉ COMPOSÉ
Elle **était** mince et grande.	Elle **est tombée** dans l'escalier.
She was slim and tall.	*She fell on the stairs.*

- ◆ The imperfect describes what *age* someone *had*
- ◆ The **passé composé** describes what *age* someone *turned* at a specific time.

IMPERFECT	PASSÉ COMPOSÉ
Elle **avait** quinze ans.	Ma fille **a eu** douze ans hier.
She was fifteen (years old).	*My daughter turned twelve yesterday.*

EXERCICE 6·15

Passé composé ou imparfait? Traduisez en français les phrases suivantes. (Do not translate the English tips in parentheses.)

1. I have never liked peanut butter (*and I still don't*). _____

2. I didn't like peanut butter when I was a child. _____

3. My daughter never played with dolls when she was little. _____

4. I have always dreamt of going on a cruise (*and I still do*). _____

5. When I was young, I always dreamt of going on a cruise. _____

6. My son turned seventeen last Wednesday. _____

7. She was eighteen years old when she arrived at the university. _____

8. Did you (*fam.*) know this woman? _____

9. Where did you (*fam.*) meet your wife? _____

10. He didn't know how to cook. _____

11. He found out that it was an error (**une erreur**). _____

12. I believed that I was going to die. _____

13. For a moment (**Un instant**), I believed that I was going to die. _____

14. She had a headache. _____

15. Suddenly, she got a headache. _____

EXERCICE 6·16

Imparfait ou passé composé? Mettez les verbes au temps qui convient.

1. Je (dormir) _____ déjà quand mon mari (rentrer) _____.

2. Quand je (habiter) _____ dans ce quartier, je (aller) _____ tous les jours au bureau à pied.

3. Il (être) _____ une fois (*Once upon a time there was*) un gros loup méchant qui (vivre) _____ dans une forêt toute noire.

4. Il (vivre) _____ au Portugal jusqu'en 2004.

5. Pour son vingtième anniversaire, ses parents lui (offrir) _____ une montre en or.

6. Quand je (être) _____ célibataire, je (penser) _____ que rien ne (être) _____ plus beau que le mariage.

7. Qu'est-ce que vous (penser) _____ de moi la première fois que vous m'avez vu(e)?

8. Tous les soirs, nous (jouer) _____ à des jeux vidéo avant de nous coucher.

9. Notre voyage à travers le Brésil (durer) _____ trente jours.

10. Je (descendre) _____ l'escalier quand je (entendre) _____ le téléphone sonner.

11. Napoléon (naître) _____ à Ajaccio et (terminer) _____ ses jours à Sainte-Hélène.

12. D'abord, ils (lire) _____ le journal, puis ils (prendre) _____ une douche, et ensuite ils (se coucher) _____.

EXERCICE
6·17

Traduction. Utilisez le passé composé et l'imparfait, selon le cas.

It was Sunday afternoon and it was raining. Everything was quiet in the city and there wasn't anyone in the streets. Suddenly, two gangsters arrived on a motorcycle. They were wearing masks and one of them held a gun in his right hand. They turned around in order to see whether someone was following them. They did not see the man who was watching them from his window. The two thieves entered the bank, opened the safe, took the money and jewelry and put everything in a big bag. In the meantime, the witness called the police who (**qui**) arrived immediately. When the robbers came out of the building, the policemen, who were waiting for them, arrested them and took them to jail.

VOCABULAIRE			
gangster	**le gangster**	safe (*noun*)	**le coffre-fort**
gun	**le pistolet**	to take (*sb somewhere*)	**emmener**
to hold	**tenir**		
in the meantime	**pendant ce temps**	thief	**le voleur, la voleuse**
mask	**le masque**	to turn around	**se retourner**
policeman	**le policier**	to watch	**observer**
quiet	**calme**	witness	**le témoin**
robbers	**les braqueurs (*m.pl.*)**		

_____

_____

_____

Dans le passage suivant, choisissez l'imparfait ou le passé composé. Faites l'élision si c'est nécessaire.

Salut Élodie,

Ton mail me (faisait / a fait) (1) _____ très plaisir. Je regrette de ne pas avoir répondu plus tôt, mais je (étais / ai été) (2) _____ très occupé et mon ordinateur (ne fonctionnait pas / n'a pas fonctionné) (3) _____ correctement. Tu (voulais / a voulu) (4) _____ savoir comment (étaient / ont été) (5) _____ mes vacances. Je vais donc essayer de te parler de tout ce que je (ai fait / faisais) (6) _____ pendant les vacances. Je (ai fini / finissais) (7) _____ les cours à l'université le 26 juin. Le 8 juillet, je (partais / suis parti) (8) _____ pour le Québec. Je (ai pu / pouvais) (9) _____ me rendre compte que la façon de vivre des Canadiens est très différente de la nôtre. Malheureusement, je (n'ai pas pu / ne pouvais pas) (10) _____ visiter beaucoup d'endroits car il (a plu / pleuvait) (11) _____ tout le temps. Je (suis resté / restais) (12) _____ au Canada trois semaines et je (suis revenu / revenais) (13) _____ en France le 28 juillet. Le 31, je (ai visité / visitais) (14) _____ Lyon. J'y (ai rencontré / rencontrais) (15) _____ mes amis, et on (s'amusait bien / s'est bien amusés) (16) _____. Puis, début août, je (allais / suis allé) (17) _____ chercher à la gare une Anglaise qui (venait / est venue) (18) _____ visiter Marseille. Je lui (ai donc montré / montrais donc) (19) _____ ma ville natale. La semaine d'après, je (l'ai laissée / la laissais) (20) _____ à l'aéroport de Nice où elle (attendait / a attendu) (21) _____ un avion pour Rome. Je (passais / ai passé) (22) _____ cinq jours merveilleux avec elle, et j'espère bien la revoir l'année prochaine. Après ça, je (ne faisais rien / n'ai rien fait) (23) _____ jusqu'au 15 août. Le lendemain, je (montais / suis monté) (24) _____ à Paris avec des amis et je (suis resté / restais) (25) _____ quelques jours là-bas. Je (allais / suis allé) (26) _____ t'envoyer une carte postale, mais je (n'avais pas / n'ai pas eu) (27) _____ le temps d'en acheter une. À mon retour, je (devais / ai dû) (28) _____ me préparer pour la rentrée. Voilà mes vacances résumées.

Bon, je vais te laisser pour aujourd'hui. J'espère avoir bientôt de tes nouvelles.

Bisous, André

P.S. Je (venais / suis venu) (29) _____ d'ouvrir mon ordinateur quand je (recevais / ai reçu) (30) _____ tes vœux d'anniversaire. Merci!

Traduisez la biographie suivante. Utilisez l'imparfait ou le passé composé, selon le cas.

Molière was born in 1622. His real name was Jean-Baptiste Poquelin. He was the son of a Parisian upholsterer who worked for the king. From 1636 until 1642, Molière went to school in Paris and then studied law in Orléans. Since he liked the theatre very much, he decided to become an actor. In fact, he became an actor, author, and the director of a theater company. He wrote plays in which he makes fun of human weaknesses and of the society of his time. Unfortunately, he had to go to prison several times because he had a lot of debts. Between 1646 and 1658, Molière and his theater company were on tour in the provinces. He was very successful. In 1662, he married Armande Béjart who was twenty years younger than he. Among the comedies he wrote, *Tartuffe, Le Bourgeois Gentilhomme, L'Avare,* and *Le Misanthrope* are the best-known. Molière died in 1673, shortly after playing in a performance of *Le Malade imaginaire.*

VOCABULAIRE			
an actor	**un acteur**	in fact	**en fait**
among	**parmi**	a performance	**une représentation**
an author	**un auteur**	several times	**plusieurs fois**
to be on tour	**être en tournée**	shortly after playing	**peu après avoir joué**
to be very successful	**avoir beaucoup de succès**	to study law	**étudier le droit**
debt	**la dette**	theater company	**la troupe (de théâtre)**
director	**le directeur, la directrice**	upholsterer	**le tapissier**
human	**humain(e)**	weakness	**la faiblesse**

_____

_____

_____

_____

_____

_____

_____

_____

_____

_____

_____

_____

_____

The pluperfect tense

Like the **passé composé,** the French *pluperfect* (also called past perfect) is a compound past tense, i.e., it consists of two words, the auxiliary and the past participle. In English, this tense is expressed by *had + past participle* (had given) or *had been . . . -ing* (had been giving). In French as in English, the pluperfect describes *what had happened before* another action in the past.

In the English sentence "I *had studied* French before I went to France" for example, the action of studying occurred prior to going to France and is therefore in the pluperfect. After we review the formation of the pluperfect, we will study its use.

The formation of the pluperfect tense

To form the pluperfect, use the imperfect tense of the auxiliary (**avoir** or **être**) and add the past participle of the verb in question.

donner *to give*	
j'avais donné	*I had given*
tu avais donné	*you had given*
il/elle/on avait donné	*he/she/it/one had given*
nous avions donné	*we had given*
vous aviez donné	*you had given*
ils/elles avaient donné	*they had given*

partir *to leave*	
j'étais parti(e)	*I had left*
tu étais parti(e)	*you had left*
il/on était parti	*he/it/one had left*
elle était partie	*she/it had left*
nous étions parti(e)s	*we had left*
vous étiez parti(e)(s)	*you had left*
ils étaient partis	*they had left*
elles étaient parties	*they had left*

se réveiller *to wake up*	
je m'étais réveillé(e)	*I had woken up*
tu t'étais réveillé(e)	*you had woken up*
il/on s'était réveillé	*he/it/one had woken up*
elle s'était réveillée	*she/it had woken up*
nous nous étions réveillé(e)s	*we had woken up*
vous vous étiez réveillé(e)(s)	*you had woken up*
ils s'étaient réveillés	*they had woken up*
elles s'étaient réveillées	*they had woken up*

Note:

◆ In the pluperfect the verb takes the same helping verb (auxiliary) as in the **passé composé.**

◆ The pluperfect is formed just like the **passé composé,** except that the auxiliary is in the imperfect.

◆ The agreement of the past participle in the pluperfect follows the same rules as in the **passé composé.**

EXERCICE
7·1

Traduisez en français les mots entre parenthèses.

1. (*They [masc.] had returned*) _____ la veille.

2. (*We had come*) _____ chez eux.

3. (*They [fem.] had chosen*) _____ de retourner.

4. (*You [pol.] had promised*) _____ de le faire.

5. (*I had laughed*) _____ de ses plaisanteries.

6. (*We had learned a lot*) _____ à l'école.

7. (*They [masc.] had been*) _____ absents.

8. (*The proposition* [**La proposition**] *had fallen*) _____ à l'eau.

9. (*It had rained*) _____ toute la journée.

10. (*You [fam.] had written*) _____ un petit mot.

11. (*He had wanted*) _____ danser avec elle.

12. (*They [masc.] had hurried*) _____ .

The uses of the pluperfect tense

The uses of the pluperfect in French and English are very similar. There are only two instances where the English past perfect will not be translated into French by the pluperfect, but rather by the imperfect.

◆ In an *affirmative* statement after **depuis, il y avait** + *time* + **que,** and **ça faisait** + *time* + **que,** the imperfect is used to refer to an action that was going on for a certain time in the past, prior to another action that interrupted it.

> He **had been working** in New York **for** five months when they offered him a job in Paris.
> Il **travaillait** à New York **depuis** cinq mois quand on lui a offert un poste à Paris.

◆ To express the English *had just* (+ *past participle*), French uses the verb **venir** in the imperfect tense + **de** (+ *infinitive*).

> He **had just left**. Il **venait de partir**.

A. The pluperfect tense is used to express an action, event, or situation which happened *before* another past action, event, or situation which may or may not be mentioned in the same sentence.

Elle **était** déjà **partie** quand
je suis arrivé.

*She **had** already **left** when I arrived.*

L'avion **avait atterri**.

*The plane **had landed**.*

EXERCICE

7·2

Traduisez en français les phrases suivantes.

1. Robert was looking for the suitcase (that) he had lost. _____

2. She finally gave me back the money (that) I had loaned (**prêter**) her a long time ago. ____

_____

3. He had an accident because he had been drinking. _____

4. The teacher was disappointed because the students had not done their homework. ____

_____

5. When they had sold their house, they moved. _____

6. When Napoleon decided to leave Moscow, the Russian winter had already started. _____

_____

7. She had lived in Africa before she came (**avant de venir**) to the United States. _____

_____

8. They (*masc.*) thought (that) he had died in the war. _____

9. She was happy because she had received an award. _____

10. I did not know where I had put my wallet. _____

B. The pluperfect is used after **si** to express a regret about something that can no longer be changed.

Si seulement j'**avais su** cela!

If only I had known that!

EXERCICE

7·3

Traduisez en français les phrases suivantes.

1. If only I had listened to him! _____

2. If only they (*masc.*) had not said that! _____

3. If only he had not driven so fast! _____

4. If only we had followed his advice! _____

5. If only you (*fam.*) had arrived on time! _____

6. If only you (*pol.*) had told me (= said it to me) earlier! _____

C. The pluperfect is used with **depuis (ça faisait... que, il y avait... que)** in a *negative* statement for an action which started in the past and continued up to a certain point in the past.

> Je ne lui **avais** pas **parlé** *depuis* trois mois quand je l'ai rencontré.
> *I had not talked to him for three months when I met him.*
> Or: *Ça faisait* trois mois *que* je ne lui **avais** pas **parlé** quand je l'ai rencontré.
> Or: *Il y avait* trois mois *que* je ne lui **avais** pas **parlé** quand je l'ai rencontré.

EXERCICE
7·4

Traduisez. (Use depuis *in all sentences.)*

1. I had not heard from him (**avoir de ses nouvelles**) for two years when he called. _____

    _____

2. They (*fem.*) had not cleaned the apartment for eight weeks when the landlord (= owner)

    came. _____

3. He had not paid his bills for three months when he received the warning. _____

    _____

4. She had not gone to work for several days when her boss fired her.

    _____

5. I hadn't seen my friends for a long time when I met them at a party. _____

    _____

D. The pluperfect is used to express a *habitual action* which happened before another habitual action (expressed by the imperfect tense) in clauses introduced by a conjunction of time such as **quand, lorsque** (*when*), **dès que, aussitôt que** (*as soon as*), **après que** (*after*), and **une fois que** (*once*).

> *Une fois que* Brice **avait fini** de travailler, il faisait la sieste.
> *Once Brice had finished working, he would take a nap.*

Traduisez en français les phrases suivantes.

1. When they (*fem.*) had eaten, they would go shopping (**faire les boutiques**). _____
   _____

2. As soon as he had left, she would open the windows. _____
   _____

3. Every Saturday, after he had mowed the lawn (**tondre la pelouse**), they (*masc.*) would go
   out together. _____

4. Once you (*fam.*) had woken up, you would always cry. _____

5. Every day, when he had finished his homework, he would surf the Net. _____
   _____

E. The pluperfect is also used after **si** in a conditional (subordinate) clause when the verb in the main clause is in the past conditional, to describe an action that did not take place (see *Past conditional*, page 000).

Les madeleines. Traduisez en français.

Stanislas, who was king of Poland and duke of Normandy, had the habit of spending the summer in a castle in Lorraine in order to go hunting. He adored desserts. His cooks tried to invent something new every day. In 1755, a maid whose name was Madeleine suggested what (**ce que**) her mother had shown her, little shell-shaped cakes, golden brown on the outside and soft inside. The king asked what the cakes which (**qu'**) he had eaten were called. And since they didn't have a name, they called them "madeleines." At the beginning of the twentieth century, "madeleines" became very famous because the writer Marcel Proust had mentioned them in his work *À la recherche du temps perdu*.

VOCABULAIRE	cook	**le cuisinier,**	to mention	**mentionner**
		la cuisinière	outside	**à l'extérieur**
	duke	**le duc**	Poland	**la Pologne**
	to go hunting	**aller à la chasse**	shell-shaped	**en forme de coquille**
	golden-brown	**doré(e)**	soft	**moelleux, moelleuse**
	inside	**à l'intérieur**	(literary) work	**l'œuvre (f.)**
	maid	**la servante**	writer	**l'écrivain (m.)**

_____

_____

_____

_____
_____
_____
_____
_____
_____

A trip. Traduisez en français.

I had always wanted to visit Europe, but we had never traveled abroad. Our daughter had already been to (in) France several times while I was still dreaming about such a trip. In order to be able to spend our vacation in a foreign country, I had started working in a bookstore downtown, and my husband, Peter, had stopped smoking to save money. Already before our wedding, he had promised me to take many trips because he knew that I like to travel.

Finally, the big day had arrived. Peter told me that he had received the plane tickets and that we were going to leave soon. Needless to say (that) I was very excited.

We left the United States on the third of August and arrived in Monaco the next morning. My husband immediately went to the casino to gamble. I had told him to be careful, but he would not (= refused to) listen. Unfortunately, he lost all the money (which = **qu'**) he had put in the bank, and we had to return home earlier than expected. Since we were broke, we sold the house (which = **que**) we had bought twenty years ago, and we rented an apartment in a neighborhood where we had lived before. If only we hadn't taken this trip!

VOCABULAIRE	all the money	**tout l'argent**	neighborhood	**le quartier**
	before	**auparavant**	never	**ne… jamais**
	casino	**le casino**	the next morning	**le lendemain matin**
	downtown	**en ville**	plane ticket	**le billet d'avion**
	earlier	**plus tôt**	to rent	**louer**
	excited	**content(e)**	to save money	**faire des économies**
	expected	**prévu(e)**	several times	**plusieurs fois**
	foreign	**étranger, étrangère**	such a trip	**un tel voyage**
	to gamble	**jouer**	to travel (to a destination)	**aller (à, en, etc.)**
	needless to say	**inutile de dire**		

_____
_____
_____
_____
_____
_____
_____
_____
_____

The *passé simple*

The **passé simple** is a literary past tense which replaces the **passé composé** in formal speeches and writing. You will never use the **passé simple** in conversation, but you will see it in newspaper articles and when you read French literature.

The formation of the *passé simple*

Regular verbs

A. The **passé simple** of all **-er** ending **verbs** (including the irregular verb **aller**) is formed by adding the endings -**ai**, -**as**, -**a**, -**âmes**, -**âtes**, -**èrent** to the stem of the infinitive.

donner *to give*			
je donn**ai**	*I gave*	nous donn**âmes**	*we gave*
tu donn**as**	*you gave*	vous donn**âtes**	*you gave*
il/elle/on donn**a**	*he/she/it/one gave*	ils/elles donn**èrent**	*they gave*

Note:

◆ -**cer** ending verbs add a **cédille** to the **c** before **a** (i.e., in all persons except the third-person plural)

commencer *to begin*		
je commençai	*I began*	nous commençâmes
tu commenças		vous commençâtes
il/elle/on commença		ils/elles commencèrent

◆ -**ger** ending verbs insert **e** after **g** before **a** (i.e., in all persons except the third-person plural)

manger *to eat*		
je mangeai	*I ate*	nous mangeâmes
tu mangeas		vous mangeâtes
il/elle/on mangea		ils/elles mangèrent

B. The **passé simple** of both **-ir** and **-re** ending verbs is formed by adding the endings -**is**, -**is**, -**it**, -**îmes**, -**îtes**, -**irent** to the stem of the infinitive.

CHOISIR *TO CHOOSE*		ENTENDRE *TO HEAR*	
je chois**is***	*I chose*	j'entend**is**	*I heard*
tu chois**is***	*you chose*	tu entend**is**	*you heard*
il/elle/on chois**it***	*he/she/it/one chose*	il/elle/on entend**it**	*he/she/it/one heard*
nous chois**îmes**	*we chose*	nous entend**îmes**	*we heard*
vous chois**îtes**	*you chose*	vous entend**îtes**	*you heard*
ils/elles chois**irent**	*they chose*	ils/elles entend**irent**	*they heard*

*Note that the singular forms of the **passé simple** of -**ir** verbs are identical to those of the present indicative.

EXERCICE

8·1

Comment dit-on en anglais?

1. ils attendirent   _____

2. nous perdîmes   _____

3. vous trouvâtes   _____

4. elles allèrent   _____

5. je cherchai   _____

6. tu nageas   _____

7. il chanta   _____

8. ils restèrent   _____

9. elle épousa   _____

10. j'obéis   _____

11. vous entendîtes   _____

12. elles descendirent   _____

13. nous allâmes   _____

14. elle vendit   _____

Irregular verbs

Some irregular verbs take the endings -**is**, -**is**, -**it**, -**îmes**,* -**îtes**,* -**irent** (as regular -**ir** and -**re** ending verbs); other irregular verbs take the endings -**us**, -**us**, -**ut**, -**ûmes**,* -**ûtes**,* -**urent**.

*Note that the **nous** and **vous** forms of all regular and irregular verbs (except **haïr** [*to hate*]) have an **accent circonflexe (â, î, û)** in the **passé simple**.

    A. The **passé simple** of the following irregular verbs can be derived from their past participle. If the past participle of the verb ends in -**i**, -**is**, or -**it**, the first series of the above mentioned endings (with **i**) form its **passé simple**. If the past participle of the verb ends in -**u**, the second series of the above mentioned endings (with **u**) form its **passé simple**.

INFINITIVE	PAST PARTICIPLE	*PASSÉ SIMPLE*	
s'asseoir *to sit down*	assis	je m'ass**is**	nous nous ass**îmes**
		tu t'ass**is**	vous vous ass**îtes**
		il/elle/on s'ass**it**	ils/elles s'ass**irent**
avoir *to have*	eu	j'**eus** [ʒy]	nous e**ûmes** [nuzym]
		tu **eus** [tyy]	vous e**ûtes** [vuzyt]
		il/elle/on **eut** [ily]	ils/elles e**urent** [ilzyʀ]
boire *to drink*	bu		
		je b**us**	nous b**ûmes**
		tu b**us**	vous b**ûtes**
		il/elle/on b**ut**	ils/elles b**urent**
connaître *to know*	connu		
		je conn**us**	nous conn**ûmes**
		tu conn**us**	vous conn**ûtes**
		il/elle/on conn**ut**	ils/elles conn**urent**
courir *to run*	couru		
		je cour**us**	nous cour**ûmes**
		tu cour**us**	vous cour**ûtes**
		il/elle/on cour**ut**	ils/elles cour**urent**
croire *to believe*	cru		
		je cr**us**	nous cr**ûmes**
		tu cr**us**	vous cr**ûtes**
		il/elle/on cr**ut**	ils/elles cr**urent**
devoir *to have to, owe*	dû		
		je d**us**	nous d**ûmes**
		tu d**us**	vous d**ûtes**
		il/elle/on d**ut**	ils/elles d**urent**
dire *to say*	dit		
		je d**is**	nous d**îmes**
		tu d**is**	vous d**îtes**
		il/elle/on d**it**	ils/elles d**irent**
dormir *to sleep*	dormi		
		je dorm**is**	nous dorm**îmes**
		tu dorm**is**	vous dorm**îtes**
		il/elle/on dorm**it**	ils/elles dorm**irent**
falloir *to be necessary*	fallu		
		il fall**ut**	
lire *to read*	lu		
		je l**us**	nous l**ûmes**
		tu l**us**	vous l**ûtes**
		il/elle/on l**ut**	ils/elles l**urent**
mettre *to put*	mis		
		je m**is**	nous m**îmes**
		tu m**is**	vous m**îtes**
		il/elle/on m**it**	ils/elles m**irent**
plaire *to please*	plu		
		je pl**us**	nous pl**ûmes**
		tu pl**us**	vous pl**ûtes**
		il/elle/on pl**ut**	ils/elles pl**urent**
pleuvoir *to rain*	plu		
		il pl**ut**	
pouvoir *to be able to*	pu		
		je p**us**	nous p**ûmes**
		tu p**us**	vous p**ûtes**
		il/elle/on p**ut**	ils/elles p**urent**

prendre *to take*	pris		
		je pris	nous prîmes
		tu pris	vous prîtes
		il/elle/on prit	ils/elles prirent
recevoir *to receive*	reçu		
		je reçus	nous reçûmes
		tu reçus	vous reçûtes
		il/elle/on reçut	ils/elles reçurent
rire *to laugh*	ri		
		je ris	nous rîmes
		tu ris	vous rîtes
		il/elle/on rit	ils/elles rirent
savoir *to know*	su		
		je sus	nous sûmes
		tu sus	vous sûtes
		il/elle/on sut	ils/elles surent
suivre *to follow*	suivi		
		je suivis	nous suivîmes
		tu suivis	vous suivîtes
		il/elle/on suivit	ils/elles suivirent
valoir *to be worth*	valu		
		je valus	nous valûmes
		tu valus	vous valûtes
		il/elle/on valut	ils/elles valurent
vivre *to live*	vécu		
		je vécus	nous vécûmes
		tu vécus	vous vécûtes
		il/elle/on vécut	ils/elles vécurent
vouloir *to want*	voulu		
		je voulus	nous voulûmes
		tu voulus	vous voulûtes
		il/elle/on voulut	ils/elles voulurent

B. The **passé simple** of the following irregular verbs cannot be derived from their past participle.

INFINITIVE	PAST PARTICIPLE	*PASSÉ SIMPLE*	
battre *to beat*	battu	je battis	nous battîmes
		tu battis	vous battîtes
		il/elle/on battit	ils/elles battirent
conduire *to drive*	conduit	je conduisis	nous conduisîmes
		tu conduisis	vous conduisîtes
		il/elle/on conduisit	ils/elles conduisirent
craindre *to fear*	craint	je craignis	nous craignîmes
		tu craignis	vous craignîtes
		il/elle/on craignit	ils/elles craignirent
écrire *to write*	écrit	j'écrivis	nous écrivîmes
		tu écrivis	vous écrivîtes
		il/elle/on écrivit	ils/elles écrivirent
être *to be*	été	je fus	nous fûmes
		tu fus	vous fûtes
		il/elle/on fut	ils/elles furent
faire *to do, make*	fait	je fis	nous fîmes
		tu fis	vous fîtes

		il/elle/on f**it**	ils/elles f**irent**
mourir *to die*	mort	je mour**us**	nous mour**ûmes**
		tu mour**us**	vous mour**ûtes**
		il/elle/on mour**ut**	ils/elles mour**urent**
naître *to be born*	né	je naqu**is**	nous naqu**îmes**
		tu naqu**is**	vous naqu**îtes**
		il/elle/on naqu**it**	ils/elles naqu**irent**
ouvrir *to open*	ouvert	j'ouvr**is**	nous ouvr**îmes**
		tu ouvr**is**	vous ouvr**îtes**
		il/elle/on ouvr**it**	ils/elles ouvr**irent**
tenir *to hold*	tenu	je t**ins** [tɛ̃]	nous t**înmes** [tɛ̃m]
		tu t**ins**	vous t**întes**
		il/elle/on t**int**	ils/elles t**inrent**
venir *to come*	venu	je v**ins** [vɛ̃]	nous v**înmes** [vɛ̃m]
		tu v**ins** [vɛ̃]	vous v**întes** [vɛ̃t]
		il/elle/on v**int** [vɛ̃]	ils/elles v**inrent** [vɛ̃ʀ]
voir *to see*	vu	je **vis**	nous **vîmes**
		tu **vis**	vous **vîtes**
		il/elle/on **vit**	ils/elles **virent**

Note:

◆ Since the **passé simple** is used in written texts telling about persons and events, you will encounter the third-person (singular and plural) forms much more often than the others.

◆ If one is familiar with the endings, the verbs in the **passé simple** are easy to identify, even if the forms are not derived from a past participle. It is evident for example, that **mourut** comes from **mourir** and **ouvrit** from **ouvrir**, etc. Only a few verbs may be difficult to recognize and should therefore be memorized: **il/elle/on fut** (**être**), **il/elle/on fit** (**faire**), **il/elle/on vit** (**voir**), **il/elle/on vint** (**venir**), **il/elle/on naquit** (**naître**).

The uses of the *passé simple*

The **passé simple** is used instead of the **passé composé** in literary and historical texts as well as in very formal speeches to state punctual and completed actions in the past.

Voltaire **mourut** en 1778.	*Voltaire died in 1778.*
L'art gothique **naquit** dans l'Île-de-France au milieu du douzième siècle.	*Gothic art originated in the Île-de-France province in the middle of the 12th century.*
Et ils **vécurent** très longtemps, **furent** très heureux et **eurent** beaucoup d'enfants.	*And they lived happily ever after. (literally: And they lived a very long time, were very happy, and had a lot of children.)*

EXERCICE
8·2

Comment dit-on en anglais?

1. il fut _____

2. il fit _____

3. il vit _____

4. nous vînmes _____

5. nous reçûmes _____

6. elle écrivit _____

7. il fallut _____

8. il prit _____

9. ils dirent _____

10. il voulut _____

11. ils mirent _____

12. elle alla _____

13. je bus _____

14. il vécut _____

15. il dut _____

16. nous eûmes _____

17. il lut _____

18. il courut _____

EXERCICE
8·3

Napoléon Bonaparte. Dans le passage suivant, mettez au passé composé les verbes qui sont au Passé simple.

Napoléon Bonaparte (naquit) (1) _____ à Ajaccio en 1769. Il (prit) (2) _____ le pouvoir en 1799 et (se maria) (3) _____ avec Joséphine de Beauharnais. Il (devint) (4) _____ _____ empereur en 1804. Quand il (se rendit) (5) _____ compte que Joséphine et lui ne pouvaient pas avoir d'enfants, il (divorça) (6) _____ d'avec sa femme et (épousa) (7) _____ la princesse Marie-Louise d'Autriche. Ils (eurent) (8) _____ un fils qui (reçut) (9) _____ immédiatement _____ le titre de «Roi de Rome». Napoléon (créa) (10) _____ le Code Civil qui reste actuellement la base de la jurisprudence française. Il (fonda) (11) _____ aussi _____ les lycées (et le baccalauréat) qui existent encore aujourd'hui. Napoléon (fit) (12) _____ beaucoup de guerres. La campagne de Russie (commença) (13) _____ en 1812 et Napoléon (gagna) (14) _____ sa première victoire importante à Borodino. Cette victoire lui (ouvrit) (15) _____ la route de Moscou. Bientôt, l'armée française (arriva) (16) _____ devant la capitale russe. Napoléon (passa) (17) _____ cinq semaines dans cette ville. Quand il (vit) (18) _____ que l'hiver russe tuait ses soldats, il (décida) (19) _____ de retourner en France. Quand il (fallut) (20) _____ traverser la Bérézina, des milliers d'hommes (perdirent) (21) _____ la vie. Après avoir perdu la bataille de Leipzig, Napoléon (abdiqua) (22) _____ et (s'en alla) (23) _____ à l'île d'Elbe dans la Méditerranée. Le frère de Louis XVI (revint) (24) _____ à Paris et (fut) (25) _____ proclamé roi de France sous le nom de Louis XVIII. Le premier mars 1815, Napoléon (s'échappa)

(26) _____ de l'île d'Elbe et (retourna) (27) _____ à Paris pour régner encore cent jours jusqu'à sa défaite à Waterloo. Finalement, Napoléon (dut) (28) _____ partir en exil à Sainte-Hélène. Il y (mourut) (29) _____ en 1821.

EXERCICE
8·4

Traduisez en anglais cette épigramme de Voltaire.

L'autre jour, au fond d'un vallon, _____

Un serpent **piqua** Jean Fréron. _____

Que pensez-vous qu'il **arriva**? _____

Ce **fut** le serpent qui **creva**. _____

THE FUTURE TENSES,
THE CONDITIONAL, AND
THE SUBJUNCTIVE

The future tenses

The future tense refers to actions or situations that will be occurring in the time to come. In French, the future has two tenses, the *simple future* (**le futur simple**) and the *future perfect* (**le futur antérieur**).

The formation of the simple future

In English, the simple future consists of *will* or *shall* + verb: *I will (shall) go, you will read, he will ask, we will (shall) know,* etc. In French, the simple future uses no auxiliary, it consists of one word only. The future meaning is expressed by a specific verb stem and certain endings.

Regular verbs

The future stem of regular **-er** and **-ir** verbs is the entire infinitive. Regular **-re** verbs drop the final **-e** of the infinitive before adding on the endings.

The future endings are: **-ai, -as, -a, -ons, -ez, -ont**. These endings, taken from the present tense of the verb **avoir,** are valid for both regular and irregular verbs. Use the following conjugations as models for all regular verbs in the future tense.

TRAVAILLER TO WORK	RÉUSSIR TO SUCCEED	PERDRE TO LOSE
je travaillerai *I will work*	je réussirai *I will succeed*	je perdrai *I will lose*
tu travailleras	tu réussiras	tu perdras
il/elle/on travaillera	il/elle/on réussira	il/elle/on perdra
nous travaillerons	nous réussirons	nous perdrons
vous travaillerez	vous réussirez	vous perdrez
ils/elles travailleront	ils/elles réussiront	ils/elles perdront

Note that the simple future also translates the English continuous or progressive future (*will be . . . -ing*) which does not exist in French (*I **will be** working* = **je travaille**rai*).

Spelling changes

Verbs that show a spelling change in the present tense (except verbs having **é** in the last syllable of the stem) show the same change in the future, but here, the change affects *all* persons of the conjugation.

Verbs that contain **-e-** in the next to last syllable of the infinitive form the future as follows:

153

1. With some of these verbs, -**e**- becomes -**è**- in all persons.

acheter *to buy*	
j'achèterai	nous achèterons
tu achèteras	vous achèterez
il/elle/on achètera	ils/elles achèteront

2. With others, the last consonant of the stem is doubled in all persons.

jeter *to throw*	
je jetterai	nous jetterons
tu jetteras	vous jetterez
il/elle/on jettera	ils/elles jetteront

Verbs ending in -**oyer** (except **envoyer** [*to send*] which is irregular) and -**uyer** change the -**y**- into an -**i**- in all persons (however, -**ayer** verbs may keep the -**y**-, as an alternate spelling).

nettoyer *to clean*	
je nettoierai	nous nettoierons
tu nettoieras	vous nettoierez
il/elle/on nettoiera	ils/elles nettoieront

essayer *to try*	
j'essaierai (or: essayerai)	nous essaierons (or: essayerons)
tu essaieras (or: essayeras)	vous essaierez (or: essayerez)
il/elle/on essaiera (or: essayera)	ils/elles essaieront (or: essayeront)

But verbs that have -**é**- in the next to last syllable of the infinitive (such as **répéter, préférer,** etc.) retain the -**é**- (exceptionally pronounced [ɛ]) in all persons.

espérer *to hope*	
j'espérerai [ʒɛspeʀəʀɛ]	nous espérerons
tu espéreras	vous espérerez
il/elle/on espérera	ils/elles espéreront

Note:

- The sound that characterizes the **futur simple** of all verbs is [ʀ]. There is an [ʀ] sound before the ending in both regular and irregular verbs. If the stem of the verb ends in **r**, there will be two [ʀ] sounds before the future ending: rent**r**e**r**ai, je mont**r**e**r**ai.
- In many instances, the -**e**- before the -**r**- is silent (especially in verbs ending in -**ier, -uer, -ouer, -éer**): j'oubli**e**rai, il/elle/on continu**e**ra, tu cré**e**ras, nous jou**e**rons, ils/elles achèt**e**ront, vous jett**e**rez, j'emploi**e**rai, etc.
- In the inverted question form, a -**t**- is inserted in the third-person singular.

| Oubliera-**t**-il? | *Will he forget?* |
| Répondra-**t**-elle? | *Will she answer?* |

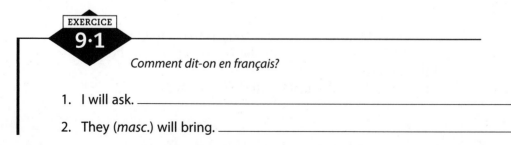

EXERCICE
9·1

Comment dit-on en français?

1. I will ask. _____

2. They (*masc.*) will bring. _____

3. Will he listen? _____

4. You (*fam.*) will not teach. _____

5. We will give. _____

6. I will wait. _____

7. Will you (*pol.*) work? _____

8. Will she answer? _____

9. You (*fam.*) will lose. _____

10. It will snow. _____

11. They (*fem.*) will forget. _____

12. I will not go to bed until (**avant**) midnight. _____

13. What will they (*masc.*) buy? _____

14. I will repeat. _____

15. We will try. _____

16. We will employ. _____

17. You (*fam.*) will remember. _____

18. They (*masc.*) will succeed. _____

19. I will obey. _____

20. Everyone will grow old. _____

Irregular verbs

Many irregular verbs have regular stems, that is, the entire infinitive or (with **-re** ending verbs) the infinitive minus final **-e**. All persons of the future tense use the same stem.

INFINITIVE	ENGLISH	FUTURE
battre	*to beat*	je **battr**ai
boire	*to drink*	je **boir**ai
conduire	*to drive*	je **conduir**ai
connaître	*to know*	je **connaîtr**ai
craindre	*to fear*	je **craindr**ai
croire	*to believe*	je **croir**ai
dire	*to say*	je **dir**ai
dormir	*to sleep*	je **dormir**ai
écrire	*to write*	j'**écrir**ai
lire	*to read*	je **lir**ai
mettre	*to put*	je **mettr**ai
naître	*to be born*	je **naîtr**ai
ouvrir	*to open*	j'**ouvrir**ai
partir	*to leave*	je **partir**ai

(continued)

INFINITIVE	ENGLISH	FUTURE
plaire	*to please*	je **plair**ai
prendre	*to take*	je **prendr**ai
rire	*to laugh*	je **rir**ai
suivre	*to follow*	je **suivr**ai
vivre	*to live*	je **vivr**ai

EXERCICE
9·2

Comment dit-on en français?

1. I will drink beer. _____

2. She will drive carefully. _____

3. You (*fam.*) will not believe this story. _____

4. You (*pol.*) will say nothing. _____

5. Will he sleep well? _____

6. We will write a term paper. _____

7. We (**On**) will read comic strips. _____

8. Everyone will take pictures. _____

9. You (*fam.*) will laugh. _____

10. They (*masc.*) will never understand. _____

The following irregular verbs have irregular stems.

INFINITIVE	ENGLISH	FUTURE
aller	*to go*	j'**ir**ai
s'asseoir	*to sit down*	je m'**assiér**ai (or: je m'**assoir**ai [without the **e** of the infinitive])
avoir	*to have*	j'**aur**ai
courir	*to run*	je **courr**ai
devoir	*to have to*	je **devr**ai
envoyer	*to send*	j'**enverr**ai
être	*to be*	je **ser**ai
faire	*to do*	je **fer**ai
falloir	*to be necessary*	il **faudr**a
mourir	*to die*	je **mourr**ai
pleuvoir	*to rain*	il **pleuvr**a
pouvoir	*to be able to*	je **pourr**ai
recevoir	*to receive*	je **recevr**ai
savoir	*to know*	je **saur**ai
tenir	*to hold*	je **tiendr**ai
valoir	*to be worth*	je **vaudr**ai
venir	*to come*	je **viendr**ai

voir	to see	je **verr**ai
vouloir	to want	je **voudr**ai

Note:

- The future of **il y a** (*there is, there are*) is **il y aura** (*there will be*).
- Most compound irregular verbs have the same future stem as the main or model verbs:

> devenir ➞ je de**viendr**ai
> revenir ➞ je re**viendr**ai
> se souvenir ➞ je me sou**viendr**ai
> promettre ➞ je pro**mettr**ai
> sourire ➞ je sou**rir**ai
> comprendre ➞ je com**prendr**ai
> apprendre ➞ j'ap**prendr**ai
> reconnaître ➞ je re**connaîtr**ai, etc.

EXERCICE 9·3

Donnez la forme correcte du verbe au futur.

1. Ils (aller) _____ à Monte Carlo.

2. Je (prendre) _____ le train.

3. Il (savoir) _____ beaucoup de choses.

4. Nous (devoir) _____ faire un choix.

5. Je (faire) _____ tout ce que tu (vouloir) _____ .

6. Elles (voir) _____ l'Airbus A380.

7. Vous (envoyer) _____ le fichier en pièce jointe.

8. (venir) _____ -tu avec moi?

9. Vous (être) _____ mieux chez vous.

10. J'(avoir) _____ trente ans en septembre.

11. Il (falloir) _____ se lever tôt.

12. Je ne (pouvoir) _____ pas venir.

EXERCICE 9·4

Vrai ou faux?

À votre avis, est-ce que les prédictions suivantes pour l'an 2050 sont bonnes?

_____ 1. On pourra éviter la guerre et on vivra en paix.

_____ 2. Nous passerons nos vacances sur la lune.

_____ 3. Les robots nettoieront nos maisons.

_____ 4. Il n'y aura plus de maladies incurables.

_____ 5. Les centrales nucléaires n'existeront plus.

_____ 6. Les éoliennes (*aerogenerators*) produiront toute notre électricité.

_____ 7. Je parlerai couramment (*fluently*) le français.

EXERCICE
9·5

Comment dit-on en français?

1. I will sit down. _____

2. We (**On**) will see. _____

3. I will go to the butcher shop. _____

4. Where will she go? _____

5. Will we have enough money? _____

6. Will there be a meeting tonight? _____

7. She will have to pay for the dinner. _____

8. They (*fem.*) will be happy. _____

9. Will that (**Ça**) be all? _____

10. What will you (*fam.*) do? _____

11. You (*pol.*) will remember. _____

12. It will be necessary to hurry. _____

13. What will the weather be like? —It will rain. _____

14. We will not be able to come. _____

15. They (*masc.*) will receive a phone call (**un coup de téléphone**). _____

The uses of the simple future

As in English, the simple future is used

1. to describe a future action or situation. Often along with expressions of time such as:

ce soir	*tonight*
demain	*tomorrow*
demain matin	*tomorrow morning*
demain après-midi	*tomorrow afternoon*

demain soir	*tomorrow night*
après-demain	*the day after tomorrow*
le lendemain	*the next day*
lundi/mardi, etc. prochain	*next Monday/Tuesday, etc.*
la semaine prochaine	*next week*
le mois prochain	*next month*
l'année prochaine	*next year*
dans quelques semaines	*in a few weeks*
dans dix ans	*in ten years, ten years from now*
dans un siècle	*in a century*
à l'avenir	*in the future*
un jour	*some day*
un de ces jours	*one of these days*
bientôt	*soon*

Il **fera** chaud **demain**.	*It will be hot tomorrow.*
J'**irai** en France la semaine prochaine.	*I will go / I will be going to France next week.*
Seul l'avenir le **dira**.	*Only time (lit.: the future) will tell.*

2. after **si** meaning *whether* if the action in the subordinate clause refers to the future, and if the introductory verb (i.e., the verb in the main clause) is in the present tense. This is also called *indirect discourse.*

Je **me demande si** elle **viendra**.	*I wonder whether she will come.*
Sais-tu s'il **pleuvra?**	*Do you know whether it will rain?*

But **si** meaning *if* (expressing a condition) can *never* be followed by the future. The present tense is used instead.

Je te **téléphonerai si** je **peux**.	*I will call you if I can.*

3. in the main clause of sentences expressing a condition when the present tense is used in the **si**-clause, and when a future action or situation is referred to.

Si le temps le **permet**, nous **ferons** du snowboard.	*If the weather allows it, we'll go snowboarding.*

Contrary to English, the simple future is used

1. in subordinate clauses, after the verb **espérer** (*to hope*) when it refers to a future action or situation. (English generally uses the present tense, not the future, in this context.)

J'**espère** que nous **gagnerons** le match.	*I hope (that) we win the game.*
Nous **espérons** que vous **passerez** une bonne soirée.	*We hope (that) you have a good evening.*

2. in subordinate clauses after the conjunctions **quand** (*when*), **lorsque** (*when*), **dès que** (*as soon as*), **aussitôt que** (*as soon as*), when the verb in the main clause is in the future or imperative and when a future action or situation is referred to. (English uses the present tense, not the future, in this context.)

Téléphonez-moi **quand** vous **serez** de retour.	*Call me when you get back.*
J'**irai** le voir **dès qu'**il **arrivera**.	*I will visit him as soon as he arrives.*

3. to express an *order* (i.e., replace an imperative).

Tu **prendras** à droite au prochain carrefour.	*Turn right at the next intersection.*
Vous lui **direz** bonjour de ma part.	*Say hello to him/her for me.*

Comment dit-on en français? Use the *futur simple* throughout.

1. Tomorrow afternoon, there will be a party. _____

2. Tonight, I will send a letter to my aunt. _____

3. I hope (that) the weather is nice next week. _____

4. In the future, he will be more careful. _____

5. When will you (*fam.*) be leaving? _____

6. I don't know whether I will go to the meeting. _____

7. Will you (*fam.*) have the time to do it? _____

8. He will come back in July. _____

9. I will never know the answer. _____

10. Will you (*fam.*) be able to join us? _____

11. Some day, this house will be worth a fortune. _____

12. He will want to see your (**votre**) passport. _____

13. My mother will buy me a laptop computer when I am fifteen. _____

14. She will call as soon as she can. _____

15. From now on (**Désormais**) take (*pol.*) the subway! _____

16. If it rains, we will stay at home. _____

17. I will leave when I want. _____

18. In a few weeks, this factory will close its doors. _____

19. The strike will only last twenty-four hours. _____

20. I will be back (**de retour**) in five minutes. _____

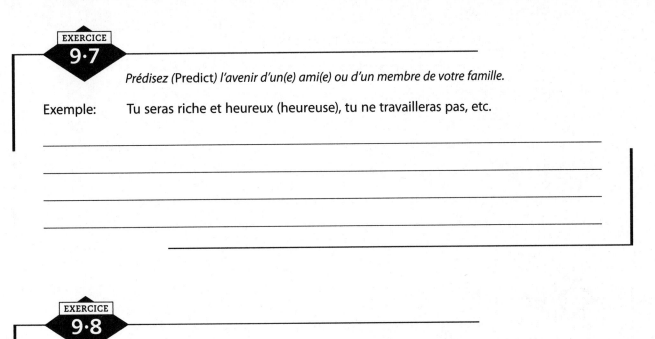

EXERCICE
9·7

Prédisez (Predict) l'avenir d'un(e) ami(e) ou d'un membre de votre famille.

Exemple: Tu seras riche et heureux (heureuse), tu ne travailleras pas, etc.

_____

_____

_____

_____

EXERCICE
9·8

Comment sera le monde dans trente ans? Utilisez votre imagination.

_____

_____

_____

_____

EXERCICE
9·9

Votre amie Anne est allée voir une diseuse de bonne aventure pour savoir ce que l'avenir lui réserve. Dites en français ce que la dame lui a dit.

You will live in Europe and you will travel a lot. You will work for a French company, and later you will become a fashion model and a movie star. You will have the lead in many movies and you will see the whole world. Everybody will admire you. You will be able to buy many things because you will be extremely rich. When you are thirty, you will meet the man of your dreams. You will get married in Paris and you will spend your honeymoon in Tahiti where the sun will shine all the time. You will have three beautiful children, one boy and two girls. The boy's name will be Antoine and the girls' names will be Chantal and Denise. Your husband will love you and you will adore your husband. You will go on many trips together. Your children will attend Harvard University. They will be successful and they will become rich and famous also. You will be very happy and you will live a long time.

VOCABULAIRE			
to attend (a school)	**aller à**	honeymoon	**la lune de miel**
to be successful	**réussir**	a movie star	**une vedette de**
a company	**une entreprise**		**cinéma**
extremely rich	**richissime**	to shine	**briller**
a fashion model	**un mannequin**	the whole world	**le monde entier**
to have the lead	**jouer le rôle**		
(in a movie or play)	**principal**		

_____

_____

_____

_____

_____

_____

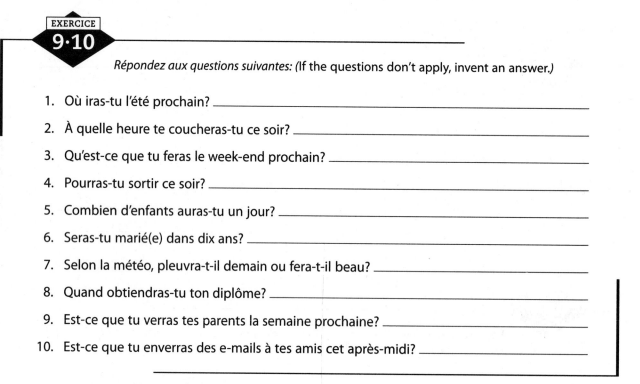

EXERCICE
9·10

Répondez aux questions suivantes: (If the questions don't apply, invent an answer.)

1. Où iras-tu l'été prochain? _____

2. À quelle heure te coucheras-tu ce soir? _____

3. Qu'est-ce que tu feras le week-end prochain? _____

4. Pourras-tu sortir ce soir? _____

5. Combien d'enfants auras-tu un jour? _____

6. Seras-tu marié(e) dans dix ans? _____

7. Selon la météo, pleuvra-t-il demain ou fera-t-il beau? _____

8. Quand obtiendras-tu ton diplôme? _____

9. Est-ce que tu verras tes parents la semaine prochaine? _____

10. Est-ce que tu enverras des e-mails à tes amis cet après-midi? _____

The close future (*le futur proche*)

An event or situation in the future, especially when it is the near future, can also be expressed by the **futur proche** which consists of the present tense of **aller** + *infinitive*. As we have seen earlier, the English equivalent of this construction is *to be going to* + *infinitive*.

Je **vais essayer**.
Ça ne **va** pas **marcher**.
Tout **va s'arranger**.
Il **va faire** froid dehors.
Comme dessert, nous **allons prendre** de la glace au chocolat.

I am going to try.
That is not going to work.
Everything is going to be all right.
It's going to be cold outside.
For dessert, we are going to have chocolate ice cream.

Remplacez le futur proche par le futur simple.

Exemple: Il **va** le **savoir**. → Il le **saura**.

1. Tu vas avoir mal au cœur. _____

2. Il va faire meilleur demain. _____

3. Elle va finir ses études dans six ans. _____

4. Nous allons nous asseoir sur un banc. _____

5. Tu vas être surpris. _____

6. Je vais me marier en octobre prochain. _____

7. Il va pleuvoir. _____

8. Il va pleurer. _____

9. Ils vont mourir. _____

10. Je vais courir. _____

11. Il va y avoir un orage. _____

12. Vous allez voir. _____

Translation difficulties

English *will* (+ *infinitive*) does not always correspond to the future tense in French. The French **futur simple** translates *will* only if a future action or situation is expressed (*I **will** ask* = **je demanderai**). Otherwise, *will* must be translated differently.

English *will* is translated by the present tense of **vouloir**:

◆ in *polite requests*

***Will** you marry me?*	**Veux**-tu m'épouser?

◆ in *refusals* (*will not* or *won't*)

*I told him repeatedly but he **won't** listen.*	Je le lui ai dit plusieurs fois mais il ne **veut** pas écouter.

English *will* is also translated by the present tense of the verb in question when repetition or habit is implied.

*I see him often but he **will** never greet me.*	Je le vois souvent mais il ne me **salue** jamais.

Comment dit-on en français?

1. Will you (*pol.*) follow me? _____

2. Will you (*fam.*) help me? _____

3. Will you (*fam.*) do me a favor? _____

4. These things (**Ce sont des choses qui**) will happen. _____

5. The car will not start (**démarrer**). _____

6. He won't (= refuses to) do it. _____

The formation of the future perfect

In English, the future perfect consists of *will have* or *shall have* + *past participle* of the verb in question *I **will** (**shall**) **have gone**, you **will have read**, he **will have known**, we **will** (**shall**) **have seen**,* etc.

In French, the future perfect (**le futur antérieur**) consists of the simple future of **avoir** or **être** + *past participle* of the verb in question. Here are two model conjugations:

travailler		aller	
j'aurai travaillé	*I will have worked*	je serai allé(e)*	*I will have gone*
tu auras travaillé		tu seras allé(e)	
il/on aura travaillé		il/on sera allé	
elle aura travaillé		elle sera allée	
nous aurons travaillé		nous serons allé(e)s	
vous aurez travaillé		vous serez allé(e)(s)	
ils auront travaillé		ils seront allés	
elles auront travaillé		elles seront allées	

*The agreement of the past participle in the future perfect is made as in all other compound tenses of verbs conjugated with **être**.

Note: Whereas the *simple future* describes an action or situation which will be taking place at some time in the future, the *future perfect* refers to an action or situation which is seen as *completed* by or at a specific time in the future. *Compare:*

Demain, je **finirai** de taper ma thèse.	*Tomorrow, I **will finish** typing my thesis.*
Demain soir, **j'aurai fini** de taper ma thèse.	*By tomorrow night, I **will have finished** typing my thesis.*

Comment dit-on en français?

1. I will have bought a car. _____

2. She will have gone to the dentist (**chez le dentiste**). _____

3. We will have gone to bed. _____

4. You (*fam.*) will already have left. _____

5. They (*masc.*) will have seen the movie. _____

6. I will have had a good time. _____

7. You (*pol.*) will have understood. _____

The uses of the future perfect

As in English, the future perfect is used for actions and situations which will be *completed* at or by a specified time in the future.

Dans trente ans, le nombre de véhicules **aura doublé** dans le monde.

*Thirty years from now, the number of vehicles in the world **will have doubled**.*

EXERCICE

9·14

Comment dit-on en français?

1. The day after tomorrow, I will have finished my report. _____

2. By the end of the year (**D'ici la fin de l'année**), we will have spent one thousand euros

   on medication (**en médicaments**). _____

3. By (**En**) July, this factory will have laid off one hundred workers. _____

   _____

4. Ten years from now (**D'ici dix ans**), these birds will have disappeared. _____

   _____

5. I hope that she will have left when you (*fam.*) come back. _____

   _____

6. Will you (*pol.*) have written the recommendation (**la recommandation**) by tonight (**ce**

   soir)? _____

EXERCICE

9·15

What will you have done by the end of the year? Answer with oui *or* non.

D'ici la fin de l'année…

_____ 1. j'aurai lu cinq livres.

_____ 2. je serai allé(e) en France.

_____ 3. je me serai marié(e).

_____ 4. j'aurai acheté une nouvelle voiture.

_____ 5. j'aurai dîné chez MacDo dix fois.

_____ 6. j'aurai gagné beaucoup d'argent.

_____ 7. j'aurai écrit mille courriels.

_____ 8. j'aurai maigri de trois kilos.

_____ 9. j'aurai vu au moins huit films étrangers.

_____ 10. j'aurai appris le français.

Contrary to English, the future perfect is used after the conjunctions **dès que** (_as soon as_), **aussitôt que** (_as soon as_), **quand** (_when_), **lorsque** (_when_), **une fois que** (_once_), **tant que** (_as long as_), and **après que** (_after_) for actions and situations which will be completed _before_ another future action. In these sentences, the verb in the main clause is in the simple future or imperative. (English uses the _present perfect_ in this context.)

Je vous **rejoindrai** _aussitôt que_   I will join you as soon as I **have eaten**.
    j'**aurai mangé**.

EXERCICE
9·16

Comment dit-on en français?

1. Call (_pol._) me as soon as you have received this message. _____

2. It will be your turn (**Ce sera votre tour**) when I have finished. _____

3. We (**On**) will know more when he has had an X-ray. _____

4. Once we have retrieved (**récupérer**) our suitcases, we will take a taxi. _____

_____

5. As long as you (_fam._) haven't done your homework, you will not be able to go out. _____

_____

6. I will write to you (_fam._) after we have arrived. _____

Contrary to English, the future perfect is used to express an assumption on the part of the speaker, i.e., the _probability_ of a past action or situation. (English uses _must have + past participle_ in this context.)

Il n'est pas encore arrivé? Il **aura manqué**   He hasn't arrived yet? He **must have missed**
    le train.   (= _he probably missed_) _the train._

Comment dit-on en français?

1. That is not possible. She must have made a mistake. _____

2. He is coming back. He must have forgotten something. _____

3. I cannot find my pen. My colleague (**Mon collègue**) must have taken it. _____

   _____

4. She hasn't called yet? You (*fam.*) must have given her the wrong (**mauvais**) number. _____

   _____

5. They (*masc.*) are not hungry? They must have already eaten. _____

   _____

The conditional

The French conditional corresponds to English *would* + *infinitive* (*I would go, she would buy*). In both languages, the conditional is used to make polite requests (*I would like a cup of coffee*), or to express what would happen if a certain condition, which may or may not be expressed in the sentence, were met: *If I had the money, I would go to France. What would you do (if you were in my place)?*

Be careful not to confuse the conditional *would* expressing a hypothetical action (*If I had the time, I would travel*) with the *would* that describes repeated action in the past and is translated with the imperfect tense:

*When I was young, I **would** (= used to) travel often.*	Quand j'étais jeune, je **voyageais** souvent.

The conditional mood has two tenses, the *present conditional* and the *past conditional*.

The formation of the present conditional

To form the present conditional, one takes the future stem of the verb and adds the endings of the imperfect tense (**-ais, -ais, -ait, -ions, -iez, -aient**).

Regular verbs

donner *to give*	
je donner**ais**	*I would give*
tu donner**ais**	*you would give*
il/elle/on donner**ait**	*he/she/it/one would give*
nous donner**ions**	*we would give*
vous donner**iez**	*you would give*
ils/elles donner**aient**	*they would give*

choisir *to choose*	
je choisir**ais**	*I would choose*
tu choisir**ais**	*you would choose*
il/elle/on choisir**ait**	*he/she/it/one would choose*
nous choisir**ions**	*we would choose*
vous choisir**iez**	*you would choose*
ils/elles choisir**aient**	*they would choose*

répondre _to answer_	
je répond**rais**	_I would answer_
tu répond**rais**	_you would answer_
il/elle/on répond**rait**	_he/she/it/one would answer_
nous répond**rions**	_we would answer_
vous répond**riez**	_you would answer_
ils/elles répond**raient**	_they would answer_

Note:

◆ As in the simple future, the ending of the present conditional is always preceded by the letter **r**. If the stem of the verb ends in **r**, there will be two [ʀ] sounds before the conditional ending: **je rent**_rerais_ (_I would go home_), **je mont**_rerais_ (_I would show_), **je rencon-**_trerais_ (_I would meet_).

◆ The stem of both regular and irregular verbs is the same in the future and in the conditional. It is the ending that differentiates the conditional from the future.

◆ Note that the pronunciation of the first-person singular in the future (**je donner**_ai_) and of the first-person singular in the present conditional (**je donner**_ais_) is identical: [ʒədɔnʀɛ].

◆ The same spelling changes that occur in the future also appear in the conditional: **acheter: j'ach**è**terais, appeler: j'appe**_ll_**erais, espérer: j'esp**é**rerais, nettoyer: je nettoie**_rais_.

EXERCICE
10·1

Comment dit-on en français?

1. We would eat. _____

2. I would not buy this rug. _____

3. You (_fam._) would ask. _____

4. I would try. _____

5. They (_masc._) would work hard. _____

6. I would be bored. _____

7. We would stay. _____

8. He would bring his grandchildren. _____

9. You (_pol._) would help. _____

10. He would remember. _____

11. You (_pol._) would succeed. _____

12. She would obey. _____

13. I would blush. _____

14. You (*fam.*) would choose. _____

15. They (*fem.*) would lose. _____

16. I wouldn't answer. _____

Irregular verbs

Some irregular verbs have regular stems (the entire infinitive or, with verbs ending in **-re**, the infinitive minus final **e**). Irregular verbs and their irregular stems in the conditional are shown in bold face in the list below. Note that the stems are the same as those for the simple future.

INFINITIVE	CONDITIONAL	ENGLISH MEANING
aller (s'en aller)	j'**ir**ais (je m'en **ir**ais)	*I would go (I would go away)*
s'asseoir	je m'**assié**rais (or: je m'**assoir**ais)	*I would sit down*
avoir	j'**aur**ais	*I would have*
battre	je battrais	*I would beat*
boire	je boirais	*I would drink*
conduire	je conduirais	*I would drive*
connaître	je connaîtrais	*I would know*
courir	je **courr**ais	*I would run*
craindre	je craindrais	*I would fear*
croire	je croirais	*I would believe*
devoir	je **devr**ais	*I ought to, I should*
dire	je dirais	*I would say*
dormir	je dormirais	*I would sleep*
écrire	j'écrirais	*I would write*
envoyer	j'**enverr**ais	*I would send*
être	je **ser**ais	*I would be*
faire	je **fer**ais	*I would do*
falloir	il **faudr**ait	*it would be necessary*
lire	je lirais	*I would read*
mettre	je mettrais	*I would put*
mourir	je **mourr**ais	*I would die*
naître	je naîtrais	*I would be born*
ouvrir	j'ouvrirais	*I would open*
plaire	je plairais	*I would please*
pleuvoir	il **pleuvr**ait	*it would rain*
pouvoir	je **pourr**ais	*I would be able, I could*
prendre	je prendrais	*I would take*
recevoir	je **recevr**ais	*I would receive*
rire	je rirais	*I would laugh*
savoir	je **saur**ais	*I would know*
suivre	je suivrais	*I would follow*
tenir	je **tiendr**ais	*I would hold*
valoir	je **vaudr**ais	*I would be worth*
venir	je **viendr**ais	*I would come*
vivre	je vivrais	*I would live*
voir	je **verr**ais	*I would see*
vouloir	je **voudr**ais	*I would like*

Note:

◆ The present conditional of the impersonal expression **il y a** (*there is/are*) is **il y aurait** (*there would be*).

◆ The present conditional of the impersonal expression **il vaut mieux** (*it is better*) is **il vaudrait mieux** (*it would be better*).

◆ Three irregular verbs have a special meaning in the present conditional.

◆ vouloir: **je voudrais** = *I would like*

◆ pouvoir: **je pourrais** = *I could*

◆ devoir: **je devrais** = *I ought to, should*

EXERCICE
10·2

Traduisez en français les mots entre parenthèses.

1. (*We would go*) _____ à la piscine.

2. (*She wouldn't have*) _____ d'argent.

3. (*There would be*) _____ une guerre.

4. (*He would be*) _____ triste.

5. (*I would drink*) _____ du jus d'orange.

6. (*Would you [fam.] run*) _____ vite?

7. (*We would send*) _____ un fax.

8. (*What would you [fam.] do*) _____ à ma place?

9. (*It would be necessary*) _____ y aller.

10. (*I would die*) _____ de peur.

11. (*It would rain*) _____ peut-être.

12. (*You [fam.] would take*) _____ le train.

13. (*You [pol.] would receive*) _____ un reçu.

14. (*He would know*) _____ la réponse.

15. (*Who would come*) _____ chez vous?

The uses of the present conditional

As in English, the present conditional expresses a *possibility* or *eventuality*.

| Ça **irait** plus vite. | *That would go faster.* |
| Qu'est-ce que je **ferais** sans toi? | *What would I do without you?* |

Contrary to English, the present conditional is always used after **au cas où** (*in case*).

| Prenez votre parapluie, **au cas où** il **pleuvrait**. | *Take your umbrella in case it rains.* |

The present conditional is used instead of the present indicative to soften a statement or a question. It expresses

1. A *polite request* (with verbs such as **vouloir, pouvoir, avoir,** and **savoir**)

Je **voudrais** une tasse de café, s'il vous plaît.	*I would like a cup of coffee please.*
Pourriez-vous m'aider?	*Could you help me?*
Est-ce que je **pourrais** avoir une place à côté de la fenêtre?	*Could I have a seat next to the window?*
Auriez-vous l'heure?	*Would you (happen to) have the (clock) time?*
Sauriez-vous où se trouve la gare?	*Would you know where the train station is?*

2. A (subdued) *wish* or *desire* (with verbs such as **aimer** and **vouloir**)

| J'**aimerais** vous parler. | *I would like to talk to you.* |
| Je **voudrais** avoir dix ans de moins. | *I would like to be ten years younger.* |

The desire can be reinforced by adding **bien** to the verb in the present conditional.

| J'**aimerais** *bien* connaître votre fille. | *I would (really) like to meet your daughter.* |
| Je **voudrais** *bien* y aller. | *I'd love to go (there). (I'd really like to go.)* |

3. An *obligation*, a *suggestion*, or *advice* (most often with the verb **devoir**, which expresses *should, ought to* in the present conditional)

Qu'est-ce que je **devrais** faire?	*What should I do?*
Vous **devriez** voir ce gratte-ciel.	*You ought to see this skyscraper.*
Tu **devrais** consulter un médecin.	*You should see a doctor.*

EXERCICE
10·3

Comment dit-on en français?

1. That (**Ce**) would be a shame (**dommage**). _____

2. That (**Ça**) wouldn't surprise (**étonner**) me. _____

3. That (**Ça**) would be (**coûter**) too expensive. _____

4. It would be better not to say anything (**ne rien dire**). _____

5. There would be riots (**des émeutes [f.pl.]**). _____

6. Here is my phone number in case you (*fam.*) need me. _____

7. In case you (*pol.*) change your mind (**changer d'avis**), let me know (**faites-le-moi savoir**).

_____

8. What would you (*pol.*) like? _____

9. I would like a piece of strawberry tart. _____

_____

10. Would you (*pol.*) like a window seat (**côté fenêtre**) or an aisle seat? _____

    _____

11. She would really like to speak French fluently. _____

    _____

12. Would you (*pol.*) have a room for two people? _____

13. Would you (*pol.*) know the address and phone number (**les coordonnées** *[f.pl.]*) of Mr.

    Avenel? _____

14. Could we see the menu please? _____

15. Could I have rice instead of (**à la place de**) the French fries? _____

16. Could I speak to Mrs. Duval? _____

17. Could you (*fam.*) close the window? _____

18. Could you (*pol.*) tell me where the nearest subway station (**la station de métro la plus**

    proche) is? _____

19. That should be forbidden (**interdit**). _____

20. I ought to go to the hairdresser (**chez le coiffeur**). _____

EXERCICE

10·4

Make the following sentences more polite by replacing the present tense of the verbs in italic with the present conditional.

1. Est-ce que je *peux* vous poser une question? _____

2. *Pouvez*-vous parler plus lentement s'il vous plaît? _____

3. *Voulez*-vous me rendre un service? _____

4. Je *veux* avoir l'addition s'il vous plaît. _____

5. Pardon Madame, *avez*-vous la monnaie de cinquante euros? _____

6. *Savez*-vous où je peux acheter des fleurs? _____

As its name indicates, the *present conditional* is mainly used to describe what would happen under a certain *condition*. This condition (which is not fulfilled at the moment of the statement, but could be fulfilled in the future) is usually introduced by **si** = *if*. In such sentences, the verb in the **si**-clause is in the *imperfect*, the verb in the main clause is in the *present conditional*. The **si**-clause can be at the beginning or at the end of the sentence.

<table>
<tr><td>Si j'**étais** malade, j'**irais** chez le médecin.</td><td>*If I were ill, I would go to the doctor.*</td></tr>
<tr><td>Je **serais** content(e) si vous **acceptiez** mon invitation.</td><td>*I would be happy if you accepted my invitation.*</td></tr>
</table>

Comment dit-on en français?

1. If I had a lot of money, I would travel around the world (**faire le tour du monde**). _____

_____

2. What would you (*pol.*) do if you won the lottery? _____

_____

3. Where would you (*fam.*) go if you had a month off (**un mois de congé**)? _____

_____

4. If I were ill, I would stay in bed. _____

5. I would be happy if you (*fam.*) came to my party. _____

6. If she had the time, she would clean (**ranger**) her room. _____

7. If I were you (**toi**), I would stop smoking. _____

8. If we went to France, we would see many beautiful cathedrals. _____

9. If he saw a black cat, he would turn around (**faire demi-tour**). _____

10. If they (*masc.*) had a satellite dish (**une parabole**), they would get (**recevoir**) this

program. _____

Qu'est-ce que vous feriez si vous étiez très riche? Qu'est-ce que vous ne feriez pas?

Si j'étais très riche,... _____

je _____ ,

je _____

et je _____ .

Complétez les phrases suivantes personnellement en utilisant le conditionnel présent.

1. Si j'étais fatigué(e), _____

2. S'il pleuvait, _____

3. Si j'avais la grippe, _____

4. Si j'étais le président des États-Unis, _____

5. Si j'habitais en France, _____

6. Si je n'apprenais pas le français, _____

7. Si je rencontrais des Français, _____

8. Si je faisais le voyage de mes rêves, _____

9. Si j'allais à la plage, _____

10. Si j'avais les moyens (*If I could afford it*), _____

EXERCICE
10·8

Si c'était à refaire, qu'est-ce que vous feriez différemment? If you had to do it all over again, what would you do differently? Say what you would do and what you would not do. Use the present conditional and fill in all lines.

Si c'était à refaire, je... _____

_____

_____

_____

EXERCICE
10·9

J'ai les problèmes suivants. Dites ce que vous feriez à ma place.

Exemple: J'ai besoin d'argent. *Si j'avais besoin d'argent, je travaillerais.*

1. Je suis fauché(e). Si _____, je _____.

2. Je suis déprimé(e). Si _____, je _____.

3. Ma voiture est en panne. Si _____, je _____.

4. Je ne réussis pas à l'examen. Si _____,
je _____.

5. J'ai mal aux dents. Si _____, je _____.

6. Je vois mal. Si _____, je _____.

7. J'ai froid. Si _____, je _____.

The present conditional is used (as in English) in a subordinate clause after the conjunction **que** (*that*) and after **si** (*whether*) to express an action or situation that occurred later in time than the verb in the main clause, if this verb is in a past tense. This is sometimes called *indirect discourse*. Here, the conditional indicates a future action in the past.

Je *savais qu*'il **serait** là.	*I knew that he would be there.*
Elle *a dit qu*'elle le **ferait**.	*She said that she would do it.*
Je *me demandais s*'il **viendrait**.	*I was wondering whether he would come.*
Ils m'*ont demandé si* j'**irais** au bal.	*They asked me whether I would go to the ball.*

EXERCICE
10·10

Comment dit-on en français?

1. I didn't think that it would snow. _____

2. I believed that this wouldn't work. _____

3. We were sure that you (*pol.*) would agree. _____

4. He had promised that he would call. _____

5. They (*masc.*) didn't think that you (*pol.*) would remember. _____

6. She didn't know whether she would have the time to do it. _____

7. He asked me whether I could help him. _____

8. I was wondering whether there would be fireworks. _____

EXERCICE
10·11

Anne parle de ses résolutions pour la nouvelle année. Traduisez ce qu'elle dit.

In a conversation with my doctor at the end of December, I had mentioned that I wanted to lose weight and remain healthy this year. I was wondering whether my New Year's resolutions would come true.

"What should I do?" I had asked Dr. Martin. He answered that if he were in my place, he would go on a diet. He would eat less and he would exercise more. He would drink only skim milk, Diet coke, and three bottles of water per day. He would avoid sweets and alcoholic beverages. Instead, he would eat lots of fruit and vegetables. He would not take the car but the bike to go to places, except if it rained. And he told me that instead of watching television, he would take walks, he would swim, and he would play tennis every day.

When I left the doctor's office, I was depressed. I knew that I wouldn't be able to change my eating habits. I would follow Dr. Martin's advice if I weren't so lazy.

alcoholic beverages	**des boissons alcoolisées**	if I were in your place	**à votre place**
at the end	**à la fin**	instead	**au lieu de cela**
to come true	**se réaliser**	instead of	**au lieu de**
Diet coke	**du coca light**	to lose weight	**maigrir**
eating habits	**les habitudes alimentaires (f.pl.)**	office (of a doctor)	**le cabinet (du médecin)**
except	**sauf**	skim milk	**du lait écrémé**
to go on a diet	**se mettre au régime**	so (+ *adjective*)	**si (+ *adjectif*)**
to go to places	**se déplacer**	sweets	**des sucreries (f.pl.)**
healthy	**en bonne santé**	to walk	**faire de la marche**

The expressions *aimer mieux* and *faire mieux* in the present conditional

When used in the present conditional,

◆ **aimer mieux** (+ *infinitive*) expresses *would rather.*

> J'**aimerais mieux** faire du shopping que de rester à la maison.   ***I'd rather** go shopping than stay at home.*

◆ **faire mieux** (+ **de** + *infinitive*) expresses *had better*

> Tu **ferais mieux** de te taire.   *You **had better** be silent.*

EXERCICE
10·12

Comment dit-on en français?

1. She'd rather chat with her friends than study. _____

2. Wouldn't you (*fam.*) rather travel? _____

3. You (*pol.*) had better follow his advice. _____

4. She had better listen to him. _____

5. They (*masc.*) had better leave. _____

6. You (*fam.*) had better wait. _____

Other uses of the present conditional

The present conditional describes a *present* action or situation, the certainty of which has not been confirmed. Since it is widely used by the news media (radio, TV, press) to report alleged facts, this use of the conditional is referred to as the "conditional of the press." (For this meaning, English uses the adverbs *supposedly, allegedly, presumably, apparently* with the verb in the present tense.)

> Il y a eu un tremblement de terre en Asie hier soir. Il y **aurait** des milliers de victimes.
> *There was an earthquake in Asia last night. There are presumably thousands of victims.*
> D'après une étude récente, les protestants **seraient** plus pratiquants que les catholiques.
> *According to a recent study, Protestants allegedly go to church more often than Catholics.*

EXERCICE
10·13

Traduisez en français les mots entre parenthèses.

1. Dans ce pays, vingt pour cent des adultes (*are allegedly*) _____ illettrés.

2. Parmi les victimes (*there are supposedly*) _____ dix enfants.

3. Selon les médecins, le blessé (*is presumably [feeling] better*) _____ .

4. D'après les médias, les speakers de la télévision (*apparently earn*) _____ plus d'argent que les vedettes de cinéma.

5. Les étudiants et les ouvriers (*are presumably on strike* [**faire grève**]) _____ .

6. L'incendie (*is allegedly*) _____ dû à une fuite (*leak*) de gaz.

The formation of the past conditional

The English equivalent of the French past conditional is *would have* + *past participle* (I **would have gone**, she **would have said**). It is used for actions or situations that would have happened but did not, because something prevented them from taking place (we **would have gone out** if it hadn't rained).

The past conditional is a compound tense formed by using the *present conditional* of **avoir** or **être** + the *past participle* of the verb.

donner to give	
j'aurais donné	*I would have given*
tu aurais donné	*you would have given*
il/elle/on aurait donné	*he/she/it/one would have given*
nous aurions donné	*we would have given*
vous auriez donné	*you would have given*
ils/elles auraient donné	*they would have given*

partir to leave	
je serais parti(e)	*I would have left*
tu serais parti(e)	*you would have left*
il/on serait parti	*he/it/one would have left*
elle serait partie	*she/it would have left*
nous serions parti(e)s	*we would have left*
vous seriez parti(e)(s)	*you would have left*
ils seraient partis	*they would have left*
elles seraient parties	*they would have left*

se réveiller *to wake up*	
je me serais réveillé(e)	*I would have woken up*
tu te serais réveillé(e)	*you would have woken up*
il/on se serait réveillé	*he/it/one would have woken up*
elle se serait réveillée	*she/it would have woken up*
nous nous serions réveillé(e)s	*we would have woken up*
vous vous seriez réveillé(e)(s)	*you would have woken up*
ils se seraient réveillés	*they would have woken up*
elles se seraient réveillées	*they would have woken up*

Note:

♦ The past conditional follows the same rules as the **passé composé** as far as the agreement of the past participle is concerned.

♦ Three irregular verbs have a special meaning in the past conditional.

> vouloir: **j'aurais voulu** = *I would have liked*
> devoir: **j'aurais dû** = *I should have*
> pouvoir: **j'aurais pu** = *I could have*

Note that in French **aurais voulu**, **aurais dû**, and **aurais pu** are followed by the infinitive whereas in English *would have*, *should have*, and *could have* are followed by the past participle.

> *J'**aurais voulu** être* infirmière. | *I **would have liked** to be a nurse.*
> *J'**aurais dû** le savoir.* | *I **should have known** it.*
> *Il **aurait pu** le faire.* | *He **could have done** it.*

♦ The past conditional of **il y a** (*there is/are*) is **il y aurait eu** (*there would have been*), the past conditional of **il faut** (*it is necessary*) is **il aurait fallu** (*it would have been necessary*), and the past conditional of **il vaut mieux** (*it is better*) is **il aurait mieux valu** (*it would have been better*).

EXERCICE
10·14

Comment dit-on en français?

1. I would have been sad. _____

2. She would have preferred to live in the country (**à la campagne**). _____

_____

3. We would have stayed longer, but we had to leave. _____

4. They (*fem.*) would have laughed. _____

5. Who would have believed that he would resign? _____

_____

6. I would have gone to bed earlier. _____

7. In your place (**À votre place**), I wouldn't have said anything. _____

8. You (*pol.*) would have died. _____

9. He would have been afraid. _____

10. Would you (*fam.*) have come? _____

11. She would have lost. _____

12. It would have been better to wait. _____

The uses of the past conditional

As in English, the past conditional expresses a *possibility* or *eventuality* in the past.

> Tôt ou tard, les gens l'**auraient su**.   *Sooner or later, people would have found out.*

Contrary to English, the past conditional is used after **au cas où** (*in case*).

> *Au cas où* vous **auriez trouvé** mes lunettes, pourriez-vous les mettre sur mon bureau?
> *In case you found my glasses, could you put them on my desk?*

The past conditional frequently expresses a *reproach* or *regret* about an action that was not performed in the past (often with the verbs **devoir,** which expresses *should have* in the past conditional; **vouloir,** which expresses *would have liked* in the past conditional; and **pouvoir,** which expresses *could have* in the past conditional).

> Je n'**aurais** pas **dû** le lui dire.   *I shouldn't have told him.*
> J'**aurais** (bien) **aimé/voulu** vous parler,   *I (really) would have liked to talk to you,*
>   mais vous n'étiez pas chez vous.   *but you weren't at home.*
> Tu **aurais pu** nous prévenir. On s'est   *You could have informed us. We were worried.*
>   fait du souci.

Comment dit-on en français?

1. Would you (*fam.*) have seen my handbag by any chance (**par hasard**)? _____

2. In case you (*pol.*) didn't notice it, it is snowing. _____

3. She should have come earlier. _____

4. You (*fam.*) should have asked. _____

5. You (*pol.*) should have left a tip. _____

6. We should have been more careful. _____

7. You (*pol.*) shouldn't have spent so much money. _____

8. They (*masc.*) would have liked to sit down. _____

9. I would have liked to know where she was born. _____

10. She would have liked to become a flight attendant. _____

11. We could have had an accident. _____

12. That could have happened to anyone (**n'importe qui**). _____

EXERCICE

10·16

Pretend that you are a grandmother or grandfather looking back on your life and expressing some regrets. Write what you should have done and what you would have liked to do.

Exemple: J'aurais dû apprendre plusieurs langues.

J'aurais voulu (aimé) partir en vacances tous les ans.

_____

_____

_____

_____

_____

_____

The past conditional also describes what would have happened in the past under a certain condition. This condition (mentioned in a **si** [*if*]-clause) was not met and can no longer be fulfilled. In such sentences, the verb in the **si**-clause is in the *pluperfect*, the verb in the main clause is in the *past conditional*. The **si**-clause can be at the beginning or at the end of the sentence.

Si tu *étais parti* plus tôt, tu n'**aurais** pas manqué l'avion.

If you had left earlier, you wouldn't have missed the plane.

Si vous *aviez su*, qu'est-ce que vous **auriez fait?**

If you had known, what would you have done?

EXERCICE

10·17

Comment dit-on en français?

1. If I had known, I wouldn't have come. _____

2. She would have earned more money if she had worked overtime (**faire des heures supplémentaires**). _____

3. If the weather had been good last weekend, we would have gone camping. _____

_____

4. If you (*fam.*) hadn't drunk so much wine, you wouldn't have had a headache. _____

5. If it hadn't rained, I would have gone swimming. _____

6. If I had heard my alarm clock, I would have woken up on time. _____

7. If she had read *Internet for Dummies* (**Internet pour les nuls**), she would have known how to surf the Net. _____

The past conditional is used (as in English) in a subordinate clause after the conjunction **que** (*that*) and after **si** (*whether*) to express an action or situation that occurred later in time than the verb in the main clause, if this verb is in a past tense. This is also called *indirect discourse*. Here, the conditional indicates a future action in the past.

J'*étais sûr qu*'il **serait parti** avant mon retour.	*I was sure that he would have left before I returned.*
Il *se demandait s*'il **aurait pu** y aller.	*He was wondering whether he could have gone there.*

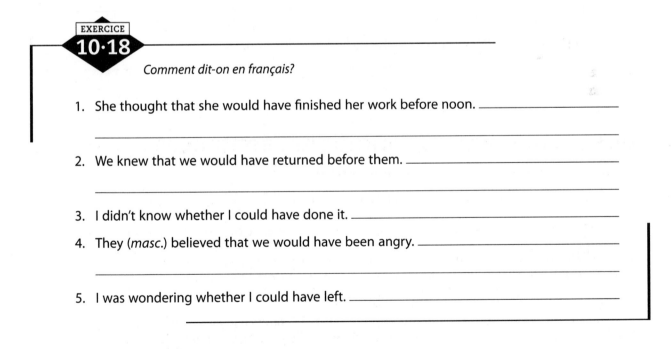

EXERCICE
10·18

Comment dit-on en français?

1. She thought that she would have finished her work before noon. _____

2. We knew that we would have returned before them. _____

3. I didn't know whether I could have done it. _____

4. They (*masc.*) believed that we would have been angry. _____

5. I was wondering whether I could have left. _____

Other uses of the past conditional

The past conditional describes a *past* action or situation the certainty of which has not been confirmed. Like the present conditional it is widely used by the news media to report alleged facts.

(English uses adverbs such as *supposedly*, *allegedly*, and *presumably* with the verb in the past tense.)

D'après ce qu'on dit dans les journaux, il **aurait tué** sa femme.	*According to what they say in the newspapers, he presumably killed his wife.*

EXERCICE
10·19

Comment dit-on en français?

1. He allegedly drowned. _____

2. She allegedly left her husband. _____

3. They (*masc.*) presumably tried to kidnap the child. _____
_____

4. The burglars supposedly took all the (**tous les**) computers. _____
_____

5. He supposedly died of a heart attack (**une crise cardiaque**). _____
_____

6. The explosion presumably caused five deaths. _____

7. Forty million readers allegedly read the novel *The Da Vinci Code*. _____
_____

8. Lightning (**La foudre**) supposedly killed four people. _____

Tense sequences in conditional sentences

A conditional sentence usually consists of two parts

1. a clause introduced by **si** = *if* (**si**-clause) which states a condition and

2. a clause (the main clause) that states the consequence or result of this condition

The conditional can never be used in the **si**-clause; it only appears in the main clause. The three most common tense sequences in conditional sentences are:

si-clause		main clause	
present tense	→	future tense	S'il **fait** beau, nous **irons** à la plage.
imperfect	→	present conditional	S'il **faisait** beau, nous **irions** à la plage.
pluperfect	→	past conditional	S'il **avait fait** beau, nous **serions allés** à la plage.

Note: **Si** followed by **il** and **ils** is elided (*s'il*, *s'ils*); **si** followed by **elle**, **elles**, and **on** is not elided (*si elle*, *si elles*, *si on*).

Comment dit-on en français?

1. If you (*fam.*) don't tell me the truth, I will get angry. _____

2. If we hurry, we will arrive on time. _____

3. If I knew him, I would speak to him. _____

4. If they (*masc.*) had gone to the cocktail party (**au cocktail**), they would have had a good

   time. _____

Remplissez les tirets avec la forme correcte du verbe entre parenthèses:

1. Si vous allez au théâtre la semaine prochaine, vous (voir) _____ une bonne pièce.

2. Si j'ai le temps, je (aller) _____ à la campagne.

3. S'il pleuvait je (mettre) _____ un imperméable.

4. Je (travailler) _____ très dur si j'étais le président des États-Unis.

5. Si vous aviez le temps, qu'est-ce que vous (faire) _____?

6. Si j'avais été fatigué(e), je (se coucher) _____.

7. Si Napoléon avait eu un fils avec Joséphine, il (ne pas épouser) _____ Marie-Louise.

8. Si on m'avait dit que je vivrais à l'étranger un jour, je (ne pas le croire) _____.

9. Si vous aviez pris un taxi, vous (arriver) _____ à temps.

10. Quelles langues parlerais-tu si tu (être) _____ suisse?

11. Avec qui seriez-vous sorti si vous (avoir) _____ le choix?

12. Si mes fleurs (être) _____ fanées, je les jetterai.

Finissez personnellement les phrases suivantes. Faites attention à la concordance des temps (*time sequence*).

1. Si j'ai l'argent, je _____.

2. Si je faisais un héritage, je _____.

3. S'il avait fait mauvais hier, _____.

4. Je serais content(e) si _____.

5. Si _____, j'arrêterais de travailler.

6. Je viendrais si _____.

7. Je serais venu(e) si _____.

8. Nous nous serions promenés si _____.

9. Qu'est-ce que vous feriez si _____?

10. Qu'est-ce que vous auriez fait si _____?

Important Note: French does *not* allow the future or conditional in the **si**-clause when **si** means *if*. Of the four tenses that may be used in the **si**-clause, the present tense, the imperfect, and the pluperfect are the most common.

Si je **suis** fatigué(e), je **m'assiérai**.	*If I am tired, I will sit down.*
S'il **neigeait,** nous ne **sortirions** pas.	*If it snowed, we wouldn't go out.*
Si elle **avait reçu** un prix, elle **aurait été** contente.	*If she had received an award, she would have been happy.*

If however **si** has the meaning *whether*, it may be followed by the future and by the conditional. This is another example of *indirect discourse*.

Je *me demande* s'il y **aura** un embouteillage aux heures de pointe.	*I am wondering whether there **will be** a traffic jam during the rush hour.*
Je *me demandais* s'il y **aurait** un embouteillage aux heures de pointe.	*I was wondering whether there **would be** a traffic jam during the rush hour.*

Note:

- After **si** (*whether*), the future tense expresses a future action or situation when the introductory verb (**se demander** in the examples above) is in the present tense, the conditional expresses a future action or situation when the introductory verb is in a past tense.
- Note also that the clause introduced by **si** (*whether*) is always at the end of the sentence.

EXERCICE
10·23

Remplissez les tirets avec la forme correcte du verbe entre parenthèses. Check whether si means "if" or "whether" before choosing the verb form.

1. S'il y (avoir) _____ un tremblement de terre, nous aurons peur.

2. S'il y (avoir) _____ un tremblement de terre, nous aurions peur.

3. S'il y (avoir) _____ un tremblement de terre, nous aurions eu peur.

4. Nous ne savons pas s'il y (avoir) _____ un tremblement de terre.

5. Elle voulait savoir s'il y (avoir) _____ un tremblement de terre.

Translation difficulties

English *would* does not always correspond to a French conditional.

1. If *would* means *used to*, i.e., if it describes a repeated, habitual action in the past, it is translated with the *imperfect* of the verb in question.

> *They **would** go to church every Sunday.*   Ils **allaient** à l'église tous les dimanches.

2. If *would* expresses a formal request, it is occasionally translated with the *present indicative* of **vouloir**.

> ***Would** you please close the door?*   **Voulez**-vous fermer la porte, s'il vous plaît?

3. If *would* is used negatively to express unwillingness, it is translated with the **passé composé** of **vouloir**.

> *He **wouldn't** tell me.*   Il **n'a pas voulu** me le dire.

EXERCICE
10·24

Comment dit-on en français?

1. Each time I saw him, he would pretend not to recognize (**reconnaître**) me. _____

2. Would you please (*pol.*) follow me? _____

3. Would you please (*pol.*) forgive me? _____

4. I gave her advice (**des conseils [m.pl.]**), but she wouldn't listen. _____

_____

5. I told him that several times, but he wouldn't believe me. _____

_____

6. I asked her to give me a hand (**un coup de main**), but she wouldn't. _____

_____

English *could*

1. *Could* is translated into French with the *present conditional* of **pouvoir** when it refers to the *future*, i.e., when it means *would be able to*.

> ***Could** you do me a favor?*   **Pourriez**-vous me rendre un service?
> *I **could** possibly do it tomorrow.*   Je **pourrais** éventuellement le faire demain.
> *I wonder whether he **could** help us.*   Je me demande s'il **pourrait** nous aider.

But: Since the conditional is not allowed after **si** meaning *if*, the *imperfect* of **pouvoir** must be used to express *could* in conditional (hypothetical) sentences.

> *I would be glad **if** you **could** be there.*   Je serais content(e) **si** tu **pouvais** être là.

2. *Could* is translated (depending on the context) with the *imperfect* or **passé composé** of **pouvoir** if it refers to the *past,* i.e., when it means *was/were able to.*

I tried to sleep but I **could***n't* (= *I failed to*).	J'ai essayé de dormir, mais je n'**ai** pas **pu**.
I **could***n't understand what he was saying.*	Je ne **pouvais** pas comprendre ce qu'il disait.

Comment dit-on en français?

1. Could I ask you (*pol.*) a question? _____

2. That could happen (**arriver**). _____

3. They (*fem.*) would come if they could. _____

4. We would be happy if you (*pol.*) could work tomorrow. _____

_____

5. I asked him whether he could (= would be able to) do it. _____

_____

6. Unfortunately, I couldn't reach you (*fam.*) (**joindre**) yesterday. _____

_____

7. Be (*pol.*) careful, the animal could become dangerous. _____

_____

The subjunctive

The *subjunctive* is one of the four personal moods which exist in French. The other three, presented earlier in this manual, are the *imperative*, the *conditional*, and the *indicative*. You are already familiar with the tenses of the indicative: the present, the passé composé, the imperfect, the pluperfect, the passé simple, the future, and the future perfect. The subjunctive has four tenses: the present subjunctive, the past subjunctive, the imperfect subjunctive, and the pluperfect subjunctive. The first two of these tenses will be discussed in this chapter since they are the only ones commonly used in today's French. There is no future tense in the subjunctive. The present subjunctive is used instead.

Contrary to English, where few subjunctive forms remain (*I wish he **were** here, they demand that she **come**, it is important that you **be** on time*, etc.), the subjunctive is widely used in French, even in everyday language. Since most French subjunctive forms have no equivalent in English, they are generally translated like the indicative.

Compare:

FRENCH	ENGLISH
Il **part**. (*indicative*)	*He **leaves** (is leaving).*
Il est possible qu'il **parte**. (*subjunctive*)	*It is possible that he **leaves** (is leaving).*
Il **est parti**. (*indicative*)	*He **left**.*
Il est possible qu'il **soit parti**. (*subjunctive*)	*It is possible that he **left**.*

The *indicative* is used by the speaker to express what he or she considers to be a fact, i.e., an action or state which occurred in the past, occurs in the present, or will occur in the future. Consider the following examples:

*She **was** ill.*	Elle **était** malade.
*They **came**.*	Ils **sont** venus.
*The weather **is** beautiful.*	Il **fait** beau.
*I **will go** to Mexico.*	J'**irai** au Mexique.

The *subjunctive* is used when the speaker expresses his, her, or someone else's personal opinion, feeling, or doubt about such an action or state. Compare the following sentences with the examples above:

*It's a shame that she **was** ill.*	*C'est **dommage** qu'elle **ait été** malade.*
*We doubt that they **came**.*	Nous *doutons* qu'ils **soient venus**.

Marie is happy that the weather is beautiful.	Marie *est heureuse* qu'il **fasse** beau.
*It is possible that I **will go** to Mexico.*	Il *est possible* que j'**aille** au Mexique.

As these sentences show, the subjunctive generally follows the conjunction **que** (*that*). But do not assume that every use of **que** is followed by the subjunctive.

It is the verbal expression preceding **que**, that is, the verb in the main clause (always at the beginning of the sentence), which determines if the indicative or the subjunctive must be used in the subordinate clause (the second part of the sentence). *Compare:*

***Je sais* que** tu **viens**. (*indicative*)	*I know (that) you are coming.*
***Je suis content* que** tu **viennes**. (*subjunctive*)	*I am glad (that) you are coming.*

In the first sentence, the main clause (**Je sais**) does *not* express an opinion, doubt, or emotion and is therefore followed by the *indicative* in the subordinate clause (**que tu viens**). In the second sentence, the main clause (**Je suis content**) expresses a feeling (happiness), and is therefore followed by the *subjunctive* in the subordinate clause (**que tu viennes**).

Detailed lists of verbs and expressions which require the use of the subjunctive in the subordinate clause after **que** will be given after the presentation of its forms.

The present subjunctive of regular verbs

The present subjunctive of regular verbs is formed by dropping the **-ent** ending from the third-person plural of the present indicative and adding the endings **-e**, **-es**, **-e**, **-ions**, **-iez**, **-ent**. Since most subjunctives follow the conjunction **que**, it is customary to use **que** when conjugating a verb in the subjunctive.

DONNER *TO GIVE*	**CHOISIR** *TO CHOOSE*	**ATTENDRE** *TO WAIT*
3rd-pers. plural present indic. (ils/elles donn**ent**)	3rd-pers. plural present indic. (ils/elles choiss**ent**)	3rd-pers. plural present indic. (ils/elles attend**ent**)
Subjunctive forms	Subjunctive forms	Subjunctive forms
que je donn**e**	que je choisiss**e**	que j'attend**e**
que tu donn**es**	que tu choisiss**es**	que tu attend**es**
qu'il/elle/on donn**e**	qu'il/elle/on choisiss**e**	qu'il/elle/on attend**e**
que nous donn**ions**	que nous choisiss**ions**	que nous attend**ions**
que vous donn**iez**	que vous choisiss**iez**	que vous attend**iez**
qu'ils/elles donn**ent**	qu'ils/elles choisiss**ent**	qu'ils/elles attend**ent**

Note:

◆ The first-, second-, and third-person singular and the third-person plural of all regular verbs in the present subjunctive have the same pronunciation.
◆ Some of the present subjunctive forms of regular verbs (the **je, tu, il/elle/on**, and **ils/elles** forms of **-er** verbs, as well as the **ils/elles** form of **-ir** and **-re** verbs) are identical to their present indicative forms. Some (the **nous** and **vous** forms) are identical to the imperfect of the indicative.
◆ Verbs whose infinitives end in **-ier** are spelled with a double **i** in the **nous** and **vous** forms in the present subjunctive.

  que nous oubl**ii**ons
  que vous étud**ii**ez

- Regular verbs that have a spelling change in the present indicative will show the same spelling change in the present subjunctive.
- Verbs ending in **-oyer**, **-uyer**, and **-ayer** change the **-y-** to an **-i-** in all persons having a silent ending, i.e., in all persons *except* **nous** and **vous**.

nettoyer *to clean*	
que je nettoie	que nous nettoyions
que tu nettoies	que vous nettoyiez
qu'il/elle/on nettoie	qu'ils/elles nettoient

Remember that with **-ayer** ending verbs this change is optional. These verbs may also retain the **-y-** throughout the conjugation: **que je paye** (or: **que je paie**). When you write, choose one or the other for a given text.

- Verbs having **-é-** in the next to last syllable change the **-é-** into an **-è-** in all persons having a silent ending.

espérer *to hope*	
que j'espère	que nous espérions
que tu espères	que vous espériez
qu'il/elle/on espère	qu'ils/elles espèrent

- Verbs having **-e-** in the next to last syllable.

    - Some of these verbs change the **-e-** into an **-è-** in all persons that have a silent ending.

acheter *to buy*	
que j'achète	que nous achetions
que tu achètes	que vous achetiez
qu'il/elle/on achète	qu'ils/elles achètent

    - Some verb forms double their final consonant in all persons that have a silent ending.

appeler *to call*	
que j'appelle	que nous appelions
que tu appelles	que vous appeliez
qu'il/elle/on appelle	qu'ils/elles appellent

But: Verbs ending in **-ger** (**nager**, etc.) do *not* add **e** to the stem of the **nous** form (**que nous nagions**), and verbs ending in **-cer** (**commencer**, etc.) do *not* add a **cédille** to the **c** in the **nous** form (**que nous commencions**). The **e** and the **cédille** are not necessary in these subjunctive forms because the ending begins with **-i.**

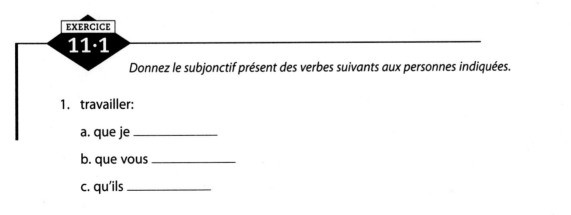

EXERCICE
11·1

Donnez le subjonctif présent des verbes suivants aux personnes indiquées.

1. travailler:

    a. que je _____

    b. que vous _____

    c. qu'ils _____

2. répondre:

a. que je _____

b. que tu _____

c. que nous _____

d. qu'elles _____

3. se lever:

a. que je _____

b. que nous _____

c. qu'ils _____

4. employer:

a. que tu _____

b. que vous _____

c. qu'ils _____

5. partager:

a. qu'elle _____

b. que nous _____

c. qu'elles _____

6. remercier:

a. que je _____

b. que tu _____

c. que nous _____

d. que vous _____

7. réussir:

a. que je _____

b. qu'elle _____

c. que nous _____

8. se rappeler:

a. que je _____

b. qu'il _____

c. que vous _____

d. qu'ils _____

9. répéter:

a. que je _____

b. qu'il _____

c. que nous _____

10. essayer:

a. que je _____

b. que nous _____

c. qu'elles _____

11. prononcer:

a. que tu _____

b. qu'elle _____

c. que nous _____

The present subjunctive of irregular verbs

While the present subjunctive *endings* of all irregular verbs (except **avoir** and **être**) are the same as those of regular verbs, their *stems* are not always derived from the third-person plural present indicative. Some irregular verbs have a subjunctive stem completely different from their indicative stem, and quite a few even have two different stems. In order not to miss a stem change, you should memorize the first-person singular (**je**) and the first-person plural (**nous**) forms of the present subjunctive of each irregular verb given below. If there is a stem change in the **nous** form, the **vous** form will have the same stem, while all other persons will have the stem of the **je** form.

Irregular verbs with a regular present subjunctive

The following irregular verbs have a *regular present subjunctive*, i.e., a stem which is derived from the third-person plural present indicative (**ils**) and which is the same for all persons. If you memorize the **je** and **nous** forms of these verbs, you will know how to conjugate them in the present subjunctive.

s'asseoir *to sit down*

que je m'asseye (or: que je m'assoie)
que nous nous asseyions (or: que nous nous assoyions)

battre *to beat*

que je batte
que nous battions

conduire *to drive*

que je conduise
que nous conduisions

Conjugated like **conduire** are: **traduire** (*to translate*), **construire** (*to build*), and **détruire** (*to destroy*)

connaître *to know*

> que je connaisse
> que nous connaissions

Conjugated like **connaître** are: **reconnaître** (*to recognize*) and **paraître** (*to seem*)

courir *to run*

> que je coure
> que nous courions

craindre *to fear*

> que je craigne
> que nous craignions

Conjugated like **craindre** are: **se plaindre** (*to complain*) and **peindre** (*to paint*)

dire *to say*

> que je dise
> que nous disions

écrire *to write*

> que j'écrive
> que nous écrivions

Conjugated like **écrire** are: **décrire** (*to describe*) and **s'inscrire** (*to register*)

lire *to read*

> que je lise
> que nous lisions

mettre *to put, put on*

> que je mette
> que nous mettions

Conjugated like **mettre** are: **promettre** (*to promise*) and **permettre** (*to allow*)

naître *to be born*

> que je naisse
> que nous naissions

ouvrir *to open*

> que j'ouvre
> que nous ouvrions

Conjugated like **ouvrir** are: **couvrir** (*to cover*), **découvrir** (*to discover*), **offrir** (*to offer*), and **souffrir** (*to suffer*)

partir *to leave*

> que je parte
> que nous partions

Conjugated like **partir** are: **dormir** (*to sleep*), **mentir** (*to lie*), **sentir** (*to feel*), **servir** (*to serve*), and **sortir** (*to go out*)

plaire *to please*

que je plaise
que nous plaisions

rire *to laugh*

que je rie
que nous riions

Conjugated like **rire** is: **sourire** (*to smile*)

suivre *to follow*

que je suive
que nous suivions

se taire *to be silent*

que je me taise
que nous nous taisions

vivre *to live*

que je vive
que nous vivions

Here is the complete conjugation of the verb **vivre** in the present subjunctive:

que je vive	que nous vivions
que tu vives	que vous viviez
qu'il/elle/on vive	qu'ils/elles vivent

Irregular verbs with two different (regular) stems

If an irregular verb shows a stem change in the **nous** and **vous** forms of the present indicative, it will also do so in the present subjunctive (*except* the verbs **savoir** and **pouvoir**, which have an irregular subjunctive stem that does not change).

The following irregular verbs have two *different stems* in the present subjunctive. One of these stems is derived from the third-person plural present indicative and used for the **je, tu, il/elle/on,** and **ils/elles** forms; the other is derived from the first-person plural present indicative and used for the **nous** and **vous** forms. If you memorize the **je** and **nous** forms of these verbs, you will know how to conjugate them in the present subjunctive.

boire *to drink*

que je **boive**
que nous **buv**ions

croire *to believe*

que je **croie**
que nous **croy**ions

devoir *to have to*

> que je **doive**
> que nous **dev**ions

envoyer *to send*

> que j'**envoie**
> que nous **envoy**ions

mourir *to die*

> que je **meure**
> que nous **mour**ions

prendre *to take*

> que je **prenne**
> que nous **pren**ions

Conjugated like **prendre** are: **apprendre** (*to learn*) and **comprendre** (*to understand*)

> **recevoir** *to receive*

> que je **reçoive**
> que nous **recev**ions

Conjugated like **recevoir** are: **apercevoir** (*to see*), **s'apercevoir** (*to notice*), and **décevoir** (*to disappoint*)

> **tenir** *to hold*

> que je **tienne**
> que nous **ten**ions

Conjugated like **tenir** are: **appartenir** (*to belong*) and **obtenir** (*to obtain, get*)

> **venir** *to come*

> que je **vienne**
> que nous **ven**ions

Conjugated like **venir** are: **devenir** (*to become*) and **revenir** (*to come back*)

> **voir** *to see*

> que je **voie**
> que nous **voy**ions

Here is the complete conjugation of the verb **boire** in the present subjunctive:

que je boive	que nous **buv**ions
que tu boives	que vous **buv**iez
qu'il/elle/on boive	qu'ils/elles boivent

Irregular verbs with an irregular stem (not derived from the indicative)

The following irregular verbs have an *irregular stem* which is the same for all persons.

faire *to do*

que je **fasse**
que nous **fass**ions

savoir *to know*

que je **sach**e
que nous **sach**ions

pouvoir *to be able to*

que je **puiss**e
que nous **puiss**ions

Here is the complete conjugation of the verb **faire** in the present subjunctive:

que je **fasse**	que nous **fassions**
que tu **fasses**	que vous **fassiez**
qu'il/elle/on **fasse**	qu'ils/elles **fassent**

The following irregular verbs have an *irregular stem* which changes in the **nous** and **vous** forms.

aller *to go*

que j'**aille**
que nous **all**ions

valoir *to be worth*

que je **vaille**
que nous **val**ions

vouloir *to want*

que je **veuille**
que nous **voul**ions

Here is the complete conjugation of the verb **aller** in the present subjunctive:

que j'**aille**	que nous **allions**
que tu **ailles**	que vous **alliez**
qu'il/elle/on **aille**	qu'ils/elles **aillent**

The following irregular verbs have an *irregular stem*. These two verbs are only conjugated in the impersonal **il** form.

pleuvoir *to rain*

qu'il **pleuve**

falloir *to be necessary*

qu'il **faille**

Avoir and être have irregular stems and irregular endings. Therefore, all forms of these two verbs must be memorized.

avoir to have	
que j'**aie**	que nous **ayons**
que tu **aies**	que vous **ayez**
qu'il/elle/on **ait**	qu'ils/elles **aient**

étre to be	
que je **sois**	que nous **soyons**
que tu **sois**	que vous **soyez**
qu'il/elle/on **soit**	qu'ils/elles **soient**

Note: The *present subjunctive* is used when the action of the subordinate clause occurs at the same time or later than the action in the main clause. Since the present subjunctive can express *present* and *future* actions and situations, it is translated into English with the present or future respectively.

Je suis triste qu'il **parte**.   *I am sad that he's leaving / will leave.*

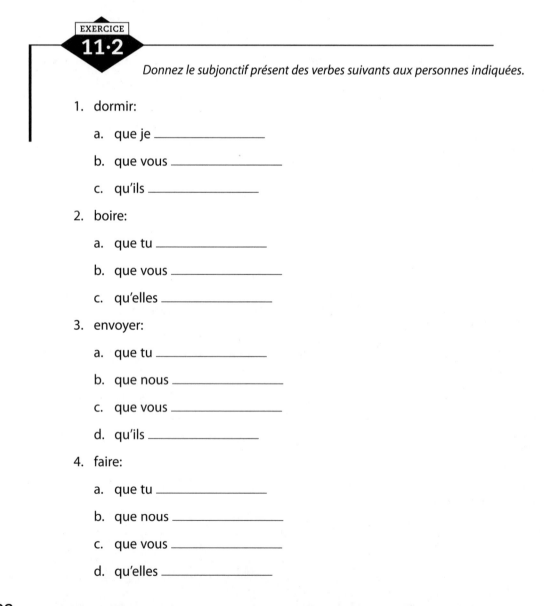

EXERCICE

11·2

Donnez le subjonctif présent des verbes suivants aux personnes indiquées.

1. dormir:

    a. que je _____

    b. que vous _____

    c. qu'ils _____

2. boire:

    a. que tu _____

    b. que vous _____

    c. qu'elles _____

3. envoyer:

    a. que tu _____

    b. que nous _____

    c. que vous _____

    d. qu'ils _____

4. faire:

    a. que tu _____

    b. que nous _____

    c. que vous _____

    d. qu'elles _____

5. aller:

   a. que je _____

   b. que vous _____

   c. qu'elles _____

6. savoir:

   a. que tu _____

   b. que nous _____

7. prendre:

   a. qu'il _____

   b. que vous _____

8. voir:

   a. que tu _____

   b. que vous _____

   c. qu'ils _____

9. pouvoir:

   a. que tu _____

   b. qu'elle _____

   c. que nous _____

10. venir:

    a. qu'il _____

    b. que nous _____

    c. que vous _____

    d. qu'elles _____

11. ouvrir:

    a. que je _____

    b. que tu _____

    c. que vous _____

    d. qu'ils _____

12. devoir:

    a. que tu _____

    b. que vous _____

    c. qu'elles _____

13. connaître:

    a. qu'il _____

    b. que vous _____

14. écrire:

    a. que tu _____

    b. que nous _____

15. dire:

    a. qu'elle _____

    b. que vous _____

16. vouloir:

    a. que tu _____

    b. que vous _____

    c. qu'ils _____

17. mettre:

    a. qu'elle _____

    b. que nous _____

    c. qu'ils _____

18. pleuvoir:

    a. qu'il _____

19. valoir:

    a. qu'il _____

20. recevoir:

    a. que tu _____

    b. que vous _____

21. avoir:

    a. que tu _____

    b. qu'elle _____

    c. que vous _____

22. être:

    a. que je _____

    b. qu'elle _____

    c. que nous _____

23. falloir:

    a. qu'il _____

The past subjunctive

The past subjunctive is formed by using the present subjunctive of the auxiliary (**avoir** or **être**) and the past participle of the verb in question.

FAIRE *TO DO*	**ALLER** *TO GO*	**S'ASSEOIR** *TO SIT DOWN*
que j'aie fait	que je sois allé(e)	que je me sois assis(e)
que tu aies fait	que tu sois allé(e)	que tu te sois assis(e)
qu'il/on ait fait	qu'il/on soit allé	qu'il/on se soit assis
qu'elle ait fait	qu'elle soit allée	qu'elle se soit assise
que nous ayons fait	que nous soyons allé(e)s	que nous nous soyons assis(es)
que vous ayez fait	que vous soyez allé(e)(s)	que vous vous soyez assis(e)(s)
qu'ils aient fait	qu'ils soient allés	qu'ils se soient assis
qu'elles aient fait	qu'elles soient allées	qu'elles se soient assises

The *past subjunctive* is used when the action of the subordinate clause occurs prior to the action in the main clause. The past subjunctive is generally translated into English with the past or pluperfect tense.

Je *regrette* que cela **soit arrivé**.   *I am sorry that this **happened**.*
Elle *était déçue* que son fils ne lui **ait**   *She was disappointed that her son **hadn't**
  pas **téléphoné**.   called her.*

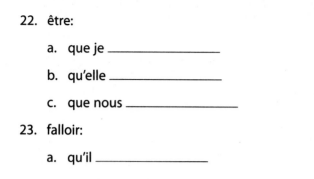

EXERCICE
11·3

Donnez le passé du subjonctif des verbes suivants aux personnes indiquées.

1. voir:

    a. que je _____

    b. que nous _____

    c. qu'ils _____

2. sortir:

    a. que tu _____

    b. qu'il _____

c. que vous _____

d. qu'ils _____

3. réussir:

    a. que je _____

    b. que tu _____

    c. qu'elle _____

    d. que nous _____

    e. qu'ils _____

4. se souvenir:

    a. que je _____

    b. qu'elle _____

    c. que nous _____

5. vendre:

    a. que tu _____

    b. qu'il _____

    c. que vous _____

    d. qu'ils _____

6. trouver:

    a. que je _____

    b. que tu _____

    c. qu'elle _____

    d. que vous _____

    e. qu'elles _____

EXERCICE
11·4

Traduisez en français les mots entre parenthèses. Utilisez le présent du subjonctif si le verbe entre parenthèses est au présent ou au futur, et le passé du subjonctif si ce verbe est au passé.

1. Je suis content que tu (*understand*) _____ mes explications.

2. Je suis content que tu (*understood*) _____ mes explications.

3. Nous sommes ravis qu'il (*can*) _____ venir.

4. Nous sommes ravis qu'il (*could*) _____ venir.

5. C'est dommage que vous (forget) _____ toujours de fermer la porte.

6. C'est dommage que vous (forgot) _____ de fermer la porte ce matin.

7. Nous regrettons qu'il (will have to) _____ partir.

8. Nous regrettons qu'il (had to) _____ partir.

9. Je suis désolé que mon oncle (is) _____ malade.

10. Je suis désolé que mon oncle (was) _____ malade.

11. Elle est déçue que tu (don't have) _____ le temps d'aller au cinéma.

12. Elle est déçue que tu (didn't have) _____ le temps d'aller au cinéma.

EXERCICE
11·5

Complétez les phrases suivantes en mettant les verbes entre parenthèses au subjonctif présent ou au subjonctif passé, selon le sens.

1. Je suis ravi qu'il (trouver) _____ un emploi le mois dernier.

2. Il est possible que cela (arriver) _____ quand elle était à Paris.

3. Nous sommes heureux que tu (pouvoir) _____ venir à notre fête demain.

4. Nous sommes heureux que tu (pouvoir) _____ venir à notre fête hier.

5. Est-ce que ta mère est triste que tu (partir) _____ demain?

6. Est-ce que ta mère est triste que tu (partir) _____ la semaine dernière?

The uses of the subjunctive

Typically, the subjunctive is used in a subordinate clause after **que** (*that*), when the preceding main clause contains a verb or expression (which itself is always in the indicative) that implies a desire, a need, an emotion (regret, joy, fear, sadness, happiness, etc.), doubt, uncertainty, or personal judgment, provided that the subjects of both clauses are *not* the same.

Consider the following example:

> *Je suis désolé* **que** nous **soyons** en retard.   *I am sorry (that) we are late.*

The main clause of this sentence is **Je suis désolé**. Since it expresses a feeling (regret), it triggers the subjunctive in the subordinate clause that follows (**que nous *soyons* en retard**).

Note that in French, main and subordinate clauses of this type are connected by the conjunction **que**. While its equivalent *that* may or may not be used in English, in French, **que** always links the two clauses.

Note also that in the example sentence above the subject of the main clause (**je**) is different from the subject in the subordinate clause (**nous**). If both sentence parts have the same subject in English (*I am sorry that I am late*), French uses an infinitive construction instead of **que** + *sub-*

junctive. One *cannot* say **Je suis désolé que *je* sois en retard**, one *must* say **Je suis désolé d'*être* en retard** *(I am sorry to be late).*

Following is a brief overview of the major uses of the subjunctive in French. The subjunctive is used in subordinate clauses following **que**:

A. after verbs expressing a *desire* or *preference*

> I **prefer** that you stay here.   Je **préfère** que vous **restiez** ici.

B. after verbs and expressions indicating an *emotion*

> We **are happy** that you feel better.   Nous **sommes contents** que vous vous **sentiez** mieux.

C. after *impersonal expressions* (beginning with **il** = *it*) indicating a *necessity,* a *possibility,* or *desirability*

> It **is possible** that it will rain tomorrow.   **Il est possible** qu'il **pleuve** demain.

D. after verbs and expressions indicating *uncertainty* and *doubt*

> They **doubt** that he is honest.   Ils **doutent** qu'il **soit** honnête.

E. after certain *conjunctions.* Here it is the conjunction itself, and *not* the verb in the main clause, that determines the mood in the subordinate clause.

> I will stay **until** he comes back.   Je resterai **jusqu'à ce qu**'il **revienne**.

F. after *negative* and *interrogative verbs of thinking*

> I **don't think** that this dress fits you well.   Je **ne pense pas** que cette robe t'**aille** bien.

Let us now examine these uses more in detail.

Verbs expressing a *wish* (except for *hope*), a *preference,* a *request,* a *need,* an *expectation,* a *permission,* or *prohibition* require the use of the subjunctive in the subordinate clause. These include:

> **aimer que** *to like*
> **aimer mieux que** *to prefer*
>
> J'aimerais mieux que...   *I would rather . . .*
>
> **attendre que** *to wait (until)*
> **s'attendre à ce que** *to expect*
> **avoir besoin que** *to need*
> **avoir envie que** *to (really) want*
> **conseiller que** *to advise*
> **défendre que** *to forbid that*
> **demander que** *to ask, request*
> **désirer que** *to wish, want*
> **exiger que** *to demand, require*
> **insister pour que** *to insist*
> **interdire que** *to forbid*
> **permettre que** *to allow, permit*
> **préférer que** *to prefer*
> **proposer que** *to suggest*

recommander que *to recommend*
souhaiter que *to wish*
suggérer que *to suggest*
tenir à ce que *to (really) want, be anxious to*
vouloir que *to want*

Je voudrais que...	*I would like . . .*
***Attends** que je **revienne**.*	*Wait 'til I come back.*
*J'**aimerais mieux** que tu n'y **ailles** pas.*	*I would rather you didn't go there.*
*Je **demande** que vous m'**aidiez**.*	*I ask that you help me.*
*Le professeur **exige** que nous **sachions** le subjonctif.*	*The teacher demands that we know the subjunctive.*
*Elle **insiste pour** que je **sois** là.*	*She insists that I be there.*
*Je **préfère** que tu le **fasses**.*	*I prefer that you do it.*

Note: The verb **espérer** (*to hope*) requires the *indicative*. The future tense is used after **espérer** when a future action or situation is referred to.

*J'**espère** que vous **allez** bien.*	*I hope (that) you are fine.*
*J'**espère** que tu te **sentiras** mieux.*	*I hope (that) you (will) feel better.*

EXERCICE
11·6

Traduisez en français les phrases suivantes.

1. I prefer that you (*fam.*) wait. _____

2. I would rather you (*fam.*) left now. _____

3. They insist that I go to church with them. _____

4. We suggest that you (*pol.*) take an early retirement (**une retraite anticipée**). _____

5. She requested that I make the decision. _____

6. We will wait till there is less traffic on the freeway. _____

7. He wishes that you (*fam.*) receive the letter tomorrow. _____

8. He hopes that you (*fam.*) receive the letter tomorrow. _____

EXERCICE
11·7

Complétez personnellement les phrases suivantes. Do not use the same subject as in the main clause.

1. J'espère que _____.

2. Veux-tu que _____?

3. Nous souhaitons que _____.

4. Je ne veux pas que _____.

5. Mes parents exigent que _____.

6. Je n'ai pas envie que _____.

7. Attends-toi à ce que _____.

With the verbs listed above, the subjunctive can only be used when the subject of the main clause is different from the subject of the subordinate clause.

> *I wish (that) **you** were in Paris.*   **Je** voudrais que **tu** sois à Paris.

When the subject of the subordinate clause would be the same as the subject of the main clause, an *infinitive* construction replaces **que** + *subjunctive*.

> *I wish (that) **I** were in Paris.*   Je **voudrais être** à Paris.
> (*And not*: **Je** voudrais que **je** sois
> à Paris.)
> ***You** wish **you** were successful in life.*   Tu **voudrais réussir** dans la vie.
> (*And not*: **Tu** voudrais que **tu**
> réussisses dans la vie.)

Sometimes, English also uses a type of infinitive construction in this case.

> *We would rather **leave**. (= We would*   Nous **aimerions mieux partir**.
> *rather **we** left.*)

EXERCICE

11·8

Subjonctif ou infinitif? Comment dit-on en français?

1. I wish I were in France. _____

2. I wish you (*fam.*) were here. _____

3. They (*masc.*) wish they had a child. _____

4. They (*masc.*) wish you (*fam.*) had a child. _____

5. We wish we knew what happened (**ce qui s'est passé**). _____

6. We wish you (*fam.*) knew what happened. _____

7. She wishes you (*fam.*) could come. _____

8. She wishes she could come. _____

9. I would like to drink some apple juice. _____

10. You (*pol.*) need to pay the bills. _____

As we have seen, French generally uses an *infinitive* construction only when the main and subordinate clauses would have the same subject. With a limited number of the verbs listed above, however, an infinitive construction can be used, even if two different subjects are present in the sentence. These verbs (**conseiller, défendre, demander, interdire, permettre, proposer, recommander, suggérer**) allow two constructions. They can either be followed by **que** + *subjunctive* or (more common in the spoken language) by **de** + *infinitive*. Note that in the infinitive construction, the object is *indirect* (**à** + noun or *indirect object pronoun* (**lui, leur**, etc.).

Il *a interdit* qu'elle **sorte**.	*He forbade her to go out.*
or: Il *lui a interdit* **de sortir**.	
Il *n'a pas permis* que son fils **ait** une voiture.	*He didn't allow his son to have a car.*
or: Il *n'a pas permis à* son fils **d'avoir** une voiture.	

EXERCICE 11·9

Traduisez en français les phrases suivantes en utilisant (a) le subjonctif et (b) l'infinitif.

1. I suggest that you (*fam.*) come with me.

   a. _____

   b. _____

2. We recommend that you (*pol.*) visit this theme park (**ce parc d'attractions**).

   a. _____

   b. _____

3. The doctor allowed him to go out.

   a. _____

   b. _____

4. I asked my sister to drive me to the airport.

   a. _____

   b. _____

5. Did you (*fam.*) forbid them to do it?

   a. _____

   b. _____

But beware of the verbs **vouloir, s'attendre à, avoir besoin,** and **tenir à**. While their English equivalents (*to want, to expect, to need, to be anxious to*) very commonly use infinitive constructions with two different subjects (*I don't want **you** to leave*), French requires these verbs to be followed by **que** + *subjunctive* when two different subjects are present (*Je ne veux pas que vous partiez*).

Compare:

ENGLISH (*INFINITIVE* CONSTRUCTION)	FRENCH (**QUE** + *SUBJUNCTIVE*)
*I want **you** to listen.* (Two different subjects: *I want that **you** listen.*)	**Je** veux que **vous** écoutiez.
*We need **him** to intervene.* (Two different subjects: *We need that **he** intervene.*]	**Nous** avons besoin qu'**il** intervienne.
*He expects **me** to be there.* (Two different subjects: *He expects that **I'll** be there.*]	**Il** s'attend à ce que **je** sois là.
*She wants (is anxious for) **her daughter** to have a normal childhood.* (Two different subjects: *She wants that **her daughter** has . . .*)	**Elle** tient à ce que **sa fille** ait une enfance normale.

When, however, the subject of the subordinate clause would be the same as the subject of the main clause, both French and English use infinitive constructions with these verbs.

*I want **to leave**. (And not: **I** want that **I** leave.)* **Je** veux **partir**. (*And not:* **Je** veux que **je** parte.)

EXERCICE
11·10

Comment dit-on en français?

1. What do you (*pol.*) want me to say? _____

2. What do you (*fam.*) want me to do? _____

3. I want you (*fam.*) to go to the bakery. _____

4. They (*masc.*) want her to drive. _____

5. My mother wants us to go to Japan this year. _____

6. My father would like me to become a computer specialist (**informaticien[ne]**). _____

_____

7. He needs you (*pol.*) to be his friend. _____

8. I would like you (*pol.*) to keep your promise. _____

9. My parents expect me to get my degree (**mon diplôme**) next month. _____

10. I don't expect this (**cela**) to be easy. _____

11. They (*masc.*) don't want us to watch soap operas. _____

12. She is anxious for you (*fam.*) to meet (**faire la connaissance de**) her parents. _____

_____

Traduisez en français le texte suivant.

My dear son,

How are you? I hope that you are fine. Your dad and I would like you to write to us more often. We worry about you and we miss you. Would you prefer that we call you once a week? We want you to know that we think of you often and that we are proud of you. What are you going to do during spring break? We suggest that you go to Switzerland to visit your uncle Paul who lives in Geneva. He wants you to come (wishes that you come) as soon as possible because you haven't seen each other for a long time. He insists that you stay with him at least two weeks. Dad will pay for the flight, but he asks that you pass your exams first. We know that you work hard because your father expects you to be a surgeon some day. Look after yourself!

Love, Mom

VOCABULAIRE	as soon as possible	**le plus tôt possible**	once a week	**une fois par semaine**
	at least	**au moins**	spring break	**les vacances (f.pl.)**
	flight	**le vol**		**de printemps**
	hard	**dur**	surgeon	**le chirurgien,**
	look after yourself	**fais attention à toi**		**la chirurgienne**
	love	**je t'embrasse**	uncle	**l'oncle (m.)**

_____

_____

_____

_____

_____

_____

Verbs or expressions indicating *feelings* or *emotions* (joy, happiness, surprise, fear, regret, sadness, anger, satisfaction, etc.) require the use of the subjunctive in the subordinate clause. These include:

être content(e) que *to be glad, pleased that*
être déçu(e) que *to be disappointed that*
être désolé(e) que *to be sorry that*
être fâché(e) que *to be angry that*
être furieux (-ieuse) que *to be furious that*
être (mal)heureux (-euse) que *to be (un)happy that*
être inquiet (inquiète) que *to be worried that*
être ravi(e) que *to be delighted that*
être surpris(e) que *to be surprised that*
être triste que *to be sad that*
il est / c'est dommage que *it is too bad that, it is a shame that*
c'est formidable/chouette que *it is great that*
avoir peur que (ne)* *to be afraid that*
craindre que (ne)* *to fear that*

s'étonner que *to be astonished that*
regretter que *to regret / be sorry that*

*Note: After expressions of *fear* (**avoir peur que, craindre que**) used in the affirmative form, the word **ne** (called *ne explétif* or *ne pléonastique*) may precede the verb in the subjunctive for stylistic reasons. This **ne** (the use of which is optional) is not followed by **pas** and does not make the sentence negative.

Elle **est contente qu**'il **fasse** beau.	*She is glad that the weather is / will be nice.*
Il **est déçu qu**'elle ne **veuille** plus sortir avec lui.	*He is disappointed that she no longer wants to date him.*
Je **suis désolé que** tu **sois tombé** malade.	*I am sorry that you became ill.*
Je **suis heureux que** vous **puissiez** venir.	*I am happy that you can come.*
J'**ai peur que** vous (**ne**) **manquiez** l'avion.	*I am afraid that you will miss the plane.*

Note:

◆ If an infinitive follows the expression of emotion, the indicative is used in the clause that follows **que**. *Compare:*

Je **suis content(e) que** tu **ailles** bien.	*I am glad that you are fine.*
Je **suis content(e) d'apprendre** que tu **vas** bien.	*I am glad to hear that you are fine.*

◆ **Être heureux (heureuse) que** is followed by the subjunctive, but **heureusement que** (*it's a good thing that, fortunately*) takes the indicative.

Heureusement qu'elle **était** là.	*It's a good thing that / Fortunately she was there.*

EXERCICE

11·12

Comment dit-on en français? Employez le subjonctif présent (phrases 1–7) et le subjonctif passé (phrases 8–12).

1. It is a shame that you (*fam.*) don't have his address. _____

2. I am glad that he is safe and sound (**sain et sauf**). _____

3. He is disappointed that she cannot go out. _____

4. I am afraid that you (*fam.*) will catch a cold (**prendre froid**). _____

5. We are sorry that you (*fam.*) have to wait. _____

6. They (*masc.*) fear that this country will lose its identity (**son identité**). _____

7. He is worried that you (*pol.*) will not accept the invitation. _____

8. Are you (*fam.*) angry that our team lost the game? _____

9. We are surprised that this (**cela**) didn't happen earlier. _____

10. He is sad that she didn't say anything. _____

11. I regret that your (*fam.*) rabbits died. _____

12. They (*masc.*) are happy that you (*pol.*) found a job. _____

Terminez personnellement les phrases suivantes. Use the subjunctive and a different subject in the subordinate clause.

1. Je suis content(e) que _____.

2. Mes parents sont inquiets que _____.

3. Je suis déçu(e) que _____.

4. Mes enfants sont heureux que _____.

5. C'est dommage que _____.

6. J'ai peur que _____.

Note: After verbs and expressions of emotion, the subjunctive can only be used if the subject in the main clause is different from the subject in the subordinate clause, as in the following sentence:

Je suis content que **vous** soyez en bonne santé.	(Two different subjects: **je** and **vous**) *I am happy that **you** are healthy.*

If both clauses have the same subject, an *infinitive* construction is used. The preposition **de** precedes the infinitive.

Je **suis content d'être** en bonne santé. (*I am happy to be healthy.*)	*I am happy that **I** am healthy.*

Subjonctif ou infinitif? Traduisez en français les mots entre parenthèses.

1. Je suis content(e) (*that I have a good salary*). _____

2. Je suis content(e) (*that you [pol.] have a good salary*). _____

3. Il regrette (*that he is old*). _____

4. Il regrette (*that his wife is old*). _____

5. Les passagers sont inquiets (*that they are late*). _____

6. Les passagers sont inquiets (*that the plane is late*) (**avoir du retard**). _____

7. Nous avons peur (*that we will miss the train*). _____

8. Nous avons peur (*that you [pol.] will miss the train*). _____

9. Je suis désolé (*that I cannot have dinner with you [pol.] tonight*). _____

10. Je suis désolé (*that you [pol.] cannot have dinner with me tonight*). _____

Traduisez en français la lettre suivante.

My dear daughter,

Thanks for your long letter. I am glad that you arrived safely at your university in France, and that your roommate, Micheline, is nice. I am delighted that you speak French together all the time. It's a shame that I cannot see you until Easter. When you start taking your classes, you will be surprised that there is little personal contact between the French professors and their students. But you will get used to it fast.

I am sorry that you forgot your cell phone, but I will send it to you tomorrow.

Do you want me to put your CD player in the package as well? I am afraid that you will not receive the package next week because of the strike. It's a good thing that you are patient.

Love, Mom

VOCABULAIRE	because of	**à cause de**	love	**bisous**
	between	**entre**	package	**le colis**
	CD player	**le lecteur de CD**	roommate	**le/la camarade**
	cell phone	**le (téléphone)**		**de chambre**
		portable	strike	**la grève**

_____

_____

_____

_____

The subjunctive is also used after *impersonal expressions* indicating *necessity, importance, desirability, possibility,* and *impossibility.* These expressions are called *impersonal* because they do not have a personal subject (such as *I, you, he, we, they,* etc.). Their subject is the impersonal **il** which corresponds to *it* in English.

Here are some common impersonal expressions that require the use of the subjunctive after **que** in the following subordinate clause.

il faut que	*it is necessary that, (so) must, has to*
il ne faut pas que	*(sb) must not*
il vaut mieux que	*it is better that*
il est bon que	*it is good that*
il est essentiel que	*it is essential that*
il est impossible que	*it is impossible that*
il est important que	*it is important that*
il est indispensable que	*it is indispensable that*
il est juste que	*it is right that*
il est nécessaire que	*it is necessary that*
il est normal que	*it is normal that*
il est possible que	*it is possible that*
il est préférable que	*it is preferable that*
il est rare que	*it is unusual, rare that*
il est (grand) temps que	*it is (about) time that*
il est (in)utile que	*it is useful (useless) that*

ce n'est pas la peine que	it's not worth the trouble that, there is no point in (doing)
Il faut qu'on **veuille** le faire.	One must want to do it.
Il ne faut pas que tu **sois** fâché.	You must not be angry.
Il vaut mieux que vous **partiez**.	It is better that you leave.
Il est essentiel que tu **aies** ton diplôme.	It is essential that you have your degree.
Il est nécessaire que tu **prennes** soin de toi.	It is necessary that you take care of yourself.
Il est temps que nous nous en **allions**.	It is time for us to leave.
Ce n'est pas la peine que je le **fasse**.	There is no point in my doing it.

Note:

◆ The expression **il est probable que** (*it is probable that*) is followed by the *indicative*.

Il est probable qu'il sera de retour demain.	It is probable that he will be back tomorrow.

But: **Il est improbable que** (*it is unlikely that*), **il n'est pas probable que** (*it is not likely that*), **il est peu probable que** (*it is not very likely that, it is unlikely that*), **est-il probable que?** (*is it probable that?*) are followed by the *subjunctive*.

Il est improbable qu'il soit de retour demain.	It is improbable/unlikely that he will be back tomorrow.

The same is true for **il est vraisemblable que** (*it is likely that*), the affirmative form of which is also followed by the indicative.

Il est vraisemblable qu'il viendra.	It is likely that he will come.

◆ In spoken French, **c'est** frequently replaces **il est** before an adjective.

C'est normal que les femmes **aient** droit au même salaire que les hommes.	It is normal that women are (be) entitled to the same salary as men.

EXERCICE

11·16

Comment dit-on en français?

1. I absolutely have to go to the dentist. _____

2. You (*fam.*) must not leave. _____

3. It is better that they (*masc.*) know the truth. _____

4. It is important that we pay attention. _____

5. Was it necessary that you (*pol.*) wake me up in the middle of the night? _____

   _____

6. It is essential that you (*pol.*) be polite. _____

7. It is possible that it will rain. _____

8. It is probable that I am late. _____

9. It is preferable that you (*fam.*) learn French. _____

10. It is useful that you (*pol.*) study a foreign language. _____

11. It is unusual that it is so cold in April. _____

12. It is normal that they (*fem.*) are on strike (**faire grève**). _____

EXERCICE
11·17

Terminez les phrases suivantes en utilisant le subjonctif ou l'indicatif, selon le cas.

1. Il faut que _____

2. Il ne faut pas que _____

3. Il vaudrait mieux que _____

4. Est-il nécessaire que _____

5. Il est impossible que _____

6. Il est probable que _____

EXERCICE
11·18

Dites à votre ami(e) ce qu'il faut qu'il/elle fasse pour être heureux (heureuse) dans la vie.

Il faut que tu...

_____

_____

EXERCICE
11·19

Complétez les phrases avec les verbes logiques qui manquent.

1. J'ai soif. Il faut que je _____ quelque chose.

2. Il a mal à la tête. Il faut qu'il _____ de l'aspirine.

3. Tous les verres et toutes les tasses sont sales. Il faut que tu _____ la vaisselle.

4. Mon travail commence à huit heures. Il faut que je _____ de chez moi à sept heures.

5. Elle a besoin de timbres. Il faut qu'elle _____ à la poste.

6. Le professeur nous a donné beaucoup de devoirs. Il faut que nous _____ deux dissertations.

7. Quand les enfants sont impatients, les parents disent: —Il faut que vous _____ de la patience.

8. On ne vous attendra pas. Il faut que vous _____ à l'heure.

9. Les invités vont arriver dans quelques minutes. Il faut encore que je _____ la table.

Note: **Que** + *subjunctive* is used after the impersonal expressions listed above when a specific person is addressed. An *infinitive* construction is used when a general statement is made. The preposition **de** precedes the infinitive except after **il faut** and **il vaut mieux**. *Compare:*

SUBJUNCTIVE (SPECIFIC SUBJECT)	INFINITIVE CONSTRUCTION (GENERAL SENSE)
Il faut que *tu* aies de la patience.	**Il faut avoir** de la patience.
You must have patience.	*One must have patience.*
Il vaut mieux qu'*il* parte.	**Il vaut mieux partir.**
*It is better that **he** leaves.*	*It is better to leave.*
Il est important que *chacun* garde son sang-froid.	**Il est important de garder** son sang-froid.
*It is important that **everyone** keep calm.*	*It is important to keep calm.*
Ce n'est pas la peine que *tu* ailles voir ce film.	**Ce n'est pas la peine d'aller** voir ce film.
*There is no point in **your** going to see this movie.*	*There is no point in going to see this movie.*

Subjonctif ou infinitif? Faites des phrases avec les éléments donnés.

1. il vaut mieux / y / aller _____

2. il vaut mieux / tu / y / aller _____

3. il est essentiel / le / faire _____

4. il est essentiel / vous / le / faire _____

5. il est inutile / se plaindre _____

6. il est inutile / vous / se plaindre _____

Traduisez en français la lettre suivante.

Dear Mom,

I just received your e-mail. I am sorry that I didn't write earlier, but I had to finish reviewing for final exams. You must understand that I am very busy at the moment.

You must not be angry. You always told me that it was important that I get good grades, didn't you? It is probable that I'll do well this year since I attended all my classes. You are asking me what I plan to do this summer. It is unlikely that I will visit you. It is better that I save some money. Otherwise, I will never be able to buy a new computer.

I've got to go now because I have a meeting in five minutes, and it is important that I be on time.

'Til next time, Martin

P.S. I have a big favor to ask you. Would it be possible that you tell Dad to send me some money? I just realized that I am completely broke.

VOCABULAIRE	broke	**fauché(e)**	a meeting	**une réunion**
	busy	**occupé(e)**	otherwise	**sinon**
	computer	**l'ordinateur** *(m.)*	to review	**réviser**
	to get	**obtenir**	to save money	**faire des économies**
	grade	**la note**	until next time	**à la prochaine**

_____

_____

_____

_____

_____

_____

The subjunctive is also used after verbs and expressions implying *uncertainty* or *doubt*. Here are some common expressions from this category.

douter que	*to doubt that*
il est douteux que	*it is doubtful that*
il n'est pas sûr/certain que	*it is not sure/certain that*
il n'est pas vrai que	*it is not true that*
je ne suis pas sûr(e)/certain(e) que	*I am not sure/certain that*
êtes-vous sûr(e)/certain(e) que... ?	*are you sure/certain that . . . ?*
est-il vrai/exact que... ?	*is it true/accurate that . . . ?*
il semble que	*it seems that*
Je **doute que** ses parents **veuillent** me connaître.	*I doubt that his parents want to meet me.*
Il **n'est pas certain qu'**il **ait** raison.	*It is not certain that he is right.*
Le professeur **n'est pas sûr que** nous le **comprenions.**	*The teacher is not sure that we understand him.*

Note: The expression **il semble que** (*it seems that*) is followed by the subjunctive since it implies uncertainty.

Il semble qu'elle **aille** mieux.   *It seems that she is feeling better.*

But if a personal indirect object pronoun is included in this expression (**il me [te, lui, nous, vous, leur] semble que**), it is followed by the *indicative* since it implies certainty on the part of the speaker.

Il me semble qu'elle **va** mieux.   *It seems **to me** that she is feeling better.*

EXERCICE
11·22

Subjonctif ou indicatif? Comment dit-on en français?

1. I doubt that this is true. _____

2. Are you (*fam.*) sure that he has a throat infection (**une angine**)? _____

3. It only seems that she is angry. _____

4. It is not certain that he said that. _____

5. Is it true that she is in love with David? _____

6. It seems that he knows her. _____

7. It seems to me that I already saw you (*pol.*) somewhere. _____

8. It is doubtful that he changed his mind _____

Note: Expressions that do not imply doubt are followed by the *indicative*. Here are some of them:

ne pas douter que	*to not doubt that*
être convaincu(e)/persuadé(e) que	*to be convinced that*
être sûr(e)/certain(e) que	*to be sure/certain that*
il n'y a aucun doute que	*there is no doubt that*
il n'est pas douteux que	*it is not doubtful that*
il est évident que	*it is evident that*
il est exact que	*it is true/correct that*
il est sûr/certain que	*it is sure/certain that*
il est vrai que	*it is true that*
il est clair que	*it is clear that*
il paraît que	*one says that / I heard that / rumor has it that*
savoir que	*to know that*

Subjonctif ou indicatif? Comment dit-on en français?

1. I am not convinced that he told the truth. _____

2. It is certain that everything will become more expensive. _____

3. It is evident that he is lazy. _____

4. We knew that it was far. _____

5. One says that he has a lot of money. _____

6. It is doubtful that she will be able to come. _____

7. Is it true that he has the flu? _____

8. I don't doubt that he will do it. _____

9. It is true that she understands Chinese. _____

10. I know that she is shy (**timide**). _____

Note: When the subject of the subordinate clause is the *same* as the subject of the main clause, an infinitive construction is used after negative or interrogative **être sûr(e)/certain(e)/ convaincu(e)** and after **douter**. The infinitive is preceded by **de**.

Je ne suis pas sûr(e)/certain(e) de vous **comprendre**.	*I am not sure I understand you.*
Elle doute de pouvoir le faire.	*She doubts that she can do it.*

Subjonctif ou infinitif? Traduisez les phrases suivantes en français.

1. She is not sure that she will be able to join us. _____

2. Are you (*fam.*) sure that you want to do that? _____

3. Are you (*fam.*) sure that he wants to do that? _____

4. I doubt that I can go there. _____

5. I doubt that he knows it. _____

6. We are not certain that we will arrive on time. _____

The subjunctive is also used after certain *conjunctions*.

pour que	*so that, in order that*
afin que	*so that, in order that*
avant que (ne)*	*before*

à condition que	on the condition that, provided that
à moins que (ne)*	unless
en attendant que	while waiting for, until
bien que	although, even though
quoique	although, even though
de crainte que (ne)*	for fear that
de peur que (ne)*	for fear that
jusqu'à ce que	until
malgré que	in spite of the fact that
pourvu que	provided that
sans que	without

*Note: The word **ne**, which, as we have seen, may precede the verb in the subjunctive after the expressions **craindre que** and **avoir peur que**, can also be placed before the verb in the subjunctive after the conjunctions **à moins que, avant que, de peur que,** and **de crainte que**. Remember that this **ne** (called *ne explétif*) has no negative value and that it is not translated into English. Since the *ne* **explétif** makes the style more elegant, it appears in written and formal language.

Nous irons à la plage **à moins qu'il (ne) fasse** mauvais.	*We will go to the beach unless the weather is bad.*
Je me dépêche **pour que ça aille** plus vite.	*I hurry so that it goes faster.*
C'est arrivé **avant que je (ne) vienne** au monde.	*That happened before I was born.*
Je vais le faire **bien que je n'en aie pas** envie.	*I am going to do it, although I don't feel like it.*
Les Français sont les gens les plus hospitaliers du monde, **pourvu que l'on ne veuille pas** entrer chez eux. (Pierre Daninos)	*The French are the most hospitable people in the world, provided that one doesn't want to enter their home.*
Elle est partie **sans que ses parents** le **sachent**.	*She left without her parents knowing it.*

Note: Whereas the conjunction **avant que** is followed by the subjunctive, **après que** is followed by the *indicative*. Today, many native speakers use the subjunctive after **après que** by analogy with **avant que**. This is however not yet accepted as formally correct.

Nous lui avons parlé **après qu'il est rentré**.	*We talked to him after he came home.*

EXERCICE

11·25

Subjonctif ou indicatif? Traduisez en français les mots en italique.

1. (Let's act *before it is too late*.) Agissons _____

2. (It started to rain *after we came home*.) Il a commencé à pleuvoir _____

3. (She never goes out *without my knowing it*.) Elle ne sort jamais _____

4. (Speak more clearly *so that we can understand you*.) Parlez plus distinctement, _____

5. (We will come *unless it rains*.) Nous viendrons _____

6. (They will go hiking *even though the weather is bad*.) Ils feront une randonnée_____

7. (Let's stay *until she is better*.) Restons _____

8. (She hides her earrings *for fear that someone will take them.*) Elle cache ses boucles

d'oreilles _____

9. (What happened *after they [masc.] left?*) Qu'est-ce qui s'est passé _____

10. (We will go on a trip *provided that you [fam.] pass your exam.*) Nous ferons un voyage _____

_____

EXERCICE

11·26

Complétez personnellement les phrases suivantes.

1. Il viendra pourvu que _____

2. Elle est allée au travail bien que _____

3. Parlez plus fort pour que _____

4. Je serai là à moins que _____

5. Continuez jusqu'à ce que _____

EXERCICE

11·27

Complétez avec la conjonction convenable d'après le sens. Choose a conjunction from the following list; do not use each conjunction more than once.

de peur que / bien que / pour que / à moins que / pourvu que

1. _____ il soit tard, il fait encore jour.

2. _____ il soit satisfait, il faudrait que tu travailles beaucoup.

3. Le week-end prochain, nous irons à la plage, _____ il ne fasse mauvais.

4. Je prends mon parapluie _____ il ne pleuve.

5. Nous pouvons échanger vos achats _____ vous ayez votre ticket de caisse.

Note: The conjunctions **afin que, avant que, à condition que, à moins que, de crainte que, de peur que, en attendant que, pour que,** and **sans que** are followed by the subjunctive when the subject of the subordinate clause is different from the subject of the main clause. When both clauses would have the same subject, the conjunctions are replaced by their corresponding prepositions and an infinitive construction is used.

CONJUNCTION (+ *SUBJUNCTIVE*)	CORRESPONDING PREPOSITION (+ *INFINITIVE*)	*ENGLISH MEANING OF THE PREPOSITION*
afin que	afin de	*in order to*
avant que (ne)	avant de	*before*
à condition que	à condition de	*on the condition*
à moins que (ne)	à moins de	*unless*
de crainte que (ne)	de crainte de	*for fear of*
de peur que (ne)	de peur de	*for fear of*
en attendant que	en attendant de	*until*
pour que	pour	*in order to*
sans que	sans	*without*

Je fais des économies **pour pouvoir** voyager.	*I save (money) in order to be able to travel.*
Elle ne manque jamais, **à moins d'être** malade.	*She never misses, unless she is ill.*
Venez nous voir **avant de partir**.	*Visit us before leaving.*
Il est parti **sans dire** au revoir.	*He left without saying good-bye.*
En attendant de déjeuner, nous allons boire un apéritif.	*While waiting for (Until we have) lunch, we are going to drink an aperitif.*

But: The conjunctions **bien que, quoique, pourvu que, malgré que,** and **jusqu'à ce que** are *always* followed by the *subjunctive*, even when the main clause has the same subject as the subordinate clause.

*J'*ai mal à la tête **bien que *j'aie pris*** deux cachets d'aspirine.	*I have a headache although **I** took two aspirin tablets.*
Nous irons en France, **pourvu que *nous* ayons** assez d'argent.	*We will go to France provided that **we** have enough money.*
Il regarde souvent la télé **jusqu'à ce *qu'il* s'endorme**.	*He often watches TV until **he** falls asleep.*

EXERCICE

11·28

Subjonctif ou infinitif? Complétez personnellement les phrases suivantes.

1. Je ferai du shopping à moins de _____.

2. Je ferai du shopping à moins que _____.

3. Il a fait ses devoirs avant de _____.

4. Rentrons vite, avant que nos parents ne _____.

5. Elle travaille pour que _____.

6. Elle travaille pour _____.

Subjonctif ou infinitif? Comment dit-on en français?

1. *They (masc.)* had lunch before *they* went to the shopping center (**le centre commercial**).

   _____

2. *They (masc.)* had lunch before *their parents* went to the shopping center. _____

   _____

3. *He* doesn't buy any clothes unless *he* absolutely needs them. _____

   _____

4. *He* doesn't buy any clothes unless *his wife* tells him to (= says it to him). _____

   _____

5. Usually, *they (fem.)* work until *they* are very tired. _____

6. *We* are happy although *we* have little money. _____

7. *I* will do it provided that *I* am not too busy. _____

8. *They (masc.)* left early for fear that *they* might be late. _____

9. *You (fam.)* will have a toy provided that *you* are good (**sage**). _____

   _____

10. *You (pol.)* can stay in the room on the condition that *you* don't make any noise. _____

    _____

Note: Besides **après que** (*after*), the following conjunctions are followed by the *indicative*.

alors que	*whereas*
aussitôt que	*as soon as*
depuis que	*since*
dès que	*as soon as*
parce que	*because*
pendant que	*while*
puisque	*since*
tandis que	*whereas*

Subjonctif ou indicatif? Remplissez les tirets avec la forme correcte du verbe entre parenthèses.

1. Elle est triste depuis qu'elle (perdre- *passé*) _____ son chien.

2. Maman m'a donné de l'argent pour que je (pouvoir) _____ acheter une montre.

3. Bien que je le (connaître) _____ depuis longtemps, je ne sais pas beaucoup de choses sur lui.

4. Je ris parce que je (être) _____ de bonne humeur.

5. Je te le dirai dès que je le (savoir) _____.

6. Tu dépenses de l'argent alors qu'il (falloir) _____ économiser.

7. Je dépense de l'argent à moins qu'il (falloir) _____ économiser.

The subjunctive is also used after the following *verbs of thinking* if they are in the *negative* or *inverted interrogative* form.

penser que *to think that*
trouver que *to think that*
croire que *to believe that*

Je ne pense/trouve pas que ce **soit** une bonne idée.	*I don't think that this is a good idea.*
Crois-tu qu'il **dise** la vérité?	*Do you think that he's telling the truth?*
Je ne crois pas qu'on **puisse** connaître un pays sans savoir sa langue.	*I don't think that one can know a country without knowing its language.*
Trouvez-vous que le français **soit** facile?	*Do you think that French is easy?*

Note:

- The affirmative and negative interrogative forms of **penser, croire,** and **trouver** are followed by the *indicative*.

Il **pense que** nous **trichons.**	*He thinks (that) we are cheating.*
Les Gaulois **croyaient que** le ciel **pouvait** leur tomber sur la tête.	*The Gauls believed the sky could fall on their heads.*
Je **trouve que** cette robe te **va** bien.	*I think (that) this dress looks good on you.*

- After verbs of thinking (**penser, croire, trouver**) **que** must always be used to introduce the subordinate clause whereas its English equivalent (*that*) can be omitted.

Je **crois/trouve/pense que** c'est vrai.	*I believe/think this is true.*

- After negative or interrogative **penser** and **croire** either the infinitive or **que** + *subjunctive* can be used if the subject of the subordinate clause is the same as the subject of the main clause.

Il ne pense pas avoir la priorité.	*He doesn't think (that) **he** has the right of way.*

Or:

Il ne pense pas qu'il ait la priorité.
Croyez-vous avoir fait de votre mieux? *Do **you** think (that) **you** did your best?*

Or:

Croyez-vous que vous ayez fait de votre mieux?

Comment dit-on en français?

1. Do you (*fam.*) think that the weather will be nice tomorrow? _____

2. I don't believe that Spanish is easier than French. _____

3. He doesn't think that we can do it. _____

4. Scientists (**Les scientifiques** *[m.pl.]*) believe that there is going to be an earthquake. _____

_____

5. Do you (*fam.*) believe (that) I made the right decision? _____

6. They don't think that there are any survivors. _____

_____

Donnez la forme correcte du verbe entre parenthèses.

1. Je ne pense pas qu'il (falloir) _____ s'inquiéter.

2. Croyez-vous que ce film (plaire) _____ aux enfants?

3. Trouves-tu que mes dissertations (être) _____ bonnes?

4. Je pense que tu (avoir) _____ tort.

5. Il croit qu'il (faire) _____ beau demain.

6. Pensez-vous vraiment que cela (pouvoir) _____ changer les choses?

7. Je ne crois pas que ce (être) _____ nécessaire.

Traduisez en français la lettre qu'Anne a écrite à son amie Mireille.

Dear Mireille,

I received your message the day before yesterday. It seems that you are very depressed at the moment because of the break-up with your fiancé. I am going to try to cheer you up a little. I am surprised that Sébastien left without your knowing it. You say that he found another woman, but I doubt that she has your charm and intelligence. Furthermore, I don't think that this young man was the ideal partner for you. You argued often, and it seems to me that he is rather selfish. Don't be sad that he left you. As one says, there are plenty more fish in the sea. I believe that it is better to be alone than in bad company.

Don't stay at home on weekends unless you don't want to get married. You will find someone good provided that you go out often. Speak to many people until you make the acquaintance of your Prince Charming. You must not be afraid of a new relationship, although you are still in a state of shock. I want you to promise me to follow my advice.

Do you still intend to go to Africa next week? You will see, that will take your mind off things. I would like you to write me a note before you leave.

You have to tell me the date and time of your return, so that I can pick you up at the airport. I can't wait to see you again. Have a good trip and good luck!

Love, Anne

VOCABULAIRE			
as	**comme**	to pick sb up	**aller/venir chercher qn**
to be in a state of shock	**être sous le choc**	Prince Charming	**le prince charmant**
break-up	**la rupture**	relationship	**la relation**
charm	**le charme**	selfish	**égoïste**
to cheer sb up	**remonter le moral à qn**	someone good	**quelqu'un de bien**
		that will take your mind off things	**ça te changera les idées**
furthermore	**de plus**		
in bad company	**mal accompagné(e)**	there are plenty of fish in the sea	**un de perdu, dix de retrouvés**
a note	**un (petit) mot**		
partner	**le/la partenaire**		

_____

_____

_____

_____

_____

_____

_____

_____

_____

_____

Révision

Before you do the next exercise, please review and compare the examples below. Both columns have similar French expressions in the main clause. But whereas the expression in italics in the left column requires the subjunctive, the expression in italics in the right column is followed by the indicative.

SUBJUNCTIVE	INDICATIVE
Je *veux que* tu me **dises** tout.	J'*espère que* tu me **diras** tout.
I want you to tell me everything.	*I hope (that) you tell me everything.*
Nous *sommes heureux que* tu **sois** là.	*Heureusement que* tu **es** là.
We are happy that you are there.	*Fortunately you are there.*

*Il est possible qu'il **boive** de la bière.*
It is possible that he drinks beer.
Je *ne pense pas qu'*elle **ait** de la fièvre.
I don't think (that) she has a fever.
***Il semble qu'**ils **soient** fâchés.*
It seems that they are angry.
Elle est venue ***avant que*** je (ne) **parte.**
She came before I left.

*Il est probable qu'il **boit** de la bière.*
It is probable that he drinks beer.
Je ***pense qu'**elle **a** de la fièvre.*
I think (that) she has a fever.
***Il me semble qu'**ils **sont** fâchés.*
It seems to me that they are angry.
Elle est venue ***après que*** je **suis parti.**
She came after I left.

EXERCICE

11·34

Complétez les phrases suivantes avec une expression convenable selon le sens. Choose the expressions from the sentences above and use each only once.

1. Il est _____ qu'il *pleut* demain.

2. Il est _____ qu'il *pleuve* demain.

3. Je _____ que tu *sois venu(e)*.

4. _____ que tu *es venu(e)*.

5. Il s'est mis à pleuvoir _____ que nous *sommes rentrés*.

6. Il s'est mis à pleuvoir _____ que nous *rentrions*.

7. Il _____ qu'il *ait* besoin de nous.

8. Il _____ qu'il *a* besoin de nous.

9. J'_____ que tu *guériras* vite.

10. Je _____ que tu *guérisses* vite.

11. Nous _____ souvent que les autres *sont* plus heureux que nous.

12. _____-tu que les autres *soient* plus heureux que nous?

Other uses of the subjunctive

The subjunctive can also be found in *relative clauses*. Relative clauses are subordinate clauses introduced by a relative pronoun (French: **qui, que, dont, où**, etc.). The relative pronouns (English: *who, which, that, whom,* etc.) refer to a thing or a person (called the *antecedent*) mentioned in the main clause. In the sentence "I want to meet a man who is famous," "who is famous" is a relative clause and "a man" is the antecedent.

The subjunctive is used in a *relative clause* if the verb or expression in the main clause indicates that the speaker is *not sure* whether the antecedent (i.e., the person or thing he talks about) exists, or that he or she would like to find it. Expressions in the main clause that will trigger the subjunctive in the relative clause include:

J'ai besoin d'un(e)…   *I need a . . .*
Je cherche un(e)…   *I am looking for a . . .*

| Connaissez-vous un(e)... | Do you know a . . . ? |
| Y a-t-il un(e)... | Is there a . . . ? |

Il cherche quelqu'un *qui* **soit** fiable.	He is looking for someone who is reliable.
Il me faut un interprète *qui* **sache** parler couramment le japonais.	I need an interpreter who knows how to speak Japanese fluently.
Connaissez-vous une personne *qui* **veuille** m'aider?	Do you know a person who would be willing to help me?
Je ne connais pas de pays *où* il **fasse** toujours beau.	I don't know a country where the weather is always good.
Y a-t-il quelque chose *que* je **puisse** faire pour vous?	Is there something I can do for you?

But: If the main clause indicates that the desired object or person has already been found or that its existence is *certain*, the *indicative* is used. *Compare:*

| Je voudrais trouver un hôtel *qui* ne **soit** pas cher. | I would like to find a hotel that is not expensive. |

(The desire is *not* fulfilled. The subjunctive is used.)

| J'ai trouvé / Je connais un hôtel *qui* n'**est** pas cher. | I found / I know a hotel that is not expensive. |

(The object is found / the speaker knows that it exists. The indicative is used.)

EXERCICE

11·35

Indicatif ou subjonctif? Comment dit-on en français?

1. We would need someone who can speak Dutch (**néerlandais**). _____

2. We know someone who can speak Dutch. _____

3. I am looking for a house that suits (**convenir à**) my parents. _____

4. We must find someone who is experienced (**expérimenté**). _____

5. He is looking for a gift that his wife will like (**plaire**). _____

The subjunctive is used in a *relative clause* if the relative clause is preceded by a *superlative* (*the best, the most beautiful,* etc.).

C'est *la plus belle ville que** je **connaisse**.	That is the most beautiful city I know.
C'est *le moins qu'**on **puisse** dire.	That is the least one can say.
C'est *le meilleur film que** j'**aie** jamais **vu**.	That is the best film I ever saw.

*Note that in English, the relative pronoun (*which, that, whom*) can be omitted. In French, **que** must *always* be used.

The choice between the subjunctive or the indicative in a relative clause after a superlative depends on whether the speaker expresses a *personal* opinion or judgment (subjunctive), or if the speaker simply states a *fact* (indicative).

Often however, the subjunctive is automatically triggered in the relative clause after a superlative, no matter whether an opinion or a fact is stated.

Cette tour est **la plus haute qu**'il y **a** (*or:* **ait**) au monde.	*This tower is the highest there is in the world.*

The subjunctive is used in a *relative clause* if the relative clause is preceded by one of the following expressions:

l'unique	*the only (one)*	ne... personne	*nobody, not anybody*
le/la seul(e)	*the only (one)*	ne... jamais	*never*
le premier, la première	*the first (one)*	ne... aucun(e)	*no, not any*
le dernier, la dernière	*the last (one)*	il n'y a que	*(there is) only*
ne... rien	*nothing, not anything*	ne... pas de	*no, not any*

Neil Armstrong est **le premier** homme **qui ait marché** sur la lune.	*Neil Armstrong is the first man who walked on the moon.*
C'est **la seule** femme **que** je **connaisse** dans cette ville.	*She is the only woman I know in this city.*
L'unique chose **dont** elle **ait** peur, c'est de se faire agresser.	*The only thing she is afraid of is getting mugged.*
Il **ne** connaît **personne qui sache** faire cela.	*He doesn't know anyone who knows how to do that.*
Il **n**'y a **aucun** médicament **qui guérisse** cette maladie.	*There is no medication that cures this disease.*
Il n'y a que Dieu **qui puisse** nous aider.	*Only God can help us.*
Je **ne** connais **pas de** musée **qui soit** plus beau.	*I don't know any museum that is more beautiful.*

EXERCICE
11·36

Comment dit-on en français?

1. That is the best pie (**tarte [f.]**) I ever ate. _____

2. You (*pol.*) are the nicest man she ever met. _____

3. That is the last craftsman (**artisan [m.]**) who knows how to do it. _____

   _____

4. I have never seen anyone who is so ambitious. _____

5. Only you (*fam.*) were successful (**réussir**). _____

6. Here are the first opinion polls (**les sondages [m.pl.]**) we received. _____

7. That is the only solution they offered. _____

8. This is the latest news (**les dernières nouvelles**) we have. _____

9. I don't know anyone (= I know nobody) who cooks better. _____

10. That is the only floor that has a balcony. _____

11. There is nothing you (*pol.*) can do to improve the situation. _____

12. Only Bertrand understood me. _____

Note: After **le premier**, **le dernier**, and **le seul** infinitive constructions (preceded by **à**) can be used instead of a relative pronoun + *subjunctive* (See *The infinitive*, page 237).

Les femmes ne sont plus *les seules* à **savoir** trouver les bonnes affaires.
Women are no longer the only ones who know how to find the good bargains.

More uses of the subjunctive

The subjunctive is also used after the following expressions:

qui que	*whoever*
où que	*wherever*
quoi que*	*whatever*

Qui que vous **soyez**, je ne vous ai jamais vu.	*Whoever you may be, I have never seen you.*
Où que tu **ailles**, je t'accompagnerai.	*Wherever you go, I will accompany you.*
Quoi que tu **dises**, je ne te crois pas.	*Whatever you may say, I don't believe you.*

qui que ce soit qui	*whoever it may be who*
qui que ce soit que	*who(m)ever it may be who(m)*
quoi que ce soit que	*whatever it may be which/that*

Qui que ce soit qui **ait** dit cela, je n'en crois rien.	*Whoever may have (it may be who) said that, I don't believe it.*
Qui que ce soit que vous **connaissiez**, je ne le connais pas.	*Whomever you may know (it may be whom you know), I don't know him.*
*Quoi que ce soit qu'*on **dise**, restez calme!	*Whatever they say (it may be that one says), stay calm!*

si (+ *adjective or adverb*) **que**	*however* (+ *adjective or adverb*)
aussi (+ *adjective or adverb*) **que**	

Si étrange *que* ça **puisse** paraître, ça marche.	*However strange it may seem, it works.*
Aussi riche *que* **soit** cette femme, elle ne peut pas nous aider.	*However rich this woman may be, she cannot help us.*

quel que **quelle que** **quels que** or: **quelles que**	+ subjunctive of **être** + noun or: + pronoun + subjunctive of « **être** »	*whatever* + *noun* *(or pronoun)* + *may be*

Les urgences accueillent tous les adultes *quel que* **soit** leur âge.	*The emergency room welcomes all adults, whatever their age may be.*
Quelle que **soit** la difficulté, il faut la surmonter.	*Whatever the difficulty may be, you must overcome it.*
Quels que **soient** vos chagrins, il faut essayer de les oublier.	*Whatever your sorrows may be, you must try to forget them.*
Les parents aiment tous leurs enfants, *quelles que* **soient** leurs aptitudes.	*Parents love all their children, whatever their capabilities may be.*

quelque (+ *singular noun*) **que**	*whatever* (+ *singular or plural noun*)
quelques (+ *plural noun*) **que**	

Quelques soucis *que* vous **ayez**, ne vous inquiétez pas trop.	*Whatever worries you may have, don't worry too much.*

*Do not confuse **quoi que** (*whatever*) and **quoique** (*although*).

Comment dit-on en français?

1. Whatever you (*fam.*) do, do it well. _____

2. Wherever you (*pol.*) are in the world, we will find you. _____

3. However incredible this may seem, everyone survived the plane crash (**l'accident d'avion**). _____

4. One must (**Il faut**) like one's work, whatever it may be. _____

5. Whatever the threats (**les menaces [f.pl.]**) may be, I will never leave! _____

6. We are going to arrest the murderers (**les assassins [m.pl.]**), whatever their age may be.

_____

7. Whoever (it may be who) did that is a coward (**un lâche**). _____

8. Whatever mistakes you (*fam.*) made, try to avoid them in the future. _____

9. However intelligent you (*fam.*) may be, you don't know everything. _____

10. No grammar book, however complete it may be, can explain everything. _____

11. I will stay by your side (**à tes côtés**), whatever happens. _____

12. One must respect people, whatever their convictions (**leurs convictions [f.pl.]**) may be.

_____

EXERCICE

11·38

Traduisez en français la lettre suivante.

Dear Françoise,

It's been a long time that I haven't heard from you. Where are you? What are you doing these days? Are you still looking for a mansion that is not too expensive? I saw a house today that you would want to buy, whatever its price may be. Unfortunately, it is not for sale.

Last night, I went to the movies (in order) to see *À la folie, pas du tout* with Audrey Tautou. It is the best psychological thriller (that) I have ever seen. I don't know any actress who can act as well as Audrey. All those who see her fall in love with her.

At work, I have some demanding customers at the moment. There is nothing (which is) more difficult than to satisfy everyone. But I try hard. That is the only thing I can do. I am proud of my work, whatever my boss may say about it (**en**).

Hoping that you are in good health, I wish you an excellent week, wherever you are.

Love, Anne

to act	**jouer**	in good health	**en bonne santé**
all those who	**tous ceux qui**	a mansion	**un manoir**
boss	**le patron,**	proud	**fier, fière**
	la patronne	psychological	**psychologique**
demanding	**exigeant(e)**	to satisfy	**satisfaire**
to fall in love with	**tomber amoureux**	these days	**ces jours-ci**
	(-euse) de	thriller	**le thriller**
for sale	**à vendre**	to try hard	**faire des efforts**

Exercices de révision

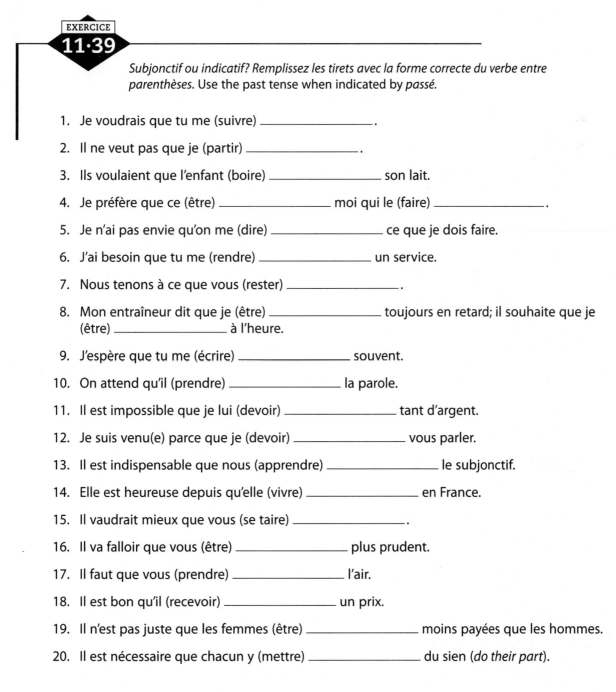

EXERCICE

11·39

Subjonctif ou indicatif? Remplissez les tirets avec la forme correcte du verbe entre parenthèses. Use the past tense when indicated by *passé.*

1. Je voudrais que tu me (suivre) _____.

2. Il ne veut pas que je (partir) _____.

3. Ils voulaient que l'enfant (boire) _____ son lait.

4. Je préfère que ce (être) _____ moi qui le (faire) _____.

5. Je n'ai pas envie qu'on me (dire) _____ ce que je dois faire.

6. J'ai besoin que tu me (rendre) _____ un service.

7. Nous tenons à ce que vous (rester) _____.

8. Mon entraîneur dit que je (être) _____ toujours en retard; il souhaite que je (être) _____ à l'heure.

9. J'espère que tu me (écrire) _____ souvent.

10. On attend qu'il (prendre) _____ la parole.

11. Il est impossible que je lui (devoir) _____ tant d'argent.

12. Je suis venu(e) parce que je (devoir) _____ vous parler.

13. Il est indispensable que nous (apprendre) _____ le subjonctif.

14. Elle est heureuse depuis qu'elle (vivre) _____ en France.

15. Il vaudrait mieux que vous (se taire) _____.

16. Il va falloir que vous (être) _____ plus prudent.

17. Il faut que vous (prendre) _____ l'air.

18. Il est bon qu'il (recevoir) _____ un prix.

19. Il n'est pas juste que les femmes (être) _____ moins payées que les hommes.

20. Il est nécessaire que chacun y (mettre) _____ du sien (*do their part*).

21. Il est important que tu t'en (souvenir) _____ .

22. Il est possible qu'elles le (savoir) _____ .

23. C'est normal que nous (défendre) _____ notre liberté.

24. Nous sommes heureux que tu (trouver- *passé*) _____ le temps de nous rendre visite.

25. C'est dommage qu'il (falloir) _____ attendre qu'il y (avoir) _____ des morts, avant que l'on (agir) _____ .

26. Nous sommes surpris que cela (ne pas arriver- *passé*) _____ plus tôt.

27. Je crois qu'il (falloir) _____ annuler le dîner.

28. L'enfant est déçu que sa mère ne lui (lire) _____ pas de contes de fées.

29. Heureusement que tu (venir -*passé*) _____ .

30. Je regrette que vous (ne pas vouloir) _____ le faire.

Subjonctif ou indicatif? Remplissez les tirets avec la forme correcte du verbe entre parenthèses. Use the past tense when indicated by *passé*.

1. Tu peux faire ce voyage pourvu que tu me (écrire) _____ souvent.

2. Maman m'a donné de l'argent pour que je (pouvoir) _____ acheter un grille-pain et un four à micro-ondes.

3. Nous irons à la plage à moins qu'il ne (pleuvoir) _____ .

4. Je vous téléphonerai avant que vous ne (partir) _____ .

5. Il a commencé à neiger après que nous (arriver- *passé*) _____ .

6. Je ne leur ai rien dit, de peur qu'ils (se faire) _____ du souci.

7. Restez jusqu'à ce que je (revenir) _____ .

8. Le bébé pleure parce qu'il (être) _____ malade.

9. Je vous dis cela afin que vous le (savoir) _____ .

10. Il est riche sans que cela (paraître) _____ .

11. Je doute que cette maison lui (appartenir) _____ .

12. Je ne suis pas sûr(e) que ce livre vous (plaire) _____ .

13. Je suis persuadé que vous (faire - *passé*) _____ tout votre possible et je vous en remercie.

14. Je sais que vous (faire) _____ très bien la cuisine.

15. Il est évident qu'il (avoir) _____ tort.

16. Il nous semble qu'il (faire) _____ très chaud.

17. Je ne crois pas qu'il (valoir) _____ la peine de se plaindre.

18. Croyez-vous qu'il (falloir) _____ être gentil avec tout le monde?

19. Je crois que ce (être) _____ vrai.

20. Je pense que vous (avoir) _____ rendez-vous chez le médecin.

21. Elle est triste que son père (mourir-passé) _____.

22. Elle est triste depuis que son père (mourir-passé) _____.

EXERCICE
11·41

Subjonctif ou indicatif? Remplissez les tirets avec la forme correcte du verbe entre parenthèses.

1. Nous espérons que vous (passer) _____ de bonnes vacances.

2. Il est nécessaire qu'on (rire) _____ pour être en bonne santé.

3. Il a disparu sans que personne ne s'en (apercevoir) _____.

4. La loi interdit que nous (conduire) _____ en état d'ivresse.

5. Ils ont peur que tout le monde (s'en aller) _____.

6. Est-il vrai qu'il (vivre) _____ seul?

7. Pensez-vous que nous (avoir) _____ le temps de visiter le château?

8. Nous sommes contents que le cadeau vous (plaire) _____.

9. Il faudrait qu'il (avoir) _____ des enfants.

10. Bien qu'il (vivre -*passé*) _____ une année en France, il ne parle pas couramment le français.

11. Je cherche quelqu'un qui (vouloir) _____ acheter ma voiture.

12. C'est le pire qui (pouvoir) _____ arriver à un pays.

13. Pierre est l'élève le plus doué que je (avoir) _____ dans ma classe.

14. L'orthographe française est l'une des orthographes les plus difficiles qui (être) _____.

15. C'est la plus belle nouvelle que nous (avoir) _____ depuis longtemps.

16. C'est la meilleure décision que tu (prendre- *passé*) _____ de ta vie.

17. Il n'y a personne qui le (savoir) _____.

18. Il n'y a aucun passager qui (sortir- *passé*) _____ indemne de cet accident.

19. Une mère aime son enfant, quoi qu'il (faire) _____.

20. C'est la seule chose qu'ils (comprendre- *passé*). _____.

The use of the subjunctive in the main clause

Use of the subjunctive in the main clause is rare.

◆ It is used in phrases (often expressing a wish) and fixed expressions (where it is not always preceded by **que**) such as:

Vive la France!	*Long live France!*
Ainsi **soit**-il!	*So be it! Amen! (end of prayer)*
Que Dieu vous **bénisse**!	*God bless you!*
Dieu **soit** loué!	*Thank God! God be praised!*
Soit! [swat]	*So be it!*
Autant que je **me (m'en) souvienne**.	*As far as I remember.*
Pas que je **sache**.	*Not that I know.*
Qu'on le **veuille** ou non.	*Whether one likes it or not.*
Que ça te **plaise** ou non.	*Whether you like it or not.*

◆ The subjunctive is also used after **que** to express an *order* or *command* in the third-person singular and plural which cannot be done with the imperative. The English equivalent is *let* (*him, her, them*) or *may* (*he, she, they*).

Qu'il se **taise**!	*May he be quiet!*
Que cela ne se **reproduise** plus!	*Don't let that happen again!*
Que personne ne **sorte**!	*May nobody leave the room!*
Que cela vous **serve** d'avertissement!	*May that serve you as a warning!*
Qu'ils **fassent** leur devoir!	*Let them do their duty!*
Qu'elle ne **dise** pas de bêtises!	*Don't let her talk nonsense!*
Dieu a dit: « Que la lumière **soit**! »	*God said: "Let there be light!"*

EXERCICE

11·42

Comment dit-on en français?

1. Long live the king! _____

2. Whether you (*fam.*) like it or not, you will go to college. _____

3. As far as I know, she no longer lives here. _____

4. Let him come as soon as possible! _____

5. May all your (*fam.*) dreams come true (**se réaliser**)! _____

6. If they don't have bread, let them eat cake (**de la brioche**)! _____

_____

7. Long live vacations! _____

THE INFINITIVE,
THE IMPERATIVE,
THE PRESENT PARTICIPLE
AND GERUND,
AND THE PASSIVE VOICE

The infinitive

In French, the infinitive has two tenses, the *present infinitive* and the *past infinitive*.

The formation of the infinitives

The present infinitive

The present infinitive is the basic, unconjugated form of the verb. Dictionaries use this form of the verb to define its meaning. In English, the present infinitive begins with "to" (*to go, to read, to ask*). In French, the present infinitive ends in **-er, -ir,** or **-re**.

1. According to the present infinitive endings, one distinguishes three groups of *regular verbs*:

   ◆ verbs ending in **-er**: **donner** (*to give*), **s'amuser** (*to have a good time*)

   ◆ verbs ending in **-ir**: **grandir** (*to grow up*), **se réunir** (*to get together*)

   ◆ verbs ending in **-re**: **attendre** (*to wait*), **se détendre** (*to relax*)

2. The present infinitive of *irregular verbs* also ends in either **-er**, such as **aller** (*to go*), **envoyer** (*to send*); **-ir**, such as **venir** (*to come*), **dormir** (*to sleep*); or **-re**, such as **prendre** (*to take*), **boire** (*to drink*), **dire** (*to say*).

The past infinitive (*l'infinitif passé*)

The past infinitive consists of the infinitive of **avoir** or **être** + *past participle* of the verb in question. It is the equivalent of English *to have / having* + *past participle*.

parler	**avoir parlé**	*to have spoken, having spoken*
arriver	**être arrivé(e)(s)**	*to have arrived, having arrived*
se dépêcher	**s'être dépêché(e)(s)**	*to have hurried, having hurried*

The past infinitive is used to express an action that occurred prior to that of the main clause. Note that English generally uses the *-ing* form in this case.

Je vous remercie d'**être venu**.	*I thank you for com**ing**.*

Important note: The preposition **après** is *always* followed by the past infinitive.

Qu'est-ce que tu vas faire **après avoir fini** tes études?	*What are you going to do after graduating?*

The verbs **se rappeler** and **se souvenir de** are generally followed by the past infinitive.

Je ne **me souviens** pas **d'avoir dit** cela.   *I don't remember saying that.*
or: Je ne **me rappelle** pas **avoir dit** cela.

Note:

◆ The same rules of agreement apply to the past participle of the past infinitive as to all other compound tenses.

Il a acheté les articles sans **les** avoir vus.   *He bought the articles without having seen them.*

◆ When a reflexive verb is used in the (present or past) infinitive form in a sentence, the reflexive pronoun must agree with the subject.

Je vais **me** fâcher.   *I am going to get angry.*
Après **nous** être amusés, nous   *After having a good time, we went home.*
   sommes rentrés.

◆ Object pronouns usually precede the infinitive (present or past).

N'hésitez pas à **le** dire.   *Don't hesitate to say it.*
Il n'aime pas **y** aller.   *He doesn't like to go there.*
Je me rappelle **les** avoir rencontrés.   *I remember meeting them.*

EXERCICE
12·1

Traduisez en français les expressions verbales en italique. Mettez le verbe à l'infinitif présent ou passé, selon le cas.

1. (He thanked me for *helping* him yesterday.) Il m'a remercié de l'_____ hier.

2. (You are going to *have a good time*.) Tu vas _____.

3. (I would like to *live there*.) Je voudrais _____.

4. (I don't remember *seeing* this movie.) Je ne me souviens pas d'_____ ce film.

5. (I am happy to *have found* this position.) Je suis content(e) d'_____ ce poste.

6. (I am sorry for *being* late.) Je suis désolé(e) d'_____ en retard.

7. (She is proud to *have received* her degree.) Elle est fière d'_____ son diplôme.

8. (Try to *remember*!) Essaie de _____.

9. (After *falling* in love, he asked her to marry him.) Après _____ amoureux, il lui a demandé la main.

10. (After *unpacking* [**défaire**] their suitcases, they (*masc.*) went out.) Après _____ leurs valises, ils sont sortis.

The negative infinitive

The negative form of the present infinitive

The present infinitive is made negative by placing both parts of the negations **ne pas** (*not*), **ne plus** (*no longer, not any more*), **ne rien** (*nothing*), **ne jamais** (*never*), **ne pas encore** (*not yet*) before it and before its object pronouns, if there are any.

Je préfère **ne plus** y *retourner*.	*I prefer not to return there any more.*
J'essaie de **ne pas** me *fâcher*.	*I try not to get angry.*
Il vaut mieux **ne rien** *dire*.	*It is better to say nothing.*

The negative form of the past infinitive

The past infinitive is made negative by placing **ne pas, ne plus, ne rien, ne jamais,** and **ne pas encore** before the auxiliary and before the object pronouns, if there are any.

Je regrette de **ne pas** *avoir lu* le livre.	*I regret not having read the book.*
Je suis triste de **ne jamais** y *être allé(e)*.	*I am sad to never have gone there.*

EXERCICE

12·2

Traduisez en français les expressions verbales en italique en donnant l'infinitif présent ou passé à la forme négative.

1. (To be or *not to be*.) Être ou _____ .

2. (I regret *not to be able* to answer this question.) Je regrette de _____ répondre à cette question.

3. (He told me *never to lie*.) Il m'a dit de _____ .

4. (She decided to *no longer eat* meat.) Elle a décidé de _____ de viande.

5. (We are glad *not to have gone* to the party.) Nous sommes contents de _____ à la fête.

6. (I am sorry *not to have written yet*.) Je suis désolé(e) de _____ .

The uses of the infinitive

Some present infinitives are used as masculine nouns.

un aller simple	*a one-way ticket*
un aller-retour	*a round-trip ticket*
le coucher du soleil	*sunset*
le devoir	*homework, assignment*

le déjeuner	*lunch*
le petit déjeuner	*breakfast*
le dîner	*dinner*
un être humain	*a human being*
le goûter	*(afternoon) snack*
le lever du soleil	*sunrise*
le pouvoir	*power*
le rire	*laughter*
le savoir	*knowledge*
le savoir-faire	*know-how*
le savoir-vivre	*manners*
le sourire	*smile*
le souvenir	*souvenir, memory*

EXERCICE 12·3

Remplissez les tirets avec les mots qui manquent.

1. Le _____, le _____ et le _____ sont les trois repas principaux de la journée.

2. Notre professeur nous donne beaucoup de _____.

3. Tôt le matin, j'aime regarder le _____ du soleil.

4. Avant de prendre la photo, le photographe nous a dit: Faites-moi un

   joli _____.

5. Ce président est très puissant, il a beaucoup de _____.

6. L'après-midi, les enfants prennent un _____ quand ils ont faim.

7. Je garderai toujours un très bon _____ de mon séjour en France.

8. Je voudrais un billet pour Nantes s'il vous plaît. —Est-ce que vous voudriez

   un _____. ou un _____?

The present infinitive is used as a subject or (after **c'est**) as an object to express a general truth. English generally uses the *-ing* form in this case.

Voir, c'est **croire**.	*Seeing is believing.*
Promettre et **tenir** sont deux.	*Promising and keeping one's promise are two different things.*
Vivre, c'est **lutter**. (Victor Hugo)	*Living is struggling.*

EXERCICE 12·4

Comment dit-on en français? Traduisez en français les mots entre parenthèses.

1. (*Eating*) _____ de la glace, ça fait grossir.

2. (*Lying*) _____ est une honte.

3. (*Building*) _____ une maison coûte cher.

4. (*Crying*) _____ ne sert à rien.

5. (*Staying*) _____ longtemps au soleil est dangereux.

6. (*Finding*) _____ un bon emploi est difficile.

7. (*Wanting*) _____ , c'est pouvoir. (*proverb*)

8. (*Walking*) _____ est bon pour la santé.

9. (*Driving*) _____ en Amérique coûte moins cher qu'en France.

10. (*Leaving*) _____ , c'est mourir un peu. (*proverb*)

The present infinitive replaces the imperative in written impersonal instructions and orders addressed to all users (in textbooks, recipes, on signs and labels).

Voir au verso.	*See on (the) back.*
Ralentir.	*Slow down.*
Mélanger le sucre et les œufs.	*Blend the sugar and the eggs.*
Ne pas marcher sur la pelouse.	*Don't walk on the grass.*
Ne pas parler au conducteur.	*Don't talk to the driver (in buses).*
En cas d'incendie **ne pas prendre** l'ascenseur.	*In case of fire don't take the elevator.*

EXERCICE 12·5

Le professeur a écrit les devoirs au tableau. Voilà ses ordres. Remplissez les tirets en utilisant l'infinitif.

1. _____ trente pages du roman *Le Père Goriot*.

2. _____ aux questions à la page dix du manuel.

3. Ensuite, _____ le vocabulaire et _____ l'exercice #3.

4. Après, _____ la cassette audio et _____ la vidéo au laboratoire.

5. Finalement, _____ une dissertation de cinq pages.

6. (*Hand in*) _____ les devoirs mardi prochain.

Donnez la recette (recipe) d'un plat que vous cuisinez souvent. Utilisez les verbes à l'infinitif.

VOCABULAIRE

to add	**ajouter**	oven	**le four**
bowl	**le bol**	to peel	**peler**
butter	**le beurre**	to pepper	**poivrer**
to cook	**faire cuire**	plate	**l'assiette** *(f.)*
to cover	**couvrir**	to pour	**verser**
to cut	**couper**	to put	**mettre**
flour	**la farine**	salt	**le sel**
frying pan	**la poêle**	to salt	**saler**
herbs	**les herbes** *(f.pl.)*	saucepan	**la casserole**
meat	**la viande**	to serve	**servir**
to mix	**mélanger**	to stir	**remuer**
mushroom	**le champignon**	to use	**utiliser**
oil	**l'huile** *(f.)*	vegetable	**le légume**
onion	**l'oignon** *(m.)*		

_____

_____

_____

_____

_____

_____

The (present or past) infinitive is used *after prepositions* or prepositional phrases such as **avant de** (*before*), **après** (*after*), **au lieu de** (*instead of*), **loin de** (*far from*), **sans** (*without*), **pour** ([*in order*] *to*), **afin de** (*in order to*), **de peur de** (*for fear of*). English uses the *-ing* form except after *to*.

Entrez *sans* **frapper**.	*Enter without **knocking**.*
Ils sont allés au cinéma *au lieu de* **travailler**.	*They went to the movies instead of **working**.*
Il s'est brossé les dents *avant de* **se coucher**.	*He brushed his teeth before **going** to bed.*
Je travaille *pour* **gagner** de l'argent.	*I work (in order) to make money.*

Remember that **après** is always followed by the *past infinitive*.

Après **être arrivés**, ils ont pris un taxi.   *After **arriving**, they took a taxi.*

Traduisez les mots entre parenthèses.

1. Il faut réfléchir (*before speaking*) _____ .

2. Il est parti (*without saying good-bye*) _____ .

3. Je n'ai pas osé entrer (*for fear of disturbing you [pol.]*) _____ .

4. Je suis (*far from sharing*) _____ votre avis.

5. Il faut manger des fruits et des légumes (*in order to be*) _____ en bonne santé.

6. (*Instead of complaining*) _____ , tu devrais nous aider.

7. (*In order to be able to do it*) _____ , il faut être habile.

8. Les Français travaillent (*in order to live*) _____ , ils ne vivent pas (*in order to work*) _____ .

9. (*After washing the dishes*) _____ , je ferai la lessive.

10. (*Before washing the dishes*) _____ , je ferai la lessive.

11. (*After switching off the light*) _____ , elle s'est couchée.

12. (*After getting up*) _____ , j'ai pris le petit déjeuner.

The infinitive is used primarily as object of a verb. When two verbs follow each other, the second verb is always in its infinitive form (*I hate to work* = **je déteste travailler**). Depending on the nature of the *first* (conjugated) verb,

- the infinitive follows it immediately

    Il aime **manger**.   *He likes to eat.*

- the infinitive is separated from it by the preposition **à**

    Il continue **à manger**.   *He continues to eat.*

- the infinitive is separated from it by the preposition **de**

    Il refuse **de manger**.   *He refuses to eat.*

Lists of the most common verbs of each of these three categories follow.

1. *No preposition* is required before the infinitive after the following verbs and expressions:

> **adorer** *to adore, love to / . . . ing*
> **aimer** *to like to*
> **aimer mieux** *to prefer to / . . . -ing*
> **aller** *to go, be going to*
> **compter** *to intend, plan to*
> **désirer** *to wish to*
> **détester** *to detest, dislike to / . . . -ing*
> **devoir** *to have to, must*
> **entendre** *to hear*
> **espérer** *to hope to*
> **falloir** *to be necessary*
> **laisser** *to let, allow to*
> **oser** *to dare*
> **pouvoir** *to be able to, can*
> **préférer** *to prefer to*
> **se rappeler** *to remember . . . -ing*

savoir *to know, know how to*
sembler *to seem to*
valoir mieux *to be better (to)*
voir *to see*
vouloir *to want to*
avoir beau (faire qch) *(to do sth) in vain*
être censé(e) (faire qch) *to be supposed (to do sth)*
faillir (faire qch) *to almost (do sth)*
(used only in the **passé composé***)*
à quoi bon (faire qch) *what's the use / the point of (doing sth), what good does it do to (do sth)*

Elle *adore* **monter** à cheval.	*She loves to go horseback riding.*
Je *vais* **oublier**.	*I am going to forget.*
Cet été, je *compte* **aller** à Paris.	*This summer, I plan to go to Paris.*
Je *déteste* me **lever** tôt.	*I hate getting up early.*
Je *dois* **aller** à la poste.	*I have to go to the post office.*
Elle *a entendu* le bébé **pleurer**.	*She heard the baby cry.*
J'*espère* **avoir** bientôt de tes nouvelles.	*I hope to hear from you soon.*
Je n'*ose* pas le **dire**.	*I don't dare to say it.*
Ils ne *savent* pas **lire**.	*They don't know how to read.*
Je l'*ai vu* **arriver**.	*I saw him arrive.*
Elle *veut* se **reposer**.	*She wants to rest.*
Il faut **être** confiant.	*One has to be confident.*
Il ne faut pas **remettre** au lendemain ce que l'on peut faire le jour même. *(proverb)*	*Do not put off till tomorrow what you can do today.*
Il vaut mieux ne pas y **aller**.	*It is better not to go there.*
Mieux vaut **prévenir** que **guérir**. *(proverb)*	*An ounce of prevention is worth a pound of cure.*
Tu *as beau* **pleurer**, personne ne t'entend.	*You're crying in vain, nobody hears you.*
Il n'*est* pas *censé* le **savoir**.	*He is not supposed to know it.*
Elle *a failli* **mourir**.	*She almost died.*
À quoi bon s'**inquiéter**?	*What good does it do to worry?*

Note: **Aller** + *infinitive* expresses the close future (*am/is/are going to* + *infinitive*) or the close future in the past (*was/were going to* + *infinitive*).

Je *vais* vous **écrire**.	*I am going to write to you.*
J'*allais* vous **écrire**.	*I was going to write to you.*

Entendre parler de means *to hear of* and is followed by a noun or stressed pronoun.

Je n'*ai* jamais *entendu* **parler** de cette actrice.	*I never heard of this actress.*
Je n'*ai* jamais *entendu* **parler** d'elle.	*I never heard of her.*

Entendre dire means *to hear (that)* and is always followed by a clause that begins with **que**.

J'*ai entendu* **dire que** le vin rouge est bénéfique pour le cœur.	*I heard that red wine is good for the heart.*

Laisser tomber means *to drop*.

Elle *a laissé* **tomber** les clés.	*She dropped the keys.*
Laisse **tomber**!	*Give it up! (Drop it! Forget it!)*

Complétez personnellement en utilisant un verbe à l'infinitif.

Exemple: Je compte *partir en vacances la semaine prochaine.*

1. Aujourd'hui, je dois absolument _____.

2. L'année prochaine, j'espère _____.

3. Ce soir, je vais _____.

4. Je n'ose pas _____.

5. Il faut _____.

6. Il vaut mieux _____.

7. Je voudrais _____.

8. Les étudiants ne peuvent pas _____.

9. Je ne sais pas _____.

10. Je déteste _____.

Traduisez en français les phrases suivantes.

1. I love to sleep late. _____

2. We cannot understand him. _____

3. My daughter plans to major in computer science. _____

4. She doesn't know how to ice skate. _____

5. I don't know what (**quoi**) to say. _____

6. We don't like to disappoint our parents. _____

7. I hope to see you (*fam.*) again soon. _____

8. The students have to write many papers. _____

9. What are you (*pol.*) going to do? _____

10. He is going to get well. _____

11. Do you (*pol.*) have to get up early tomorrow? _____

12. I don't dare to admit it. _____

13. What would you (*pol.*) like to drink? _____

14. It will be better to wait. _____

15. He prefers to pay cash (**en espèces**). _____

EXERCICE
12·10

Traduisez en français les phrases suivantes.

1. Can I ask you (*pol.*) a favor? _____

2. Could I borrow your (**votre**) umbrella? _____

3. One cannot please everyone. _____

4. She wants to speak with you (*fam.*). _____

5. The Internet surfers (**Les internautes** *[m.pl.]*) are going to know this website (**ce site Web**). _____

6. She doesn't let her children watch television. _____

7. The little girl dropped her teddy bear. _____

8. Did you (*fam.*) drop the course? _____

9. I heard that you (*pol.*) wrote a book. _____

10. Have you (*fam.*) ever heard of this writer? —Yes, I have heard of him. _____

11. She didn't hear the alarm clock ring. _____

12. You (*pol.*) are not supposed to download (**télécharger**) this music. _____

13. We almost missed the plane. _____

14. I almost made a mistake (**se tromper**). _____

15. What good does it do to continue? _____

Faire + infinitive (causative *faire*)

If, in a sentence, the subject does not perform the action, but *causes* it to be done by someone else, French uses the verb **faire** + *infinitive*.

In English, this idea is expressed by *to have* + *object* + *past participle* (*to have something done*) or by *to make* + *object* + *infinitive* (*to make someone do something*).

Je **fais** *développer* les photos.	*I **have / am having** the pictures **developed**.*
Elle **fera** *nettoyer* son tailleur.	*She will **have** her suit **cleaned**.*
Nous **avons fait** *réparer* le lave-vaisselle.	*We **had** the dishwasher **repaired**.*
Il **a fait** *chanter* les enfants.	*He **made** the children **sing**.*
Tu me **fais** *rire*.	*You **make** me **laugh**.*

Ça me **fait** *pleurer*.
Qu'est-ce qui l'a **fait** *changer* d'avis?

*That **makes** me cry.*
*What **made** him **change** his mind?*

EXERCICE
12·11

Traduisez en français les phrases suivantes.

1. He is having his car repaired (*to repair* = **réparer**). _____

2. They are having a castle built (*to build* = **construire**). _____

3. He will have a suit made. _____

4. We are going to have Internet installed (*to install* = **installer**). _____

5. We just had the lock (**la serrure**) changed. _____

6. She had flowers delivered (*to deliver* = **livrer**) to her mother's home (**domicile** *[m.]*). ___

   _____

7. I must have my passport renewed. (*to renew* = **renouveler**) _____

8. The magician made the rabbit disappear. _____

9. He makes his wife laugh. _____

10. Don't make (*fam.*) me wait! _____

Idiomatic expressions with causative faire

faire attendre qn *to keep sb waiting*
faire chanter qn *to blackmail sb*
faire marcher qn *to pull sb's leg*
faire savoir qch à qn *to let sb know, inform sb of sth*
faire venir qn *to send for sb*
faire visiter qch à qn *to show sb around sth*
faire voir qch à qn *to show sth to sb*

Note: **Se faire** is used to show that the subject has, had or will have something done for himself or to himself.

se faire couper les cheveux *to have one's hair cut, get a haircut*
se faire comprendre *to make oneself understood*

EXERCICE
12·12

Comment dit-on en français?

1. They (*fem.*) blackmailed their boss. _____

2. They (*masc.*) kept me waiting for three hours. _____

3. I will show you (*fam.*) the pictures. _____

4. I will let you (*pol.*) know (it). _____

5. We sent for the doctor. _____

6. He showed his friends around Bordeaux. _____

7. I can make myself understood in French. _____

8. She had her hair cut. _____

Verb + *de quoi* (something, enough) + infinitive

Avez-vous *de quoi* vivre?	*Do you have enough to live on?*
Apportez *de quoi* lire.	*Bring something to read.*
(= Apportez quelque chose à lire.)	

Comment dit-on en français?

1. Do you (*fam.*) have something to wear? _____

2. He doesn't have enough to pay the rent (**le loyer**). _____

3. I hope that you (*fam.*) bring something to drink. _____

4. There will be something to do for everyone. _____

5. You (*pol.*) will find something to eat in the freezer (**le congélateur**). _____

6. The artists come here to find something to paint. _____

7. He was so poor that he didn't even have enough to buy himself a shirt. _____

8. She earns enough to feed herself (**se nourrir**). _____

2. The preposition **à** is required before the infinitive after the following verbs and expressions:

> **aider qn à** *to help sb to*
> **s'amuser à** *to have a good time, have fun, to enjoy . . . -ing*
> **apprendre à** *to learn to, teach to*
> **arriver à** *to succeed in . . . -ing, manage to, can*
> **ne pas arriver à** *to be unable to, cannot*
> **s'attendre à** *to expect to*
> **avoir (qch) à** *to have (sth) to*

avoir du mal à *to have trouble, have a hard time . . . -ing*
commencer à *to begin to, start . . . -ing*
continuer à *to continue to*
forcer qn à *to force sb to*
s'habituer à *to get used to / accustomed to . . . -ing*
hésiter à *to hesitate to*
inviter qn à *to invite, ask sb to*
mettre (du temps) à *to take (time) to*
se mettre à *to begin to, start . . . -ing*
passer (du temps) à *to spend (time) (doing)*
penser à *to be thinking of (doing)*
réussir à *to succeed in . . . -ing, be able to*
tenir à *to be anxious/eager to, insist on . . . -ing*

Elle *aide* sa mère *à faire* la vaisselle.	*She helps her mother (to) do the dishes.*
Mon frère *apprend à conduire*.	*My brother is learning to drive.*
Je vais t'*apprendre à cuisiner*.	*I am going to teach you to cook.*
Je n'*arrive* pas *à* y **croire**.	*I can't believe it.*
Je ne m'*attendais* pas *à* vous **voir**.	*I didn't expect to see you.*
Il *a* d'autres chats *à* **fouetter**.	*He has other fish to fry. (lit.: He has other cats to whip.)*
J'*ai du mal à* vous **entendre**.	*I'm having trouble hearing you.*
N'*hésite* pas *à* **venir** me voir.	*Don't hesitate to come see me.*
J'*ai mis* une heure *à* m'**endormir**.	*It took me an hour to go to sleep.*
Je *tiens à* le **dire**.	*I insist on saying it.*

EXERCICE
12·14

Complétez personnellement en utilisant une préposition et un verbe à l'infinitif.

Exemple: Il continue _____.

         *Il continue **à** pleuvoir.*

1. J'hésite _____.

2. J'ai du mal _____.

3. J'apprends _____.

4. Je n'arrive pas _____.

5. Je commence _____.

6. Puis-je vous aider _____.

7. Je passe beaucoup de temps _____.

8. J'ai _____.

Comment dit-on en français?

1. Help (*fam.*) me (to) get up. _____

2. I have a big favor to ask you (*fam.*). _____

3. You (*fam.*) have nothing to fear. _____

4. Do you (*fam.*) have something to do at the moment? _____

5. They (*masc.*) have trouble walking. _____

6. He learns to ride a bike (**monter à vélo**). _____

7. It started to rain. _____

8. I cannot (can't manage to) sleep. _____

9. We hesitate to ask this question. _____

10. I am beginning to understand. _____

11. We did not succeed in convincing (**convaincre**) her. _____

12. One must get used to living in a dangerous world. _____

13. They (*fem.*) forced the children to obey. _____

14. He invited us to have a drink (**prendre un verre**). _____

15. I spent my vacation doing nothing. _____

3. The preposition **de** is required before the infinitive after the following verbs and expressions:

> **accepter de** *to accept, agree to*
> **(s')arrêter de** *to stop, quit (doing)*
> **conseiller à qn de** *to advise sb to*
> **continuer de** (or: **à**) *to continue to*
> **décider de** *to decide to*
> **defendre/interdire à qn de** *to forbid sb to*
> **demander à qn de** *to ask sb to*
> **dire à qn de** *to tell sb to*
> **essayer de** *to try to*
> **être en train de** *to be in the process of . . . -ing*
> **éviter de** *to avoid . . . -ing, take care not to*
> **s'excuser de** *to apologize for . . . -ing*
> **faire semblant de** *to pretend to*
> **finir de** *to finish . . . -ing*
> **oublier de** *to forget to*
> **permettre à qn de** *to allow sb to*
> **promettre (à qn) de** *to promise (sb) to*
> **proposer/suggérer à qn de** *to propose to sb to, suggest that sb do*

refuser de *to refuse to do*
regretter de *to regret to, be sorry for . . . -ing*
remercier qn de *to thank sb for . . . -ing / having done*
rêver de *to dream of . . . -ing*
risquer de *to risk / run the risk of . . . -ing, probably (do)*
se souvenir de *to remember . . . -ing*
valoir la peine de *to be worth . . . -ing*
venir de *(+ infinitive) (recent past) to have just (+ past participle)*
avoir l'air de *to look like, seem to*
avoir besoin de *to need to, have to*
avoir envie de *to feel like . . . -ing*
avoir hâte de *to look forward to . . . -ing, be anxious to*
avoir honte de *to be ashamed to*
avoir peur de *to be afraid to*
avoir raison de *to be right to*
avoir tort de *to be wrong in . . . -ing*
avoir l'intention de *to have the intention to*
avoir l'habitude de *to be used to . . . -ing*
avoir l'occasion de *to have the opportunity to*
avoir le temps de *to have the time to*

Arrêtez de vous **moquer** de moi!	*Stop making fun of me!*
Vous *avez eu raison de* vous **plaindre**.	*You were right to complain.*
J'*ai hâte d'avoir* de tes nouvelles.	*I can't wait (am anxious) to hear from you.*
Dites-lui *de* m'attendre.	*Tell him to wait for me.*
Elle *a essayé de* se **suicider**.	*She tried to commit suicide.*
Je m'excuse d'arriver si tard.	*I apologize for arriving so late.*
Il *a fait semblant de* **dormir**.	*He pretended to sleep.*
L'enquête *risque d'être* longue.	*The investigation will probably be long.*
Il *vient de* partir.	*He (has) just left.*
La vie *vaut la peine d'être* vécue.	*Life is worth living.*

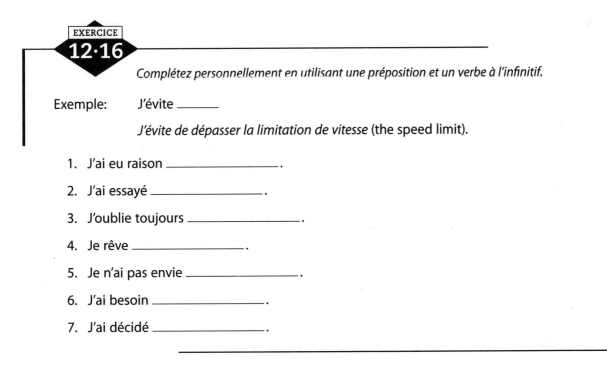

EXERCICE
12·16

Complétez personnellement en utilisant une préposition et un verbe à l'infinitif.

Exemple: J'évite _____

J'évite de dépasser la limitation de vitesse (the speed limit).

1. J'ai eu raison _____.

2. J'ai essayé _____.

3. J'oublie toujours _____.

4. Je rêve _____.

5. Je n'ai pas envie _____.

6. J'ai besoin _____.

7. J'ai décidé _____.

Comment dit-on en français? Use infinitive constructions throughout.

1. She needs to pay for college (**ses études** [*f.pl.*]). _____

2. They (*masc.*) refused to take the exam. _____

3. He decided to accept the gift. _____

4. I can't wait to know more (**plus de choses**) about (**sur**) you (*fam.*). _____

5. We are not used to working every day. _____

6. I tried to warn you (*pol.*). _____

7. I am in the process of translating these sentences. _____

8. We just received the package. _____

9. I dream of living abroad. _____

10. The waitress forgot to bring the cheese tray. _____

11. He pretends to be poor. _____

12. The old lady is afraid to go out. _____

13. I don't have the time to rest. _____

14. I feel like crying. _____

15. You (*fam.*) don't seem to realize the danger. _____

16. Promise (*fam.*) me to be nice to the students. _____

17. I advise you (*pol.*) to pay attention. _____

18. The doctor has forbidden him to drink alcohol (**de l'alcool**). _____

19. He told me not to worry. _____

20. We asked the teacher to be lenient (**indulgent**). _____

Est-ce vrai ou faux, pour vous?

_____ 1. Je viens de rentrer.

_____ 2. Demain, je vais assister à un concert.

_____ 3. Hier, j'ai essayé de conduire un camion (*truck*).

_____ 4. Je suis en train de faire cet exercice.

_____ 5. Ce matin, j'ai oublié de prendre le petit déjeuner.

_____ 6. Je rêve de fonder une famille.

_____ 7. J'ai appris à conjuguer les verbes français.

_____ 8. Je n'ai pas besoin de travailler.

_____ 9. Je n'ai pas le temps de m'amuser.

_____ 10. J'ai du mal à joindre les deux bouts (*make ends meet*).

_____ 11. J'ai des enfants à élever.

_____ 12. Je commence à comprendre la grammaire française.

_____ 13. J'aime faire du vélo.

_____ 14. J'espère me perfectionner en français.

_____ 15. Je n'ai jamais entendu parler du Louvre.

Exercices de révision

EXERCICE

12·19

Remplissez les tirets avec à *ou de* si c'est nécessaire.

1. Elle aime _____ aller au théâtre.

2. Vous pouvez _____ compter sur moi.

3. Voulez-vous que je vous aide _____ porter vos valises?

4. J'adore _____ faire du vélo.

5. N'oublie pas _____ prendre tes médicaments.

6. Nous essayons _____ faire de notre mieux.

7. Il faut _____ respecter les gens.

8. Elle déteste _____ être seule.

9. Vous n'avez rien _____ perdre.

10. Ils ont décidé _____ se marier.

11. Je m'excuse _____ être en retard.

12. Nous apprenons _____ parler français.

13. Je dois _____ me dépêcher.

14. J'espère _____ faire de bonnes affaires.

15. Les vacances viennent _____ commencer.

16. Elle rêve _____ devenir actrice.

17. J'ai une proposition _____ vous faire.

18. Je n'ose pas _____ lui dire la vérité.

19. Si tu as besoin de moi, n'hésite pas _____ le dire.

20. Est-ce que je peux _____ prendre un message?

21. Ma mère m'a appris _____ coudre.

22. J'ai besoin _____ faire des économies.

23. Je préfère _____ ne pas y aller.

24. Il s'est mis _____ pleurer.

25. Je ne m'attendais pas _____ vous voir.

26. Je regrette _____ ne pas avoir écrit plus tôt.

27. Je ne sais pas _____ skier.

28. Vous ne réussirez jamais _____ me convaincre.

29. Évitez _____ brûler le feu rouge (*run a red light*).

30. Je commençais _____ me faire du souci.

31. Qu'est-ce que tu vas _____ faire? —Je vais _____ réfléchir.

32. Nous finissons _____ travailler à huit heures.

33. Ils invitent leurs amis _____ faire une promenade.

34. Je vous promets _____ venir.

35. Ils ont eu raison _____ manifester.

36. Je refuse _____ assister à ce mariage.

37. Il vaut mieux _____ quitter la ville.

38. Je n'arrivais pas _____ me faire comprendre.

39. Vous avez tort _____ fumer.

40. Ils veulent _____ continuer _____ travailler ensemble.

EXERCICE

12·20

Remplissez les tirets avec à ou de si c'est nécessaire.

1. Ça semble _____ fonctionner.

2. Il risque _____ perdre son travail.

3. Nous sommes en train _____ laver la voiture.

4. Les élèves entendent la cloche _____ sonner.

5. Il a l'intention _____ arrêter _____ fumer.

6. Il a peur _____ perdre les élections.

7. Permettez-moi _____ me présenter.

8. Je vous remercie _____ m'avoir aidé.

9. Je n'ai pas l'habitude _____ me lever tôt le matin.

10. Veux-tu _____ boire quelque chose?

11. On l'a forcé _____ démissionner.

12. Ce livre ne vaut pas la peine _____ être lu.

13. J'ai envie _____ m'amuser.

14. On a demandé aux personnes âgées _____ ne pas sortir pendant la canicule (*heat wave*).

15. J'ai hâte _____ vous connaître.

16. J'ai accepté _____ le faire.

17. Nous commençons _____ regretter _____ être venus.

18. J'allais _____ rentrer.

19. Mes parents comptent _____ faire un voyage

20. Je vous propose _____ écouter.

21. Je me souviens _____ l'avoir vu.

22. Nous nous amusons _____ le taquiner (*tease*).

23. Je tiens _____ vous remercier pour votre gentillesse.

24. Il a fait semblant _____ ne pas nous voir.

25. As-tu le temps _____ m'aider pour mes devoirs?

26. Les enfants autistes ont du mal _____ communiquer.

27. Tu as beau _____ chercher ton portefeuille, tu ne le trouveras pas.

28. Les brins de muguet sont censés _____ porter chance.

29. Il faudra _____ se mettre au travail.

30. Elle a failli _____ avoir un accident.

Faites des phrases personnelles avec les verbes suivants en utilisant une construction verbe + verbe. *Mettez une preposition (à ou de/d') entre les deux verbes si c'est nécessaire.*

Exemple: oublier: *Les enfants ont oublié de dire merci.*

1. espérer _____

2. apprendre _____

3. refuser _____

4. avoir du mal _____

5. vouloir _____

6. il faut _____

7. pouvoir _____

8. (ne pas) avoir le temps _____

9. avoir envie _____

10. devoir _____

11. aller _____

12. regretter _____

13. aimer _____

14. hésiter _____

15. savoir _____

16. décider _____

17. aider _____

18. avoir besoin _____

The infinitive is used as the object of an adjectival phrase.

1. The infinitive following an adjective is preceded by **de**.

◆ The following common **être** + *adjective* expressions (partial list)

être content(e) de *to be satisfied to*
être déçu(e) de *to be disappointed to*
être désolé(e) de *to be sorry to*
être enchanté(e) de *to be delighted to*
être fier (fière) de *to be proud to*
être forcé(e) de *to be forced to*
être heureux (heureuse) de *to be happy to*
être libre de *to be free to*
être obligé(e) de *to be forced to, have to*
être (im)patient(e) de *to be (im)patient, anxious to*
être ravi(e) de *to be delighted to*
être reconnaissant(e) à qn de *to be thankful to sb for . . . -ing*
être satisfait(e) de *to be satisfied to*
être sûr(e) de *to be sure of . . . -ing*
être surpris(e) de *to be surprised to*
être triste de *to be sad to*

Il est *content d'avoir gagné* le prix.   *He is happy to have won the prize.*
Je suis *ravi/enchanté de* vous **connaître**.   *I am delighted to meet you.*
Vous êtes *libre de* **dire** ce que vous pensez.   *You are free to say what you think.*
Je vous suis *reconnaissant de* m'**avoir embauché**.   *I am grateful to you for having hired me.*

◆ After the impersonal **il est** + *adjective*

il est bon **de**	*it is good to*
il est dangereux **de**	*it is dangerous to*
il est défendu **de** / il est interdit **de**	*it is forbidden to*
il est difficile (à qn) **de**	*it is difficult (for sb) to*
il est dur **de**	*it is hard to*
il est facile **de**	*it is easy to*
il est important **de**	*it is important to*
il est nécessaire **de**	*it is necessary to*
il est (im)possible **de**	*it is (im)possible to*
il est (in)utile **de**	*it is useful (useless) to*

*Il **est interdit de** marcher* sur la pelouse.	*It's forbidden to walk on the grass.*
*Il **est difficile d'apprendre** une langue étrangère.*	*It's difficult to learn a foreign language.*

Note: In informal French, **ce (c')** + **être** (+ *adjective* + **de**) frequently replaces the impersonal **il** + **être** (+ *adjective* + **de**).

*C'est **interdit de** fumer.*	*It's forbidden to smoke.*
*C'est **dur de** plaire* à tout le monde.	*It's hard to please everyone.*

EXERCICE
12·22

Comment dit-on en français?

1. We had to do it. _____

2. I am sorry to disturb you (*pol.*). _____

3. He is sad he forgot the appointment. _____

4. I am delighted to make your (*pol.*) acquaintance. _____

5. It is forbidden to park here. _____

6. It is useful to know a foreign language. _____

7. It is easy to learn French. _____

8. It is dangerous to drive without a seat belt. _____

---

2. The infinitive following an *adjective* is preceded by the preposition **à**

◆ when the subject (noun or pronoun) of the sentence or clause *precedes* the infinitive.

Cette voiture est difficile *à réparer.*	*This car is difficult to repair.*

◆ when **ce (c')** + **être** + *adjective* refers to a previously mentioned idea, i.e., is the speaker's reaction to what has already been said.

C'est bon à savoir.	*That's good to know.*
C'est impossible à dire.	*That's impossible to say.*

◆ when the infinitive follows one of these adjectives and past participles (partial list).

être autorisé(e) à *to be authorized to*

être déterminé(e) à *to be determined to*

être habitué(e) à *to be used to . . . -ing*

être lent(e) à *to be slow in . . . -ing*

être long(ue) à *to take a long time to*

être occupé(e) à *to be busy (doing)*

être prêt(e) à *to be ready/prepared/willing to*

Je *suis habitué à* travailler dur.	*I am used to working hard.*
C'est *long à* faire.	*It takes a long time to do it.*
Elle *est occupée à* nettoyer sa chambre.	*She is busy cleaning her room.*

◆ after **(le) seul, (la) seule, (les) seuls, (les) seules,** and after **nombreux.**

Vous êtes *le seul à* me comprendre.	*You are the only one who understands me.*
Les gens sont *nombreux à* être inquiets.	*Numerous people are worried.*

◆ after an *ordinal number* (**le premier, la première, les premiers, les premières, le/la deuxième,** etc.) and after **le dernier, la dernière, les derniers, les dernières** with or without a noun.

Nous sommes *les premiers à* arriver et *les derniers à* partir.	*We are the first to arrive and the last to leave.*

Note: Adjectives preceded by **trop** (*too*) or **assez** (*enough*) take **pour** before the following infinitive.

C'est *trop beau pour* être vrai.	*That's too good to be true.*
Tu es *assez grand pour* comprendre ça.	*You are old enough to understand this.*

EXERCICE
12·23

Comment dit-on en français?

1. We are ready to leave. _____

2. The taxi is slow in coming. _____

3. She is busy doing the laundry. _____

4. I am used to seeing him every day. _____

5. She was the only one who knew the answer. _____

6. You (*fam.*) are the first one (*fem.*) to contact me. _____

7. They (*fem.*) will not be the last ones to ask me that question. _____

8. He is too young to get married. _____

Remplissez les tirets avec à *ou* de/d', *selon le cas.*

1. Ils sont déçus _____ avoir perdu le match.

2. Je suis désolé _____ avoir été si long _____ te donner de mes nouvelles.

3. Je suis autorisé _____ visiter cet endroit.

4. Elle est fière _____ avoir obtenu la meilleure note.

5. Je suis impatient _____ te voir.

6. Ce serait trop long _____ expliquer.

7. Il est impossible _____ prédire l'avenir.

8. Quand est-ce qu'il va y avoir un tremblement de terre dans cette région? —C'est impossible _____ prédire.

9. Suivez mon conseil! —C'est plus facile _____ dire qu' _____ faire!

10. Elle est triste _____ le voir partir.

11. C'est triste _____ voir.

12. Les hôtels sont prêts _____ vous accueillir.

13. C'est difficile _____ croire.

14. Ce plat est lourd _____ digérer.

15. Il est facile _____ réparer cette voiture.

16. En 1980, Marguerite Yourcenar devient la première femme _____ être admise à l'Académie Française.

17. Je suis toujours le dernier _____ le savoir.

18. Ils étaient nombreux _____ manifester.

19. Il était obligé _____ démissionner.

20. La décision n'était pas facile _____ prendre.

21. Il est interdit _____ fumer dans les lieux publics.

22. La dernière personne _____ l'avoir vu, c'est sa secrétaire.

23. « Il est bon _____ parler et meilleur _____ se taire. » (La Fontaine)

24. Nos voisins étaient les seuls _____ avoir la climatisation (*air conditioning*).

25. On est heureux _____ être vivants.

The infinitive is used as the object of a noun. When used after a noun, the infinitive is most often preceded by the preposition **de**, especially after **il est** or **c'est**.

le besoin de *the need to*

J'éprouve le besoin *de* **me reposer**.　　　*I feel the need to rest.*

c'est dommage de *it's a pity to*

Ce serait dommage *de* **perdre** cet argent.　　*It would be a pity to lose that money.*

ce n'est pas la peine de *there is no need to, there is no point in . . . -ing*

Ce n'est pas la peine *de* **parler** si fort.　　*There is no need to speak so loud.*

il n'est pas question de *it's out of the question to*

Il n'est pas question *de* **céder**.　　　*It's out of the question to yield.*

il est (grand) temps de *it's (about) time to*

Il est temps *de* **partir**.　　　*It's time to leave.*

c'est un plaisir de *it's a pleasure to*

C'est un plaisir *de* vous **connaître**.　　*It's a pleasure to meet you.*

c'est mon (ton, son...) tour de *it's my (your, his, her . . .) turn to*

C'est mon tour *de* **parler**.　　　*It's my turn to speak.*

The infinitive is used after **merci.** After the word **merci**, the infinitive is preceded by **de**.

Merci *de* **fumer** dehors.	*Thanks for smoking outside.*
Merci *d'***être** avec nous.	*Thanks for being with us.*
Merci *d'***avoir** appelé.	*Thanks for calling.*
Merci *de* m'**avoir** invité(e).	*Thanks for inviting me.*

Note: The *past infinitive* is used after **merci de** if the action (that someone is being thanked for) happened before the statement is made.

EXERCICE
12·25

Remplissez les tirets avec la préposition correcte.

1. Ce n'est pas le moment _____ parler.

2. C'est ton tour _____ jouer.

3. C'est un régal (*a delight*) _____ entendre ce pianiste.

4. C'est le seul moyen _____ trouver sa trace.

5. C'est l'heure _____ aller au lit.

6. La chance _____ trouver des survivants s'aménuise (*is diminishing*).

7. Ne manquez pas l'occasion _____ participer.

8. C'est une erreur _____ croire que le subjonctif ne s'utilise qu'à l'écrit.

9. Merci _____ avoir accepté notre invitation.

10. Ce n'est pas la peine _____ t'excuser.

Sébastien parle de ses projets d'avenir. Traduisez en français ce qu'il dit.

Today, I feel like talking to you about my plans for the immediate future.

After graduating, I plan to rest a little. Before beginning to work, I want to have a good time. In order to be happy in life, one must try to fulfill one's dreams. Instead of searching for a job, I prefer to go abroad for a while. I hope to see many countries. I told my friends to come with me, but they thought that it was better to go to graduate school right away. That's a shame! While they will be writing their boring term papers, I will spend my time reading good books, because I intend to learn something new every day. I will be able to listen to the radio without having to do my homework. I will no longer have to take required courses, and I will no longer be afraid to flunk a test. I will be free to do what (**ce que**) I want! Time will fly by (I will not see the time go by). My friends are going to be green with envy when they hear me describe my adventures. I am sure (that) I will always have good memories of this vacation.

I am going to let you go now. Before flying to Asia, I still have to pack my suitcases.

Good-bye! Sébastien

VOCABULAIRE			
to be green with envy	**pâlir d'envie**	to go to graduate school	**faire des études supérieures**
course	**le cours**	to graduate	**obtenir son diplôme**
to describe	**décrire**	to have good memories of	**garder un bon souvenir de**
to flunk a test	**rater un examen**	immediate	**immédiat(e)**
to fly (to a place)	**prendre l'avion pour**	a job	**un emploi**
for a while	**pendant un certain temps**	plans	**les projets** *(m.pl.)*
to fulfill	**réaliser**	required	**obligatoire**

_____

_____

_____

_____

_____

_____

_____

_____

_____

_____

_____

The imperative

One uses the imperative to give directions, orders, suggestions, and advice. *Wait!*, *Let's see!*, and *Don't forget!* are imperatives in English. In French, the imperative has three forms, the second-person singular (which is used to give a command to one person the speaker would address with **tu**), the first-person plural (which is used to give a command to two or more people including the speaker [**nous**]), and the second-person plural (which is used to give a command to one person the speaker would address with **vous** and to any group of people).

Regular forms of the imperative

To find the imperative, simply take the **tu**, **nous**, and **vous** forms of the present tense and drop the subject pronouns. This rule holds true for all regular and irregular verbs except for **être**, **avoir**, **savoir**, and **vouloir** which have irregular imperatives.

Note that with all **-er** ending verbs—as well as with the verbs **ouvrir** (*to open*), **souffrir** (*to suffer*), **offrir** (*to offer*)—you will also drop the **s** from the conjugated verb form in the second-person singular to create the imperative.

PRESENT TENSE		IMPERATIVE
tu donnes (*you give*)	→	donne! (*give!*)
nous finissons (*we finish*)	→	finissons! (*let's finish!*)
vous faites (*you do*)	→	faites! (*do!*)

Note: Regular verbs that show spelling changes in the present indicative conserve these changes in the *imperative*.

appelle!	*call!*
achète!	*buy!*
avançons!	*let's advance (go forward)!*
répète!	*repeat!*
nettoie!	*clean!*
mangeons!	*let's eat!*

Comment dit-on en français?

1. Listen (*pol.*)! _____

2. Slow down (*pol.*)! _____

3. Wait (*fam.*)! _____

4. Speak (*fam.*) louder (**plus fort**)! _____

5. Speak (*pol.*) more slowly please! _____

6. Stay (*fam.*) here! _____

7. Pay (*fam.*) the bill! _____

8. Buy (*fam.*) some stamps! _____

9. Help (*pol.*) the poor (**les pauvres [m.pl.]**)! _____

10. Answer (*pol.*) the question! _____

11. Try on (*fam.*) this coat _____

12. Continue (*pol.*) straight ahead, then turn left. _____

13. Let's eat at McDonald's (**chez MacDo**). _____

14. Come in (*pol.*)! _____

15. Get home (*fam.*) safely! _____

16. Close (*pol.*) the door! _____

17. Open (*fam.*) the window! _____

18. Ask (*pol.*) the teacher! _____

19. Let's leave! _____

20. Come here (*fam.*)! _____

21. Let's see! _____

22. Sleep (*fam.*) well! _____

23. Drink (*fam.*) your milk! _____

24. Take (*fam.*) your time! _____

25. Take (*pol.*) the second street on the right! _____

The negative imperative

To form the *negative imperative*, one surrounds the verb with the negative expression: **ne... pas, ne... jamais, ne... plus**, etc.

Ne bouge **pas**!	*Don't move!*
Ne quittez **pas**!	*Please hold! (Don't hang up! Stay on the line!)*
Ne dis **rien**!	*Don't say anything!*
Ne rions **plus**!	*Let's not laugh any more!*

EXERCICE
13·2

Comment dit-on en français?

1. Don't forget (*fam.*)! _____

2. Let's not waste (**perdre**) our time! _____

3. Don't drive (*fam.*) so (**si**) fast! _____

4. Don't work (*fam.*) so hard! _____

5. Don't disobey (*fam.*)! _____

6. Let's not travel any more! _____

7. Let's not exaggerate (anything)! _____

8. Don't drink (*pol.*) this water! _____

9. Don't say anything (*pol.*)! _____

10. Don't leave! (*fam.*)! _____

11. Don't (*pol.*) make any noise! _____

12. Don't (*pol.*) laugh! _____

Irregular forms of the imperative

Four verbs have an irregular imperative; the command forms cannot be derived from the present tense conjugation but must be memorized.

ÊTRE	AVOIR	SAVOIR	VOULOIR
sois! *be!*	aie! *have!*	sache! *know!*	(veuille!)
soyons! *let's be!*	ayons! *let's have!*	sachons! *let's know!*	(veuillons!)
soyez! *be!*	ayez! *have!*	sachez! *know!*	veuillez!

Soyez gentil avec moi!	*Be nice to me!*
Sois sage!	*Be good! (= well-behaved)*
Soyons raisonnables!	*Let's be reasonable.*
Ayons de la patience!	*Let's have patience!*
N'**ayez** pas honte!	*Don't be ashamed!*
Ne **soyez** jamais en retard!	*Never be late!*
Sachez que je suis là pour vous!	*Know that I am there for you!*

Note: Of the three imperative forms of **vouloir**, only **veuillez** is used. The others are extremely rare. The form **veuillez** is used (followed by an infinitive) in polite requests (meaning *please*) and in numerous final formulas of formal letters.

Veuillez me suivre.	*Please follow me! (Would you be so kind as to follow me?)*
Veuillez agréer, Madame/Monsieur, l'expression de mes sentiments distingués.	*Sincerely (yours),*

EXERCICE
13·3

Comment dit-on en français?

1. Be (*fam.*) careful! _____

2. Be (*pol.*) good! _____

3. Let's be courageous! _____

4. Don't be (*fam.*) afraid! _____

5. Have (*pol.*) courage! _____

6. Have (*fam.*) faith (**confiance**) in me! _____

7. Know (*fam.*) the truth! _____

8. Be (*fam.*) proud! _____

9. Don't be (*pol.*) late! _____

10. Let's not be disappointed! _____

11. Please sit down (*pol.*)! _____

12. Please leave (*pol.*) a message after the beep (**le bip**)! _____

EXERCICE
13·4

Choisissez la bonne traduction.

1. _____ Faites de beaux rêves!   a. Get well soon!

2. _____ Croisons les doigts!   b. Please wait!

3. _____ Revenons à nos moutons!   c. Take care of yourself!

4. _____ Veuillez attacher votre ceinture de sécurité!   d. Let's keep our fingers crossed!

5. _____ Veuillez patienter!   e. Please fasten your seat belts!

6. _____ Faites comme chez vous!   f. (Let's) knock on wood!

7. _____ Prends soin de toi!   g. Make yourself at home!

8. _____ Touchons du bois!

9. _____ Appelons un chat un chat!

10. _____ Soyez le/la bienvenu(e)!

11. _____ Répondez s'il vous plaît. (= R.S.V.P.)!

12. _____ Guéris vite!

13. _____ Prenez place!

14. _____ Ayez pitié de lui!

h. Let's get back to our subject!

i. Have pity on him!

j. Please respond!

k. Let's call a spade a spade!

l. Have a seat!

m. Welcome!

n. Sweet dreams!

EXERCICE

13·5

Votre ami(e) vous parle de ses problèmes. Donnez-lui des conseils. (Give advice to your friend who complains about various things.)

Exemple: J'ai faim.

Mange quelque chose!

1. Je n'ai pas d'argent. _____

2. Je suis fatigué(e). _____

3. Je suis déprimé(e) (*depressed*). _____

4. J'ai froid. _____

5. J'ai chaud. _____

6. J'ai soif. _____

7. Je voudrais maigrir. _____

8. Je ne peux pas dormir. _____

9. J'ai la grippe. _____

10. J'ai mal à la tête. _____

11. J'ai peur de l'avion. _____

12. Je suis en retard. _____

The position of object pronouns with the imperative

In the *affirmative imperative* the object pronoun follows the verb and is joined to it by a hyphen (**me** becomes **moi**).

Attendez-**moi**!   *Wait for me!*
Regarde-**nous**!   *Look at us!*

Aidez-**les**!	*Help them!*
Demande-**lui**!	*Ask him!*
Allons-**y**!	*Let's go!*
Allez-**y**!	*Go ahead!*
Excusez-**moi**!	*Excuse me!*
Tenez-**moi** au courant!	*Keep me posted!*
Prévenez-**moi**!	*Inform me!*
Faites-**moi** confiance!	*Trust me!*
Bois-**en**!	*Drink some!*
Laissez-**moi** tranquille!	*Leave me alone!*

Note: If the familiar command is followed by the pronouns **y** or **en**, all **-er** ending verbs and those **-ir** ending verbs that are conjugated like **-er** verbs in the present tense (**ouvrir, souffrir**, and **offrir**) *retain* the -**s** in the second-person singular for phonetic reasons. Don't forget to make the liaison sound [z] between the -**s** and **y** or **en**.

vas-**y**!	*go ahead!*
mange**s**-**en**!	*eat some!*
reste**s**-**y**!	*stay there!*
ouvre**s**-**en**!	*open some!*
profite**s**-**en**!	*make the most of it!*

EXERCICE 13·6

Comment dit-on en français?

1. Listen to me (*fam.*)! _____

2. Trust me (*fam.*)! _____

3. Follow me (*pol.*)! _____

4. Let's hope so (**le**)! _____

5. Ask her (*pol.*)! _____

6. Go ahead (*fam.*)! _____

7. Help me (*fam.*)! _____

8. Phone them (*pol.*)! _____

9. Pass me (*fam.*) the salt! _____

10. Buy some (*fam.*)! _____

11. Do it (*pol.*)! _____

12. Keep me posted (*fam.*)! _____

13. Excuse me (*fam.*)! _____

14. Wait for me (*fam.*)! _____

15. Look at her (*fam.*)! _____

16. Try it (*pol.*)! _____

If there are two object pronouns with the imperative form, the direct object pronoun precedes the indirect object pronoun, but **y** and **en** always come last. The pronouns are joined to each other and to the verb by a hyphen. Note that before **en**, **moi** becomes **m'**.

Dis-**le-moi**!	*Tell me!*
Donnez-**m'en**!	*Give me some!*
Donnez-**les-leur**!	*Give them to them!*
Passez-**le-moi**!	*Let me talk to him! (on the phone)*
Dites-**le-lui**!	*Say it to him!*
Emmène-**les-y**!	*Take them there!*

EXERCICE
13·7

Comment dit-on en français?

1. Give (*fam.*) it (*masc.*) to them! _____

2. Put (*pol.*) them there! _____

3. Give (*pol.*) him some! _____

4. Bring (*pol.*) it (*masc.*) to me! _____

5. Show (*pol.*) it (*fem.*) to them! _____

6. Lend (*fam.*) me some! _____

In the *negative imperative,* the object pronoun or pronouns precede the verb. There is no hyphen.

Ne **le** regarde pas!	*Don't look at him!*
N'**y** pensez plus!	*Don't think of it any more!*

EXERCICE
13·8

Comment dit-on en français?

1. Don't leave (*fam.*) (**quitter**) me! _____

2. Don't believe (*pol.*) her! _____

3. Don't disturb (*pol.*) us! _____

4. Don't answer (*fam.*) him! _____

5. Don't make (*pol.*) me laugh! _____

6. Don't listen (*fam.*) to them! _____

7. Don't lie (*fam.*) to me! _____

If there are two object pronouns in the negative imperative, they have the same order as in a normal declarative sentence.

me (m')	before	le (l')	before	lui	before	y	before	en
te (t')		la (l')		leur				
se (s')		les						
nous								
vous								

Ne **me le** dites pas!	*Don't tell (it to) me!*
Ne **m'en** parlez pas!	*Don't talk to me about it!*
Ne **vous y** mariez pas!	*Don't get married there!*

EXERCICE 13·9

Dites en français.

1. Don't (*fam.*) show them to him! _____

2. Don't (*pol.*) sell it (*fem.*) to them! _____

3. Let's not offer it (*masc.*) to her! _____

4. Don't (*fam.*) give me any! _____

5. Let's not send it (*fem.*) to her! _____

The imperative of reflexive verbs

In the *negative imperative*, the reflexive pronoun precedes the verb.

Ne **te** dépêche pas!	*Don't hurry!*
Ne **nous** dépêchons pas!	*Let's not hurry!*
Ne **vous** dépêchez pas!	*Don't hurry!*
Ne **t'en** va pas!	*Don't go away!*
Ne **nous** en allons pas!	*Let's not go away!*
Ne **vous** en allez pas!	*Don't go away!*

In the *affirmative imperative*, the reflexive pronoun follows the verb and is attached to it by a hyphen. The pronoun **te** becomes **toi** except before **en,** when it shortens to **t'**.

Dépêche-**toi**!	*Hurry!*
Dépêchons-**nous**!	*Let's hurry!*
Dépêchez-**vous**!	*Hurry!*
Assieds-**toi**!	*Sit down!*
Asseyons-**nous**!	*Let's sit down!*
Asseyez-**vous**!	*Sit down!*
Va **t'en**!	*Go away!*
Allons-**nous**-en!	*Let's go away!*
Allez-**vous**-en!	*Go away!*
Soignez-**vous** bien!	*Look after yourself!*
Méfiez-**vous**!	*Watch out! (Be careful!)*
Imaginez-**vous**!	*(Just) Imagine!*

Comment dit-on en français?

1. Sit down (*pol.*)! _____

2. Let's hurry! _____

3. Hide (*pol.*)! _____

4. Wake up (*fam.*)! _____

5. Let's introduce ourselves! _____

6. Go away (*fam.*)! _____

7. Be quiet (*fam.*)! _____

8. Have a good time (*pol.*)! _____

9. Make yourself (*pol.*) comfortable! _____

10. Remember (*fam.*)!

    a. (se rappeler) _____

    b. (se souvenir) _____

11. Relax (*pol.*)! _____

12. Don't complain (*fam.*)! _____

13. Don't make fun of me (*fam.*)! _____

14. Don't fall asleep (*pol.*)! _____

15. Don't worry (*fam.*)! _____

16. Don't get angry (*pol.*). _____

The present participle and the gerund

The formation of the present participle

The present participle ends in -**ant** in French and in -*ing* in English (*seeing, writing, working*). But do not assume that every English -*ing* form is the equivalent of a French verb form ending in -**ant**. As we shall see later in this chapter, most English -*ing* forms are *not* translated by the French present participle.

To form the *present participle*, drop the ending -**ons** from the present tense of the first-person plural (**nous**) form and replace it by -**ant**.

INFINITIVE	*NOUS* FORM		PRESENT PARTICIPLE	ENGLISH MEANING
donner	nous donnons	→	donn**ant**	*giving*
finir	nous finissons	→	finiss**ant**	*finishing*
vendre	nous vendons	→	vend**ant**	*selling*
boire	nous buvons	→	buv**ant**	*drinking*

The present participle of verbs ending in -**cer** has a **cédille**.

> **commencer** (nous commençons): commen**ç**ant   *beginning*

The present participle of verbs ending in -**ger** ends in -**eant**.

> **manger** (nous mang**e**ons) → mang**eant**   *eating*

The following three verbs have irregular present participles:

avoir	→	**ayant**	*having*
être	→	**étant**	*being*
savoir	→	**sachant**	*knowing*

Note: **Ne... pas** surrounds the present participle:

> **ne** voyant **pas**   *not seeing*

EXERCICE
14·1

Comment dit-on en français?

1. walking _____

2. reflecting _____

3. waiting _____

4. traveling _____

5. hoping _____

6. pronouncing _____

7. coming _____

8. going _____

9. believing _____

10. having _____

11. being _____

12. understanding _____

13. doing _____

14. laughing _____

15. seeing _____

16. reading _____

17. writing _____

18. fearing _____

19. not knowing (**savoir**) _____

20. wanting _____

The present participle also has a compound form, the *perfect participle* which consists of the present participle of **avoir** or **être** and the past participle of the verb.

ayant appris	*having learned*
étant parti(e)(s)	*having left*

The perfect participle is used to indicate an action which precedes the action expressed by the main verb.

Ayant beaucoup **travaillé** pendant deux mois, elle **est partie** en vacances. — *Having worked a lot for two months, she left on a vacation.*

Note: **Ne... pas** surrounds the auxiliary of the perfect participle.

n'ayant **pas** vu — *not having seen*

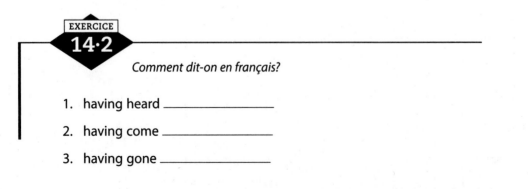

Comment dit-on en français?

1. having heard _____

2. having come _____

3. having gone _____

4. having been _____

5. having fallen _____

6. having lost _____

7. having slept _____

8. not having gone out _____

9. having chosen _____

10. not having seen _____

11. having lived (**vivre**) _____

12. having left _____

The uses of the present participle

The present participle (which is invariable) can be used alone or with the preposition **en** to form the *gerund*.

The *present participle* (without **en**) occurs mainly in written French (in the press, literature, correspondence, or administrative language). It is used

- to indicate a *cause*, a reason for something (English: *because, since*)

    Voyant le danger, le chauffeur a ralenti.   *Seeing the danger, the driver slowed down. (Since he saw the danger, . . .)*

- to replace a *relative clause* introduced by **qui** (English: *which, who*)

    J'aimerais trouver un correspondant **parlant** (= **qui** parle) grec.   *I would like to find a pen pal who speaks Greek.*

    Les passagers **ayant** (= **qui** ont) déjà **enregistré** leurs bagages peuvent se rendre directement à la porte d'embarquement.   *The passengers having (= who have) already checked in their baggage may go directly to the gate.*

EXERCICE
14·3

Traduisez en français les mots entre parenthèses, en utilisant le participe présent.

1. (*Not knowing what to say*) _____, il s'est tu.

2. (*Being hungry*) _____, il est rentré.

3. (*Being tired*) _____, je n'ai pas couru.

4. (*Wishing [***souhaiter***] to spend the weekend in your region*) _____, je vous serais reconnaissante de bien vouloir me réserver une chambre.

5. (*Not being able to finish his studies*) _____, il doit trouver un emploi.

6. (*Not wanting to disturb her*) _____, il restait silencieux.

7. (*Having American citizenship*) _____, il peut voter aux États-Unis.

8. (*Seeing the red light [**le feu rouge**]*) _____, le conducteur s'est arrêté.

9. (*The subway being on strike*) _____, il a dû prendre un taxi.

10. (*Having missed the bus*) _____, j'ai pris le métro.

11. (*Not having received my fax*) _____, il n'a pas pu finir le travail.

12. (*Having lived in Japan for ten years*) _____, elle parle couramment le japonais.

13. Elle a acheté une voiture (*which consumes little gasoline*) _____.

14. Il a percuté (*He hit*) un camion (*coming in the opposite direction [**en sens inverse**]*) _____.

15. (*The plane arriving from Madrid*) _____ a trente minutes de retard.

Other uses of the present participle

The *present participle* is also used

- to indicate the *manner* in which something is done or the accompanying circumstances

  Regardant par la fenêtre, il a vu deux policiers.   *Looking out of the window, he saw two policemen.*

- to express an action which happened *immediately before* the action of the main verb (at the beginning of the sentence)

  Arrivant à la maison, il s'est déshabillé.   *He arrived at home and then got undressed.* (= *After arriving . . .*)

- to indicate an action which *immediately follows* the main action, expressing the *result* of the main action.

  Il est parti, me **laissant** toute seule.   *He left, leaving me all alone.*

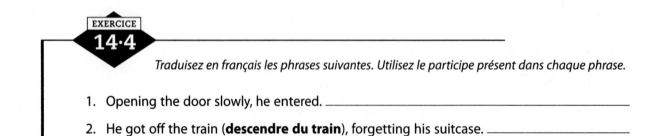

EXERCICE

14·4

Traduisez en français les phrases suivantes. Utilisez le participe présent dans chaque phrase.

1. Opening the door slowly, he entered. _____

2. He got off the train (**descendre du train**), forgetting his suitcase. _____

3. Taking his hat, he went out. _____

4. Having finished his speech, he sat down. _____

5. The bomb exploded, killing eighty people. _____

The gerund and its uses

The present participle following the preposition **en** (*while, by, on, upon*) is called the *gerund* (**le gérondif**). Unlike the present participle alone which is rarely used in conversation, the gerund frequently occurs in the written as well as in the spoken language.

♦ The *gerund* serves to express an action that happens at the *same time* as the action of the main verb. (English: *while + present participle*)

En France, il est interdit d'utiliser le téléphone portable **en roulant.**	*In France, it is forbidden to use the cell phone while driving.*
L'appétit vient **en mangeant.** (*proverb*)	*Eating stimulates the appetite. (literally: The appetite comes while eating.)*

Note: The word **tout** is sometimes used before the gerund to emphasize the simultaneity of the gerund and the main verb.

Il étudiait *tout* **en écoutant** la radio.	*He studied while (at the same time) listening to the radio.*

Tout before a gerund can also express an opposition (*although, even though*).

Tout **en sachant** que c'était dangereux, il y est allé.	*Although he knew that it was dangerous, he went there.*

♦ The *gerund* serves to indicate the *manner* or the *means* by which an action is, was, or will be completed. (English: *by + present participle*)

Ils ont appris le français **en écoutant** des chansons.	*They learned French by listening to songs.*
C'est **en forgeant** qu'on devient forgeron. (*proverb*)	*Practice makes perfect. (literally: It's by working the forge that one becomes a blacksmith.)*

♦ The *gerund* serves to indicate a *particular moment* when the main action takes, took, or will take place. (English: *when, as, on, upon + present participle*)

Faites attention **en reculant.**	*Be careful when you back up.*
Ferme la porte **en sortant.**	*Close the door as you go out.*

EXERCICE 14·5

Traduisez en français les mots entre parenthèses en utilisant le gérondif.

1. On s'instruit (*by traveling*) _____ .

2. J'ai eu la voiture moins chère (*by bargaining*) _____ .

3. Renvoyez dès aujourd'hui ce bulletin (*by using*) _____ l'enveloppe ci-jointe.

4. Roméo s'est tué (*by drinking*) _____ une potion contenant un poison.

5. Il a trouvé sa montre (*when he tidied up*) _____ ses affaires.

6. Ne le dites pas (*while laughing*) _____ .

7. Il est parti (*while crying*) _____ .

8. Je vous quitte pour ce jour, (*[while] hoping*) _____ avoir bien vite de vos nouvelles.

9. (*[By] thanking you*) _____ à l'avance, je vous prie d'agréer, cher Monsieur, l'expression de mes sentiments les meilleurs.

10. Ils sont sortis de l'appartement (*by slamming* [**claquer**] *the door*). _____ .

11. Ce qui m'a frappé (*while listening to this song*) _____ c'est la belle voix de la chanteuse.

12. (*Upon entering the house*) _____ , j'ai remarqué qu'on avait été cambriolés.

13. (*On receiving the award*) _____ elle a pleuré de joie.

14. Si nous parlions (*while having lunch*) _____ ?

15. Conduire (*while telephoning*) _____ est interdit en France.

EXERCICE
14·6

Traduisez en français en utilisant le gérondif.

1. Switch off the light as you (*pol.*) go out. _____

2. One must not speak while eating. _____

3. It is by visiting France that one learns best (**le mieux**) how to speak French. _____

_____

4. You (*pol.*) succeeded by making an effort. _____

5. I earn my living by working. _____

6. He fell when he went down the stairs. _____

7. He broke his leg while skiing. _____

8. She found this job by reading the want ads (**les petites annonces**). _____

_____

9. I lost weight (**maigrir**) by exercising (**faire du sport**) every day. _____

_____

10. Nowadays, one often telephones while walking and one eats one's meals while watching television. _____

Complétez personnellement en employant en + *participe présent.*

Exemple: Ils se promènent _____ .

Ils se promènent en bavardant.

1. Je fais mes devoirs _____ .

2. J'écoute souvent la radio _____ .

3. Quelquefois, je parle au téléphone _____ .

4. Parfois, je conduis à l'école _____ .

5. De temps en temps, je regarde la télé _____ .

6. La chanteuse joue du piano _____ .

Faites une seule phrase en employant en + *participe présent. Suivez le modèle.*

Exemple: Anne faisait la vaisselle. Elle a cassé une assiette.

En faisant la vaisselle, Anne a cassé une assiette.

1. Brice allait au théâtre. Il a rencontré un ami. _____

2. Mireille lisait le journal. Elle a découvert un article intéressant. _____

3. On regarde le journal télévisé. On se tient au courant de l'actualité. _____

4. Nous travaillons dur. Nous réussirons. _____

5. Je fais du yoga. Je me détends. _____

6. Les joueurs s'entraînent tous les jours. Ils ont gagné le match. _____

7. J'ai couru très vite. J'ai attrapé le bus. _____

8. Vous prenez la deuxième rue à droite. Vous arriverez à la gare. _____

Translation difficulties

The English -*ing* form of the verb rarely corresponds to a French verb form ending in -**ant**.

English frequently combines the verb *to be* with the present participle to form the present, past, and future continuous tenses (I am go*ing*, he was / has been / had been drink*ing*, we will be leav*ing*). These constructions have no equivalent in French where the verb **être** cannot be followed by a present participle.

When the English -*ing* form follows the verb *to be*, French does the following:

- To translate *am/is/are -ing*, French uses the *present tense* of the verb.

I am leaving.	Je **pars**.
He is writing.	Il **écrit**.

  If the speaker wants to emphasize that the action *is* in progress, the expression **être** (in the present) **en train de** + *infinitive* can be used.

He is (in the process of) recovering.	Il **est en train de** se remettre.

- To translate *was, were . . . -ing*, French uses the *imperfect tense.*

I was working in the garden when the phone rang.	Je **travaillais** dans le jardin quand le téléphone a sonné.

  If the speaker wants to emphasize that the action *was* in progress, the expression **être** (in the imperfect) **en train de** + *infinitive* can be used.

I was (in the process of) changing (clothes).	J'**étais en train de** me changer.

- To translate *have/has been -ing*, French uses

  - the **passé composé** if the action was in the past.

I have been working all day.	J'**ai travaillé** toute la journée.

  - the *present tense* if the action continues in the present (with **depuis** and **ça fait… que**).

I have been living in Paris for three years.	J'**habite** à Paris **depuis** trois ans.

- To translate *had been -ing*, French uses

  - the *pluperfect tense* if the action was completed before another past action.

He had been dating her for three years when she left him.	Il **était sorti** avec elle **pendant** trois ans quand elle l'a quitté.

  - the *imperfect tense* when the action was interrupted by another past action. (with **depuis** and **ça fait…que**).

I had been living in Paris for three years when I met you.	J'**habitais** à Paris **depuis** trois ans quand je vous ai connu.

- To translate *will be . . . -ing* French uses the *future tense.*

He will be leaving tomorrow.	Il **partira** demain.

- To translate *to be going to* + *infinitive*, French uses **aller** + *infinitive.*

  - The present tense of **aller** is used to translate *is/are going to* + *infinitive.*

He is going to leave.	Il **va partir**.

  - The imperfect tense of **aller** is used to translate *was/were going to* + *infinitive.*

He was going to leave.	Il **allait partir**.

Comment dit-on en français?

1. He is sleeping. _____

2. What are you (*pol.*) doing? _____

3. I am dying of fear. _____

4. She is in the process of sweeping the patio (**la terrasse**). _____

5. We were watching TV when he called. _____

6. He was in the process of shaving when the light went out (**s'éteindre**). _____

7. They (*fem.*) have been saying it for a long time. _____

8. How long have you (*pol.*) been living here? _____

9. I have been walking all morning. _____

10. The police stopped him because he had been speeding (**dépasser la limitation de vitesse**). _____

11. He had been living in New Orleans (**la Nouvelle-Orléans**) for forty years when the hurricane destroyed his house. _____

12. She will be celebrating (**fêter**) her thirtieth birthday. _____

French uses an *infinitive* to translate an English *-ing* form

◆ when the English *-ing* form follows a *preposition*, and when the subject of the main clause is the same as the subject of the subordinate clause. Whereas the use of the *-ing* form after a preposition is very common in English, where all prepositions (except *to*) are followed by the present participle (*without* think*ing*, *before* eat*ing*, *by* say*ing*, *upon* arriv*ing*, *while* speak*ing*, *through* work*ing*, *after* graduat*ing*, etc.), the only preposition that can precede a present participle in French is **en**. All other (French) prepositions are followed by the infinitive.

*Come and see me **before leaving**.*	Venez me voir ***avant de** partir.*
*He won **without knowing** it.*	Il a gagné ***sans** le **savoir**.*
*That goes **without saying**.*	Cela va ***sans** dire.*

◆ when the English *-ing* form follows another verb, verbal expression, adjective, or *thank you / thanks*.

*It started **raining**.*	Il a commencé à **pleuvoir**.
*It stopped **snowing**.*	Il a cessé de **neiger**.
*I don't feel like **going** out.*	Je n'ai pas envie de **sortir**.
*This film is worth **seeing**.*	Ce film vaut la peine d'**être vu**.
*She is busy **doing** the housework.*	Elle est occupée à **faire** le ménage.
*Thanks for **stopping** by.*	Merci d'**être passé**.
*Thanks for **waiting**.*	Merci de **patienter**.

◆ when the English *-ing* form is the subject or object of a verb.

Swimming is healthy.   **Nager** est bon pour la santé.

French uses a *past participle* to translate an English present participle used as an adjective and denoting a position already assumed (*sitting, lying*).

*She is **sitting** in the first row.*   Elle est **assise** au premier rang.
*He was **lying** on the floor.*   Il était **allongé** (**couché**) par terre.

But the word *standing* is translated by the adverb **debout**:

*The children remained **standing**.*   Les enfants restaient **debout**.

EXERCICE
14·10

Comment dit-on en français?

1. Come in (*pol.*) without making any noise. _____

2. That goes without saying. _____

3. Phone (*fam.*) me before leaving. _____

4. I love riding (horses). _____

5. He doesn't like flying (**prendre l'avion**). _____

6. Have you (*pol.*) finished painting? _____

7. I prefer staying here. _____

8. I saw him crossing the street. _____

9. After entering the house, he took off (**enlever**) his coat. _____

10. After getting dressed, I combed my hair. _____

11. I have trouble breathing (**respirer**). _____

12. We don't feel like playing. _____

13. He spends his time studying. _____

14. This novel isn't worth reading. _____

15. Thanks for coming. _____

16. They (*fem.*) are sitting in the last row. _____

The passive voice

A verb may be either in the active or in the passive voice. In a sentence using the *active voice*, the subject performs the action expressed by the verb and the object receives it. The following sentences are in the active voice.

> *The Chinese* **make** *these clothes.*
> (subject)   (verb)   (object)
> Les Chinois **font** ces vêtements.

In a sentence using the *passive voice*, the subject receives the action. The performer of this action is called the agent and is introduced with *by* in English and with the preposition **par** in French. If a sentence using the active voice is transformed into one using the passive voice, the object of the active sentence becomes the subject of the passive sentence, and the subject of the active sentence becomes the agent of the passive sentence. Here is the passive version of the active sentences above.

> *These clothes* **are made by** *the Chinese.*
> (subject)   (verb)   (agent)
> Ces vêtements **sont faits par** les Chinois.

Note that the agent is not always mentioned, as is the case in the following passive sentences.

> Ces vêtements **sont faits** en Chine.   *These clothes* **are made** *in China.*
> La décision **sera prise** demain.   *The decision* **will be made**
>   *tomorrow.*

The formation of the passive voice

As the examples above show, the passive voice is formed by combining the desired tense of **être** with the *past participle* of the verb in question. English does the same using the verb *to be*. Here are the forms of the passive voice in the first-person singular:

INDICATIVE		
MOOD	TENSE	
present tense	je suis invité(e)	*I am invited*
imperfect:	j'étais invité(e)	*I was being invited*
passé composé:	j'ai été invité(e)	*I was / have been invited*
recent past:	je viens d'être invité(e)	*I have just been invited*
		(continued)

283

MOOD	TENSE		
pluperfect:	j'avais été invité(e)	*I had been invited*	
Passé simple:	je fus invité(e)	*I was invited*	
simple future:	je serai invité(e)	*I will be invited*	
future perfect:	j'aurai été invité(e)	*I will have been invited*	
close future:	je vais être invité(e)	*I am going to be invited*	

CONDITIONAL

MOOD	TENSE		
present:	je serais invité(e)	*I would be invited*	
past:	j'aurais été invité(e)	*I would have been invited*	

SUBJUNCTIVE

MOOD	TENSE		
present :	(que) je sois invité(e)	*(that) I am invited*	
past:	(que) j'aie été invité(e)	*(that) I have been invited*	

INFINITIVE

MOOD	TENSE		
present:	être invité(e)(s)	*(to) be invited*	
past:	avoir été invité(e)(s)	*(to) have been invited*	

Note: The past participle of the verb in the passive voice *agrees* in gender and number with the subject of the sentence.

En France, le menu **est affiché** à l'extérieur des restaurants.	*In France, the menu **is posted** outside the restaurants.*
Les articles ne **sont** ni **repris** ni **échangés**.	*The merchandise is neither **taken back** nor **exchanged**.*
Le baccalauréat **a été créé** par Napoléon en 1808.	*The baccalaureate exam **was created** by Napoleon in 1808.*
Elle **vient d'être mutée** à Paris.	*She **has just been transferred** to Paris.*
L'Empire allemand **fut proclamé** en 1871.	*The German Empire **was proclaimed** in 1871.*
L'obélisque **avait été érigé** place de la Concorde en 1836.	*The obelisk **had been put up** on the Place de la Concorde in 1836.*
Le voyage **va être annulé**.	*The trip **is going to be canceled**.*
Les matchs **seront reportés**.	*The games **will be postponed**.*
Je regrette qu'elle **ait été renversée** par un camion.	*I regret that she **has been run over** by a truck.*

Note: Although the verb **être** may be used in any tense in the passive voice, it occurs most frequently in the present, future, and **passé composé**.

When an active sentence is transformed into a passive one, the verb **être** is always in the same tense as the verb in the original, active sentence. The past participle of this verb follows **être**. *Compare:*

Active voice:	Une voiture **a percuté** deux personnes. (verb tense: **passé composé**)	*A car **hit** two people.*
Passive voice:	Deux personnes **ont été percutées** par une voiture. (tense of **être**: **passé composé**)	*Two people **were hit** by a car.*

Mettez les phrases suivantes à la forme passive.

1. La police arrête le cambrioleur. _____

2. Richelieu a fondé l'Académie Française. _____

3. Les ravisseurs (*The kidnappers*) ont battu les otages. _____

4. Le tramway avait écrasé le chien. _____

5. La vendeuse mettra les pantalons en solde demain. _____

6. Il est important que les ouvriers fassent le travail. _____

Comment dit-on en français?

1. The vaccine (**Le vaccin**) against rabies (**la rage**) was invented by Louis Pasteur. _____

_____

2. The movie star is followed by the photographers. _____

3. One out of every ten women (**Une femme sur dix**) is beaten by her husband. _____

_____

4. Fifty people were hired by the airline company. (*to hire* = **embaucher**) _____

_____

5. They (*masc.*) were forced to work. _____

6. In France, the death penalty (**la peine de mort**) was abolished in 1981. _____

_____

7. Some day, a cure (**un remède**) for AIDS (**le SIDA**) will be discovered. _____

_____

8. The visit has been postponed several times. _____

9. Thanksgiving is celebrated on the last Thursday in November. _____

10. The class (**Le cours**) has just been canceled. (*to cancel* = **supprimer**) _____

_____

11. Fortunately, nobody was injured in the accident. (*to injure* = **blesser**) _____

_____

12. The ATM (**Le distributeur de billets**) was damaged. _____

13. You (*pol.*) are fired. (*to fire* = **renvoyer**) _____

14. That (**Cela**) has never been done. _____

15. She hopes to be invited. _____

Écrivez des phrases à la forme active et à la forme passive avec les éléments donnés. Utilisez le passé composé.

Exemple: Le roman *Madame Bovary* / écrire / Flaubert.

　　　　　 a. Flaubert a écrit le roman *Madame Bovary*.

　　　　　 b. Le roman *Madame Bovary* a été écrit par Flaubert.

1. La tour Eiffel / construire / en 1889 / Gustave Eiffel.

    a. _____

    b. _____

2. Les rayons X / découvrir / l'Allemand Roentgen.

    a. _____

    b. _____

3. « La Marseillaise »* / composer / Rouget de Lisle.

    a. _____

    b. _____

4. Le tableau « Impression, soleil levant » / peindre / Monet.

    a. _____

    b. _____

5. Le poème « Le Lac » / écrire / Lamartine.

    a. _____

    b. _____

———————
*"La Marseillaise" is the name of the French national anthem.

Est-ce vrai ou faux?

_____ 1. Le château de Versailles a été construit par le Roi Soleil.

_____ 2. La première ligne du métro parisien a été ouverte en 1900.

_____ 3. La pénicilline a été découverte par Alexander Fleming.

_____ 4. La pièce « Hamlet » a été écrite par Molière.

_____ 5. Les présidents américains sont élus par un collège électoral.

_____ 6. Le président français est élu au suffrage universel direct.

_____ 7. La Bastille a été démolie par les révolutionnaires en 1900.

_____ 8. L'écriture pour les aveugles a été inventée par Louis Braille.

_____ 9. Le roi Louis XVI et sa femme Marie Antoinette ont été guillotinés.

_____ 10. La Statue de la liberté a été sculptée par un Français.

EXERCICE

15·5

Traduisez en français le texte suivant.

During the last riots, many cars were set on fire and numerous display windows were broken by the rioters. Several stores were looted and merchandise worth several thousand euros was stolen. When the riot police arrived, one person was seriously injured by a Molotov cocktail. The victim (**La victime**) was taken to the hospital where he (**elle**) was operated on immediately. According to the doctors, he is in critical condition. A few people (**personnes** _[f.]_) were taken into custody. They (**Elles**) were sentenced to five months in jail. The juvenile delinquent who had thrown the Molotov cocktail ran away and has not yet been found by the police. As soon as the culprit is caught, he will be arrested and punished. The precise number of victims will be known in the coming days.

VOCABULAIRE	as soon as	**aussitôt que**	to operate	**opérer**
	to be in critical condition	**être dans un état critique**	to punish	**sanctionner**
			riot police	**les CRS** _(m.pl.)_
	to break	**briser**	rioter	**l'émeutier** _(m.)_
	to catch	**attraper**	riots	**les émeutes** _(f.pl.)_
	the culprit	**le/la coupable**	to run away	**s'enfuir**
	display window	**la vitrine**	to sentence	**condamner**
	during	**lors de**	seriously	**grièvement**
	in the coming days	**dans les jours qui viennent**	to set on fire	**incendier**
			to take (to the hospital)	**transporter (à l'hôpital)**
	juvenile delinquent	**le/la jeune délinquant(e)**	to take into custody	**interpeller**
	to loot	**piller**		
	merchandise	**les marchandises** _(m.pl.)_	to throw	**lancer**
			worth	**d'une valeur de**
	a Molotov cocktail	**un cocktail Molotov**		

_____

_____

_____

_____

_____
_____
_____
_____

The uses of the passive voice

If the agent of the passive sentence is expressed, it is introduced by **par**, sometimes by **de** (English: _by_). **Par** is used with verbs expressing _physical action_.

Il a été **mordu par** un chien.	_He was bitten **by** a dog._

De is generally used instead of **par** with verbs indicating a _state_ (rather than an action), such as **aimer, adorer, détester, admirer, respecter, apprécier, connaître**, etc.

Elle est **aimée de** nous tous.	_She is liked **by** us all._
Les boulangers français sont très **appréciés des** Anglais.	_French bakers are much appreciated **by** the English._

EXERCICE
15·6

Est-ce par _ou_ de? _Traduisez en français._

1. The thief is already known _by_ the police. _____

2. My backpack was stolen _by_ a hoodlum (**un voyou**). _____

3. Our secretary will always be appreciated _by_ everybody. _____

4. We were punished _by_ the teacher. _____

5. This man is respected _by_ all. _____

6. President Kennedy was very admired _by_ the French. _____

Translation difficulties

Whereas in English, any object (direct or indirect) of an active sentence can become the subject of a passive sentence, French only allows a _direct object_ to become the subject of a passive sentence. Verbs that take an _indirect object_ (remember that a noun object is indirect when it is preceded by the preposition **à**), such as **téléphoner** (_to call_), **demander** (_to ask_), **répondre** (_to answer_), are never used in a passive construction. Therefore, common English statements such as "I was told / asked / allowed / given / offered / promised," cannot be translated literally into French. _Compare:_

Active voice:	_He answered the letter._	Il a répondu **à** la lettre.
Passive voice:	_The letter was answered by him._	impossible in French

| | Active voice: | *They offered Paul a job.* | Ils ont offert un emploi **à** Paul. |
| | Passive voice: | *Paul was offered a job by them.* | impossible in French |

Since in French the active verb must take a direct object to make a passive construction possible, verbs such as **donner** (*to give*), **écrire** (*to write*), **envoyer** (*to send*), **expliquer** (*to explain*), **montrer** (*to show*), **offrir** (*to offer*), **permettre** (*to allow*), **promettre** (*to promise*), etc., which can take two objects, one direct (a thing) and one indirect (a person), allow only a thing to become the subject of a passive sentence.

Of the two objects in the active sentence **On offrira *une collation aux* passagers** (*One [They] will offer a snack to the passengers*), only the direct object (**une collation**) can become the subject of a passive sentence:

Une collation **sera offerte** aux passagers.   *A snack will be offered to the passengers.*

In English, one can also say: "The passengers will be offered a snack." In French, this is not possible, because **passagers** is an indirect object in the active sentence. Note also that **on** cannot become the agent of a passive sentence. One cannot say "**par on**."

EXERCICE
15·7

Traduisez les phrases suivantes en utilisant le passif. Si le passif n'est pas possible en français, écrivez « impossible ».

1. She was not invited. _____

2. They (*masc.*) will be laid off. (*to lay sb off* = **licencier qn**) _____

3. The deadline will be postponed by a week. (*to postpone sth* = **repousser** qch) _____

_____

4. The shop was just closed. _____

5. This novel was written by Balzac. _____

6. The president is going to be elected by the French. (*to elect sb* = **élire qn**) _____

_____

7. We were told to leave. (*to tell sb sth* = **dire qch à qn**) _____

8. They (*fem.*) were promised a reward. _____

9. A reward was promised to them. _____

10. Numerous flights have been cancelled. (*to cancel sth* = **annuler qch**) _____

_____

11. The TV program (**L'émission [f.] de télévision**) was interrupted. (*to interrupt sth* =

interrompre qch) _____

12. She was mugged by a stranger. (*to mug sb* = **agresser qn**) _____

_____

Traduisez en français les phrases suivantes en utilisant le passif. Si le passif n'est pas possible en français, écrivez « impossible ».

1. New snowfalls (**De nouvelles chutes [f.pl.] de neige**) are expected in the evening. (*to expect sth* = **attendre qch**) _____

2. She was given a gift by her sister. _____

3. I was offered a job. _____

4. The cat was run over by a bus (*to run over sb/sth* = **écraser qn/qch**). _____

_____

5. Were you (*pol.*) allowed to smoke? _____

6. The plane has been hijacked by terrorists (*to hijack sth* = **détourner qch**). _____

_____

7. Credit cards are not accepted in this restaurant. _____

8. The demonstration was forbidden (*to forbid sth* = **interdire qch**). _____

_____

9. The lyrics (**Les paroles [f.pl.]**) of this song were written by the singer. _____

_____

10. Three people were taken hostage (*to take sb hostage* = **prendre qn en otage**). _____

_____

11. The principal (**Le proviseur**) was hit by a student (*to hit sb* = **frapper qn**). _____

_____

12. We have been lied to (*to lie to sb* = **mentir à qn**). _____

Translating the English passive voice into French

Although the passive voice can be found in French (especially in the press and in the news on television), passive constructions are used less frequently in French than in English. French generally prefers the active voice, particularly in everyday conversation.

Here is how an English passive sentence is likely to be rendered into French:

1. If the agent of the action is expressed. French *frequently* uses the *active* instead of the passive voice (unless the agent who performs the action needs to be emphasized). *Compare:*

English (passive voice)   The mail **is distributed** by the mailman.
French (active voice)   Le facteur **distribue** le courrier.
                     The mailman distributes the mail.

French *always* uses the *active voice* with verbs that do not allow a passive construction, i.e., with verbs that take an *indirect object*. *Compare:*

English (passive voice)	*I **was asked** by the police officer to stay in the car.*
French (active voice)	Le policier **m'a demandé** de rester dans la voiture.
	The police officer asked me to stay in the car.

2. If the agent of the action is *not* expressed. French *frequently* uses **on** (= *one*) + *active voice* instead of the passive voice.

| *He was kidnapped.* | On l'a kidnappé. |
| *French is spoken here.* | On parle français ici. |

French *always* uses **on** (= *one*) + *active voice* with verbs that do not allow a passive construction.

They were told to wait.	On **leur** a dit d'attendre.
You are wanted on the phone.	On **vous** demande au téléphone.
She was given a raise.	On **lui** a donné une augmentation.

Note: **On** can be used only if the unexpressed agent refers implicitly to a *person.* If this agent refers implicitly to a thing, the passive voice must be used.

| *The valley was flooded.* | La vallée a été inondée. |

EXERCICE 15·9

Comment dit-on en français?

1. We were asked to leave by the police. _____

2. We were asked to leave. _____

3. The question was answered. _____

4. The question was answered by the teacher. _____

5. They (*masc.*) were promised a good salary. _____

6. They (*masc.*) were promised a good salary by the boss. _____

7. He was allowed to stay. _____

8. We have been lied to. _____

9. She will be remembered (*to remember sb* = **se souvenir de qn**). _____

10. Were you (*pol.*) given a warning (**un avertissement**)? _____

11. Chinese is taught in these high schools. _____

12. We were advised to stay at home. _____

If the performer of the action (i.e., the agent) is not expressed, and if the subject of the passive verb is a *thing*, French frequently uses a *reflexive construction* (**se** + *verb*) to translate an English passive sentence.

*French **is spoken** in Quebec.*	Le français **se parle** au Québec.
*Strawberries **are harvested** in June.*	Les fraises **se récoltent** en juin.
*How **is** that **spelled**?*	Comment (est-ce que) ça **s'écrit**?

The passive voice   **291**

The passive voice **is used** more often in English than in French.	Le passif **s'emploie** plus souvent en anglais qu'en français.
*Revenge is a dish (which **is**) best **served** cold.*	*La vengeance est un plat qui **se mange** froid.*

Note that the reflexive construction is used only in the third-person singular and plural (**se**), and that usually a well-known fact or habit is stated in such sentences.

EXERCICE
15·10

Traduisez en français en utilisant se + verbe.

1. These cars sell (are sold) like hotcakes (**des petits pains**). _____

2. That is no longer done. _____

3. White wine is drunk chilled (**frais**). _____

4. Portuguese is spoken in Brazil (**au Brésil**). _____

5. How is that spelled (= written)? _____

6. It is written like it is pronounced. _____

EXERCICE
15·11

Est-ce vrai ou faux?

_____ 1. "I visit my parents" se traduit par « je visite mes parents ».

_____ 2. En France, le fromage se mange avant le dessert.

_____ 3. Les apéritifs se prennent après le repas.

_____ 4. « Manger le petit déjeuner » ne se dit pas.

_____ 5. Le « l » du mot « fusil » ne se prononce pas.

_____ 6. Le vin blanc se boit avec les fruits de mer.

_____ 7. Les journaux se vendent dans les kiosques.

_____ 8. Les vrais amis se comptent sur les doigts d'une seule main.

Joan of Arc and the Hundred Years War. Traduisez en français le texte suivant.

It is the beginning of the fifteenth century. A big part of France is occupied by the English. Is France going to become English? The French are waiting for a miracle. At this time, Joan of Arc appears. She had been told by voices to save her country. She therefore leaves her home town in order to go and see king Charles. She is offered a horse by some peasants who feel sorry for her. She has a lot of trouble convincing (to convince) Charles of her mission. But in the end, she is given the soldiers (whom [**dont**]) she needs. Many French think that she is sent by God. The city of Orléans is liberated, and the king crowned in Reims, thanks to Joan of Arc. After the coronation, Joan continues to fight. When she tries to take Paris, she is wounded. Then, she is betrayed, made a prisoner and accused of witchcraft. She is interrogated by judges who are convinced that she is inspired by the devil. At the end of the trial, she is condemned to death. She is only nineteen years old when she is burned alive in Rouen in 1421.

    Today, Joan of Arc is the patron saint of France.

VOCABULAIRE			
alive	**vif, vive**	the Hundred Year's War	**la Guerre de Cent Ans**
to appear	**apparaître**		
to be convinced	**être convaincu(e)**	to inspire	**inspirer**
beginning	**le début**	to interrogate	**interroger**
to betray	**trahir**	to liberate	**libérer**
to burn	**brûler**	patron saint *(f.)*	**la sainte patronne**
to condemn to death	**condamner à mort**	peasant	**le paysan, la paysanne**
to convince	**convaincre**	prisoner	**le prisonnier, la prisonnière**
coronation	**le sacre**		
to crown	**couronner**	to save	**sauver**
the devil	**le diable**	soldier	**le soldat**
to feel sorry for sb	**avoir pitié de qn**	thanks to	**grâce à**
to fight	**se battre**	trial	**le procès**
to go and see	**aller voir**	witchcraft	**la sorcellerie**

_____

_____

_____

_____

_____

_____

_____

_____

_____

APPENDIX A
Numbers, dates, time

Cardinal numbers

0	zéro	41	quarante et un	82	quatre-vingt-deux
1	un	42	quarante-deux	83	quatre-vingt-trois
2	deux	43	quarante-trois	84	quatre-vingt-quatre
3	trois	44	quarante-quatre	85	quatre-vingt-cinq
4	quatre	45	quarante-cinq	86	quatre-vingt-six
5	cinq	46	quarante-six	87	quatre-vingt-sept
6	six	47	quarante-sept	88	quatre-vingt-huit
7	sept	48	quarante-huit	89	quatre-vingt-neuf
8	huit	49	quarante-neuf	90	quatre-vingt-dix
9	neuf	50	cinquante	91	quatre-vingt-onze
10	dix	51	cinquante et un	92	quatre-vingt-douze
11	onze	52	cinquante-deux	93	quatre-vingt-treize
12	douze	53	cinquante-trois	94	quatre-vingt-quatorze
13	treize	54	cinquante-quatre	95	quatre-vingt-quinze
14	quatorze	55	cinquante-cinq	96	quatre-vingt-seize
15	quinze	56	cinquante-six	97	quatre-vingt-dix-sept
16	seize	57	cinquante-sept	98	quatre-vingt-dix-huit
17	dix-sept	58	cinquante-huit	99	quatre-vingt-dix-neuf
18	dix-huit	59	cinquante-neuf	100	cent
19	dix-neuf	60	soixante	101	cent un
20	vingt	61	soixante et un	102	cent deux
21	vingt et un	62	soixante-deux		
22	vingt-deux	63	soixante-trois	120	cent vingt
23	vingt-trois	64	soixante-quatre	190	cent quatre-vingt-dix
24	vingt-quatre	65	soixante-cinq		
25	vingt-cinq	66	soixante-six	200	deux cents
26	vingt-six	67	soixante-sept	201	deux cent un
27	vingt-sept	68	soixante-huit		
28	vingt-huit	69	soixante-neuf	302	trois cent deux
29	vingt-neuf	70	soixante-dix	400	quatre cents
30	trente	71	soixante et onze	500	cinq cents
31	trente et un	72	soixante-douze	600	six cents
32	trente-deux	73	soixante-treize	700	sept cents
33	trente-trois	74	soixante-quatorze	800	huit cents
34	trente-quatre	75	soixante-quinze	900	neuf cents
35	trente-cinq	76	soixante-seize		
36	trente-six	77	soixante-dix-sept	1000	mille
37	trente-sept	78	soixante-dix-huit	1001	mille un
38	trente-huit	79	soixante-dix-neuf	1100	mille cent (onze cents)
39	trente-neuf	80	quatre-vingts	1200	mille deux cents
40	quarante	81	quatre-vingt-un	1900	mille neuf cents

2000	deux mille	
1.000.000	un million	
2.000.000	deux millions	
1.000.000.000	un milliard (*English: a billion*)	
1.000.000.000.000	un billion (*English: a trillion*)	

Ordinal numbers

first	1er	premier (première)
second	2e	deuxième, second(e)
third	3e	troisième
fourth	4e	quatrième
fifth	5e	cinquième
sixth	6e	sixième
seventh	7e	septième
eighth	8e	huitième
ninth	9e	neuvième
tenth	10e	dixième
eleventh	11e	onzième
twentieth	20e	vingtième
twenty-first	21e	vingt-et-unième
one hundredth	100e	centième

Note: In titles and dates, cardinal numbers are always used, except for *the first*.

Louis the Fourteenth	Louis XIV (Louis Quatorze)
Napoleon the First	Napoléon I (Napoléon Premier)
(on) the third of March	le 3 (trois) mars
(on) the first of April	le 1er (premier) avril

Days of the week

Monday	lundi
Tuesday	mardi
Wednesday	mercredi
Thursday	jeudi
Friday	vendredi
Saturday	samedi
Sunday	dimanche

Note that *on* with weekdays is not translated into French:

on Monday	lundi

except if the day is repeated:

on Mondays (= every Monday)	**le** lundi
on Tuesdays (= every Tuesday)	**le** mardi

Months of the year

January	janvier	*July*	juillet
February	février	*August*	août
March	mars	*September*	septembre
April	avril	*October*	octobre
May	mai	*November*	novembre
June	juin	*December*	décembre

Note that the days of the week and the months are not capitalized in French. The French equivalent of *in* before the name of a month is **en**:

in January   en janvier

Seasons of the year

spring	le printemps
summer	l'été
fall	l'automne
winter	l'hiver
in spring	au printemps
in summer	en été
in the fall	en automne
in winter	en hiver

Time

What time is it?	Quelle heure est-il?
It is one o'clock.	Il est une heure.
2 h	deux heures
3 h 10	trois heures dix
4 h 50	cinq heures moins dix
6 h 15	six heures et quart
8 h 30	huit heures et demie
9 h 45	dix heures moins le quart
noon	midi
midnight	minuit
at one o'clock	à une heure

Note: The French equivalent of A.M. is **du matin** (*literally: of the morning*).

At six A.M.   À six heures du matin.

The equivalent of P.M. is **de l'après-midi** (*literally: of the afternoon*) for the afternoon hours, and **du soir** (*literally: of the evening*) for the evening hours.

From two P.M. until nine P.M.   De deux heures de l'après-midi à neuf heures du soir.

The 24-hour system is also used, especially for schedules.

one P.M.	treize heures
five P.M.	dix-sept heures
eight P.M.	vingt heures

APPENDIX B
Verb tables

Regular verbs
Regular *-er* ending verbs

travailler (*to work*)

Present indicative	je travaille, tu travailles, il/elle/on travaille, nous travaillons, vous travaillez, ils/elles travaillent
Imperative	travaille, travaillons, travaillez
Passé composé	j'ai travaillé, tu as travaillé, il/elle/on a travaillé, nous avons travaillé, vous avez travaillé, ils/elles ont travaillé
Imperfect	je travaillais, tu travaillais, il/elle/on travaillait, nous travaillions, vous travailliez, ils/elles travaillaient
Pluperfect	j'avais travaillé, tu avais travaillé, il/elle/on avait travaillé, nous avions travaillé, vous aviez travaillé, ils/elles avaient travaillé
Passé simple	je travaillai, tu travaillas, il/elle/on travailla, nous travaillâmes, vous travaillâtes, ils/elles travaillèrent
Future	je travaillerai, tu travailleras, il/elle/on travaillera, nous travaillerons, vous travaillerez, ils/elles travailleront
Futur antérieur	j'aurai travaillé, tu auras travaillé, il/elle/on aura travaillé, nous aurons travaillé, vous aurez travaillé, ils/elles auront travaillé
Present conditional	je travaillerais, tu travaillerais, il/elle/on travaillerait, nous travaillerions, vous travailleriez, ils/elles travailleraient
Past conditional	j'aurais travaillé, tu aurais travaillé, il/elle/on aurait travaillé, nous aurions travaillé, vous auriez travaillé, ils/elles auraient travaillé
Present subjunctive	que je travaille, que tu travailles, qu'il/elle/on travaille, que nous travaillions, que vous travailliez, qu'ils/elles travaillent
Past subjunctive	que j'aie travaillé, que tu aies travaillé, qu'il/elle/on ait travaillé, que nous ayons travaillé, que vous ayez travaillé, qu'ils/elles aient travaillé

Regular -ir ending verbs

finir (*to finish*)

Present indicative	je finis, tu finis, il/elle/on finit, nous finissons, vous finissez, ils/elles finissent
Imperative	finis, finissons, finissez
Passé composé	j'ai fini, tu as fini, il/elle/on a fini, nous avons fini, vous avez fini, ils/elles ont fini
Imperfect	je finissais, tu finissais, il/elle/on finissait, nous finissions, vous finissiez, ils/elles finissaient
Pluperfect	j'avais fini, tu avais fini, il/elle/on avait fini, nous avions fini, vous aviez fini, ils/elles avaient fini
Passé simple	je finis, tu finis, il/elle/on finit, nous finîmes, vous finîtes, ils/elles finirent
Future	je finirai, tu finiras, il/elle/on finira, nous finirons, vous finirez, ils/elles finiront
Futur antérieur	j'aurai fini, tu auras fini, il/elle/on aura fini, nous aurons fini, vous aurez fini, ils/elles auront fini
Present conditional	je finirais, tu finirais, il/elle/on finirait, nous finirions, vous finiriez, ils/elles finiraient
Past conditional	j'aurais fini, tu aurais fini, il/elle/on aurait fini, nous aurions fini, vous auriez fini, ils/elles auraient fini
Present subjunctive	que je finisse, que tu finisses, qu'il/elle/on finisse, que nous finissions, que vous finissiez, qu'ils/elles finissent
Past subjunctive	que j'aie fini, que tu aies fini, qu'il/elle/on ait fini, que nous ayons fini, que vous ayez fini, qu'ils/elles aient fini

Regular -re ending verbs

vendre (*to sell*)

Present indicative	je vends, tu vends, il/elle/on vend, nous vendons, vous vendez, ils/elles vendent
Imperative	vends, vendons, vendez
Passé composé	j'ai vendu, tu as vendu, il/elle/on a vendu, nous avons vendu, vous avez vendu, ils/elles ont vendu
Imperfect	je vendais, tu vendais, il/elle/on vendait, nous vendions, vous vendiez, ils/elles vendaient
Pluperfect	j'avais vendu, tu avais vendu, il/elle/on avait vendu, nous avions vendu, vous aviez vendu, ils/elles avaient vendu
Passé simple	je vendis, tu vendis, il/elle/on vendit, nous vendîmes, vous vendîtes, ils/elles vendirent
Future	je vendrai, tu vendras, il/elle/on vendra, nous vendrons, vous vendrez, ils/elles vendront
Futur antérieur	j'aurai vendu, tu auras vendu, il/elle/on aura vendu, nous aurons vendu, vous aurez vendu, ils/elles auront vendu
Present conditional	je vendrais, tu vendrais, il/elle/on vendrait, nous vendrions, vous vendriez, ils/elles vendraient
Past conditional	j'aurais vendu, tu aurais vendu, il/elle/on aurait vendu, nous aurions vendu, vous auriez vendu, ils/elles auraient vendu
Present subjunctive	que je vende, que tu vendes, qu'il/elle/on vende, que nous vendions, que vous vendiez, qu'ils/elles vendent
Past subjunctive	que j'aie vendu, que tu aies vendu, qu'il/elle/on ait vendu, que nous ayons vendu, que vous ayez vendu, qu'ils/elles aient vendu

Regular reflexive verbs

se coucher (*to go to bed*)

Present indicative	je me couche, tu te couches, il/elle/on se couche, nous nous couchons, vous vous couchez, ils/elles se couchent
Imperative	couche-toi, couchons-nous, couchez-vous
Passé composé	je me suis couché(e), tu t'es couché(e), il/elle/on s'est couché(e), nous nous sommes couché(e)s, vous vous êtes couché(e)(s), ils/elles se sont couché(e)s
Imperfect	je me couchais, tu te couchais, il/elle/on se couchait, nous nous couchions, vous vous couchiez, ils/elles se couchaient
Pluperfect	je m'étais couché(e), tu t'étais couché(e), il/elle/on s'était couché(e), nous nous étions couché(e)s, vous vous étiez couché(e)(s), ils/elles s'étaient couché(e)s
Passé simple	je me couchai, tu te couchas, il/elle/on se coucha, nous nous couchâmes, vous vous couchâtes, ils/elles se couchèrent
Future	je me coucherai, tu te coucheras, il/elle/on se couchera, nous nous coucherons, vous vous coucherez, ils/elles se coucheront
Futur antérieur	je me serai couché(e), tu te seras couché(e), il/elle/on se sera couché(e), nous nous serons couché(e)s, vous vous serez couché(e)(s), ils/elles se seront couché(e)s
Present conditional	je me coucherais, tu te coucherais, il/elle/on se coucherait, nous nous coucherions, vous vous coucheriez, ils/elles se coucheraient
Past conditional	je me serais couché(e), tu te serais couché(e), il/elle/on se serait couché(e), nous nous serions couché(e)s, vous vous seriez couché(e)(s) ils/elles se seraient couché(e)s
Present subjunctive	que je me couche, que tu te couches, qu'il/elle/on se couche, que nous nous couchions, que vous vous couchiez, qu' ils/elles se couchent
Past subjunctive	que je me sois couché(e), que tu te sois couché(e), qu'il/elle/on se soit couché(e), que nous nous soyons couché(e)s, que vous vous soyez couché(e)(s), qu'ils/elles se soient couché(e)s

Regular verbs with spelling changes

acheter (*to buy*)

Present indicative	j'achète, tu achètes, il/elle/on achète, nous achetons, vous achetez, ils/elles achètent
Imperative	achète, achetons, achetez
Passé composé	j'ai acheté, tu as acheté, il/elle/on a acheté, nous avons acheté, vous avez acheté, ils/elles ont acheté
Imperfect	j'achetais, tu achetais, il/elle/on achetait, nous achetions, vous achetiez, ils/elles achetaient
Pluperfect	j'avais acheté, tu avais acheté, il/elle/on avait acheté, nous avions acheté, vous aviez acheté, ils/elles avaient acheté
Passé simple	j'achetai, tu achetas, il/elle/on acheta, nous achetâmes, vous achetâtes, ils/elles achetèrent
Future	j'achèterai, tu achèteras, il/elle/on achètera, nous achèterons, vous achèterez, ils/elles achèteront
Futur antérieur	j'aurai acheté, tu auras acheté, il/elle/on aura acheté, nous aurons acheté, vous aurez acheté, ils/elles auront acheté
Present conditional	j'achèterais, tu achèterais, il/elle/on achèterait, nous achèterions, vous achèteriez, ils/elles achèteraient

Past conditional	j'aurais acheté, tu aurais acheté, il/elle/on aurait acheté, nous aurions acheté, vous auriez acheté, ils/elles auraient acheté
Present subjunctive	que j'achète, que tu achètes, qu'il/elle/on achète, que nous achetions, que vous achetiez, qu'ils/elles achètent
Past subjunctive	que j'aie acheté, que tu aies acheté, qu'il/elle/on ait acheté, que nous ayons acheté, que vous ayez acheté, qu'ils/elles aient acheté

Verbs conjugated like **acheter**: **amener** (*to bring*), **emmener** (*to take*), **peser** (*to weigh*)

appeler (*to call*)

Present indicative	j'appelle, tu appelles, il/elle/on appelle, nous appelons, vous appelez, ils/elles appellent
Imperative	appelle, appelons, appelez
Passé composé	j'ai appelé, tu as appelé, il/elle/on a appelé, nous avons appelé, vous avez appelé, ils/elles ont appelé
Imperfect	j'appelais, tu appelais, il/elle/on appelait, nous appelions, vous appeliez, ils/elles appelaient
Pluperfect	j'avais appelé, tu avais appelé, il/elle/on avait appelé, nous avions appelé, vous aviez appelé, ils/elles avaient appelé
Passé simple	j'appelai, tu appelas, il/elle/on appela, nous appelâmes, vous appelâtes, ils/elles appelèrent
Future	j'appellerai, tu appelleras, il/elle/on appellera, nous appellerons, vous appellerez, ils/elles appelleront
Futur antérieur	j'aurai appelé, tu auras appelé, il/elle/on aura appelé, nous aurons appelé, vous aurez appelé, ils/elles auront appelé
Present conditional	j'appellerais, tu appellerais, il/elle/on appellerait, nous appellerions, vous appelleriez, ils/elles appelleraient
Past conditional	j'aurais appelé, tu aurais appelé, il/elle/on aurait appelé, nous aurions appelé, vous auriez appelé, ils/elles auraient appelé
Present subjunctive	que j'appelle, que tu appelles, qu'il/elle/on appelle, que nous appelions, que vous appeliez, qu'ils/elles appellent
Past subjunctive	que j'aie appelé, que tu aies appelé, qu'il/elle/on ait appelé, que nous ayons appelé, que vous ayez appelé, qu'ils/elles aient appelé

Verbs conjugated like **appeler**: **jeter** (*to throw*)

commencer (*to begin*)

Present indicative	je commence, tu commences, il/elle/on commence, nous commençons, vous commencez, ils/elles commencent
Imperative	commence, commençons, commencez
Passé composé	j'ai commencé, tu as commencé, il/elle/on a commencé, nous avons commencé, vous avez commencé, ils/elles ont commencé
Imperfect	je commençais, tu commençais, il/elle/on commençait, nous commencions, vous commenciez, ils/elles commençaient
Pluperfect	j'avais commencé, tu avais commencé, il/elle/on avait commencé, nous avions commencé, vous aviez commencé, ils/elles avaient commencé
Passé simple	je commençai, tu commenças, il/elle/on commença, nous commençâmes, vous commençâtes, ils/elles commencèrent
Future	je commencerai, tu commenceras, il/elle/on commencera, nous commencerons, vous commencerez, ils/elles commenceront
Futur antérieur	j'aurai commencé, tu auras commencé, il/elle/on aura commencé, nous aurons commencé, vous aurez commencé, ils/elles auront commencé

Present conditional	je commencerais, tu commencerais, il/elle/on commencerait, nous commencerions, vous commenceriez, ils/elles commenceraient
Past conditional	j'aurais commencé, tu aurais commencé, il/elle/on aurait commencé, nous aurions commencé, vous auriez commencé, ils/elles auraient commencé
Present subjunctive	que je commence, que tu commences, qu'il/elle/on commence, que nous commencions, que vous commenciez, qu'ils/elles commencent
Past subjunctive	que j'aie commencé, que tu aies commencé, qu'il/elle/on ait commencé, que nous ayons commencé, que vous ayez commencé, qu'ils/elles aient commencé

Verbs conjugated like **commencer: effacer** (*to erase*), **forcer** (*to force*), **placer** (*to place*), **remplacer** (*to replace*)

essayer (*to try*)

Present indicative	j'essaie, tu essaies, il/elle/on essaie, nous essayons, vous essayez, ils/elles essaient
Imperative	essaie, essayons, essayez
Passé composé	j'ai essayé, tu as essayé, il/elle/on a essayé, nous avons essayé, vous avez essayé, ils/elles ont essayé
Imperfect	j'essayais, tu essayais, il/elle/on essayait, nous essayions, vous essayiez, ils/elles essayaient
Pluperfect	j'avais essayé, tu avais essayé, il/elle/on avait essayé, nous avions essayé, vous aviez essayé, ils/elles avaient essayé
Passé simple	j'essayai, tu essayas, il/elle/on essaya, nous essayâmes, vous essayâtes, ils/elles essayèrent
Future	j'essaierai, tu essaieras, il/elle/on essaiera, nous essaierons, vous essaierez, ils/elles essaieront
Futur antérieur	j'aurai essayé, tu auras essayé, il/elle/on aura essayé, nous aurons essayé, vous aurez essayé, ils/elles auront essayé
Present conditional	j'essaierais, tu essaierais, il/elle/on essaierait, nous essaierions, vous essaieriez, ils/elles essaieraient
Past conditional	j'aurais essayé, tu aurais essayé, il/elle/on aurait essayé, nous aurions essayé, vous auriez essayé, ils/elles auraient essayé
Present subjunctive	que j'essaie, que tu essaies, qu'il/elle/on essaie, que nous essayions, que vous essayiez, qu'ils/elles essaient
Past subjunctive	que j'aie essayé, que tu aies essayé, qu'il/elle/on ait essayé, que nous ayons essayé, que vous ayez essayé, qu'ils/elles aient essayé

Verbs conjugated like **essayer: balayer** (*to sweep*), **payer** (*to pay*)

lever (*to lift*)

Present indicative	je lève, tu lèves, il/elle/on lève, nous levons, vous levez, ils/elles lèvent
Imperative	lève, levons, levez
Passé composé	j'ai levé, tu as levé, il/elle/on a levé, nous avons levé, vous avez levé, ils/elles ont levé
Imperfect	je levais, tu levais, il/elle/on levait, nous levions, vous leviez, ils/elles levaient
Pluperfect	j'avais levé, tu avais levé, il/elle/on avait levé, nous avions levé, vous aviez levé, ils/elles avaient levé
Passé simple	je levai, tu levas, il/elle/on leva, nous levâmes, vous levâtes, ils/elles levèrent
Future	je lèverai, tu lèveras, il/elle/on lèvera, nous lèverons, vous lèverez, ils/elles lèveront

Futur antérieur	j'aurai levé, tu auras levé, il/elle/on aura levé, nous aurons levé, vous aurez levé, ils/elles auront levé
Present conditional	je lèverais, tu lèverais, il/elle/on lèverait, nous lèverions, vous lèveriez, ils/elles lèveraient
Past conditional	j'aurais levé, tu aurais levé, il/elle/on aurait levé, nous aurions levé, vous auriez levé, ils/elles auraient levé
Present subjunctive	que je lève, que tu lèves, qu'il/elle/on lève, que nous levions, que vous leviez, qu'ils/elles lèvent
Past subjunctive	que j'aie levé, que tu aies levé, qu'il/elle/on ait levé, que nous ayons levé, que vous ayez levé, qu'ils/elles aient levé

Verbs conjugated like **lever: élever** (*to raise*), **enlever** (*to take off, kidnap*)

manger (*to eat*)

Present indicative	je mange, tu manges, il/elle/on mange, nous mangeons, vous mangez, ils/elles mangent
Imperative	mange, mangeons, mangez
Passé composé	j'ai mangé, tu as mangé, il/elle/on a mangé, nous avons mangé, vous avez mangé, ils/elles ont mangé
Imperfect	je mangeais, tu mangeais, il/elle/on mangeait, nous mangions, vous mangiez, ils/elles mangeaient
Pluperfect	j'avais mangé, tu avais mangé, il/elle/on avait mangé, nous avions mangé, vous aviez mangé, ils/elles avaient mangé
Passé simple	je mangeai, tu mangeas, il/elle/on mangea, nous mangeâmes, vous mangeâtes, ils/elles mangèrent
Future	je mangerai, tu mangeras, il/elle/on mangera, nous mangerons, vous mangerez, ils/elles mangeront
Futur antérieur	j'aurai mangé, tu auras mangé, il/elle/on aura mangé, nous aurons mangé, vous aurez mangé, ils/elles auront mangé
Present conditional	je mangerais, tu mangerais, il/elle/on mangerait, nous mangerions, vous mangeriez, ils/elles mangeraient
Past conditional	j'aurais mangé, tu aurais mangé, il/elle/on aurait mangé, nous aurions mangé, vous auriez mangé, ils/elles auraient mangé
Present subjunctive	que je mange, que tu manges, qu'il/elle/on mange, que nous mangions, que vous mangiez, qu'ils/elles mangent
Past subjunctive	que j'aie mangé, que tu aies mangé, qu'il/elle/on ait mangé, que nous ayons mangé, que vous ayez mangé, qu'ils/elles aient mangé

Verbs conjugated like **manger: changer** (*to change*), **nager** (*to swim*), **partager** (*to share*), **ranger** (*to arrange, tidy up*), **voyager** (*to travel*)

préférer (*to prefer*)

Present indicative	je préfère, tu préfères, il/elle/on préfère, nous préférons, vous préférez, ils/elles préfèrent
Imperative	préfère, préférons, préférez
Passé composé	j'ai préféré, tu as préféré, il/elle/on a préféré, nous avons préféré, vous avez préféré, ils/elles ont préféré
Imperfect	je préférais, tu préférais, il/elle/on préférait, nous préférions, vous préfériez, ils/elles préféraient
Pluperfect	j'avais préféré, tu avais préféré, il/elle/on avait préféré, nous avions préféré, vous aviez préféré, ils/elles avaient préféré
Passé simple	je préférai, tu préféras, il/elle/on préféra, nous préférâmes, vous préférâtes, ils/elles préférèrent

Future	je préférerai, tu préféreras, il/elle/on préférera, nous préférerons, vous préférerez, ils/elles préféreront
Futur antérieur	j'aurai préféré, tu auras préféré, il/elle/on aura préféré, nous aurons préféré, vous aurez préféré, ils/elles auront préféré
Present conditional	je préférerais, tu préférerais, il/elle/on préférerait, nous préférerions, vous préféreriez, ils/elles préféreraient
Past conditional	j'aurais préféré, tu aurais préféré, il/elle/on aurait préféré, nous aurions préféré, vous auriez préféré, ils/elles auraient préféré
Present subjunctive	que je préfère, que tu préfères, qu'il/elle/on préfère, que nous préférions, que vous préfériez, qu'ils/elles préfèrent
Past subjunctive	que j'aie préféré, que tu aies préféré, qu'il/elle/on ait préféré, que nous ayons préféré, que vous ayez préféré, qu'ils/elles aient préféré

Verbs conjugated like **préférer: espérer** (*to hope*), **posséder** (*to possess, own*), **répéter** (*to repeat*)

Irregular verbs

aller (*to go*)

Present indicative	je vais, tu vas, il/elle/on va, nous allons, vous allez, ils/elles vont
Imperative	va, allons, allez
Passé composé	je suis allé(e), tu es allé(e), il/elle/on est allé(e), nous sommes allé(e)s, vous êtes allé(e)(s), ils/elles sont allé(e)s
Imperfect	j'allais, tu allais, il/elle/on allait, nous allions, vous alliez, ils/elles allaient
Pluperfect	j'étais allé(e), tu étais allé(e), il/elle/on était allé(e), nous étions allé(e)s, vous étiez allé(e)(s), ils/elles étaient allé(e)s
Passé simple	j'allai, tu allas, il/elle/on alla, nous allâmes, vous allâtes, ils/elles allèrent
Future	j'irai, tu iras, il/elle/on ira, nous irons, vous irez, ils/elles iront
Futur antérieur	je serai allé(e), tu seras allé(e), il/elle/on sera allé(e), nous serons allé(e)s, vous serez allé(e)(s), ils/elles seront allé(e)s
Present conditional	j'irais, tu irais, il/elle/on irait, nous irions, vous iriez, ils/elles iraient
Past conditional	je serais allé(e), tu serais allé(e), il/elle/on serait allé(e), nous serions allé(e)s, vous seriez allé(e)(s), ils/elles seraient allé(e)s
Present subjunctive	que j'aille, que tu ailles, qu'il/elle/on aille, que nous allions, que vous alliez, qu'ils/elles aillent
Past subjunctive	que je sois allé(e), que tu sois allé(e), qu'il/elle/on soit allé(e), que nous soyons allé(e)s, que vous soyez allé(e)(s), qu'ils/elles soient allé(e)s

s'asseoir (*to sit down*)

Present indicative	je m'assieds (m'assois), tu t'assieds (t'assois), il/elle/on s'assied (s'assoit), nous nous asseyons (nous assoyons), vous vous asseyez (vous assoyez), ils/elles s'asseyent (s'assoient)
Imperative	assieds-toi, asseyons-nous, asseyez-vous
Passé composé	je me suis assis(e), tu t'es assis(e), il/elle/on s'est assis(e), nous nous sommes assis(es), vous vous êtes assis(e)(es), ils/elles se sont assis(es)
Imperfect	je m'asseyais, tu t'asseyais, il/elle/on s'asseyait, nous nous asseyions, vous vous asseyiez, ils/elles s'asseyaient
Pluperfect	je m'étais assis(e), tu t'étais assis(e), il/elle/on s'était assis(e), nous nous étions assis(es), vous vous étiez assis(e)(es), ils/elles s'étaient assis(es)
Passé simple	je m'assis, tu t'assis, il/elle/on s'assit, nous nous assîmes, vous vous assîtes, ils/elles s'assirent

Future	je m'assiérai, tu t'assiéras, il/elle/on s'assiéra, nous nous assiérons, vous vous assiérez, ils/elles s'assiéront
Futur antérieur	je me serai assis(e), tu te seras assis(e), il/elle/on se sera assis(e), nous nous serons assis(es), vous vous serez assis(e)(es), ils/elles se seront assis(es)
Present conditional	je m'assiérais, tu t'assiérais, il/elle/on s'assiérait, nous nous assiérions, vous vous assiériez, ils/elles s'assiéraient
Past conditional	je me serais assis(e), tu te serais assis(e), il/elle/on se serait assis(e), nous nous serions assis(es), vous vous seriez assis(e)(es), ils/elles se seraient assis(es)
Present subjunctive	que je m'asseye, que tu t'asseyes, qu'il/elle/on s'asseye, que nous nous asseyions, que vous vous asseyiez, qu'ils/elles s'asseyent
Past subjunctive	que je me sois assis(e), que tu te sois assis(e), qu'il/elle/on se soit assis(e), que nous nous soyons assis(es), que vous vous soyez assis(e)(es), qu'ils/elles se soient assis(es)

avoir (*to have*)

Present indicative	j'ai, tu as, il/elle/on a, nous avons, vous avez, ils/elles ont
Imperative	aie, ayons, ayez
Passé composé	j'ai eu, tu as eu, il/elle/on a eu, nous avons eu, vous avez eu, ils/elles ont eu
Imperfect	j'avais, tu avais, il/elle/on avait, nous avions, vous aviez, ils/elles avaient
Pluperfect	j'avais eu, tu avais eu, il/elle/on avait eu, nous avions eu, vous aviez eu, ils/elles avaient eu
Passé simple	j'eus, tu eus, il/elle/on eut, nous eûmes, vous eûtes, ils/elles eurent
Future	j'aurai, tu auras, il/elle/on aura, nous aurons, vous aurez, ils/elles auront
Futur antérieur	j'aurai eu, tu auras eu, il/elle/on aura eu, nous aurons eu, vous aurez eu, ils/elles auront eu
Present conditional	j'aurais, tu aurais, il/elle/on aurait, nous aurions, vous auriez, ils/elles auraient
Past conditional	j'aurais eu, tu aurais eu, il/elle/on aurait eu, nous aurions eu, vous auriez eu, ils/elles auraient eu
Present subjunctive	que j'aie, que tu aies, qu'il/elle/on ait, que nous ayons, que vous ayez, qu'ils/elles aient
Past subjunctive	que j'aie eu, que tu aies eu, qu'il/elle/on ait eu, que nous ayons eu, que vous ayez eu, qu'ils/elles aient eu

boire (*to drink*)

Present indicative	je bois, tu bois, il/elle/on boit, nous buvons, vous buvez, ils/elles boivent
Imperative	bois, buvons, buvez
Passé composé	j'ai bu, tu as bu, il/elle/on a bu, nous avons bu, vous avez bu, ils/elles ont bu
Imperfect	je buvais, tu buvais, il/elle/on buvait, nous buvions, vous buviez, ils/elles buvaient
Pluperfect	j'avais bu, tu avais bu, il/elle/on avait bu, nous avions bu, vous aviez bu, ils/elles avaient bu
Passé simple	je bus, tu bus, il/elle/on but, nous bûmes, vous bûtes, ils/elles burent
Future	je boirai, tu boiras, il/elle/on boira, nous boirons, vous boirez, ils/elles boiront
Futur antérieur	j'aurai bu, tu auras bu, il/elle/on aura bu, nous aurons bu, vous aurez bu, ils/elles auront bu

Present conditional	je boirais, tu boirais, il/elle/on boirait, nous boirions, vous boiriez, ils/elles boiraient
Past conditional	j'aurais bu, tu aurais bu, il/elle/on aurait bu, nous aurions bu, vous auriez bu, ils/elles auraient bu
Present subjunctive	que je boive, que tu boives, qu'il/elle/on boive, que nous buvions, que vous buviez, qu'ils/elles boivent
Past subjunctive	que j'aie bu, que tu aies bu, qu'il/elle/on ait bu, que nous ayons bu, que vous ayez bu, qu'ils/elles aient bu

conduire (*to drive*)

Present indicative	je conduis, tu conduis, il/elle/on conduit, nous conduisons, vous conduisez, ils/elles conduisent
Imperative	conduis, conduisons, conduisez
Passé composé	j'ai conduit, tu as conduit, il/elle/on a conduit, nous avons conduit, vous avez conduit, ils/elles ont conduit
Imperfect	je conduisais, tu conduisais, il/elle/on conduisait, nous conduisions, vous conduisiez, ils/elles conduisaient
Pluperfect	j'avais conduit, tu avais conduit, il/elle/on avait conduit, nous avions conduit, vous aviez conduit, ils/elles avaient conduit
Passé simple	je conduisis, tu conduisis, il/elle/on conduisit, nous conduisîmes, vous conduisîtes, ils/elles conduisirent
Future	je conduirai, tu conduiras, il/elle/on conduira, nous conduirons, vous conduirez, ils/elles conduiront
Futur antérieur	j'aurai conduit, tu auras conduit, il/elle/on aura conduit, nous aurons conduit, vous aurez conduit, ils/elles auront conduit
Present conditional	je conduirais, tu conduirais, il/elle/on conduirait, nous conduirions, vous conduiriez, ils/elles conduiraient
Past conditional	j'aurais conduit, tu aurais conduit, il/elle/on aurait conduit, nous aurions conduit, vous auriez conduit, ils/elles auraient conduit
Present subjunctive	que je conduise, que tu conduises, qu'il/elle/on conduise, que nous conduisions, que vous conduisiez, qu'ils/elles conduisent
Past subjunctive	que j'aie conduit, que tu aies conduit, qu'il/elle/on ait conduit, que nous ayons conduit, que vous ayez conduit, qu'ils/elles aient conduit

Verbs conjugated like **conduire: construire** (*to build, construct*), **traduire** (*to translate*)

connaître (*to know*)

Present indicative	je connais, tu connais, il/elle/on connaît, nous connaissons, vous connaissez, ils/elles connaissent
Imperative	connais, connaissons, connaissez
Passé composé	j'ai connu, tu as connu, il/elle/on a connu, nous avons connu, vous avez connu, ils/elles ont connu
Imperfect	je connaissais, tu connaissais, il/elle/on connaissait, nous connaissions, vous connaissiez, ils/elles connaissaient
Pluperfect	j'avais connu, tu avais connu, il/elle/on avait connu, nous avions connu, vous aviez connu, ils/elles avaient connu
Passé simple	je connus, tu connus, il/elle/on connut, nous connûmes, vous connûtes, ils/elles connurent
Future	je connaîtrai, tu connaîtras, il/elle/on connaîtra, nous connaîtrons, vous connaîtrez, ils/elles connaîtront
Futur antérieur	j'aurai connu, tu auras connu, il/elle/on aura connu, nous aurons connu, vous aurez connu, ils/elles auront connu
Present conditional	je connaîtrais, tu connaîtrais, il/elle/on connaîtrait, nous connaîtrions, vous connaîtriez, ils/elles connaîtraient

Past conditional	j'aurais connu, tu aurais connu, il/elle/on aurait connu, nous aurions connu, vous auriez connu, ils/elles auraient connu
Present subjunctive	que je connaisse, que tu connaisses, qu'il/elle/on connaisse, que nous connaissions, que vous connaissiez, qu'ils/elles connaissent
Past subjunctive	que j'aie connu, que tu aies connu, qu'il/elle/on ait connu, que nous ayons connu, que vous ayez connu, qu'ils/elles aient connu

courir (*to run*)

Present indicative	je cours, tu cours, il/elle/on court, nous courons, vous courez, ils/elles courent
Imperative	cours, courons, courez
Passé composé	j'ai couru, tu as couru, il/elle/on a couru, nous avons couru, vous avez couru, ils/elles ont couru
Imperfect	je courais, tu courais, il/elle/on courait, nous courions, vous couriez, ils/elles couraient
Pluperfect	j'avais couru, tu avais couru, il/elle/on avait couru, nous avions couru, vous aviez couru, ils/elles avaient couru
Passé simple	je courus, tu courus, il/elle/on courut, nous courûmes, vous courûtes, ils/elles coururent
Future	je courrai, tu courras, il/elle/on courra, nous courrons, vous courrez, ils/elles courront
Futur antérieur	j'aurai couru, tu auras couru, il/elle/on aura couru, nous aurons couru, vous aurez couru, ils/elles auront couru
Present conditional	je courrais, tu courrais, il/elle/on courrait, nous courrions, vous courriez, ils/elles courraient
Past conditional	j'aurais couru, tu aurais couru, il/elle/on aurait couru, nous aurions couru, vous auriez couru, ils/elles auraient couru
Present subjunctive	que je coure, que tu coures, qu'il/elle/on coure, que nous courions, que vous couriez, qu'ils/elles courent
Past subjunctive	que j'aie couru, que tu aies couru, qu'il/elle/on ait couru, que nous ayons couru, que vous ayez couru, qu'ils/elles aient couru

craindre (*to fear*)

Present indicative	je crains, tu crains, il/elle/on craint, nous craignons, vous craignez, ils/elles craignent
Imperative	crains, craignons, craignez
Passé composé	j'ai craint, tu as craint, il/elle/on a craint, nous avons craint, vous avez craint, ils/elles ont craint
Imperfect	je craignais, tu craignais, il/elle/on craignait, nous craignions, vous craigniez, ils/elles craignaient
Pluperfect	j'avais craint, tu avais craint, il/elle/on avait craint, nous avions craint, vous aviez craint, ils/elles avaient craint
Passé simple	je craignis, tu craignis, il/elle/on craignit, nous craignîmes, vous craignîtes, ils/elles craignirent
Future	je craindrai, tu craindras, il/elle/on craindra, nous craindrons, vous craindrez, ils/elles craindront
Futur antérieur	j'aurai craint, tu auras craint, il/elle/on aura craint, nous aurons craint, vous aurez craint, ils/elles auront craint
Present conditional	je craindrais, tu craindrais, il/elle/on craindrait, nous craindrions, vous craindriez, ils/elles craindraient
Past conditional	j'aurais craint, tu aurais craint, il/elle/on aurait craint, nous aurions craint, vous auriez craint, ils/elles auraient craint
Present subjunctive	que je craigne, que tu craignes, qu'il/elle/on craigne, que nous craignions, que vous craigniez, qu'ils/elles craignent

| Past subjunctive | que j'aie craint, que tu aies craint, qu'il/elle/on ait craint, que nous ayons craint, que vous ayez craint, qu'ils/elles aient craint |

Verbs conjugated like **craindre: plaindre** (*to pity, feel sorry for sb*)

croire (*to believe*)

Present indicative	je crois, tu crois, il/elle/on croit, nous croyons, vous croyez, ils/elles croient
Imperative	crois, croyons, croyez
Passé composé	j'ai cru, tu as cru, il/elle/on a cru, nous avons cru, vous avez cru, ils/elles ont cru
Imperfect	je croyais, tu croyais, il/elle/on croyait, nous croyions, vous croyiez, ils/elles croyaient
Pluperfect	j'avais cru, tu avais cru, il/elle/on avait cru, nous avions cru, vous aviez cru, ils/elles avaient cru
Passé simple	je crus, tu crus, il/elle/on crut, nous crûmes, vous crûtes, ils/elles crurent
Future	je croirai, tu croiras, il/elle/on croira, nous croirons, vous croirez, ils/elles croiront
Futur antérieur	j'aurai cru, tu auras cru, il/elle/on aura cru, nous aurons cru, vous aurez cru, ils/elles auront cru
Present conditional	je croirais, tu croirais, il/elle/on croirait, nous croirions, vous croiriez, ils/elles croiraient
Past conditional	j'aurais cru, tu aurais cru, il/elle/on aurait cru, nous aurions cru, vous auriez cru, ils/elles auraient cru
Present subjunctive	que je croie, que tu croies, qu'il/elle/on croie, que nous croyions, que vous croyiez, qu'ils/elles croient
Past subjunctive	que j'aie cru, que tu aies cru, qu'il/elle/on ait cru, que nous ayons cru, que vous ayez cru, qu'ils/elles aient cru

devoir (*to have to, must*)

Present indicative	je dois, tu dois, il/elle/on doit, nous devons, vous devez, ils/elles doivent
Imperative	dois, devons, devez
Passé composé	j'ai dû, tu as dû, il/elle/on a dû, nous avons dû, vous avez dû, ils/elles ont dû
Imperfect	je devais, tu devais, il/elle/on devait, nous devions, vous deviez, ils/elles devaient
Pluperfect	j'avais dû, tu avais dû, il/elle/on avait dû, nous avions dû, vous aviez dû, ils/elles avaient dû
Passé simple	je dus, tu dus, il/elle/on dut, nous dûmes, vous dûtes, ils/elles durent
Future	je devrai, tu devras, il/elle/on devra, nous devrons, vous devrez, ils/elles devront
Futur antérieur	j'aurai dû, tu auras dû, il/elle/on aura dû, nous aurons dû, vous aurez dû, ils/elles auront dû
Present conditional	je devrais, tu devrais, il/elle/on devrait, nous devrions, vous devriez, ils/elles devraient
Past conditional	j'aurais dû, tu aurais dû, il/elle/on aurait dû, nous aurions dû, vous auriez dû, ils/elles auraient dû
Present subjunctive	que je doive, que tu doives, qu'il/elle/on doive, que nous devions, que vous deviez, qu'ils/elles doivent
Past subjunctive	que j'aie dû, que tu aies dû, qu'il/elle/on ait dû, que nous ayons dû, que vous ayez dû, qu'ils/elles aient dû

dire (*to say, tell*)

Present indicative	je dis, tu dis, il/elle/on dit, nous disons, vous dites, ils/elles disent
Imperative	dis, disons, dites
Passé composé	j'ai dit, tu as dit, il/elle/on a dit, nous avons dit, vous avez dit, ils/elles ont dit
Imperfect	je disais, tu disais, il/elle/on disait, nous disions, vous disiez, ils/elles disaient
Pluperfect	j'avais dit, tu avais dit, il/elle/on avait dit, nous avions dit, vous aviez dit, ils/elles avaient dit
Passé simple	je dis, tu dis, il/elle/on dit, nous dîmes, vous dîtes, ils/elles dirent
Future	je dirai, tu diras, il/elle/on dira, nous dirons, vous direz, ils/elles diront
Futur antérieur	j'aurai dit, tu auras dit, il/elle/on aura dit, nous aurons dit, vous aurez dit, ils/elles auront dit
Present conditional	je dirais, tu dirais, il/elle/on dirait, nous dirions, vous diriez, ils/elles diraient
Past conditional	j'aurais dit, tu aurais dit, il/elle/on aurait dit, nous aurions dit, vous auriez dit, ils/elles auraient dit
Present subjunctive	que je dise, que tu dises, qu'il/elle/on dise, que nous disions, que vous disiez, qu'ils/elles disent
Past subjunctive	que j'aie dit, que tu aies dit, qu'il/elle/on ait dit, que nous ayons dit, que vous ayez dit, qu'ils/elles aient dit

dormir (*to sleep*)

Present indicative	je dors, tu dors, il/elle/on dort, nous dormons, vous dormez, ils/elles dorment
Imperative	dors, dormons, dormez
Passé composé	j'ai dormi, tu as dormi, il/elle/on a dormi, nous avons dormi, vous avez dormi, ils/elles ont dormi
Imperfect	je dormais, tu dormais, il/elle/on dormait, nous dormions, vous dormiez, ils/elles dormaient
Pluperfect	j'avais dormi, tu avais dormi, il/elle/on avait dormi, nous avions dormi, vous aviez dormi, ils/elles avaient dormi
Passé simple	je dormis, tu dormis, il/elle/on dormit, nous dormîmes, vous dormîtes, ils/elles dormirent
Future	je dormirai, tu dormiras, il/elle/on dormira, nous dormirons, vous dormirez, ils/elles dormiront
Futur antérieur	j'aurai dormi, tu auras dormi, il/elle/on aura dormi, nous aurons dormi, vous aurez dormi, ils/elles auront dormi
Present conditional	je dormirais, tu dormirais, il/elle/on dormirait, nous dormirions, vos dormiriez, ils/elles dormiraient
Past conditional	j'aurais dormi, tu aurais dormi, il/elle/on aurait dormi, nous aurions dormi, vous auriez dormi, ils/elles auraient dormi
Present subjunctive	que je dorme, que tu dormes, qu'il/elle/on dorme, que nous dormions, que vous dormiez, qu'ils/elles dorment
Past subjunctive	que j'aie dormi, que tu aies dormi, qu'il/elle/on ait dormi, que nous ayons dormi, que vous ayez dormi, qu'ils/elles aient dormi

écrire (*to write*)

Present indicative	j'écris, tu écris, il/elle/on écrit, nous écrivons, vous écrivez, ils/elles écrivent
Imperative	écris, écrivons, écrivez
Passé composé	j'ai écrit, tu as écrit, il/elle/on a écrit, nous avons écrit, vous avez écrit, ils/elles ont écrit

Imperfect	j'écrivais, tu écrivais, il/elle/on écrivait, nous écrivions, vous écriviez, ils/elles écrivaient	
Pluperfect	j'avais écrit, tu avais écrit, il/elle/on avait écrit, nous avions écrit, vous aviez écrit, ils/elles avaient écrit	
Passé simple	j'écrivis, tu écrivis, il/elle/on écrivit, nous écrivîmes, vous écrivîtes, ils/elles écrivirent	
Future	j'écrirai, tu écriras, il/elle/on écrira, nous écrirons, vous écrirez, ils/elles écriront	
Futur antérieur	j'aurai écrit, tu auras écrit, il/elle/on aura écrit, nous aurons écrit, vous aurez écrit, ils/elles auront écrit	
Present conditional	j'écrirais, tu écrirais, il/elle/on écrirait, nous écririons, vous écririez, ils/elles écriraient	
Past conditional	j'aurais écrit, tu aurais écrit, il/elle/on aurait écrit, nous aurions écrit, vous auriez écrit, ils/elles auraient écrit	
Present subjunctive	que j'écrive, que tu écrives, qu'il/elle/on écrive, que nous écrivions, que vous écriviez, qu'ils/elles écrivent	
Past subjunctive	que j'aie écrit, que tu aies écrit, qu'il/elle/on ait écrit, que nous ayons écrit, que vous ayez écrit, qu'ils/elles aient écrit	

Verbs conjugated like **écrire: décrire** (*to describe*)

être (*to be*)

Present indicative	je suis, tu es, il/elle/on est, nous sommes, vous êtes, ils/elles sont
Imperative	sois, soyons, soyez
Passé composé	j'ai été, tu as été, il/elle/on a été, nous avons été, vous avez été, ils/elles ont été
Imperfect	j'étais, tu étais, il/elle/on était, nous étions, vous étiez, ils/elles étaient
Pluperfect	j'avais été, tu avais été, il/elle/on avait été, nous avions été, vous aviez été, ils/elles avaient été
Passé simple	je fus, tu fus, il/elle/on fut, nous fûmes, vous fûtes, ils/elles furent
Future	je serai, tu seras, il/elle/on sera, nous serons, vous serez, ils/elles seront
Futur antérieur	j'aurai été, tu auras été, il/elle/on aura été, nous aurons été, vous aurez été, ils/elles auront été
Present conditional	je serais, tu serais, il/elle/on serait, nous serions, vous seriez, ils/elles seraient
Past conditional	j'aurais été, tu aurais été, il/elle/on aurait été, nous aurions été, vous auriez été, ils/elles auraient été
Present subjunctive	que je sois, que tu sois, qu'il/elle/on soit, que nous soyons, que vous soyez, qu'ils/elles soient
Past subjunctive	que j'aie été, que tu aies été, qu'il/elle/on ait été, que nous ayons été, que vous ayez été, qu'ils/elles aient été

faire (*to do, make*)

Present indicative	je fais, tu fais, il/elle/on fait, nous faisons, vous faites, ils/elles font
Imperative	fais, faisons, faites
Passé composé	j'ai fait, tu as fait, il/elle/on a fait, nous avons fait, vous avez fait, ils/elles ont fait
Imperfect	je faisais, tu faisais, il/elle/on faisait, nous faisions, vous faisiez, ils/elles faisaient
Pluperfect	j'avais fait, tu avais fait, il/elle/on avait fait, nous avions fait, vous aviez fait, ils/elles avaient fait
Passé simple	je fis, tu fis, il/elle/on fit, nous fîmes, vous fîtes, ils/elles firent
Future	je ferai, tu feras, il/elle/on fera, nous ferons, vous ferez, ils/elles feront

Futur antérieur	j'aurai fait, tu auras fait, il/elle/on aura fait, nous aurons fait, vous aurez fait, ils/elles auront fait
Present conditional	je ferais, tu ferais, il/elle/on ferait, nous ferions, vous feriez, ils/elles feraient
Past conditional	j'aurais fait, tu aurais fait, il/elle/on aurait fait, nous aurions fait, vous auriez fait, ils/elles auraient fait
Present subjunctive	que je fasse, que tu fasses, qu'il/elle/on fasse, que nous fassions, que vous fassiez, qu'ils/elles fassent
Past subjunctive	que j'aie fait, que tu aies fait, qu'il/elle/on ait fait, que nous ayons fait, que vous ayez fait, qu'ils/elles aient fait

falloir (*to be necessary*)

Present indicative	il faut
Passé composé	il a fallu
Imperfect	il fallait
Pluperfect	il avait fallu
Passé simple	il fallut
Future	il faudra
Futur antérieur	il aura fallu
Present conditional	il faudrait
Past conditional	il aurait fallu
Present subjunctive	qu'il faille
Past subjunctive	qu'il ait fallu

lire (*to read*)

Present indicative	je lis, tu lis, il/elle/on lit, nous lisons, vous lisez, ils/elles lisent
Imperative	lis, lisons, lisez
Passé composé	j'ai lu, tu as lu, il/elle/on a lu, nous avons lu, vous avez lu, ils/elles ont lu
Imperfect	je lisais, tu lisais, il/elle/on lisait, nous lisions, vous lisiez, ils/elles lisaient
Pluperfect	j'avais lu, tu avais lu, il/elle/on avait lu, nous avions lu, vous aviez lu, ils/elles avaient lu
Passé simple	je lus, tu lus, il/elle/on lut, nous lûmes, vous lûtes, ils/elles lurent
Future	je lirai, lu liras, il/elle/on lira, nous lirons, vos lirez, ils/elles liront
Futur antérieur	j'aurai lu, tu auras lu, il/elle/on aura lu, nous aurons lu, vous aurez lu, ils/elles auront lu
Present conditional	je lirais, tu lirais, il/elle/on lirait, nous lirions, vous liriez, ils/elles liraient
Past conditional	j'aurais lu, tu aurais lu, il/elle/on aurait lu, nous aurions lu, vous auriez lu, ils/elles auraient lu
Present subjunctive	que je lise, que tu lises, qu'il/elle/on lise, que nous lisions, que vous lisiez, qu'ils/elles lisent
Past subjunctive	que j'aie lu, que tu aies lu, qu'il/elle/on ait lu, que nous ayons lu, que vous ayez lu, qu'ils/elles aient lu

Verbs conjugated like **lire: élire** (*to elect*)

mentir (*to lie, tell a lie*)

Present indicative	je mens, tu mens, il/elle/on ment, nous mentons, vous mentez, ils/elles mentent
Imperative	mens, mentons, mentez
Passé composé	j'ai menti, tu as menti, il/elle/on a menti, nous avons menti, vous avez menti, ils/elles ont menti

Imperfect	je mentais, tu mentais, il/elle/on mentait, nous mentions, vous mentiez, ils/elles mentaient
Pluperfect	j'avais menti, tu avais menti, il/elle/on avait menti, nous avions menti, vous aviez menti, ils/elles avaient menti
Passé simple	je mentis, tu mentis, il/elle/on mentit, nous mentîmes, vous mentîtes, ils/elles mentirent
Future	je mentirai, tu mentiras, il/elle/on mentira, nous mentirons, vous mentirez, ils/elles mentiront
Futur antérieur	j'aurai menti, tu auras menti, il/elle/on aura menti, nous aurons menti, vous aurez menti, ils/elles auront menti
Present conditional	je mentirais, tu mentirais, il/elle/on mentirait, nous mentirions, vous mentiriez, ils/elles mentiraient
Past conditional	j'aurais menti, tu aurais menti, il/elle/on aurait menti, nous aurions menti, vous auriez menti, ils/elles auraient menti
Present subjunctive	que je mente, que tu mentes, qu'il/elle/on mente, que nous mentions, que vous mentiez, qu'ils/elles mentent
Past subjunctive	que j'aie menti, que tu aies menti, qu'il/elle/on ait menti, que nous ayons menti, que vous ayez menti, qu'ils/elles aient menti

mettre (*to put, to put on*)

Present indicative	je mets, tu mets, il/elle/on met, nous mettons, vous mettez, ils/elles mettent
Imperative	mets, mettons, mettez
Passé composé	j'ai mis, tu as mis, il/elle/on a mis, nous avons mis, vous avez mis, ils/elles ont mis
Imperfect	je mettais, tu mettais, il/elle/on mettait, nous mettions, vous mettiez, ils/elles mettaient
Pluperfect	j'avais mis, tu avais mis, il/elle/on avait mis, nous avions mis, vous aviez mis, ils/elles avaient mis
Passé simple	je mis, tu mis, il/elle/on mit, nous mîmes, vous mîtes, ils/elles mirent
Future	je mettrai, tu mettras, il/elle/on mettra, nous mettrons, vous mettrez, ils/elles mettront
Futur antérieur	j'aurai mis, tu auras mis, il/elle/on aura mis, nous aurons mis, vous aurez mis, ils/elles auront mis
Present conditional	je mettrais, tu mettrais, il/elle/on mettrait, nous mettrions, vous mettriez, ils/elles mettraient
Past conditional	j'aurais mis, tu aurais mis, il/elle/on aurait mis, nous aurions mis, vous auriez mis, ils/elles auraient mis
Present subjunctive	que je mette, que tu mettes, qu'il/elle/on mette, que nous mettions, que vous mettiez, qu'ils/elles mettent
Past subjunctive	que j'aie mis, que tu aies mis, qu'il/elle/on ait mis, que nous ayons mis, que vous ayez mis, qu'ils/elles aient mis

Verbs conjugated like **mettre: admettre** (*to admit*), **commettre** (*to commit*), **permettre** (*to allow*), **promettre** (*to promise*), **remettre** (*to put back*)

mourir (*to die*)

Present indicative	je meurs, tu meurs, il/elle/on meurt, nous mourons, vous mourez, ils/elles meurent
Imperative	meurs, mourons, mourez
Passé composé	je suis mort(e), tu es mort(e), il/elle/on est mort(e), nous sommes mort(e)s, vous êtes mort(e)(s), ils/elles sont mort(e)s
Imperfect	je mourais, tu mourais, il/elle/on mourait, nous mourions, vous mouriez, ils/elles mouraient

Pluperfect	j'étais mort(e), tu étais mort(e), il/elle/on était mort(e), nous étions mort(e)s, vous étiez mort(e)(s), ils/elles étaient mort(e)s
Passé simple	je mourus, tu mourus, il/elle/on mourut, nous mourûmes, vous mourûtes, ils/elles moururent
Future	je mourrai, tu mourras, il/elle/on mourra, nous mourrons, vous mourrez, ils/elles mourront
Futur antérieur	je serai mort(e), tu seras mort(e), il/elle/on sera mort(e), nous serons mort(e)s, vous serez mort(e)(s), ils/elles seront mort(e)s
Present conditional	je mourrais, tu mourrais, il/elle/on mourrait, nous mourrions, vous mourriez, ils/elles mourraient
Past conditional	je serais mort(e), tu serais mort(e), il/elle/on serait mort(e), nous serions mort(e)s, vous seriez mort(e)(s), ils/elles seraient mort(e)s
Present subjunctive	que je meure, que tu meures, qu'il/elle/on meure, que nous mourions, que vous mouriez, qu'ils/elles meurent
Past subjunctive	que je sois mort(e), que tu sois mort(e), qu'il/elle/on soit mort(e), que nous soyons mort(e)s, que vous soyez mort(e)(s), qu'ils/elles soient mort(e)s

naître (*to be born*)

Present indicative	je nais, tu nais, il/elle/on naît, nous naissons, vous naissez, ils/elles naissent
Imperative	nais, naissons, naissez
Passé composé	je suis né(e), tu es né(e), il/elle/on est né(e), nous sommes né(e)s, vous êtes né(e)(s), ils/elles sont né(e)s
Imperfect	je naissais, tu naissais, il/elle/on naissait, nous naissions, vous naissiez, ils/elles naissaient
Pluperfect	j'étais né(e), tu étais né(e), il/elle/on était né(e), nous étions né(e)s, vous étiez né(e)(s), ils/elles étaient né(e)s
Passé simple	je naquis, tu naquis, il/elle/on naquit, nous naquîmes, vous naquîtes, ils/elles naquirent
Future	je naîtrai, tu naîtras, il/elle/on naîtra, nous naîtrons, vous naîtrez, ils/elles naîtront
Futur antérieur	je serai né(e), tu seras né(e), il/elle/on sera né(e), nous serons né(e)s, vous serez né(e)(s), ils/elles seront né(e)s
Present conditional	je naîtrais, tu naîtrais, il/elle/on naîtrait, nous naîtrions, vous naîtriez, ils/cllcs naîtraicnt
Past conditional	je serais né(e), tu serais né(e), il/elle/on serait né(e), nous serions né(e)s, vous seriez né(e)(s), ils/elles seraient né(e)s
Present subjunctive	que je naisse, que tu naisses, qu'il/elle/on naisse, que nous naissions, que vous naissiez, qu'ils/elles naissent
Past subjunctive	que je sois né(e), que tu sois né(e), qu'il/elle/on soit né(e), que nous soyons né(e)s, que vous soyez né(e)(s), qu'ils/elles soient né(e)s

ouvrir (*to open*)

Present indicative	j'ouvre, tu ouvres, il/elle/on ouvre, nous ouvrons, vous ouvrez, ils/elles ouvrent
Imperative	ouvre, ouvrons, ouvrez
Passé composé	j'ai ouvert, tu as ouvert, il/elle/on a ouvert, nous avons ouvert, vous avez ouvert, ils/elles ont ouvert
Imperfect	j'ouvrais, tu ouvrais, il/elle/on ouvrait, nous ouvrions, vous ouvriez, ils/elles ouvraient
Pluperfect	j'avais ouvert, tu avais ouvert, il/elle/on avait ouvert, nous avions ouvert, vous aviez ouvert, ils/elles avaient ouvert

Passé simple	j'ouvris, tu ouvris, il/elle/on ouvrit, nous ouvrîmes, vous ouvrîtes, ils/elles ouvrirent
Future	j'ouvrirai, tu ouvriras, il/elle/on ouvrira, nous ouvrirons, vous ouvrirez, ils/elles ouvriront
Futur antérieur	j'aurai ouvert, tu auras ouvert, il/elle/on aura ouvert, nous aurons ouvert, vous aurez ouvert, ils/elles auront ouvert
Present conditional	j'ouvrirais, tu ouvrirais, il/elle/on ouvrirait, nous ouvririons, vous ouvririez, ils/elles ouvriraient
Past conditional	j'aurais ouvert, tu aurais ouvert, il/elle/on aurait ouvert, nous aurions ouvert, vous auriez ouvert, ils/elles auraient ouvert
Present subjunctive	que j'ouvre, que tu ouvres, qu'il/elle/on ouvre, que nous ouvrions, que vous ouvriez, qu'ils/elles ouvrent
Past subjunctive	que j'aie ouvert, que tu aies ouvert, qu'il/elle/on ait ouvert, que nous ayons ouvert, que vous ayez ouvert, qu'ils/elles aient ouvert

Verbs conjugated like **ouvrir: couvrir** (*to cover*), **découvrir** (*to discover*), **offrir** (*to offer*), **souffrir** (*to suffer*)

partir (*to leave*)

Present indicative	je pars, tu pars, il/elle/on part, nous partons, vous partez, ils/elles partent
Imperative	pars, partons, partez
Passé composé	je suis parti(e), tu es parti(e), il/elle/on est parti(e), nous sommes parti(e)s, vous êtes parti(e)(s), ils/elles sont parti(e)s
Imperfect	je partais, tu partais, il/elle/on partait, nous partions, vous partiez, ils/elles partaient
Pluperfect	j'étais parti(e), tu étais parti(e), il/elle/on était parti(e), nous étions parti(e)s, vous étiez parti(e)(s), ils/elles étaient parti(e)s
Passé simple	je partis, tu partis, il/elle/on partit, nous partîmes, vous partîtes, ils/elles partirent
Future	je partirai, tu partiras, il/elle/on partira, nous partirons, vous partirez, ils/elles partiront
Futur antérieur	je serai parti(e), tu seras parti(e), il/elle/on sera parti(e), nous serons parti(e)s, vous serez parti(e)(s), ils/elles seront parti(e)s
Present conditional	je partirais, tu partirais, il/elle/on partirait, nous partirions, vous partiriez, ils/elles partiraient
Past conditional	je serais parti(e), tu serais parti(e), il/elle/on serait parti(e), nous serions parti(e)s, vous seriez parti(e)(s), ils/elles seraient parti(e)s
Present subjunctive	que je parte, que tu partes, qu'il/elle/on parte, que nous partions, que vous partiez, qu'ils/elles partent
Past subjunctive	que je sois parti(e), que tu sois parti(e), qu'il/elle/on soit parti(e), que nous soyons parti(e)s, que vous soyez parti(e)(s), qu'ils/elles soient parti(e)s

Verbs conjugated like **partir: sortir** (*to go out*)

peindre (*to paint*)

Present indicative	je peins, tu peins, il/elle/on peint, nous peignons, vous peignez, ils/elles peignent
Imperative	peins, peignons, peignez
Passé composé	j'ai peint, tu as peint, il/elle/on a peint, nous avons peint, vous avez peint, ils/elles ont peint
Imperfect	je peignais, tu peignais, il/elle/on peignait, nous peignions, vous peigniez, ils/elles peignaient

Pluperfect	j'avais peint, tu avais peint, il/elle/on avait peint, nous avions peint, vous aviez peint, ils/elles avaient peint
Passé simple	je peignis, tu peignis, il/elle/on peignit, nous peignîmes, vous peignîtes, ils/elles peignirent
Future	je peindrai, tu peindras, il/elle/on peindra, nous peindrons, vous peindrez, ils/elles peindront
Futur antérieur	j'aurai peint, tu auras peint, il/elle/on aura peint, nous aurons peint, vous aurez peint, ils/elles auront peint
Present conditional	je peindrais, tu peindrais, il/elle/on peindrait, nous peindrions, vous peindriez, ils/elles peindraient
Past conditional	j'aurais peint, tu aurais peint, il/elle/on aurait peint, nous aurions peint, vous auriez peint, ils/elles auraient peint
Present subjunctive	que je peigne, que tu peignes, qu'il/elle/on peigne, que nous peignions, que vous peigniez, qu'ils/elles peignent
Past subjunctive	que j'aie peint, que tu aies peint, qu'il/elle/on ait peint, que nous ayons peint, que vous ayez peint, qu'ils/elles aient peint

Verbs conjugated like **peindre: atteindre** (*to reach, attain*), **éteindre** (*to switch off*)

plaire (*to please*)

Present indicative	je plais, tu plais, il/elle/on plaît, nous plaisons, vous plaisez, ils/elles plaisent
Imperative	plais, plaisons, plaisez
Passé composé	j'ai plu, tu as plu, il/elle/on a plu, nous avons plu, vous avez plu, ils/elles ont plu
Imperfect	je plaisais, tu plaisais, il/elle/on plaisait, nous plaisions, vous plaisiez, ils/elles plaisaient
Pluperfect	j'avais plu, tu avais plu, il/elle/on avait plu, nous avions plu, vous aviez plu, ils/elles avaient plu
Passé simple	je plus, tu plus, il/elle/on plut, nous plûmes, vous plûtes, ils/elles plurent
Future	je plairai, tu plairas, il/elle/on plaira, nous plairons, vous plairez, ils/elles plairont
Futur antérieur	j'aurai plu, tu auras plu, il/elle/on aura plu, nous aurons plu, vous aurez plu, ils/elles auront plu
Present conditional	je plairais, tu plairais, il/elle/on plairait, nous plairions, vous plairiez, ils/elles plairaient
Past conditional	j'aurais plu, tu aurais plu, il/elle/on aurait plu, nous aurions plu, vous auriez plu, ils/elles auraient plu
Present subjunctive	que je plaise, que tu plaises, qu'il/elle/on plaise, que nous plaisions, que vous plaisiez, qu'ils/elles plaisent
Past subjunctive	que j'aie plu, que tu aies plu, qu'il/elle/on ait plu, que nous ayons plu, que vous ayez plu, qu'ils/elles aient plu

pleuvoir (*to rain*)

Present indicative	il pleut
Passé composé	il a plu
Imperfect	il pleuvait
Pluperfect	il avait plu
Passé simple	il plut
Future	il pleuvra
Futur antérieur	il aura plu

Present conditional	il pleuvrait
Past conditional	il aurait plu
Present subjunctive	qu'il pleuve
Past subjunctive	qu'il ait plu

pouvoir (can, to be able to)

Present indicative	je peux or je puis, tu peux, il/elle/on peut, nous pouvons, vous pouvez, ils/elles peuvent
Passé composé	j'ai pu, tu as pu, il/elle/on a pu, nous avons pu, vous avez pu, ils/elles ont pu
Imperfect	je pouvais, tu pouvais, il/elle/on pouvait, nous pouvions, vous pouviez, ils/elles pouvaient
Pluperfect	j'avais pu, tu avais pu, il/elle/on avait pu, nous avions pu, vous aviez pu, ils/elles avaient pu
Passé simple	je pus, tu pus, il/elle/on put, nous pûmes, vous pûtes, ils/elles purent
Future	je pourrai, tu pourras, il/elle/on pourra, nous pourrons, vous pourrez, ils/elles pourront
Futur antérieur	j'aurai pu, tu auras pu, il/elle/on aura pu, nous aurons pu, vous aurez pu, ils/elles auront pu
Present conditional	je pourrais, tu pourrais, il/elle/on pourrait, nous pourrions, vous pourriez, ils/elles pourraient
Past conditional	j'aurais pu, tu aurais pu, il/elle/on aurait pu, nous aurions pu, vous auriez pu, ils/elles auraient pu
Present subjunctive	que je puisse, que tu puisses, qu'il/elle/on puisse, que nous puissions, que vous puissiez, qu'ils/elles puissent
Past subjunctive	que j'aie pu, que tu aies pu, qu'il/elle/on ait pu, que nous ayons pu, que vous ayez pu, qu'ils/elles aient pu

prendre (to take)

Present indicative	je prends, tu prends, il/elle/on prend, nous prenons, vous prenez, ils/elles prennent
Imperative	prends, prenons, prenez
Passé composé	j'ai pris, tu as pris, il/elle/on a pris, nous avons pris, vous avez pris, ils/elles ont pris
Imperfect	je prenais, tu prenais, il/elle/on prenait, nous prenions, vous preniez, ils/elles prenaient
Pluperfect	j'avais pris, tu avais pris, il/elle/on avait pris, nous avions pris, vous aviez pris, ils/elles avaient pris
Passé simple	je pris, tu pris, il/elle/on prit, nous prîmes, vous prîtes, il/elle/on prirent
Future	je prendrai, tu prendras, il/elle/on prendra, nous prendrons, vous prendrez, ils/elles prendront
Futur antérieur	j'aurai pris, tu auras pris, il/elle/on aura pris, nous aurons pris, vous aurez pris, ils/elles auront pris
Present conditional	je prendrais, tu prendrais, il/elle/on prendrait, nous prendrions, vous prendriez, ils/elles prendraient
Past conditional	j'aurais pris, tu aurais pris, il/elle/on aurait pris, nous aurions pris, vous auriez pris, ils/elles auraient pris
Present subjunctive	que je prenne, que tu prennes, qu'il/elle/on prenne, que nous prenions, que vous preniez, qu'ils/elles prennent
Past subjunctive	que j'aie pris, que tu aies pris, qu'il/elle/on ait pris, que nous ayons pris, que vous ayez pris, qu'ils/elles aient pris

Verbs conjugated like **prendre: apprendre** (*to learn*), **comprendre** (*to understand*), **surprendre** (*to surprise*)

recevoir (*to receive*)

Present indicative	je reçois, tu reçois, il/elle/on reçoit, nous recevons, vous recevez, ils/elles reçoivent
Imperative	reçois, recevons, recevez
Passé composé	j'ai reçu, tu as reçu, il/elle/on a reçu, nous avons reçu, vous avez reçu, ils/elles ont reçu
Imperfect	je recevais, tu recevais, il/elle/on recevait, nous recevions, vous receviez, ils/elles recevaient
Pluperfect	j'avais reçu, tu avais reçu, il/elle/on avait reçu, nous avions reçu, vous aviez reçu, ils/elles avaient reçu
Passé simple	je reçus, tu reçus, il/elle/on reçut, nous reçûmes, vous reçûtes, ils/elles reçurent
Future	je recevrai, tu recevras, il/elle/on recevra, nous recevrons, vous recevrez, ils/elles recevront
Futur antérieur	j'aurai reçu, tu auras reçu, il/elle/on aura reçu, nous aurons reçu, vous aurez reçu, ils/elles auront reçu
Present conditional	je recevrais, tu recevrais, il/elle/on recevrait, nous recevrions, vous recevriez, ils/elles recevraient
Past conditional	j'aurais reçu, tu aurais reçu, il/elle/on aurait reçu, nous aurions reçu, vous auriez reçu, ils/elles auraient reçu
Present subjunctive	que je reçoive, que tu reçoives, qu'il/elle/on reçoive, que nous recevions, que vous receviez, qu'ils/elles reçoivent
Past subjunctive	que j'aie reçu, que tu aies reçu, qu'il/elle/on ait reçu, que nous ayons reçu, que vous ayez reçu, qu'ils/elles aient reçu

Verbs conjugated like **recevoir: apercevoir** (*to perceive*), **décevoir** (*to disappoint*)

rire (*to laugh*)

Present indicative	je ris, tu ris, il/elle/on rit, nous rions, vous riez, ils/elles rient
Imperative	ris, rions, riez
Passé composé	j'ai ri, tu as ri, il/elle/on a ri, nous avons ri, vous avez ri, ils/elles ont ri
Imperfect	je riais, tu riais, il/elle/on riait, nous riions, vous riiez, ils/elles riaient
Pluperfect	j'avais ri, tu avais ri, il/elle/on avait ri, nous avions ri, vous aviez ri, ils/elles avaient ri
Passé simple	je ris, tu ris, il/elle/on rit, nous rîmes, vous rîtes, ils/elles rirent
Future	je rirai, tu riras, il/elle/on rira, nous rirons, vous rirez, ils/elles riront
Futur antérieur	j'aurai ri, tu auras ri, il/elle/on aura ri, nous aurons ri, vous aurez ri, ils/elles auront ri
Present conditional	je rirais, tu rirais, il/elle/on rirait, nous ririons, vous ririez, ils/elles riraient
Past conditional	j'aurais ri, tu aurais ri, il/elle/on aurait ri, nous aurions ri, vous auriez ri, ils/elles auraient ri
Present subjunctive	que je rie, que tu ries, qu'il/elle/on rie, que nous riions, que vous riiez, qu'ils/elles rient
Past subjunctive	que j'aie ri, que tu aies ri, qu'il/elle/on ait ri, que nous ayons ri, que vous ayez ri, qu'ils/elles aient ri

Verbs conjugated like **rire: sourire** (*to smile*)

savoir (*to know*)

Present indicative	je sais, tu sais, il/elle/on sait, nous savons, vous savez, ils/elles savent
Imperative	sache, sachons, sachez
Passé composé	j'ai su, tu as su, il/elle/on a su, nous avons su, vous avez su, ils/elles ont su
Imperfect	je savais, tu savais, il/elle/on savait, nous savions, vous saviez, ils/elles savaient
Pluperfect	j'avais su, tu avais su, il/elle/on avait su, nous avions su, vous aviez su, ils/elles avaient su
Passé simple	je sus, tu sus, il/elle/on sut, nous sûmes, vous sûtes, ils/elles surent
Future	je saurai, tu sauras, il/elle/on saura, nous saurons, vous saurez, ils/elles sauront
Futur antérieur	j'aurai su, tu auras su, il/elle/on aura su, nous aurons su, vous aurez su, ils/elles auront su
Present conditional	je saurais, tu saurais, il/elle/on saurait, nous saurions, vous sauriez, ils/elles sauraient
Past conditional	j'aurais su, tu aurais su, il/elle/on aurait su, nous aurions su, vous auriez su, ils/elles auraient su
Present subjunctive	que je sache, que tu saches, qu'il/elle/on sache, que nous sachions, que vous sachiez, qu'ils/elles sachent
Past subjunctive	que j'aie su, que tu aies su, qu'il/elle/on ait su, que nous ayons su, que vous ayez su, qu'ils/elles aient su

sentir (*to feel, to smell*)

Present indicative	je sens, tu sens, il/elle/on sent, nous sentons, vous sentez, ils/elles sentent
Imperative	sens, sentons, sentez
Passé composé	j'ai senti, tu as senti, il/elle/on a senti, nous avons senti, vous avez senti, ils/elles ont senti
Imperfect	je sentais, tu sentais, il/elle/on sentait, nous sentions, vous sentiez, ils/elles sentaient
Pluperfect	j'avais senti, tu avais senti, il/elle/on avait senti, nous avions senti, vous aviez senti, ils/elles avaient senti
Passé simple	je sentis, tu sentis, il/elle/on sentit, nous sentîmes, vous sentîtes, ils/elles sentirent
Future	je sentirai, tu sentiras, il/elle/on sentira, nous sentirons, vous sentirez, ils/elles sentiront
Futur antérieur	j'aurai senti, tu auras senti, il/elle/on aura senti, nous aurons senti, vous aurez senti, ils/elles auront senti
Present conditional	je sentirais, tu sentirais, il/elle/on sentirait, nous sentirions, vous sentiriez, ils/elles sentiraient
Past conditional	j'aurais senti, tu aurais senti, il/elle/on aurait senti, nous aurions senti, vous auriez senti, ils/elles auraient senti
Present subjunctive	que je sente, que tu sentes, qu'il/elle/on sente, que nous sentions, que vous sentiez, qu'ils/elles sentent
Past subjunctive	que j'aie senti, que tu aies senti, qu'il/elle/on ait senti, que nous ayons senti, que vous ayez senti, qu'ils/elles aient senti

servir (*to serve*)

Present indicative	je sers, tu sers, il/elle/on sert, nous servons, vous servez, ils/elles servent
Imperative	sers, servons, servez

Passé composé	j'ai servi, tu as servi, il/elle/on a servi, nous avons servi, vous avez servi, ils/elles ont servi
Imperfect	je servais, tu servais, il/elle/on servait, nous servions, vous serviez, ils/elles servaient
Pluperfect	j'avais servi, tu avais servi, il/elle/on avait servi, nous avions servi, vous aviez servi, ils/elles avaient servi
Passé simple	je servis, tu servis, il/elle/on servit, nous servîmes, vous servîtes, ils/elles servirent
Future	je servirai, tu serviras, il/elle/on servira, nous servirons, vous servirez, ils/elles serviront
Futur antérieur	j'aurai servi, tu auras servi, il/elle/on aura servi, nous aurons servi, vous aurez servi, ils/elles auront servi
Present conditional	je servirais, tu servirais, il/elle/on servirait, nous servirions, vous serviriez, ils/elles serviraient
Past conditional	j'aurais servi, tu aurais servi, il/elle/on aurait servi, nous aurions servi, vous auriez servi, ils/elles auraient servi
Present subjunctive	que je serve, que tu serves, qu'il/elle/on serve, que nous servions, que vous serviez, qu'ils/elles servent
Past subjunctive	que j'aie servi, que tu aies servi, qu'il/elle/on ait servi, que nous ayons servi, que vous ayez servi, qu'ils/elles aient servi

suivre (*to follow, to take [a class]*)

Present indicative	je suis, tu suis, il/elle/on suit, nous suivons, vous suivez, ils/elles suivent
Imperative	suis, suivons, suivez
Passé composé	j'ai suivi, tu as suivi, il/elle/on a suivi, nous avons suivi, vous avez suivi, ils/elles ont suivi
Imperfect	je suivais, tu suivais, il/elle/on suivait, nous suivions, vous suiviez, ils/elles suivaient
Pluperfect	j'avais suivi, tu avais suivi, il/elle/on avait suivi, nous avions suivi, vous aviez suivi, ils/elles avaient suivi
Passé simple	je suivis, tu suivis, il/elle/on suivit, nous suivîmes, vous suivîtes, ils/elles suivirent
Future	je suivrai, tu suivras, il/elle/on suivra, nous suivrons, vous suivrez, ils/elles suivront
Futur antérieur	j'aurai suivi, tu auras suivi, il/elle/on aura suivi, nous aurons suivi, vous aurez suivi, ils/elles auront suivi
Present conditional	je suivrais, tu suivrais, il/elle/on suivrait, nous suivrions, vous suivriez, ils/elles suivraient
Past conditional	j'aurais suivi, tu aurais suivi, il/elle/on aurait suivi, nous aurions suivi, vous auriez suivi, ils/elles auraient suivi
Present subjunctive	que je suive, que tu suives, qu'il/elle/on suive, que nous suivions, que vous suiviez, qu'ils/elles suivent
Past subjunctive	que j'aie suivi, que tu aies suivi, qu'il/elle/on ait suivi, que nous ayons suivi, que vous ayez suivi, qu'ils/elles aient suivi

tenir (*to hold*)

Present indicative	je tiens, tu tiens, il/elle/on tient, nous tenons, vous tenez, ils/elles tiennent
Imperative	tiens, tenons, tenez
Passé composé	j'ai tenu, tu as tenu, il/elle/on a tenu, nous avons tenu, vous avez tenu, ils/elles ont tenu
Imperfect	je tenais, tu tenais, il/elle/on tenait, nous tenions, vous teniez, ils/elles tenaient

	Pluperfect	j'avais tenu, tu avais tenu, il/elle/on avait tenu, nous avions tenu, vous aviez tenu, ils/elles avaient tenu
	Passé simple	je tins, tu tins, il/elle/on tint, nous tînmes, vous tîntes, ils/elles tinrent
	Future	je tiendrai, tu tiendras, il/elle/on tiendra, nous tiendrons, vous tiendrez, ils/elles tiendront
	Futur antérieur	j'aurai tenu, tu auras tenu, il/elle/on aura tenu, nous aurons tenu, vous aurez tenu, ils/elles auront tenu
	Present conditional	je tiendrais, tu tiendrais, il/elle/on tiendrait, nous tiendrions, vous tiendriez, ils/elles tiendraient
	Past conditional	j'aurais tenu, tu aurais tenu, il/elle/on aurait tenu, nous aurions tenu, vous auriez tenu, ils/elles auraient tenu
	Present subjunctive	que je tienne, que tu tiennes, qu'il/elle/on tienne, que nous tenions, que vous teniez, qu'ils/elles tiennent
	Past subjunctive	que j'aie tenu, que tu aies tenu, qu'il/elle/on ait tenu, que nous ayons tenu, que vous ayez tenu, qu'ils/elles aient tenu

valoir (*to be worth*)

	Present indicative	je vaux, tu vaux, il/elle/on vaut, nous valons, vous valez, ils/elles valent
	Imperative	vaux, valons, valez
	Passé composé	j'ai valu, tu as valu, il/elle/on a valu, nous avons valu, vous avez valu, ils/elles ont valu
	Imperfect	je valais, tu valais, il/elle/on valait, nous valions, vous valiez, ils/elles valaient
	Pluperfect	j'avais valu, tu avais valu, il/elle/on avait valu, nous avions valu, vous aviez valu, ils/elles avaient valu
	Passé simple	je valus, tu valus, il/elle/on valut, nous valûmes, vous valûtes, ils/elles valurent
	Future	je vaudrai, tu vaudras, il/elle/on vaudra, nous vaudrons, vous vaudrez, ils/elles vaudront
	Futur antérieur	j'aurai valu, tu auras valu, il/elle/on aura valu, nous aurons valu, vous aurez valu, ils/elles auront valu
	Present conditional	je vaudrais, tu vaudrais, il/elle/on vaudrait, nous vaudrions, vous vaudriez, ils/elles vaudraient
	Past conditional	j'aurais valu, tu aurais valu, il/elle/on aurait valu, nous aurions valu, vous auriez valu, ils/elles auraient valu
	Present subjunctive	que je vaille, que tu vailles, qu'il/elle/on vaille, que nous valions, que vous valiez, qu'ils/elles vaillent
	Past subjunctive	que j'aie valu, que tu aies valu, qu'il/elle/on ait valu, que nous ayons valu, que vous ayez valu, qu'ils/elles aient valu

venir (*to come*)

	Present indicative	je viens, tu viens, il/elle/on vient, nous venons, vous venez, ils/elles viennent
	Imperative	viens, venons, venez
	Passé composé	je suis venu(e), tu es venu(e), il/elle/on est venu(e), nous sommes venu(e)s, vous êtes venu(e)(s), ils/elles sont venu(e)s
	Imperfect	je venais, tu venais, il/elle/on venait, nous venions, vous veniez, ils/elles venaient
	Pluperfect	j'étais venu(e), tu étais venu(e), il/elle/on était venu(e), nous étions venu(e)s, vous étiez venu(e)(s), ils/elles étaient venu(e)s
	Passé simple	je vins, tu vins, il/elle/on vint, nous vînmes, vous vîntes, ils/elles vinrent
	Future	je viendrai, tu viendras, il/elle/on viendra, nous viendrons, vous viendrez, ils/elles viendront

Futur antérieur	je serai venu(e), tu seras venu(e), il/elle/on sera venu(e), nous serons venu(e)s, vous serez venu(e)(s), ils/elles seront venu(e)s
Present conditional	je viendrais, tu viendrais, il/elle/on viendrait, nous viendrions, vous viendriez, ils/elles viendraient
Past conditional	je serais venu(e), tu serais venu(e), il/elle/on serait venu(e), nous serions venu(e)s, vous seriez venu(e)(s), ils/elles seraient venu(e)s
Present subjunctive	que je vienne, que tu viennes, qu'il/elle/on vienne, que nous venions, que vous veniez, qu'ils/elles viennent
Past subjunctive	que je sois venu(e), que tu sois venu(e), qu'il/elle/on soit venu(e), que nous soyons venu(e)s, que vous soyez venu(e)(s), qu'ils/elles soient venu(e)s

Verbs conjugated like **venir: devenir** (*to become*), **revenir** (*to come back*)

vivre (*to live*)

Present indicative	je vis, tu vis, il/elle/on vit, nous vivons, vous vivez, ils/elles vivent
Imperative	vis, vivons, vivez
Passé composé	j'ai vécu, tu as vécu, il/elle/on a vécu, nous avons vécu, vous avez vécu, ils/elles ont vécu
Imperfect	je vivais, tu vivais, il/elle/on vivait, nous vivions, vous viviez, ils/elles vivaient
Pluperfect	j'avais vécu, tu avais vécu, il/elle/on avait vécu, nous avions vécu, vous aviez vécu, ils/elles avaient vécu
Passé simple	je vécus, tu vécus, il/elle/on vécut, nous vécûmes, vous vécûtes, ils/elles vécurent
Future	je vivrai, tu vivras, il/elle/on vivra, nous vivrons, vous vivrez, ils/elles vivront
Futur antérieur	j'aurai vécu, tu auras vécu, il/elle/on aura vécu, nous aurons vécu, vous aurez vécu, ils/elles auront vécu
Present conditional	je vivrais, tu vivrais, il/elle/on vivrait, nous vivrions, vous vivriez, ils/elles vivraient
Past conditional	j'aurais vécu, tu aurais vécu, il/elle/on aurait vécu, nous aurions vécu, vous auriez vécu, ils/elles auraient vécu
Present subjunctive	que je vive, que tu vives, qu'il/elle/on vive, que nous vivions, que vous viviez, qu'ils/elles vivent
Past subjunctive	que j'aie vécu, que tu aies vécu, qu'il/elle/on ait vécu, que nous ayons vécu, que vous ayez vécu, qu'ils/elles aient vécu

Verbs conjugated like **vivre: survivre** (*to survive*)

voir (*to see*)

Present indicative	je vois, tu vois, il/elle/on voit, nous voyons, vous voyez, ils/elles voient
Imperative	vois, voyons, voyez
Passé composé	j'ai vu, tu as vu, il/elle/on a vu, nous avons vu, vous avez vu, ils/elles ont vu
Imperfect	je voyais, tu voyais, il/elle/on voyait, nous voyions, vous voyiez, ils/elles voyaient
Pluperfect	j'avais vu, tu avais vu, il/elle/on avait vu, nous avions vu, vous aviez vu, ils/elles avaient vu
Passé simple	je vis, tu vis, il/elle/on vit, nous vîmes, vous vîtes, ils/elles virent
Future	je verrai, tu verras, il/elle/on verra, nous verrons, vous verrez, ils/elles verront
Futur antérieur	j'aurai vu, tu auras vu, il/elle/on aura vu, nous aurons vu, vous aurez vu, ils/elles auront vu

Present conditional	je verrais, tu verrais, il/elle/on verrait, nous verrions, vous verriez, ils/elles verraient
Past conditional	j'aurais vu, tu aurais vu, il/elle/on aurait vu, nous aurions vu, vous auriez vu, ils/elles auraient vu
Present subjunctive	que je voie, que tu voies, qu'il/elle/on voie, que nous voyions, que vous voyiez, qu'ils/elles voient
Past subjunctive	que j'aie vu, que tu aies vu, qu'il/elle/on ait vu, que nous ayons vu, que vous ayez vu, qu'ils/elles aient vu

Verbs conjugated like **voir: revoir** (*to see again*)

vouloir (*to want*)

Present indicative	je veux, tu veux, il/elle/on veut, nous voulons, vous voulez, ils/elles veulent
Imperative	veuille, veuillons, veuillez
Passé composé	j'ai voulu, tu as voulu, il/elle/on a voulu, nous avons voulu, vous avez voulu, ils/elles ont voulu
Imperfect	je voulais, tu voulais, il/elle/on voulait, nous voulions, vous vouliez, ils/elles voulaient
Pluperfect	j'avais voulu, tu avais voulu, il/elle/on avait voulu, nous avions voulu, vous aviez voulu, ils/elles avaient voulu
Passé simple	je voulus, tu voulus, il/elle/on voulut, nous voulûmes, vous voulûtes, ils/elles voulurent
Future	je voudrai, tu voudras, il/elle/on voudra, nous voudrons, vous voudrez, ils/elles voudront
Futur antérieur	j'aurai voulu, tu auras voulu, il/elle/on aura voulu, nous aurons voulu, vous aurez voulu, ils/elles auront voulu
Present conditional	je voudrais, tu voudrais, il/elle/on voudrait, nous voudrions, vous voudriez, ils/elles voudraient
Past conditional	j'aurais voulu, tu aurais voulu, il/elle/on aurait voulu, nous aurions voulu, vous auriez voulu, ils/elles auraient voulu
Present subjunctive	que je veuille, que tu veuilles, qu'il/elle/on veuille, que nous voulions, que vous vouliez, qu'ils/elles veuillent
Past subjunctive	que j'aie voulu, que tu aies voulu, qu'il/elle/on ait voulu, que nous ayons voulu, que vous ayez voulu, qu'ils/elles aient voulu

French-English glossary

An asterisk follows expressions of informal or colloquial French. Regular adjectives are listed in their masculine singular form.

A

abdiquer to abdicate
accident *(m.)* accident
   accident de voiture car accident
achat *(m.)* purchase
acheter to buy
achever to finish
acteur *(m.)* actor
actrice *(f.)* actress
actuellement presently
addition *(f.)* bill (in a restaurant), check
admettre to admit
admirer to admire
adolescent *(m.)*, **adolescente** *(f.)* teenager
adresse *(f.)* address
adulte *(m./f.)* adult
aéroport *(m.)* airport
affaires *(f.pl.)* personal effects, business
Afrique *(f.)* Africa
âge *(m.)* age
agent immobilier *(m.)* real-estate agent
agir to act
agrafeuse *(f.)* stapler
agréable pleasant
aider to help
aimer to like, love
   aimer mieux to prefer
alcool *(m.)* alcohol
Allemagne *(f.)* Germany
allemand *(m.)* German
aller to go
   aller chercher qch to get sth
   aller chercher qn to pick up sb
allumer to switch on
ambassade *(f.)* embassy
(s')améliorer to improve
amener to bring (a person)
Amérique *(f.)* America
ami *(m.)*, **amie** *(f.)* friend

amoureux, amoureuse (de) in love (with)
amuser to amuse
   s'amuser to have a good time, have fun
an *(m.)* year
analphabète *(m./f.)* illiterate person
anglais *(m.)* English
Angleterre *(f.)* England
animal *(m.) (plur.:* **animaux***)* animal
   animal domestique pet
anniversaire *(m.)* birthday
annuler to cancel
anorak *(m.)* anorak
août August
apéritif *(m.)* before-dinner drink
appareil photo *(m.)* camera
appartement *(m.)* apartment
appartenir à to belong to
appeler to call
apporter to bring
apprenant *(m.)*, **apprenant(e)** *(f.)* learner
apprendre to learn
après after
après-demain the day after tomorrow
après-midi *(m.)* afternoon
arbre *(m.)* tree
arc-en-ciel *(m.)* rainbow
argent *(m.)* money, silver
armée *(f.)* army
(s')arrêter to stop, arrest
arriver to arrive, happen
ascenseur *(m.)* elevator
Asie *(f.)* Asia
aspirateur *(m.)* vacuum cleaner
s'asseoir to sit down
assiette *(f.)* plate
assister à to attend
attendre to wait (for)
atterrir to land
attraper to catch

aujourd'hui today
aussitôt que as soon as
autobus *(m.)* bus
automne *(m.)* fall
autoroute *(f.)* freeway
autre other
autrefois formerly, in the past
Autriche *(f.)* Austria
avant (que) before
avec with
avenir *(m.)* future
avertissement *(m.)* warning
aveugle blind
avion *(m.)* airplane
avis *(m.)* opinion
    à mon/ton avis in my/your opinion
avocat *(m.),* **avocate** *(f.)* lawyer
avoir to have
    avoir besoin de to need
    avoir chaud to be hot (people)
    avoir envie de to feel like, want to
    avoir faim to be hungry
    avoir froid to be cold (people)
    avoir lieu to take place
    avoir mal (à) to have a pain (in)
    avoir mal au cœur to feel nauseated
    avoir peur to be afraid
    avoir raison to be right (people)
    avoir soif to be thirsty
    avoir tort to be wrong (people)
avril April

B

balayer to sweep
balle *(f.)* ball, bullet
banc *(m.)* bench
bande dessinée *(f.)* comic strip
bande sonore *(f.)* soundtrack
banque *(f.)* bank
barre *(f.)* bar *(candy)*
    barre de céréales granola bar
bataille *(f.)* battle
bateau *(m.)* ship
bâtir to build
    bâtir des châteaux en Espagne to build castles in the air
battre to beat
bavarder to chat
beau, bel, belle beautiful, handsome
beaucoup (de) a lot (of), many, much
bébé *(m.)* baby
Belgique *(f.)* Belgium
belle-mère *(f.)* mother-in-law
beurre *(m.)* butter
    beurre de cacahuètes peanut butter
bibliothèque *(f.)* library
biche *(f.)* doe

bicyclette *(f.)* bicycle
bien well
bien que although
bientôt soon
    à bientôt see you soon
bienvenue welcome
bière *(f.)* beer
billet *(m.)* ticket
bisou* *(m.)* kiss
blanc, blanche white
blessé *(adj.)* wounded, injured
blessé *(m.)* *(noun)* injured (person)
blesser to wound, injure
bleu blue
blouson *(m.)* jacket, windbreaker
boire to drink
bois *(m.)* wood
boisson *(f.)* drink, beverage
boîte *(f.)* box
bon, bonne good
bonbons *(m. pl.)* candy
bottes *(f.pl.)* boots
boucherie *(f.)* butcher shop
bougie *(f.)* candle
boulanger *(m.),* **boulangère** *(f.)* baker
boulangerie *(f.)* bakery
boum* *(f.)* party *(teenagers')*
bourse *(f.)* scholarship
bouteille *(f.)* bottle
boutique *(f.)* shop
bouton *(m.)* button
braqueur* *(m.)* robber
bras *(m.)* arm
Brésil *(m.)* Brazil
brosser to brush
    se brosser les dents to brush one's teeth
brouillard *(m.)* fog
bruit *(m.)* noise
brûler to burn
    brûler un feu rouge to run a red light
bûche *(f.)* **de Noël** Yule log *(traditional French Christmas pastry in the shape of a log richly decorated with frosting)*
bureau *(m.)* office, desk

C

ça (cela) that
    ça m'est égal it's all the same to me
cabine téléphonique *(f.)* phone booth
cadeau *(m.)* gift
café *(m.)* coffee, café
cahier *(m.)* notebook
calculatrice *(f.)* calculator
camarade *(m./f.)* **de chambre** roommate
cambrioler to burglarize
cambrioleur *(m.),* **cambrioleuse** *(f.)* burglar
canapé *(m.)* sofa, couch

canard *(m.)* duck

    il fait un froid de canard* *it is freezing cold*

caniche *(m.)* poodle

car because

carotte *(f.)* carrot

carrefour *(m.)* intersection

carte *(f.)* menu, map

    carte de crédit *credit card*

    carte postale *postcard*

cauchemar *(m.)* nightmare

cave *(f.)* cellar

ce, cet, cette this, that

céder to yield

ceinture *(f.)* belt

    ceinture de sécurité *safety belt, seat belt*

cela (ça) that

célèbre famous

céleri *(m.)* celery

célibataire single

centre commercial *(m.)* shopping center, mall

c'est-à-dire that is to say

chair *(f.)* **de poule** goose bumps

chaise *(f.)* chair

chambre *(f.)* room, bedroom

chance *(f.)* luck

    bonne chance! *good luck!*

chanceux, chanceuse lucky

changer to change

    changer d'avis *to change one's mind*

chanson *(f.)* song

chanter to sing

chanteur *(m.)*, **chanteuse** *(f.)* singer

chapeau *(m.)* hat

chaque each, every

chasseur *(m.)* hunter

chat *(m.)*, **chatte** *(f.)* cat

château *(m.)* castle

chaud hot, warm

chaussettes *(f.pl.)* socks

chaussures *(f.pl.)* shoes

chemise *(f.)* shirt

cher, chère expensive, dear

chercher to look for

cheval *(m.)* *(plur.:* **chevaux***)* horse

cheveux *(m.pl.)* hair

chez at (to, in) the home of

chien *(m.)*, **chienne** *(f.)* dog

Chine *(f.)* China

chinois *(m.)* Chinese

chocolat *(m.)* chocolate

choisir to choose

choix *(m.)* choice

chômage *(m.)* unemployment

chose *(f.)* thing

chute *(f.)* fall, descent

ciel *(m.)* sky

cinéma *(m.)* movie theater, movies

circulation *(f.)* traffic

cirque *(m.)* circus

ciseaux *(m.pl.)* scissors

classe *(f.)* class

    en classe *in, to class*

clé *(f.)* key

client *(m.)*, **cliente** *(f.)* customer

climatisation *(f.)* air conditioning

clôture *(f.)* fence

coiffeur *(m.)*, **coiffeuse** *(f.)* hairdresser

colis *(m.)* package

colline *(f.)* hill

colocataire *(m./f.)* housemate

combien (de) how much, how many

comédie musicale *(f.)* musical

comique *(m./f.)* comedian

commander to order

commencer to begin

comment how

commode *(f.)* chest of drawers

comprendre to understand

compter to count, plan (on, to)

concert *(m.)* concert

conducteur *(m.)*, **conductrice** *(f.)* driver

conduire to drive

conférence *(f.)* lecture

confiture *(f.)* jam

congé *(m.)* vacation, time off work, leave

congrès *(m.)* conference

connaître to know

conseil *(m.)* (piece of) advice

conseiller to advise

conte *(m.)* story

    conte de fées *fairy tale*

content happy

contravention *(f.)* traffic ticket

convaincre to convince

coordonnées *(f.pl.)* address and phone number

copain *(m.)* friend, boyfriend

copine *(f.)* friend, girlfriend

corne *(f.)* horn *(animal)*

costume *(m.)* suit *(men's)*

côte *(f.)* coast

    Côte d'Azur *French Riviera*

côté *(m.)* side

se coucher to go to bed

coudre to sew

couleur *(f.)* color

Coupe *(f.)* **du monde** World Cup

courage *(m.)* courage

couramment fluently

courir to run

courriel *(m.)* e-mail

courrier *(m.)* mail

    courrier électronique *e-mail*

cours *(m.)* course, class

course *(f.)* errand, race
cousin *(m.)*, **cousine** *(f.)* cousin
coût *(m.)* cost
    coût de la vie cost of living
couteau *(m.)* knife
coûter to cost
    coûter les yeux de la tête* to cost an arm and a leg
couverture *(f.)* blanket
couvrir to cover
craindre to fear
cravate *(f.)* tie
crever* to die
croire to believe
cuiller (cuillère) *(f.)* spoon
cuisine *(f.)* kitchen, cooking, food
cuisiner to cook
cuisse *(f.)* **de grenouille** frog leg
curriculum vitae *(m.)* résumé, CV

D

d'abord at first
d'accord okay, O.K.
    être d'accord (avec) to agree (with)
dame *(f.)* lady, woman
dangereux, dangereuse dangerous
dans in
danser to dance
d'après according to
de from, of
début *(m.)* beginning
décembre December
déçu disappointed
défaite *(f.)* defeat
défendre to forbid
dehors outside
déjà already
déjeuner *(m.)* lunch
déjeuner to have lunch
demain tomorrow
demander to ask
déménager to move (change residence)
dent *(f.)* tooth
se dépêcher to hurry
dépenser to spend *(money)*
déposer (qn) to drop (sb) off
déprimé depressed
depuis since, for
déranger to disturb, bother
dernier, dernière last
derrière behind
dès que as soon as
descendre to go down, get out of (a vehicle)
désolé sorry
dessert *(m.)* dessert
dessin animé *(m.)* cartoon
se détendre to relax
détester to hate, detest

dette *(f.)* debt
devant in front of
devenir to become
deviner to guess
devoir *(verb)* to have to, must, owe
devoirs *(m.pl.)* homework
diable *(m.)* devil
Dieu God
difficile hard, difficult
dimanche *(m.)* Sunday
dîner *(m.)* dinner
dîner *(verb)* to have, eat dinner
diplôme *(m.)* diploma, (university) degree
dire to say
diseuse *(f.)* **de bonne aventure** fortune teller
se disputer to argue
dissertation *(f.)* term paper
doigt *(m.)* finger
dommage *(m.)* pity, shame
    c'est dommage that's too bad
donner to give
dormir to sleep
dos *(m.)* back
douane *(f.)* customs
douche *(f.)* shower
douter to doubt
drapeau *(m.)* flag
droit right
tout droit straight ahead
droite: à droite on (to) the right
drôle funny
dur hard
durer to last

E

eau *(f.)* water
échecs *(m.pl.)* chess
échouer to fail
    échouer à un (l') examen to fail an (the) exam
école *(f.)* school
Écosse *(f.)* Scotland
écouter to listen (to)
écrire to write
écrivain *(m.)* writer
église *(f.)* church
Égypte *(f.)* Egypt
électricité *(f.)* electricity
élève *(m./f.)* student, pupil *(primary and secondary school)*
e-mail *(m.)* e-mail
embouteillage *(m.)* traffic jam
embrasser to hug, kiss
emmener to take (sb somewhere)
empêchement *(m.)* unforeseen difficulty
emprunter to borrow
enceinte pregnant
encore still, again

s'endormir to fall asleep
endroit (m.) place
enfance (f.) childhood
enfant (m./f.) child
enfin finally
ennuyeux, ennuyeuse boring
enseigner to teach
ensemble together
ensuite then
entendre to hear
s'entraîner to practice
entrer (dans) to enter
enveloppe (f.) envelope
envoyer to send
épeler to spell
épouser to marry
équipe (f.) team
erreur (f.) error
escalier (m.) stairs
escargot (m.) snail
Espagne (f.) Spain
espagnol (m.) Spanish
espérer to hope
essayer to try (on)
essence (f.) gasoline
et and
étage (m.) floor (of a building)
état (m.) state, condition
États-Unis (m.pl.) United States
été (m.) summer
éternuer to sneeze
étoile (f.) star
    étoile filante shooting star
étranger (m.), étrangère (f.) stranger, foreigner
étranger, étrangère (adj.) foreign
    à l'étranger abroad
être to be
    être à to belong to
    être à l'aise to be comfortable
    être à l'heure to be on time
    être chanceux, chanceuse to be lucky
    être de bonne/mauvaise humeur to be in a good/bad mood
    être en retard to be late
    être en train de to be in the process of
    être sur le point de to be about to
études (f.pl.) studies
étudiant (m.), étudiante (f.) student (*at university*)
étudier to study
Europe (f.) Europe
européen, européenne European
événement (m.) event
exagérer to exaggerate
examen (m.) exam, test
exiger (que) to demand (that)
exil (m.) exile
explication (f.) explanation

F

fâché angry
se fâcher to get angry
facile easy
facilement easily
façon (f.) manner, way
facteur (m.) mailman
facture (f.) the bill
faire to do, make
    faire attention to pay attention
    faire de son mieux to do one's best
    faire des courses to run errands
    faire des économies to save money
    faire du lèche-vitrines to do window-shopping
    faire la cuisine to cook
    faire la fête to party, celebrate
    faire la grasse matinée to sleep late
    faire (la) grève to be on strike
    faire la lessive to do the laundry
    faire la queue to stand in line
    faire la sieste to take a nap
    faire la vaisselle to do the dishes
    faire le ménage to do the housework
    faire un stage to do an internship
    faire ses valises to pack (one's suitcases)
    faire un voyage to go on a trip, take a trip
falloir to be necessary
fané wilted
fatigué tired
fauché* broke, without money
faute (f.) mistake, fault
fauteuil (m.) armchair
faux, fausse false, wrong
femme (f.) woman, wife
    femme de ménage cleaning woman
fenêtre (f.) window
fermé closed
fermer to close
fête (f.) holiday, party, celebration
    fête nationale national holiday
feu (m.) traffic light, fire
    feu d'artifice fireworks
    feu rouge red light
feuilleton (m.) soap opera, serial
février February
fiable reliable
fier, fière proud
fièvre (f.) fever
fille (f.) daughter, girl
film (m.) movie, film
fils (m.) son
fin (f.) end
finir to finish
fleur (f.) flower
foie (m.) liver
    foie gras goose liver pâté, foie gras

fois *(f.)* time
    la prochaine fois next time
    une fois one time, once
fonctionner to work, function
fonder to found
football *(m.)* soccer
forêt *(f.)* forest
fort strong
four *(m.)* **à micro-ondes** microwave oven
fourchette *(f.)* fork
foyer *(m.)* home, fireplace, hearth
frais, fraîche fresh
fraise *(f.)* strawberry
franc, franche frank
français *(m.)* French
France *(f.)* France
frapper to strike, hit
    ce qui m'a frappé* what struck me
fréquemment frequently
frère *(m.)* brother
frigo* *(m.)* fridge
frites *(f.pl.)* French fries
froid *(adj.)* cold
fromage *(m.)* cheese
fruit *(m.)* (a piece of) fruit
    fruits de mer seafood
fuite *(f.)* leak, flight, escape
fumer to smoke
furieux, furieuse angry, furious
fusil *(m.)* gun, rifle

G

gagnant *(m.),* **gagnante** *(f.)* winner
gagner to win, earn
    gagner à la loterie to win the lottery
    gagner sa vie to make, earn a living
gant *(m.)* glove
garage *(m.)* garage
garçon *(m.)* boy, waiter
garder to look after, keep
gare *(f.)* train station
gâteau *(m.)* cake
gâter to spoil
gauche left
    à gauche on (to) the left
gens *(m.pl.)* people
glace *(f.)* mirror, ice cream
gorge *(f.)* throat
grand big, tall
    grand magasin (m.) department store
grand-mère *(f.)* grandmother
grand-père *(m.)* grandfather
gratte-ciel *(m.)* skyscraper
gratuit free (of charge)
gravement (malade) seriously (ill)
grec *(m.)* Greek
Grèce *(f.)* Greece

grenier *(m.)* attic
grève *(f.)* strike
grille-pain *(m.)* toaster
grippe *(f.)* flu
gros, grosse big, fat
guérir to cure, get well
guerre *(f.)* war
gymnase *(m.)* gymnasium

H

habile skillful
s'habiller to get dressed
habiter to live, reside
habitude *(f.)* habit
    d'habitude usually
haut high
herbe *(f.)* grass
héritage *(m.)* inheritance
heure *(f.)* hour, time, o'clock
    à l'heure on time
    à quelle heure (at) what time
    quelle heure est-il? what time is it?
heureux, heureuse happy
hier yesterday
    hier soir last night
histoire *(f.)* story, history
hiver *(m.)* winter
homme *(m.)* man
hôpital *(m.)* hospital
horoscope *(m.)* horoscope
hors-d'œuvre *(m.)* appetizer
hôtel *(m.)* hotel
hôtesse *(f.)* **de l'air** *(female)* flight attendant

I

ici here
idée *(f.)* idea
il faut it is necessary
il vaut mieux it is better
il y a there is, there are, ago
île *(f.)* island
illettré illiterate
immeuble *(m.)* building, apartment building
imperméable *(m.)* raincoat
impôt *(m.)* tax
incendie *(m.)* fire
Inde *(f.)* India
infirmier *(m.),* **infirmière** *(f.)* nurse
informatique *(f.)* computer science
inquiet, inquiète worried
s'inquiéter to worry
intentionnellement intentionally
interdire to forbid
interdit forbidden
internaute *(m./f.)* Web surfer
Internet *(m.)* Internet
interrompre to interrupt

inutile useless
invité *(m.)*, **invitée** *(f.)* guest
inviter to invite
Irlande *(f.)* Ireland
Italie *(f.)* Italy
italien, italienne *(adj.)* Italian

J

jamais ever, never
    ne... jamais never
jambe *(f.)* leg
janvier January
Japon *(m.)* Japan
japonais *(m.)* Japanese
jardin *(m.)* garden, yard
jaune yellow
jean *(m.)* jeans
jeter to throw
    jeter par la fenêtre to throw out the window
jeu *(m.)* *(plur.:* **jeux***)* game
jeu vidéo video game
jeudi *(m.)* Thursday
jeune young
joie *(f.)* joy
joindre to reach, join
joli pretty
jouer to play
jouet *(m.)* toy
joueur *(m.)*, **joueuse** *(f.)* player
jour *(m.)* day
    un jour some day
journal *(m.)* *(plur.:* **journaux***)* newspaper
juillet July
juin June
jupe *(f.)* skirt
jus *(m.)* juice
jusqu'à until

K

kilo *(m.)* kilogram
kiosque *(m.)* newsstand

L

là there
lâche coward, cowardly
laisser to leave, let
lait *(m.)* milk
langue *(f.)* language
    langue maternelle mother tongue
lapin *(m.)* rabbit
lave-vaisselle *(m.)* dishwasher
laver to wash
légume *(m.)* vegetable
lendemain *(m.)* next day
lent slow
lentement slowly
lettre *(f.)* letter

leur *(pron.)* (to) them
leur, leurs *(adj.)* their
se lever to get up
librairie *(f.)* bookstore
libre free
lire to read
lit *(m.)* bed
littérature *(f.)* literature
livre *(m.)* book
logiciel *(m.)* software
loi *(f.)* law
loin (de) far (from)
long, longue long
longtemps a long time
lorsque when
louer to rent
loup *(m.)* wolf
lui (to) him, (to) her
lumière *(f.)* light
lundi *(m.)* Monday
lune *(f.)* moon
    lune de miel honeymoon
lunettes *(f.pl.)* (eye)glasses
lutter (contre) to fight (against), struggle
lycée *(m.)* high school

M

machine *(f.)* **à laver** washing machine
magasin *(m.)* store
    grand magasin department store
magnétoscope *(m.)* VCR
mai May
maigre skinny
maigrir to lose weight
mail (= **mél**) *(m.)* e-mail
maillot *(m.)* **de bain** bathing suit
main *(f.)* hand
maintenant now
mairie *(f.)* city hall
mais but
maison *(f.)* house
    à la maison home, at home
mal badly
malade *(adj.)* ill
malade *(m./f.)* sick person, patient
maladie *(f.)* disease, illness
malentendu *(m.)* misunderstanding
malgré in spite of
malheureusement unfortunately
manger to eat
    manger sur le pouce* to have a quick bite to eat
manifester to demonstrate
mannequin *(m.)* fashion model, store dummy
manquer (à) to miss
manteau *(m.)* coat
marcher to walk, work (= function)
mardi *(m.)* Tuesday

mari *(m.)* husband
mariage *(m.)* marriage, wedding
marié *(adj.)* married
marié *(m.)* bridegroom
mariée *(f.)* bride
se marier (avec) to get married (to)
marron brown
mars March
match *(m.)* game
matin *(m.)* morning
mauvais bad
méchant mean, vicious
médecin *(m.)* doctor
meilleur better
même same, even
mendiant *(m.)*, **mendiante** *(f.)* beggar
menu *(m.)* (fixed price) menu
mercredi *(m.)* Wednesday
mère *(f.)* mother
merveilleux, merveilleuse marvelous, wonderful
message *(m.)* message
météo *(f.)* weather forecast, weather
métier *(m.)* profession, trade
métro *(m.)* subway, metro
mettre to put
    se mettre à (+ inf.) to begin (doing)
meubles *(m.pl.)* furniture
Mexique *(m.)* Mexico
midi *(m.)* noon
mieux better
milieu *(m.)* middle
(des) milliers *(m.pl.)* thousands
mince slim, thin
minuit midnight
moins less, minus
mois *(m.)* month
mon, ma, mes *(adj.)* my
monde *(m.)* world
    tout le monde everybody
monnaie *(f.)* (small) change, currency
monsieur (M.) *(m.)* sir, gentleman (Mr.)
monstre *(m.)* monster
montagne *(f.)* mountain
monter to go up, get into (*a vehicle*)
montre *(f.)* watch
montrer to show
morceau *(m.)* piece
mordre to bite
mot *(m.)* word, (written) note
moto(cylette) *(f.)* motorcycle
mourir to die
mouton *(m.)* sheep
muguet *(m.)* lily-of-the-valley
mur *(m.)* wall
musée *(m.)* museum
musique *(f.)* music

N

nager to swim
nappe *(f.)* tablecloth
neige *(f.)* snow
neiger to snow
ne… jamais never
ne… pas not
ne… personne no one, nobody, not anyone
ne… que only
ne… rien nothing, not anything
Net *(m.)* Net (= Internet)
nettoyer to clean
neveu *(m.)* *(plur.:* **neveux***)* nephew
nièce *(f.)* niece
Noël *(m.)* Christmas
    père Noël (m.) Santa Claus
noir black
nom *(m.)* name
note *(f.)* grade (*in a course*)
nouveau, nouvel, nouvelle new
nouvelle *(f.)* (a piece of) news, short story
novembre November
nuage *(m.)* cloud
numéro *(m.)* **de téléphone** telephone number

O

obéir to obey
obtenir to get
occupé busy
octobre October
œil *(m.)* *(plur.:* **les yeux***)* eye
offrir to offer
oiseau *(m.)* bird
oncle *(m.)* uncle
ongle *(m.)* finger nail
opéra *(m.)* opera
or *(m.)* gold
orage *(m.)* thunderstorm
ordinateur *(m.)* computer
oser to dare
otage *(m.)* hostage
ou or
où where
oublier to forget
ouvert open
ouvrier *(m.)*, **ouvrière** *(f.)* worker
ouvrir to open

P

pain *(m.)* bread
paix *(f.)* peace
pâle pale
pamplemousse *(m.)* grapefruit
panne: tomber en panne to break down (*car*)
pantalon *(m.)* (pair of) pants
papillon *(m.)* butterfly

Pâques *(f.pl.)* Easter
paquet *(m.)* package
parabole *(f.)* satellite dish
parapluie *(m.)* umbrella
parce que because
parents *(m.pl.)* parents, relatives
paresseux, paresseuse lazy
parler to speak
partager to share
partir to leave
partout everywhere
passager *(m.)*, **passagère** *(f.)* passenger
passer to pass, spend *(time)*, take *(a test)*
   se passer to happen
patiemment patiently
patience *(f.)* patience
patient *(adj.)* patient
patienter to wait
patiner to ice skate
pâtisserie *(f.)* pastry shop, pastry
patron *(m.)*, **patronne** *(f.)* boss
pauvre poor
payer to pay (for)
   payer en espèces to pay cash
pays *(m.)* country
peau *(f.)* skin
pelouse *(f.)* lawn
pendant during, for
penser to think
perdre to lose
   perdre la tête to lose one's mind, one's temper
père *(m.)* father
   père Noël Santa Claus
permettre to allow
permis *(m.)* **de conduire** driver's license
personne *(f.)* person
peser to weigh
petit small, short
   petit ami (m.), petite amie (f.) boyfriend, girlfriend
   petit déjeuner (m.) breakfast
   petit pain (m.) roll (bread)
peur *(f.)* fear
peut-être perhaps, maybe
pharmacie *(f.)* pharmacy
piano *(m.)* piano
pièce *(f.)* play *(theater)*, coin, room *(of a house)*
   pièce montée tiered wedding cake
piège *(m.)* trap
pied *(m.)* foot
   à pied on foot
piquer to sting, bite
pire worse, worst
piscine *(f.)* swimming pool
place *(f.)* seat, room (space), (public) square
plage *(f.)* beach
plaire à to please

plaisanter to joke
plaisanterie *(f.)* joke
plaisir *(m.)* pleasure
plancher *(m.)* floor (*of a room*)
plat *(m.)* dish, course
   plat principal main course
pleurer to cry
pleuvoir to rain
   pleuvoir à verse to rain hard, pour
   pleuvoir des cordes* to rain cats and dogs
pluie *(f.)* rain
plus more
   plus longtemps longer
   plus vite faster
plusieurs several
poème *(m.)* poem
poignée *(f.)* handle, doorknob
poisson *(m.)* fish
policier *(m.)* policeman
pomme *(f.)* apple
pompier *(m.)* firefighter
pont *(m.)* bridge
(téléphone) portable *(m.)* cell phone
porte *(f.)* door
portefeuille *(m.)* wallet
porte-monnaie *(m.)* coin purse
porter to wear, carry
   porter bonheur to bring good luck
portugais *(m.)* Portuguese
posséder to own
poste *(f.)* post office
poster to mail
poubelle *(f.)* garbage can
poupée *(f.)* doll
pour for, in order to
   pour que so that
pourboire *(m.)* tip *(waiter)*
pourquoi why
pouvoir *(m.)* power
pouvoir *(verb)* to be able to
prédire to predict
préférer to prefer
premier, première first
prendre to take
   prendre une décision to make a decision
presque almost
pressé in a hurry
prêter to loan, lend
prier to pray, beg
printemps *(m.)* spring
prison *(f.)* prison, jail
priver to deprive
prix *(m.)* price, prize, award
prochain next
professeur *(m.)* teacher, professor
projet *(m.)* plan

se promener to take a walk
promesse (*f.*) promise
promettre to promise
prononcer to pronounce
proposer to suggest
propre clean, own
prudemment carefully
prudent careful
puis then
puissant powerful
pull-over (pull) (*m.*) sweater
PV (procès verbal) (*m.*) (traffic) ticket

Q

quand when
quartier (*m.*) neighborhood
que that, which; what?
quel, quelle which? what?
quelque chose something
quelque part somewhere
quelquefois sometimes
quelques some, a few
quelqu'un someone, somebody
qu'est-ce que what?
questionnaire (*m.*) questionnaire
queue (*f.*) line
qui who, whom; who? whom?
quitter to leave
quoi what?
quoique although

R

raconter to tell
radio (*f.*) radio
ragots* (*m.pl.*) gossip
rappeler to call back, remind
    se rappeler to remember
rarement rarely
ravi delighted
recevoir to receive
recherche (*f.*) search
    recherches (f.pl.) research
recommander to recommend
récompense (*f.*) reward
reçu (*m.*) receipt
rédaction (*f.*) composition, essay
réfrigérateur (*m.*) refrigerator
refuser to refuse
regarder to look at, watch
regretter to regret, be sorry
remède (*m.*) cure
remercier to thank
rencontrer to meet
rendez-vous (*m.*) (social) date, appointment
rendre to give back, hand in (*homework*)
rentrée (*f.*) beginning of the (new) school year
rentrer to go home, come home

repas (*m.*) meal
répéter to repeat
répondeur (*m.*) answering machine
répondre (à) to answer
réponse (*f.*) answer
se reposer to rest
représentation (*f.*) performance
respirer to breathe
rester to stay, remain
resto-U* (**= restaurant universitaire**) (*m.*) dining commons, university cafeteria
résultat (*m.*) result
retour (*m.*) return
retourner to return, go back
réunion (*f.*) meeting
réussir (à) to succeed, pass (*a test*)
rêve (*m.*) dream
réveil (*m.*) alarm clock
se réveiller to wake up
revenir to come back
réviser to review
revue (*f.*) magazine
rez-de-chaussée (*m.*) first floor, ground floor
rhume (*m.*) cold
rire to laugh
riz (*m.*) rice
robe (*f.*) dress
roi (*m.*) king
roman (*m.*) novel
rouge red
rougir to blush
roux, rousse red (-haired)
rue (*f.*) street
russe (*m.*) Russian
Russie (*f.*) Russia

S

sac (*m.*) bag, handbag
    sac à dos backpack
    sac à main handbag
    sac de couchage sleeping bag
sage well-behaved, wise
salaire (*m.*) salary
sale dirty
salle (*f.*) room; hall
    salle à manger dining room
    salle de bains bathroom
    salle de classe classroom
salon (*m.*) living room
saluer to greet
samedi (*m.*) Saturday
sans without
santé (*f.*) health
sapeur-pompier (*m.*) firefighter
savoir to know
savon (*m.*) soap
selon according to

semaine *(f.)* week
sembler to seem
septembre September
serpent *(m.)* snake
serveur *(m.)*, **serveuse** *(f.)* waiter, waitress
service *(m.)* favor, service
serviette *(f.)* napkin, towel
seul alone
seulement only
short *(m.)* (pair of) shorts
si if, whether
siècle *(m.)* century
singe *(m.)* monkey
skier to ski
smoking *(m.)* tuxedo
sœur *(f.)* sister
soin *(m.)* care
soir *(m.)* evening
    ce soir tonight
soldat *(m.)* soldier
solde: en solde on sale
soleil *(m.)* sun
sonner to ring (*bell, telephone, alarm clock*)
sortie *(f.)* exit, outing
sortir to go out, exit
souffrir to suffer
souhaiter (que) to wish (that)
sourire to smile
souris *(f.)* mouse
sous under
sous-sol *(m.)* basement
se souvenir (de) to remember
souvent often
spectacle *(m.)* show
stage *(m.)* internship
    faire un stage to do an internship
stylo *(m.)* pen
suggérer to suggest
Suisse *(f.)* Switzerland
suisse *(adj.)* Swiss
suivre to follow, take (*a course*)
supermarché *(m.)* supermarket
sur on
sûr sure, safe
surpris surprised
survivre to survive

T

table *(f.)* table
tableau *(m.)* blackboard; painting
tant (de) so much, so many
tante *(f.)* aunt
tapis *(m.)* rug
tard late
    plus tard later
tarte *(f.)* pie, tart
tasse *(f.)* cup

taureau *(m.)* bull
tee-shirt *(m.)* tee-shirt
télé* *(f.)* TV
télécarte *(f.)* (prepaid) phone card
télécharger to download
télécommande *(f.)* remote control
téléphone *(m.)* telephone
    (téléphone) portable (m.) cell phone
téléphoner (à) to call, phone
téléviseur *(m.)* television set
télévision *(f.)* television
tempête *(f.)* storm
    tempête de neige snowstorm, blizzard
temps *(m.)* time, weather
    à temps in time
tenir to hold
    tenir à to insist on, be anxious to
terminaison *(f.)* ending
terminer to end
terre *(f.)* earth, land
tête *(f.)* head
TGV (train *[m.]* **à grande vitesse)** French high-speed train
thé *(m.)* tea
théâtre *(m.)* theater
ticket *(m.)* **de caisse** sales slip, receipt
timbre *(m.)* (postage) stamp
tirer to pull
tiroir *(m.)* drawer
toilettes *(f.pl.)* restroom
tomber to fall
    tomber à l'eau* to fall through (plans)
    tomber dans les pommes* to faint, pass out
    tomber en panne to break down (car)
    tomber malade to become, fall ill
tondre la pelouse to mow the lawn
tôt early
    plus tôt earlier
toujours always
tour *(f.)* tower
tour *(m.)* turn, walk, ride
tourner to turn
tout everything
    tout à coup suddenly
    tout le monde everybody
    tout le temps all the time
train *(m.)* train
tramway *(m.)* streetcar, light rail
travail *(m.)* work
travailler to work
travers: à travers across
traverser to cross
tremblement *(m.)* **de terre** earthquake
très very
trésor *(m.)* treasure
triste sad
trop (de) too, too much, too many

trou *(m.)* hole
trouver to find
tuer to kill
Turquie *(f.)* Turkey

U

université *(f.)* university
usine *(f.)* factory
utile useful
utiliser to use

V

vacances *(f.pl.)* vacation
vaisselle *(f.)* dishes
valeur *(f.)* value
valise *(f.)* suitcase
   faire ses valises to pack one's
      suitcase(s)
valoir to be worth
   valoir mieux to be better
vedette *(f.)* star, movie star
veille (la) *(f.)* the night before
vélo* *(m.)* bike
vendeur *(m.)* salesperson, salesman
vendeuse *(f.)* saleslady, saleswoman
vendre to sell
vendredi *(m.)* Friday
venir to come
vent *(m.)* wind
vérité *(f.)* truth
verre *(m.)* glass
vers toward, at about (with clock time)
verser to pour

vert green
veste *(f.)* jacket
vêtements *(m.pl.)* clothes, clothing
viande *(f.)* meat
victoire *(f.)* victory
vie *(f.)* life
vieux, vieil, vieille old
ville *(f.)* city, town
   ville natale home town
vin *(m.)* wine
violet, violette purple
visiter to visit (*a place*)
vite fast, quickly
vitre *(f.)* (window) pane
vivre to live
vœu *(m.)* wish
voir to see
voisin *(m.)*, **voisine** *(f.)* neighbor
voiture *(f.)* car
voix *(f.)* voice
volant *(m.)* steering wheel
voler to fly, steal
volontiers gladly
vouloir to want
voyage *(m.)* trip
voyager to travel
vrai true
vue *(f.)* view
   de vue by sight

Y

y there
yeux *(m.pl.)* eyes

English-French glossary

A

a lot (of) beaucoup
abolish abolir
about environ
abroad à l'étranger
accident accident *(m.)*
acquaintance connaissance *(f.)*
   make the acquaintance of faire la
    connaissance de
across à travers
act jouer, agir
actor acteur *(m.)*
actress actrice *(f.)*
address adresse *(f.)*
admit admettre
adult adulte *(m./f.)*
adventure aventure *(f.)*
advice (piece of) conseil *(m.)*
advise conseiller
advisor conseiller *(m.)*, conseillère *(f.)*
Africa Afrique *(f.)*
afraid: be afraid avoir peur, craindre
after après (que)
afternoon après-midi *(m.)*
age âge *(m.)*
ago il y a
agree (with) être d'accord (avec)
air conditioning climatisation *(f.)*
airline company compagnie aérienne
   (f.)
airplane avion *(m.)*
airport aéroport *(m.)*
aisle couloir *(m.)*
alarm (clock) réveil *(m.)*
alive en vie, vivant
allow permettre, laisser
almost presque
alone seul
already déjà
also aussi
although bien que, quoique
always toujours
America Amérique *(f.)*

and et
angry fâché; furieux, furieuse
   get angry se fâcher
animal animal *(m.) (plur.:* animaux*)*
answer *(noun)* réponse *(f.)*
answer *(verb)* répondre
answering machine répondeur *(m.)*
apartment appartement *(m.)*
apologize s'excuser
appetizer hors-d'œuvre *(m.)*
applaud applaudir
apple pomme *(f.)*
appointment rendez-vous *(m.)*
appreciate apprécier
April avril
argue se disputer
armchair fauteuil *(m.)*
arrest *(verb)* arrêter
arrive arriver
article article *(m.)*
Asia Asie *(f.)*
ask demander
   ask a question poser une question
assignment devoir *(m.)*
at à
   at first d'abord
   at least au moins
ATM (automated teller machine) distributeur
   (automatique) *(m.)* de billets
attend assister (à)
attention: pay attention faire attention
attentively attentivement
attic grenier *(m.)*
August août
aunt tante *(f.)*
Austria Autriche *(f.)*
autumn automne *(m.)*
avoid éviter
award *(noun)* prix *(m.)*

B

baby bébé *(m.)*
backpack sac *(m.)* à dos

bad mauvais
badly mal
bag sac *(m.)*
baker boulanger *(m.)*, boulangère *(f.)*
bakery boulangerie *(f.)*
balcony balcon *(m.)*
bank banque *(f.)*
bar bar *(m.)*
   (candy) bar barre *(f.)*
bargain *(noun)* bonne affaire *(f.)*
bargain *(verb)* marchander
basement sous-sol *(m.)*
basket panier *(m.)*
bathing suit maillot *(m.)* de bain
bathroom salle *(f.)* de bains
be être
   be able to ("can") *pouvoir*
   be afraid *avoir peur*
   be hungry *avoir faim*
   be interested in *s'intéresser à*
   be lucky *avoir de la chance; être chanceux, chanceuse*
   be mistaken *se tromper*
   be named *s'appeler*
   be quiet *se taire*
   be right *avoir raison*
   be situated *se trouver*
   be sleepy *avoir sommeil*
   be thirsty *avoir soif*
   be wrong (person) *avoir tort*
beach plage *(f.)*
bear *(noun)* ours *(m.)*
beat *(verb)* battre, frapper
beautiful beau, bel, belle
because parce que, car
   because of *à cause de*
become devenir
bed lit *(m.)*
bedroom chambre *(f.)* à coucher
beer bière *(f.)*
before avant (que)
begin commencer, se mettre à
behave se comporter, se conduire
Belgium Belgique *(f.)*
believe croire
belong to appartenir à , être à
belt ceinture *(f.)*
   seat belt, safety belt *ceinture de sécurité*
bench banc *(m.)*
better *(adj.)* meilleur
better *(adv.)* mieux
between entre
bicycle bicyclette *(f.)*, vélo* *(m.)*
big grand
bike vélo* *(m.)*
bill facture *(f.)*, *(in restaurant)* addition *(f.)*
bird oiseau *(m.)*
birthday anniversaire *(m.)*

bite *(verb)* mordre
black noir
blackboard tableau noir *(m.)*
blanket couverture *(f.)*
blue bleu
blush *(verb)* rougir
boat bateau *(m.)*, *(small)* barque *(f.)*
bomb *(noun)* bombe *(f.)*
book livre *(m.)*
bookstore librairie *(f.)*
boots bottes *(f.pl.)*
boring ennuyeux, ennuyeuse
borrow emprunter
boss patron *(m.)*, patronne *(f.)*
both (tous) les deux *(m.pl.)*, (toutes) les deux *(f.pl.)*
bother *(verb)* déranger
bottle bouteille *(f.)*
box boîte *(f.)*
boy garçon *(m.)*
boyfriend petit ami *(m.)*, copain *(m.)*
Brazil Brésil *(m.)*
bread pain *(m.)*
break *(verb)* casser
   break down *(car)* tomber en panne
breakfast petit déjeuner *(m.)*
bride mariée *(f.)*
bridegroom marié *(m.)*
bridge pont *(m.)*
bring apporter
broke *(no money)* fauché*
broken cassé
brother frère *(m.)*
brush *(verb)* (se) brosser
building bâtiment *(m.)*
burglar cambrioleur *(m.)*, cambrioleuse *(f.)*, braqueur* *(m.)*
bus autobus *(m.)*
busy occupé
but mais
butcher shop boucherie *(f.)*
butter beurre *(m.)*
   peanut butter *beurre de cacahuètes*
butterfly papillon *(m.)*
buy acheter

C

cake gâteau *(m.)*
calculator calculatrice *(f.)*
call *(verb)* appeler, téléphoner (à)
camera appareil photo *(m.)*
camping camping *(m.)*
   go camping *faire du camping*
can (be able to) pouvoir
cancel annuler, supprimer
candle bougie *(f.)*
candy bonbons *(m.pl.)*
car voiture *(f.)*

card carte *(f.)*
> ***credit card*** *carte de crédit*
> ***postcard*** *carte postale*

careful prudent
carefully prudemment
carry porter
cartoon dessin animé *(m.)*
cash register caisse *(f.)*
castle château *(m.)*
cat chat *(m.)*, chatte *(f.)*
catch attraper
cathedral cathédrale *(f.)*
cause *(verb)* causer
celebrate fêter, célébrer, faire la fête
cell phone (téléphone) portable *(m.)*
cellar cave *(f.)*
century siècle *(m.)*
chair chaise *(f.)*
champagne champagne *(m.)*
change changer
> ***change one's mind*** *changer d'avis*

chat *(verb)* bavarder
cheese fromage *(m.)*
chicken poulet *(m.)*
child enfant *(m./f.)*
childhood enfance *(f.)*
Chinese chinois *(m.)*
chocolate chocolat *(m.)*
choice choix *(m.)*
choose choisir
Christmas Noël *(m.)*
church église *(f.)*
citizenship nationalité *(f.)*
city ville *(f.)*
class classe *(f.)*, cours *(m.)*
classroom salle *(f.)* de classe
clean *(verb)* nettoyer
clean *(adj.)* propre
clock *(big)* horloge *(f.)*, *(small)* pendule *(f.)*
close *(verb)* fermer
closed fermé
clothes, clothing vêtements *(m.pl.)*
cloud nuage *(m.)*
coach *(sports)* entraîneur *(m.)*
coat manteau *(m.)*
coffee café *(m.)*
cold froid *(m.)*
> ***be cold*** *(person) avoir froid*
> ***be cold*** *(weather) faire froid*

college université *(f.)*
color couleur *(f.)*
comb *(verb)* se peigner
come venir
comedy comédie *(f.)*
comic strip bande dessinée *(f.)*
complain (about) se plaindre (de)
composition *(writing)* rédaction *(f.)*

computer ordinateur *(m.)*
> ***computer science*** *informatique **(f.)***
> ***laptop computer*** *ordinateur portable*

concert concert *(m.)*
consume consommer
continue continuer
cook *(noun)* cuisinier *(m.)*, cuisinière *(f.)*
cook *(verb)* cuisiner, faire la cuisine
cooking cuisine *(f.)*
correctly correctement
cost *(noun)* coût *(m.)*
cost *(verb)* coûter
country pays *(m.)*
cousin cousin *(m.)*, cousine *(f.)*
crazy fou, folle
credit card carte *(f.)* de credit
cross *(verb)* traverser
cruise *(noun)* croisière *(f.)*
> ***go on a cruise*** *faire une croisière*

cry *(verb)* pleurer
cup tasse *(f.)*
cure remède *(m.)*
customer client *(m.)*, cliente *(f.)*
cut *(verb)* couper

D

dad papa *(m.)*
damage *(verb)* endommager
dance *(verb)* danser
dangerous dangereux, dangereuse
dare *(verb)* oser
date *(noun)* date *(f.)*, *(social)* rendez-vous *(m.)*
daughter fille *(f.)*
day jour *(m.)*, journée *(f.)*
> ***every day*** *chaque jour*
> ***some day*** *un jour*
> ***the day before yesterday*** *avant-hier*

deadline date limite *(f.)*
dear cher, chère
death mort *(f.)*
debt dette *(f.)*
decade décennie *(f.)*
December décembre
deer *(female)* biche *(f.)*
delicious délicieux, délicieuse
delighted ravi
demand *(verb)* exiger (que)
demonstrate *(protest)* manifester
demonstration *(protest)* manifestation *(f.)*
dentist dentiste *(m./f.)*
department *(of a store)* rayon *(m.)*
> ***department store*** *grand magasin **(m.)***
> ***shoe department*** *rayon des chaussures*

depressed déprimé
desk bureau *(m.)*
dessert dessert *(m.)*
destroy détruire

detest détester
devil diable *(m.)*
die mourir
difficult difficile
dining room salle *(f.)* à manger
dinner dîner *(m.)*
diploma diplôme *(m.)*
dirty sale
disappear disparaître
disappoint décevoir
disappointed déçu
dish plat *(m.)*
dishes vaisselle *(f.)*
dishwasher lave-vaisselle *(m.)*
disturb déranger
divorce *(noun)* divorce *(m.)*
divorce *(verb)* divorcer
do faire
doctor médecin *(m.)*
doe biche *(f.)*
dog chien *(m.)*, chienne *(f.)*
doll poupée *(f.)*
door porte *(f.)*
doubt *(noun)* doute *(m.)*
doubt *(verb)* douter
dream *(noun)* rêve *(m.)*
dream *(verb)* rêver
dress *(noun)* robe *(f.)*
drink *(noun)* boisson *(f.)*
drink *(verb)* boire
drive conduire, rouler
driver conducteur *(m.)*, conductrice *(f.)*
    driver's license permis **(m.)** de conduire
drown se noyer
during pendant

E

each chaque
early tôt, de bonne heure
earn gagner
earring boucle *(f.)* d'oreille
earthquake tremblement *(m.)* de terre
easy facile
Easter Pâques *(f.pl.)*
eat manger
    eat dinner dîner
    eat lunch déjeuner
    eat out dîner au restaurant
effort effort *(m.)*
Egypt Égypte *(f.)*
elevator ascenseur *(m.)*
e-mail courrier électronique *(m.)*, e-mail *(m.)*, mail *(m.)*, courriel *(m.)*
employ employer
engineer ingénieur *(m.)*
England Angleterre *(f.)*

English anglais *(m.)*
enough assez (de)
enter entrer (dans)
envelope enveloppe *(f.)*
Europe Europe *(f.)*
    in/to Europe en Europe
European *(adj.)* européen, européenne
even même
evening soir *(m.)*, soirée *(f.)*
event événement *(m.)*
every chaque
everybody tout le monde
everyone tout le monde
everything tout
everywhere partout
exaggerate exagérer
exam examen *(m.)*
except sauf
exit *(noun)* sortie *(f.)*
expect s'attendre à
expensive cher, chère
experienced expérimenté
explode exploser
explosion explosion *(f.)*
eye œil *(m.)* *(plur.: yeux)*
eyeglasses lunettes *(f.pl.)*

F

face visage *(m.)*
factory usine *(f.)*
fail échouer
    fail an exam échouer à un examen, rater* un examen
fall *(verb)* tomber
    fall asleep s'endormir
fall *(noun)* *(season)* automne *(m.)*, *(snow-, water-)* chute *(f.)*
false faux, fausse
family famille *(f.)*
famous célèbre
far (from) loin (de)
fashion model mannequin *(m.)*
fast rapide *(adj.)*, vite *(adv.)*
father père *(m.)*
father-in-law beau-père *(m.)*
favor service *(m.)*
favorite favori, favorite; préféré
fax *(noun)* fax *(m.)*
fear *(noun)* peur *(f.)*
fear *(verb)* craindre, avoir peur
February février
feel (se) sentir
fence *(noun)* clôture *(f.)*
fever fièvre *(f.)*
fill (up, out) remplir
finally enfin
find trouver

finger doigt (m.)
fingernail ongle (m.)
finish finir, terminer, achever
fire (from a job) licencier, renvoyer, virer*
firefighter pompier (m.), sapeur-pompier (m.)
fireworks feu (m.) d'artifice
first premier, première
    at first d'abord
fish (noun) poisson (m.)
flag drapeau (m.)
flight vol (m.)
    flight attendant (female) hôtesse (**f.**) de l'air
floor (of a building) étage (m.)
    on the ground (first) floor au rez-de-chaussée
    on the second floor au premier étage
    on the third floor au deuxième étage
floor (of a room) plancher (m.)
flower fleur (f.)
flu grippe (f.)
fluently couramment
fly (verb) voler
fog brouillard (m.)
foggy: be foggy out faire du brouillard
follow suivre
foot pied (m.)
    on foot à pied
for pour, depuis, pendant
forbid défendre, interdire
foreign (adj.) étranger, étrangère
forest forêt (f.)
forget oublier
forgive pardonner
fork fourchette (f.)
fortune fortune (f.)
France France (f.)
frank franc, franche
free libre
free (of charge) gratuit
freeway autoroute (f.)
French fries frites (f.pl.)
Friday vendredi (m.)
friend ami (m.), amie (f.), copain (m.), copine (f.)
frog grenouille (f.)
from de
front: in front of devant
furniture meubles (m.pl.)
furthermore de plus
future avenir (m.)

G

game jeu (m.), (football, basketball) match (m.)
garage garage (m.)
garden jardin (m.)
gasoline essence (f.)
gentleman monsieur (m.)
German allemand (m.)

Germany Allemagne (f.)
get obtenir, recevoir
    get along (with) s'entendre (avec)
    get angry se fâcher
    get bored s'ennuyer
    get dressed s'habiller
    get engaged se fiancer
    get lost se perdre
    get married se marier
    get undressed se déshabiller
    get up se lever
    get used to s'habituer à
gift cadeau (m.)
girl fille (f.), jeune fille (f.)
girlfriend petite amie (f.), copine (f.)
give donner
    give back rendre
glass verre (m.)
glasses (eye) lunettes (f.pl.)
glove gant (m.)
go aller
    go away s'en aller
    go down descendre
    go for a walk se promener
    go out sortir
    go swimming se baigner
    go to bed se coucher
    go up monter
God Dieu
gold or (m.)
good bon, bonne; (well-behaved) sage
good-bye au revoir
goose bumps chair (f.) de poule
grade (in course) note (f.)
graduate (verb) obtenir son diplôme, finir ses
    études
grandchildren petits-enfants (m.pl.)
grandfather grand père (m.)
grandmother grand-mère (f.)
grass herbe (f.)
Greece Grèce (f.)
Greek (adj.) grec, grecque
green vert
greet saluer
gun pistolet (m.), fusil (m.)
gym(nasium) gymnase (m.)

H

hair cheveux (m.pl.)
half moitié (f.)
hallway couloir (m.)
ham jambon (m.)
hand main (f.)
hand in (homework) rendre, remettre
handbag sac (m.) à main
handsome beau, bel

happen arriver, se passer
happy heureux, heureuse; content
hard dur, difficile
hat chapeau (m.)
hate (verb) détester
have avoir
   have a good time / have fun s'amuser
   have lunch déjeuner
   have to (do something) devoir
head tête (f.)
health santé (f.)
healthy en bonne santé
hear entendre
help (verb) aider
her (adj.) son, sa, ses
here ici
hesitate hésiter
hide (verb) (se) cacher
high school lycée (m.)
hijack détourner
his (adj.) son, sa, ses
hit (crash into) percuter, (beat) frapper,
   battre
hold tenir
home town ville natale (f.)
homework devoirs (m.pl.)
honeymoon lune (f.) de miel
hope (verb) espérer
horse cheval (m.) (plur.: chevaux)
hostage otage (m.)
hot chaud
hotel hôtel (m.)
hour heure (f.)
house maison (f.)
housemate colocataire (m./f.)
housework ménage (m.)
how comment
   how many combien
   how much combien
hug (verb) embrasser
hunger faim (f.)
hungry: be hungry avoir faim
hurricane ouragan (m.)
hurry se dépêcher
   be in a hurry être pressé
husband mari (m.)

I

ice cream glace (f.)
ice skate (verb) patiner
if si
ill malade
immediately immédiatement
important important
improve (s')améliorer
in dans
   + city à

+ feminine country *en*
+ masculine country *au*
   in a hurry pressé
   in love (with) amoureux, amoureuse (de)
injure blesser
inspector inspecteur (m.), inspectrice (f.)
instead of au lieu de
interested: be . . . in être intéressé par
Internet Internet (m.)
introduce (oneself) (se) présenter
invent inventer
invite inviter
Ireland Irlande (f.)
island île (f.)
Italian italien (m.)
Italy Italie (f.)

J

jacket blouson (m.), veste (f.), anorak (m.)
jail prison (f.)
jam (fruit) confiture (f.)
January janvier
Japan Japon (m.)
Japanese japonais (m.)
jeans (pair of) jean (m.)
jewelry bijoux (m.pl.)
job travail (m.), emploi (m.)
join rejoindre
joke (noun) plaisanterie (f.)
joke (verb) plaisanter
judge juge (m.)
juice jus (m.)
July juillet
June juin

K

keep garder, tenir (promise)
key clé (f.)
kidnap enlever
kill tuer
kilogram kilo (m.)
king roi (m.)
kiss (verb) (s')embrasser
kitchen cuisine (f.)
knife couteau (m.)
knock (verb) frapper
know savoir, (person or place) connaître

L

lady dame (f.)
lake lac (m.)
land (verb) atterrir
landscape paysage (m.)
language langue (f.)
laptop computer ordinateur portable (m.)
last (adj.) dernier, dernière
   last night hier soir

last *(verb)* durer
late tard
    be late être en retard
later plus tard
laugh *(verb)* rire
laundry lessive *(f.)*
lawn pelouse *(f.)*
lawyer avocat *(m.)*, avocate *(f.)*
lay off *(work)* licencier
lay the table mettre la table
lazy paresseux, paresseuse
learn apprendre
learner apprenant *(m.)*, apprenante *(f.)*
leave *(verb)* partir, quitter *(place or a person)*, laisser *(tip, message)*
lecture conférence *(f.)*
left gauche *(f.)*
    on/to the left à gauche
    turn left tourner à gauche
leg jambe *(f.)*
lend prêter
less moins
let laisser, permettre
letter lettre *(f.)*
library bibliothèque *(f.)*
license: driver's license permis *(m.)* de conduire
lie *(verb)* mentir
life vie *(f.)*
light *(noun)* lumière *(f.)*
like *(verb)* aimer
link *(noun)* lien *(m.)*
listen to écouter
little: a little (un) peu (de)
live *(verb)* habiter, vivre
live habiter, vivre
living room salon *(m.)*, séjour *(m.)*
loan *(verb)* prêter
long time: a long time longtemps
look (at) regarder
    look for chercher
lose perdre
    lose patience perdre patience
    lose weight maigrir
lot: a lot beaucoup
love *(verb)* aimer
luck chance *(f.)*
    good luck bonne chance
luckily heureusement
lucky: be lucky avoir de la chance, être chanceux, chanceuse
lunch déjeuner *(m.)*
    have/eat lunch déjeuner

M

magazine magazine *(m.)*
mail courrier *(m.)*
mailman facteur *(m.)*

major in se spécialiser en
make faire
    make a decision prendre une décision
    make fun of se moquer de
    make oneself comfortable se mettre à l'aise
man homme *(m.)*
many beaucoup (de)
March mars
marriage mariage *(m.)*
married marié
marry se marier, épouser
mask masque *(m.)*
May mai
maybe peut-être
meal repas *(m.)*
mean *(adj.)* méchant
measure *(verb)* mesurer
meat viande *(f.)*
meet rencontrer
meeting réunion *(f.)*
memory souvenir *(m.)*
mention mentionner
menu carte *(f.)*
merchant commerçant *(m.)*, commerçante *(f.)*
message message *(m.)*
Mexico Mexique *(m.)*
middle milieu *(m.)*
midnight minuit
milk lait *(m.)*
minute minute *(f.)*
miracle miracle *(m.)*
mirror miroir *(m.)*
miss manquer
Miss Mlle (mademoiselle)
mistake faute *(f.)*
model: fashion model mannequin *(m.)*
mom maman *(f.)*
Monday lundi *(m.)*
money argent *(m.)*
month mois *(m.)*
moon lune *(f.)*
more plus (de)
morning matin *(m.)*
mother mère *(f.)*
mother-in-law belle-mère *(f.)*
motorcycle motocyclette *(f.)*, moto* *(f.)*
mountain montagne *(f.)*
mouse souris *(f.)*
move bouger, déménager *(change residence)*
movie film *(m.)*
    movie star vedette *(f.)* de cinéma
    movie theater cinéma *(m.)*
    movies cinéma *(m.)*
mow the lawn tondre la pelouse
Mr. M. (monsieur)
Mrs. Mme (madame)
much beaucoup (de)

museum musée *(m.)*
music musique *(f.)*
musical (comedy) comédie musicale *(f.)*
must *(have to)* devoir
my *(adj.)* mon, ma, mes

N

name *(noun)* nom *(m.)*
napkin serviette *(f.)*
near près (de)
necklace collier *(m.)*
need *(verb)* avoir besoin (de)
neighbor voisin *(m.)*, voisine *(f.)*
nephew neveu *(m.)* *(plur.: neveux)*
Net (= **Internet**) Net *(m.)*
never ne… jamais
new nouveau, nouvel, nouvelle
news informations *(f.pl.)*, nouvelle(s) *(f.)*
newspaper journal *(m.)* *(plur.: journaux)*
newsstand kiosque *(m.)*
next prochain
nice gentil, gentille
niece nièce *(f.)*
night nuit *(f.)*
    at night le soir
    last night hier soir
nightmare cauchemar *(m.)*
no longer, not any more ne… plus
no one ne… personne
nobody ne… personne
noise bruit *(m.)*
noon midi
north nord *(m.)*
not ne… pas
    not any more ne… plus
notebook cahier *(m.)*
nothing ne… rien
notice *(verb)* remarquer, s'apercevoir
novel *(noun)* roman *(m.)*
November novembre
now maintenant
nowadays de nos jours
nurse infirmier *(m.)*, infirmière *(f.)*

O

obey obéir (à)
object *(noun)* objet *(m.)*
October octobre
of de
offer *(verb)* offrir
office bureau *(m.)*
often souvent
old vieux, vieil, vieille
on sur
    on sale en solde
    on/to the left à gauche
    on/to the right à droite

once une fois
only seulement, ne… que
open *(verb)* ouvrir
open *(adj.)* ouvert
opinion avis *(m.)*
    in my (your, etc.) opinion à mon (ton, etc.)
      avis
or ou
other autre
our *(adj.)* notre, nos
outside dehors
owe devoir
own *(verb)* posséder, avoir
owner propriétaire *(m./f.)*

P

package paquet *(m.)*, colis *(m.)*
paint *(verb)* peindre
pants *(pair of)* pantalon *(m.)*
paper papier *(m.)*, *(term)* dissertation *(f.)*
parents parents *(m.pl.)*
park *(noun)* parc *(m.)*
park *(verb)* stationner, se garer
parliament parlement *(m.)*
party fête *(f.)*, boum* *(f.)*, soirée *(f.)*
pass an exam réussir à un examen
passenger passager *(m.)*, passagère *(f.)*
passport passeport *(m.)*
pastry pâtisserie *(f.)*
pastry shop pâtisserie *(f.)*
patience patience *(f.)*
    lose patience perdre patience
pay payer
peanut butter beurre *(m.)* de cacahuètes
pedagogy pédagogie *(f.)*
pen stylo *(m.)*
people gens *(m.pl.)*, *(with a number)* personnes
    (f.pl.)
per par
performance représentation *(f.)*
perhaps peut-être
person *(male or female)* personne *(f.)*
pet animal domestique *(m.)*
pharmacy pharmacie *(f.)*
piano piano *(m.)*
pick up sb aller/venir chercher qn
picture photo *(f.)*, image *(f.)*
pie tarte *(f.)*
piece morceau *(m.)*
place endroit *(m.)*, lieu *(m.)*
plan *(to do)* compter (+ *inf.*)
plate assiette *(f.)*
play *(noun)* pièce (de théâtre) *(f.)*
play *(verb)* jouer (à, de)
player joueur *(m.)*, joueuse *(f.)*
please *(interj.)* s'il vous plaît
please *(verb)* plaire à

pleasure plaisir *(m.)*
poem poème *(m.)*
police police *(f.)*
polite poli
political science sciences politiques *(f.pl.)*
politics politique *(f.)*
poor pauvre
Portuguese portugais *(m.)*
post office bureau *(m.)* de poste
postcard carte postale *(f.)*
postman facteur *(m.)*
postpone remettre, reporter, repousser
pour verser
prefer préférer
pregnant enceinte
prepare préparer
pretend (to) faire semblant (de)
pretty joli
previews *(movies)* bande annonce *(f.)*
price prix *(m.)*
prince prince *(m.)*
principal *(school)* proviseur *(m.)*
printer *(equipment)* imprimante *(f.)*
prize prix *(m.)*
promise *(noun)* promesse *(f.)*
promise *(verb)* promettre
pronounce prononcer
proof preuve *(f.)*
protect protéger
proud fier, fière
provided that pourvu que
purple violet, violette
put mettre

Q

question *(noun)* question *(f.)*
questionnaire questionnaire *(m.)*
quick rapide
quickly vite, rapidement

R

rabbit lapin *(m.)*
radio radio *(f.)*
rain *(noun)* pluie *(f.)*
rain *(verb)* pleuvoir
raincoat imperméable *(m.)*
raise (a child) élever (un enfant)
rarely rarement
rather assez
read lire
reader lecteur *(m.)*, lectrice *(f.)*
realize *(notice)* se rendre compte (de)
really vraiment
receive recevoir
reception réception *(f.)*
recommend recommander
recreational vehicle (RV) camping-car *(m.)*

red rouge
refrigerator réfrigérateur *(m.)*, frigo* *(m.)*
region région *(f.)*
regret *(verb)* regretter
relax se détendre
remember se rappeler, se souvenir (de)
remote control télécommande *(f.)*
rent *(noun)* loyer *(m.)*
rent *(verb)* louer
repeat *(verb)* répéter
report *(noun)* rapport *(m.)*
resign démissionner
responsible responsable
rest *(verb)* se reposer
restaurant restaurant *(m.)*
restroom toilettes *(f.pl.)*
résumé curriculum vitae *(m.)*
return retourner, revenir, *(home)* rentrer
reward récompense *(f.)*
rice riz *(m.)*
rich riche
right droit *(m.)* droite *(f.)*
   on/to the right à droite
right away tout de suite
ring *(bell, telephone, alarm clock)* sonner
riot émeute *(f.)*
road route *(f.)*
roof toit *(m.)*
room chambre *(f.)*, pièce *(f.)*, salle *(f.)*
roommate camarade *(m./f.)* de chambre
row *(tier)* rang *(m.)*
rug tapis *(m.)*
run *(verb)* courir
Russia Russie *(f.)*
Russian russe *(m.)*

S

sad triste
safe *(adj.)* sûr
   feel safe se sentir en sécurité
safe *(noun)* coffre-fort *(m.)*
salad salade *(f.)*
salary salaire *(m.)*
salesman vendeur *(m.)*
saleswoman vendeuse *(f.)*
salt sel *(m.)*
same même
sandwich sandwich *(m.)*
Santa Claus père Noël *(m.)*
satisfy satisfaire
Saturday samedi *(m.)*
say dire
scallops coquilles Saint.-Jacques *(f.pl.)*
scholarship bourse *(f.)*
school école *(f.)*
   high school lycée (m.)
   middle school collège (m.)

seafood fruits *(m.pl.)* de mer
seat place *(f.)*
   aisle seat place *(f.)* côte couloir
   seat belt ceinture *(f.)* de sécurité
   window seat place *(f.)* côte fenêtre
secret secret *(m.)*
secretary secrétaire *(m./f.)*
see voir
seem sembler, paraître
selfish égoïste
sell vendre
semester semestre *(m.)*
send envoyer
sentence phrase *(f.)*
September septembre
serial feuilleton *(m.)*
set the table mettre la table
several plusieurs
share *(verb)* partager
shave *(verb)* se raser
ship *(noun)* bateau *(m.)*, *(small)* barque *(f.)*
shirt chemise *(f.)*
shoes chaussures *(f.pl.)*
shop *(noun)* magasin *(m.)*, *(small)* boutique *(f.)*
shopping center centre commercial *(m.)*
short court *(hair)*, petit *(person)*
shorts *(pair of)* short *(m.)*
show *(noun)* spectacle *(m.)*
show *(verb)* montrer
shower *(noun)* douche *(f.)*
sick malade
since depuis, *(because)* puisque
sing chanter
singer chanteur *(m.)*, chanteuse *(f.)*
single *(unmarried)* célibataire
sister sœur *(f.)*
sit down s'asseoir
ski *(verb)* skier
skin peau *(f.)*
skirt jupe *(f.)*
sky ciel *(m.)*
skyscraper gratte-ciel *(m.)*
sleep *(noun)* sommeil *(m.)*
sleep *(verb)* dormir
slim mince
slow lent
slowly lentement
small petit
snail escargot *(m.)*
snow *(noun)* neige *(f.)*
snow *(verb)* neiger
so *(+ adj.)* si *(+ adj.)*
   so that pour que
soap opera feuilleton *(m.)*
society société *(f.)*
socks chaussettes *(f.pl.)*

software logiciel *(m.)*
soldier soldat *(m.)*
somebody quelqu'un
someone quelqu'un
something quelque chose
sometimes quelquefois
somewhere quelque part
son fils *(m.)*
song chanson *(f.)*
soon bientôt
sorry désolé
soup soupe *(f.)*
Spain Espagne *(f.)*
Spanish espagnol *(m.)*
speak parler
speaker conférencier *(m.)*, conférencière *(f.)*
speech discours *(m.)*
speed vitesse *(f.)*
spend *(money)* dépenser
spend *(time)* passer
spoil gâter
spoon cuiller (cuillère) *(f.)*
spring printemps *(m.)*
squirrel écureuil *(m.)*
stairs escalier *(m.)*
stamp *(postage)* timbre *(m.)*
stapler agrafeuse *(f.)*
star étoile *(f.)*
start commencer, se mettre à
stay *(noun)* séjour *(m.)*
stay *(verb)* rester
steal voler
stewardess hôtesse *(f.)* de l'air
still encore, toujours
stop (s')arrêter
store magasin *(m.)*
   department store grand magasin
story histoire *(f.)*, conte *(m.)*
straight ahead tout droit
stranger inconnu *(m.)*, inconnue *(f.)*, étranger *(m.)*,
   étrangère *(f.)*
strawberry fraise *(f.)*
street rue *(f.)*
strike *(noun)* grève *(f.)*
strike *(verb)* frapper, battre
strong fort
student élève *(m./f.)*, *(university)* étudiant *(m.)*, étudiante
   (f.)
studies études *(f.pl.)*
study *(verb)* étudier
subway métro *(m.)*
succeed réussir
successful: be successful réussir, avoir du succès
suddenly soudain, tout à coup
suffer souffrir
suggest proposer, suggérer

suit (*men's*) costume (*m.*)
  suit (*women's*) tailleur (**m.**)
  bathing suit maillot (**m.**) *de bain*
suitcase valise (*f.*)
summer été (*m.*)
sun soleil (*m.*)
Sunday dimanche (*m.*)
supermarket supermarché (*m.*)
supposed: be supposed to être censé, devoir
sure sûr
surf (*verb*) surfer
  surf the Net surfer sur Internet
surgeon chirurgien (*m.*), chirurgienne (*f.*)
survive survivre (à)
survivor survivant (*m.*), survivante (*f.*)
suspect (*verb*) se douter (de)
suspicious suspect
sweater pull(-over) (*m.*)
sweep balayer
swim nager
swimming pool piscine (*f.*)
swimsuit maillot (*m.*) de bain
switch off éteindre
Swiss (*adj.*) suisse
Switzerland Suisse (*f.*)

T

T-shirt tee-shirt (*m.*)
table table (*f.*)
  set the table mettre la table
tablecloth nappe (*f.*)
take prendre
  take (a class) suivre (un cours)
  take (sb somewhere) emmener (qn quelque part)
  take a nap faire la sieste
  take a test passer un examen
  take a trip faire un voyage
  take a walk faire une promenade
  take care of s'occuper de
  take place avoir lieu
talk (*verb*) parler
tall grand
tea thé (*m.*)
teach enseigner
teacher professeur (*m.*)
team équipe (*f.*)
teddy bear ours (*m.*) en peluche
teenager adolescent (*m.*), adolescente (*f.*)
telephone (*noun*) téléphone (*m.*)
telephone (*verb*) téléphoner à
television télévision (*f.*)
tell raconter, dire
terrorist terroriste (*m./f.*)
thank remercier
the le, la, l', les
theater théâtre (*m.*)

their (*adj.*) leur, leurs
then puis, ensuite
there là, y
there is/are il y a
these (*adj.*) ces
thief voleur (*m.*), voleuse (*f.*)
thing chose (*f.*)
think penser, trouver, croire
thirst soif (*f.*)
thirsty: be thirsty avoir soif
this (*adj.*) ce, cet, cette
throat gorge (*f.*)
throw jeter
Thursday jeudi (*m.*)
ticket contravention (*f.*) (*traffic*), billet (*m.*) (*train, plane, etc.*)
tidy up ranger
tie (*noun*) cravate (*f.*)
time temps (*m.*), heure (*f.*), fois (*f.*)
  a long time longtemps
  all the time tout le temps
  from time to time de temps en temps
tip (*waiter*) pourboire (*m.*)
tired fatigué
toast (*noun*) pain grillé (*m.*)
today aujourd'hui
together ensemble
tomorrow demain
tonight ce soir
too trop, (*also*) aussi
  too many trop (*de*)
  too much trop (*de*)
tooth dent (*f.*)
towel serviette (*f.*)
tower tour (*f.*)
town ville (*f.*)
toy jouet (*m.*)
traffic circulation (*f.*)
  traffic jam embouteillage (**m.**)
  traffic light feu (**m.**) (*de signalisation*)
train train (*m.*)
  train station gare (**f.**)
translate traduire
trap piège (*m.*)
travel (*verb*) voyager
tray plateau (*m.*)
tree arbre (*m.*)
trip voyage (*m.*)
truck camion (*m.*)
true vrai
truth vérité (*f.*)
try, try on essayer
Tuesday mardi (*m.*)
Turkey Turquie (*f.*)
turn tourner
tuxedo smoking (*m.*)

U

umbrella parapluie (*m.*)
uncle oncle (*m.*)
under sous
understand comprendre
unfortunately malheureusement
United States États-Unis (*m.pl.*)
    in/to the United States aux États-Unis
university université (*f.*)
unless à moins que
until jusqu'à (ce que)
use (*verb*) se servir de, utiliser, employer
useful utile
usually d'habitude, en général

V

vacation vacances (*f.pl.*)
vegetable légume (*m.*)
very très
victim victime (*f.*)
video game jeu vidéo (*m.*)
visit (*noun*) visite (*f.*)
visit (*verb*) visiter (*places*), rendre visite à (*people*)
voice voix (*f.*)

W

wait (for) attendre
waiter serveur (*m.*), garçon (*m.*)
waitress serveuse (*f.*)
wake up se réveiller
walk marcher, aller à pied
wallet portefeuille (*m.*)
want (to) vouloir, avoir envie de
war guerre (*f.*)
warning avertissement (*m.*)
wash (se) laver
washing machine machine (*f.*) à laver
watch (*noun*) montre (*f.*)
watch (*verb*) regarder
water eau (*f.*)
wear porter
weather temps (*m.*)
wedding mariage (*m.*)
Wednesday mercredi (*m.*)
week semaine (*f.*)
weekend week-end (*m.*)
weigh peser
well bien
what que, qu'est-ce que, quel, quoi
    what is the weather like? quel temps fait-il?
    what time is it? quelle heure est-il?

when quand, lorsque
where où
whether si
which quel, quelle, quels, quelles
while pendant que
white blanc, blanche
who qui
why pourquoi
wife femme (*f.*), épouse (*f.*)
win gagner
    win the lottery gagner à la loterie
wind vent (*m.*)
windbreaker blouson (*m.*), anorak (*m.*)
window fenêtre (*f.*)
wine vin (*m.*)
winter hiver (*m.*)
wish (*noun*) souhait (*m.*), vœu (*m.*)
    make a wish faire un vœu
wish (to) (*verb*) vouloir, avoir envie de
with avec
without sans
witness témoin (*m.*)
wolf loup (*m.*)
woman femme (*f.*)
wonder (*verb*) se demander
word mot (*m.*)
work (*noun*) travail (*m.*)
work (*verb*) travailler, (*function*) marcher, fonctionner
world monde (*m.*)
worried inquiet, inquiète
worry (*verb*) s'inquiéter
wound (*verb*) blesser
write écrire
writer écrivain (*m.*)
wrong faux, fausse
    be wrong (person) avoir tort

X

X-ray radio (*f.*)
    have an X-ray passer la radio

Y

yard jardin (*m.*)
year an (*m.*), année (*f.*)
yellow jaune
yes oui
yesterday hier
yogurt yaourt (*m.*)
young jeune
your (*adj.*) ton, ta, tes, votre, vos

Answer key

Note that some highly personalized exercises have been omitted from this answer key.

Unit 1 The present tense of regular verbs

1-1 1. habite 2. travaille 3. coûte 4. jouent 5. sonne 6. écoutons 7. tournes 8. dansez 9. adore 10. aime

1-2 1. Nous visitons 2. Elle enseigne 3. Vous chantez 4. Je pense 5. Nous montons 6. Nous montrons 7. Il embrasse 8. Ils trouvent 9. Ils embrassent 10. Je tombe 11. Il raconte 12. Elle regarde 13. Nous dînons 14. Ils déjeunent 15. Il pleure 16. Tu joues 17. Je reste 18. Elles étudient 19. Il habite 20. Tu fermes 21. J'oublie 22. Ils aident 23. Vous apportez 24. Tu donnes 25. J'aime 26. Ils gagnent 27. Nous remercions 28. Ils traversent 29. Elle porte 30. Il travaille

1-4 1. regardons 2. enseignent 3. danse 4. aime 5. chante 6. pleurent 7. jouez 8. parlent 9. écoutes 10. habite

1-6 1. Je ne tombe pas souvent malade. 2. Je n'aime pas les chats. 3. Il ne travaille pas dur. 4. Nous ne parlons pas chinois. 5. Les Français ne dînent pas à cinq heures. 6. Le livre ne coûte pas cher. 7. Vous n'habitez pas ici.

1-7 1. Je ne déteste pas le lait. 2. Je n'arrive pas demain. 3. Il n'admire pas son frère. 4. Vous n'étudiez pas trop. (or: Tu n'étudies pas trop.) 5. Vous ne parlez pas mal. (or: Tu ne parles pas mal.)

1-8 1. appellent 2. promène 3. pèses 4. emmenons 5. enlève 6. épelez 7. gèle 8. mènent 9. achètent

1-9 1. Elle achète 2. Elles jettent 3. Nous jetons 4. J'appelle 5. Il amène 6. Nous élevons 7. Elle lève 8. Vous rappelez

1-10 1. protègent 2. exagérez 3. considère 4. cède 5. préférons 6. répète

1-11 1. J'espère 2. Tu préfères 3. Ils ne répètent pas 4. Nous célébrons 5. Il possède 6. Elle exagère

1-12 1. paie (or: paye) 2. essayons 3. appuie 4. envoient 5. rangeons 6. effaçons 7. téléchargeons 8. emploie

1-13 1. Nous prononçons 2. Nous partageons 3. Il voyage 4. Nous mangeons 5. Les végétariens ne mangent pas 6. J'essaie 7. Elle envoie 8. Nous envoyons 9. Tu nettoies 10. Nous commençons 11. Nous nageons 12. Nous ne dérangeons pas 13. Ils balaient 14. Vous téléchargez 15. Je paie (or: je paye)

1-14 1. remplissez 2. réussis 3. choisis 4. guérit 5. rougissons 6. obéissent 7. vieillit 8. grossissent

1-15 1. Nous choisissons 2. Ils grandissent 3. On ne grossit pas 4. Ils réfléchissent 5. Nous applaudissons 6. Vous bâtissez 7. Elle ne punit pas 8. Je rougis 9. Tu ralentis 10. Elle ne maigrit pas

1-16 1. descends 2. interrompt 3. entendons 4. rends 5. perd 6. vendent 7. rend

1-17 1. Nous ne vendons pas 2. Je rends 3. Vous descendez 4. Elle perd 5. Tu entends 6. Je n'attends pas 7. Il ne répond pas 8. Ils perdent 9. Nous rendons visite à

1-18 *Most answers will vary.* 2. vrai 3. faux 4. vrai 9. vrai 10. vrai

1-19 Ma tante Élodie habite à Lyon. Elle travaille dans un collège où elle enseigne l'espagnol. Elle ne gagne pas beaucoup d'argent, mais elle aime beaucoup son travail. Tous les matins, elle quitte la maison de bonne heure, et elle arrive à l'école à sept heures et demie. Elle monte au premier étage où ses élèves attendent. Pendant qu'elle parle, les élèves écoutent. Quelquefois, ils chantent une chanson que leur maîtresse choisit. Les classes d'Élodie finissent à trois heures de l'après-midi. En général, elle reste à l'école jusqu'à quatre heures et aide les élèves. Certains d'entre eux pensent qu'elle donne trop de devoirs. Quand elle entend la cloche, Élodie ferme la porte de son bureau et rentre à la maison.

Marc, le mari d'Élodie, travaille dans le rayon des chaussures d'un grand magasin qui emploie plus de cinq cents personnes. Il porte toujours un costume et une cravate. Ses clients essaient des sandales, des bottes, des tennis et des tongs, mais ils n'achètent rien s'ils ne trouvent pas la couleur et le style qu'ils cherchent. De temps en temps, Marc perd patience. Néanmoins, il vend au moins cent paires de chaussures chaque jour.

1-20 1. Est-ce que tu aimes les hamburgers? 2. Aimes-tu les hamburgers? 3. Tu aimes les hamburgers?

1-21 1. Est-ce que vous étudiez le français? / Étudiez-vous le français? 2. Est-ce qu'il regarde la télévision? / Regarde-t-il la télévision? 3. Est-ce qu'ils visitent le Louvre? / Visitent-ils le Louvre? 4. Est-ce que je danse bien? / (Inversion impossible) 5. Est-ce que nous perdons? / Perdons-nous? 6. Est-ce que tu habites au Mexique? / Habites-tu au Mexique? 7. Est-ce que je mange trop? / (Inversion impossible) 8. Est-ce que tu restes à la maison? / Restes-tu à la maison? 9. Est-ce que le professeur gagne beaucoup d'argent? / Le professeur gagne-t-il beaucoup d'argent? 10. Est-ce que les bénévoles aident? / Les bénévoles aident-ils?

1-22 1. Tu aimes la cuisine italienne (Vous aimez la cuisine italienne), n'est-ce pas? 2. Pierre n'habite pas à Paris, n'est-ce pas? 3. Le cours commence à huit heures, n'est-ce pas? 4. Vous visitez la France, n'est-ce pas? 5. Marie porte des lunettes, n'est-ce pas?

1-23 1. Où est-ce que tu travailles? / Où travailles-tu? 2. Quand est-ce que nous retournons? / Quand retournons-nous? 3. Comment est-ce qu'il voyage? / Comment voyage-t-il? 4. Combien de maisons est-ce qu'ils possèdent? / Combien de maisons possèdent-ils? 5. Pourquoi est-ce que vous demandez? / Pourquoi demandez-vous? 6. Où est-ce que votre sœur habite? / Où habite votre sœur? 7. Quand est-ce que j'arrive? / (Inversion impossible) 8. Pourquoi est-ce que le garçon pleure? / Pourquoi le garçon pleure-t-il?

1-24 1. Qu'est-ce qu'ils achètent? (Qu'achètent-ils?) 2. Qu'est-ce qu'il étudie? (Qu'étudie-t-il?) 3. Qu'est-ce que nous aimons? (Qu'aimons-nous?) 4. Qui réussit? 5. Qui aimes-tu? 6. Qu'est-ce que vous attendez? (Qu'attendez-vous?) 7. Qu'est-ce que vous cherchez? (Que cherchez-vous?) 8. De quoi parles-tu?

1-25 1. Quels journaux vendent-ils? (Quels journaux est-ce qu'ils vendent?) 2. À quelle heure dînes-tu? (À quelle heure est-ce que tu dînes?) 3. Dans quelle ville habites-tu? (Dans quelle ville est-ce que tu habites?) 4. Quel est votre numéro de téléphone? 5. Quel dessert choisissez-vous? (Quel dessert est-ce que vous choisissez?) 6. Quelle est la date de ton anniversaire? 7. Quels sont vos loisirs préférés? 8. Quelle est votre taille?

1-26 1. Oui, j'habite à Paris. (Non, je n'habite pas à Paris.) 2. Je cherche… *Answers will vary.* 3. Oui, je parle italien. (Non, je ne parle pas italien.) 4. Oui, je réussis toujours aux examens. (Non, je ne réussis pas toujours aux examens.) 5. En général, je déjeune à… *Answers will vary.* 6. D'habitude, je dîne à… *Answers will vary.* 7. J'étudie… (les mathématiques? la chimie?) *Answers will vary.* 8. Oui, je mange beaucoup. (Non, je ne mange pas beaucoup.) 9. J'attends… (mon ami[e]? le professeur?) *Answers will vary.* 10. J'étudie le français parce que… *Answers will vary.*

1-27 1. Où habites-tu? (Où habitez-vous?) 2. Qui attends-tu? (Qui attendez-vous?) 3. Comment voyage-t-elle? (Comment est-ce qu'elle voyage?) 4. Pourquoi étudies-tu le français? (Pourquoi étudiez-vous le français?) 5. Qu'est-ce que vous détestez? (Que détestez-vous?) 6. Quelle est votre (ta) nationalité? 7. À quelle heure dînent-ils? (À quelle heure est-ce qu'ils dînent?) 8. Combien coûte la voiture? 9. Combien de personnes invite-t-il? (Combien de personnes est-ce qu'il invite?) 10. Quand arrive-t-elle? (Quand est-ce qu'elle arrive?)

1-28 1. Nous regardons les photos. 2. Ils écoutent la radio. 3. Je paie le repas. 4. Il attend l'autobus. 5. Elle cherche son chien. 6. Vous payez les boissons.

1-29 1. Est-ce que tu obéis à ton père? 2. Les enfants obéissent aux parents. 3. Nous répondons à la lettre. 4. Il répond à Marie. 5. Nous demandons au garçon. 6. Elle téléphone à son petit ami. 7. Ils entrent dans la maison. 8. Je rends visite à ma tante. 9. Elle ressemble à son frère. 10. Nous assistons au mariage. 11. Ils réussissent toujours à l'examen.

1-30   1. Denise joue aux cartes. 2. Ils ne jouent pas aux échecs. 3. Nous jouons au billard. 4. Est-ce que tu joues au golf? 5. Est-ce que vous jouez au volley-ball? 6. Ils jouent à un jeu. 7. Les enfants jouent au football. 8. Notre équipe joue très bien au basket-ball.

1-31   1. Il joue au golf. 2. Ils jouent au football. 3. Il joue au base-ball. 4. Il joue au basket-ball. 5. Ils jouent aux échecs. 6. Ils jouent au tennis. 7. Il joue au football américain.

1-32   1. Qui joue de la guitare? 2. Mon frère joue du piano et de la flûte. 3. Est-ce que tu joues du violon? 4. Je ne joue pas de la trompette. 5. Antoine joue de l'orgue. 6. Ils ne jouent pas de la harpe.

1-33   1. Les étudiants demandent aux professeurs. 2. Anne répond au téléphone. 3. Nous attendons le train. 4. J'écoute la musique. 5. David téléphone à ses copains. 6. Vous entrez dans la chambre. 7. Tu joues du piano. 8. Sébastien joue au tennis. 9. Les enfants cherchent les jouets.

1-34   1. Paris me manque. 2. Je manque à mes amis. 3. Elle manque à ses parents. 4. Les moustiques ne leur manquent pas. 5. Est-ce qu'elle te manque? 6. Est-ce que tu lui manques? 7. Est-ce que tu lui manques? 8. Est-ce que je vous manque? —Oui, vous me manquez. 9. Il lui manque. 10. Elle ne lui manque pas.

1-35   1. Mon lit me manque. 2. Mes amis me manquent. 3. Mon ordinateur me manque. 4. Mon pays me manque. 5. Ma voiture me manque. 6. Ma chambre me manque.

1-36   Anne, Mary, Bill et Tom étudient le français dans un lycée privé en Oregon. Ils adorent cette langue et ils ne manquent jamais la classe. Tous les jours leur professeur de français, Mlle Dutronc, entre dans le bâtiment à huit heures précises. Pendant qu'elle attend l'ascenseur, elle cherche la clé de son bureau. Quelquefois, elle téléphone à ses parents en Belgique. Ils lui manquent beaucoup. Heureusement, son père paie (paye) ces appels, parce qu'ils coûtent cher. Les élèves de Mlle Dutronc obéissent toujours à leur professeur, et la plupart du temps ils répondent correctement à ses questions. Ils demandent souvent à Mlle Dutronc de jouer du piano, et ils écoutent attentivement la musique. Une fois par mois, ils regardent des diapositives que leur professeur apporte en classe. Le vendredi, pour récompenser ses élèves, Mademoiselle Dutronc joue à des jeux avec eux.

Unit 2 The present tense of irregular verbs

2-1   1. Je vais 2. Ils vont 3. Ils ont 4. Elle va 5. J'ai 6. Nous avons 7. Nous allons 8. Il a 9. Nous buvons 10. Bois-tu (Est-ce que tu bois) 11. Ils ne boivent pas 12. Est-ce que je conduis 13. Il conduit 14. Je connais 15. Ils connaissent 16. Est-ce qu'il court (Court-il) 17. Nous devons 18. Ils craignent 19. Je crains 20. Est-ce que tu crois (Crois-tu)

2-2   *Possible answers:* 1. Oui, je vais souvent au cinéma. (Non, je ne vais pas souvent au cinéma.) 2. Je bois… (du café au lait) *Answers will vary.* 3. Oui, je cours vite. (Non, je ne cours pas vite.) 4. Oui, je dis toujours la vérité, (Non, je ne dis pas toujours la vérité.) 5. Oui, je crois aux horoscopes. (Non, je ne crois pas aux horoscopes.) 6. Oui, je connais Paris. (Non, je ne connais pas Paris.) 7. Aujourd'hui, je dois… (aller chez le coiffeur) *Answers will vary.* 8. Je conduis prudemment. (Je ne conduis pas prudemment.) 9. Oui, j'éteins la lumière (Non, je n'éteins pas la lumière) quand je quitte la chambre. 10. Oui, j'ai des frères et sœurs. (Non je n'ai pas **de** frères et sœurs.) (J'ai… sœur[s], mais je n'ai pas de frère.)

2-3   1. Elle dort 2. Ils dorment 3. Nous sortons 4. Je pars 5. Elles ne partent pas 6. Ça sent 7. J'écris 8. Ils écrivent 9. Êtes-vous (Est-ce que vous êtes) 10. Je suis 11. Il est 12. Ils sont 13. Je fais 14. Fait-il (Est-ce qu'il fait) 15. Nous faisons 16. Elles font 17. Qu'est-ce que vous faites (Que faites-vous) 18. Je lis 19. Nous lisons 20. Ils ne comprennent pas 21. Elle met 22. Je meurs 23. Est-ce que tu promets (Promets-tu) 24. Elles mettent 25. J'ouvre 26. Prenez-vous (Est-ce que vous prenez) 27. Il pleut 28. Ils ne peuvent pas 29. Est-ce que vous pouvez (Pouvez-vous) 30. Est-ce que je peux (Puis-je)

2-4   *Possible answers:* 1. Je dors bien. (Je dors mal.) 2. J'écris beaucoup de courriels à mes amis. (Je n'écris pas beaucoup de courriels à mes amis.) 3. Je suis optimiste (pessimiste). 4. En ce moment, je réponds aux questions de cet exercice. 5. Je lis… livres par an. 6. Oui, je mets un pull-over en hiver. 7. J'apprends le français. 8. Les magasins ouvrent à… heures. 9. Il pleut souvent (Il ne pleut pas souvent) dans la région où j'habite. 10. Oui, je peux sortir ce soir. (Non, je ne peux pas sortir ce soir.)

2-5   1. Je reçois 2. Recevez-vous 3. Nous ne rions pas 4. Pourquoi riez-vous (Pourquoi est-ce que vous riez) 5. Elle ne sait pas 6. Savez-vous 7. Ils suivent 8. La maison vaut 9. Je viens 10. Viennent-ils (Est-ce qu'ils viennent) 11. Elle vit 12. Les gens vivent 13. Qu'est-ce que tu veux 14. Est-ce que vous voyez (Voyez-vous) 15. On voit

2-6   *Most answers will vary.* 7. vrai

2-7   1. allons 2. avons 3. vont 4. boit 5. conduisent 6. cours 7. connaît 8. croyons 9. croient 10. devez 11. dit 12. dites 13. dormez 14. pars 15. voient 16. voyez 17. voyons 18. vient 19. venez 20. écrivez 21. sommes 22. êtes

23. sont 24. fait 25. font 26. faites 27. faut 28. Lis 29. mets 30. permettez 31. ouvre 32. offre 33. Puis 34. peuvent 35. Pouvez 36. peut 37. peux 38. prends 39. prenons 40. prennent 41. reçoivent 42. reçoit 43. Ris 44. vaut 45. valez 46. voulons 47. veut 48. savent 49. sais 50. pleut 51. vis 52. vivez

2-8   Aujourd'hui c'est mercredi et j'ai un jour de congé. Les enfants ne vont pas à l'école non plus. Ils sont ravis parce qu'ils peuvent faire ce qu'ils veulent. D'habitude, le mercredi, nous dormons jusqu'à dix heures. Ensuite, nous prenons le petit déjeuner. Nous mangeons des gaufres ou du pain grillé avec du beurre et de la confiture, et nous buvons du chocolat chaud ou du café au lait. Plus tard, nous allons souvent au musée ou à la bibliothèque. Quelquefois, nous faisons une promenade dans la forêt. Là, nous voyons des écureuils, des ours, des biches et de jolis papillons. De temps en temps, mes neveux viennent avec nous. Notre endroit préféré est un petit lac pittoresque entouré de hautes montagnes. On peut prendre une barque et pêcher la truite. Si on a une belle pêche, on est, comme le dit le dicton, « heureux comme un poisson dans l'eau ». Quand nous revenons le soir, nous sommes fatigués. Je dis « bonne nuit » à mes fils parce que je dois être au bureau à huit heures du matin le jeudi.

2-9   1. Est-ce qu'il vient? (Vient-il?) 2. Elle lit un roman. 3. Maintenant je comprends. 4. Actuellement, le président français est aux États-Unis. 5. Aujourd'hui, je dois écrire une dissertation. 6. Nous sommes en train de nettoyer la maison. 7. Ils sont sur le point de commencer.

2-10   1. La France est un beau pays. 2. Bill Gates a beaucoup d'argent. 3. Elle va à l'église le dimanche. 4. Il dit toujours la vérité. 5. Ils vont au cinéma ce soir. 6. Je pars demain. 7. Elles viennent la semaine prochaine.

2-11   1. a. Depuis combien de temps habitez-vous ici? b. Ça fait combien de temps que vous habitez ici? c. Il y a combien de temps que vous habitez ici? 2. a. J'habite ici depuis cinq ans. b. Ça fait cinq ans que j'habite ici. c. Il y a cinq ans que j'habite ici. d. Voilà cinq ans que j'habite ici. 3. Nous sortons ensemble depuis août. 4. Je connais son mari depuis janvier. 5. Est-ce que vous attendez (Attendez-vous) depuis longtemps?

2-12   1. J'ai le permis de conduire depuis… 2. Ça fait… que je travaille. 3. Il y a… que j'étudie le français. 4. Je suis malade depuis… 5. Ça fait… que j'habite dans cette ville. 6. Il y a… que je joue du piano.

2-13   1. Depuis combien de temps êtes-vous (es-tu) marié(e)? 2. Depuis combien de temps joue-t-il du violon? 3. Ça fait combien de temps qu'ils cherchent du travail? 4. Depuis combien de temps connaissez-vous (connais-tu) son père? 5. Ça fait combien de temps que vous sortez ensemble? 6. Depuis quand est-elle malade? 7. Depuis quand travaillez-vous (travailles-tu)? 8. Depuis quand attendez-vous la lettre? 9. Depuis quand apprenez-vous (apprends-tu) l'italien? 10. Depuis quand est-il au chômage?

2-14   Mes parents ont une grande maison près de Tours. Ils y habitent depuis plus de trente ans. Mon papa dit qu'il ne veut pas déménager parce qu'il préfère la campagne à la ville. À son avis, la vie est beaucoup plus agréable dans un petit village. En semaine, mon père monte dans sa voiture à sept heures et quart du matin et va au travail. D'habitude, il prend l'autoroute parce qu'il peut conduire plus vite. Pendant ce temps, ma maman conduit ses filles (mes sœurs cadettes) à l'école. Quand elle revient vers huit heures, elle nettoie la cuisine et la salle de bains. Après, elle sort pour acheter de la viande et du pain. Elle est de retour une heure plus tard et prépare le déjeuner. À midi, mes sœurs prennent l'autobus. Quand elles arrivent à la maison, elles sont affamées. Mon papa ne peut pas déjeuner avec elles parce qu'il n'a pas assez de temps. C'est la raison pour laquelle il ne voit pas sa famille avant six heures du soir. L'après-midi, ma mère lit son courrier électronique et écrit à ses amis. Je crois qu'elle est toujours très occupée parce qu'elle connaît beaucoup de monde. Le soir, mon père met la table et ma mère sert le dîner. Pendant le repas, ils rient beaucoup. Si le temps le permet, ils mangent sur le balcon, mais quand il pleut, ils restent dans la salle à manger. Plus tard, mes sœurs font leurs devoirs et mes parents lisent le journal ou regardent la télévision. À minuit, tout le monde est au lit et dort jusqu'au lendemain matin.

2-15   1. Je vais essayer. 2. Est-ce qu'il va pleuvoir (Va-t-il pleuvoir) la semaine prochaine? 3. Tu vas avoir une contravention. 4. Est-ce qu'ils vont aller (Vont-ils aller) au cinéma? 5. Qu'est-ce que nous allons faire demain? (Qu'allons-nous faire demain?) 6. Elles ne vont pas attendre. 7. Qui va gagner? 8. Ça ne va pas marcher. 9. Il va neiger ce soir. 10. Où vas-tu manger?

2-16   1. Ils viennent d'acheter un camping-car. 2. Nous venons de recevoir un fax. 3. C'est ce que je viens de dire. 4. Je viens de lire l'article. 5. Il vient d'écrire une rédaction. 6. L'enquête vient de commencer. 7. Est-ce que vous venez de déménager? 8. Est-ce que tu sais ce qui vient d'arriver? 9. Il vient de passer une semaine à la montagne. 10. Elle vient d'avoir son permis de conduire.

2-17   *Possible answers:* 1. Cet après-midi, je vais assister à un mariage et je vais manger de la glace. 2. L'été prochain, je vais aller au Canada. 3. Je vais dîner à sept heures ce soir. 4. Je vais déjeuner à midi demain. 5. Oui, je vais sortir (Non, je ne vais pas sortir) le week-end prochain. 6. Oui, je vais étudier (Non, je ne vais pas étudier) l'allemand l'année prochaine. 7. Je viens de répondre aux questions de cet exercice.

2-18   1. Je ne sais pas son nom. 2. Est-ce que tu sais (sais-tu) la date de la Révolution française? 3. Nous ne savons pas son âge. 4. Savez-vous l'heure? 5. Sait-il (Est-ce qu'il sait) le poème par cœur? 6. Qui sait la réponse à cette question? 7. Est-ce qu'ils savent (Savent-ils) la vérité?

2-19   1. Elles savent lire et écrire. 2. Je ne sais pas nager. 3. Sais-tu skier? 4. Il ne sait pas conduire. 5. Nous savons piloter un avion. 6. Savez-vous préparer ce plat?

2-20   1. Nous ne savons pas où il travaille. 2. Ils savent que vous êtes exigeant(e). 3. Je ne sais pas s'il vient à la soirée. 4. Sais-tu quand le film commence? 5. Il sait qui est responsable. 6. Elle ne sait pas pourquoi le bébé pleure. 7. Savez-vous combien il gagne? 8. Sait-elle combien de temps il va rester?

2-21   1. Où sont mes clés? —Je ne sais pas. 2. C'est vrai, tu sais. 3. Est-ce qu'il va pleuvoir demain? —Qui sait? 4. Elles ne savent pas quoi dire. 5. Tu sais quoi? Il vient de téléphoner. 6. Nous ne savons rien.

2-22   1. Connais-tu tes voisins? —Oui, je les connais très bien. 2. Je ne connais pas cet endroit. 3. Il ne connaît pas cette femme, mais moi, je la connais. 4. Connaissez-vous cet hôtel? 5. Nous connaissons très bien cette rue. 6. Elle connaît cette ville comme sa poche. 7. Les étudiants connaissent la pièce *Huis clos*. 8. Ma sœur connaît la musique classique. 9. Je connais quelqu'un en Angleterre. 10. Connais-tu le Japon? 11. Nous ne vous connaissons pas. 12. Est-ce que je vous connais?

2-23   1. Connaissez 2. connais 3. sait 4. connais, sais 5. sait, connaît 6. connaissent 7. sais 8. savent 9. sait 10. connaissent 11. sais 12. sait 13. connaissons, savons 14. Connais, connais 15. sais 16. Sais 17. savez 18. Sais, sais 19. Savez 20. savent

2-24   Je connais mon amie Sandrine depuis plusieurs années. Elle sait faire la cuisine mais (et je ne sais pas pourquoi) elle ne connaît pas la cuisine française. C'est pour ça (cela) que je vais emmener Sandrine dans un restaurant français que je connais très bien. Je connais le propriétaire, mais je ne sais pas s'il est français. Je sais que mon amie va aimer la cuisine de ce restaurant car elle connaît l'art culinaire. Et qui sait, elle va peut-être parler français un jour. On ne sait jamais.

2-25   1. J'ai mal à la tête. 2. Avez-vous faim? —Non, mais j'ai très soif. 3. Elle a froid. 4. Il a raison et tu as tort. 5. Elle n'a pas sommeil. 6. J'ai très peur. 7. Quel âge avez-vous? —J'ai trente ans. 8. Quel âge a votre patron? —Il a quarante ans. 9. J'ai besoin d'une agrafeuse. 10. Nous avons besoin de vacances. 11. Il a besoin d'étudier. 12. Ils n'ont pas envie de voyager. 13. Tu as l'air fatigué. 14. J'ai hâte d'ouvrir mes cadeaux. 15. Vous avez de la chance!

2-26   1. a besoin d'argent 2. ai faim 3. as soif 4. a froid 5. avons chaud 6. as tort 7. avez raison 8. a (treize) ans 9. a de la chance 10. ont envie de 11. ai mal aux 12. ai peur 13. a l'air 14. ai… ans 15. a mal à

2-27   1. vrai 2. faux 3. vrai 4. vrai 5. vrai

2-28   1. faire la grasse matinée 2. font (la) grève 3. fais (souvent) la sieste 4. font le pont 5. fait (quelquefois) l'école buissonnière 6. fait exprès

2-29   1. Il fait semblant d'être riche. 2. Je fais la cuisine et les enfants font la vaisselle. 3. Qui fait la lessive chez vous? 4. Mon mari fait le ménage et je fais les provisions. 5. Il fait l'école buissonnière aujourd'hui. 6. Est-ce que vous faites souvent la sieste? 7. On fait la queue à la poste et à la banque.

2-30   1. Ils font rarement de l'auto-stop. 2. Je fais du lèche-vitrines tout le temps. 3. Quand est-ce que nous faisons des courses? 4. Je vais faire des économies. 5. Vous faites des progrès. 6. Le mois prochain, nous faisons un voyage. 7. Est-ce que tu fais (Fais-tu) une promenade? 8. Elles font une pause à midi. 9. Je fais toujours de mon mieux. 10. Il fait ses valises. 11. Elle fait un stage cet été. 12. Quand est-ce que tu fais du baby-sitting?

2-31   1. Il fait de alpinisme. 2. Elle fait de la natation. 3. Ils font de la gymnastique tous les jours. 4. Où font-elles du ski? 5. Dimanche, nous faisons du vélo. 6. De temps en temps, je fais du cheval. 7. Elle fait du footing (du jogging) tous les matins. 8. Ça ne fait rien. 9. Ça fait combien? 10. Qu'est-ce que tu fais dans la vie?

2-32   1. La montre est à elle. 2. Le chien est à eux. 3. Le parapluie est à Véronique. 4. Ces cahiers sont aux étudiants. 5. L'ordinateur n'est pas à moi. 6. Je ne suis pas d'accord avec lui. 7. Je suis quelquefois en retard. 8. Elle est toujours à l'heure. 9. Ils sont au chômage. 10. Pourquoi es-tu en colère? 11. Elle est au régime. 12. Etes-vous (Est-ce que vous êtes) de mauvaise humeur? 13. Nous sommes originaires de Vancouver. 14. Je suis pressé(e) 15. Les otages sont toujours en vie.

2-33   *Possible answers:* 1. Je suis originaire de New York (or: des États-Unis). 2. Je suis très en colère quand mes copains me posent un lapin (*stand me up*). 3. Je suis en train d'apprendre le français. 4. Quand je suis enrhumé(e), j'achète des mouchoirs (*handkerchiefs, tissues*). 5. Quand je suis pressé(e), je cours!

2-34   1. est au régime 2. sont au chômage 3. m'est égal 4. est au courant 5. sommes en avance

2-35   1. Comment vas-tu? 2. Comment va votre sœur? 3. Elle ne va pas bien (Elle va mal), elle a la grippe. 4. Nous allons mieux. 5. Comment ça va?

2-36   1. Qu'est-ce que tu veux dire? 2. Savez-vous ce que je veux dire? 3. Que veut dire « porte » en anglais? 4. Qui prend la décision? 5. Quand est-ce que nous prenons (Quand prenons-nous) le petit déjeuner? 6. Les Français prennent le dîner à vingt heures (à huit heures du soir). 7. Nous prenons un verre au bar. 8. Il va prendre sa retraite en mai. 9. Tu vas prendre froid. 10. Nous ne prenons pas Pierre au sérieux.

2-37   Bon anniversaire, Anne! Aujourd'hui, c'est l'anniversaire de ma sœur Anne. Elle a seize ans.
Anne a hâte de manger le gâteau. Elle vient de souffler les bougies et elle a l'air heureux (heureuse). Les cadeaux sont sur la table et elle doit ouvrir les boîtes. Anne a de la chance parce qu'il y a beaucoup de cadeaux et de cartes. Ce soir, nous allons faire la fête. Maman va faire la cuisine et je vais faire la vaisselle.
J'espère qu'Anne ne va pas avoir mal à l'estomac parce qu'elle mange toujours trop. Heureusement, elle n'est pas au régime. Demain, Anne va faire l'école buissonnière et elle va faire la grasse matinée. Le professeur va être en colère, mais ça ne fait rien. Après-demain, nous n'avons pas besoin d'aller à l'école parce que c'est samedi.

2-38   1. Est-ce que la comédie musicale vous plaît? 2. Il plaît aux femmes. 3. Est-ce que ça leur plaît? 4. Ces lunettes lui plaisent. 5. Votre maison me plaît beaucoup. 6. Ce plat ne nous plaît pas. 7. Mon nouveau travail me plaît. 8. Tu ne me plais pas avec des cheveux courts. 9. Est-ce que ce genre de musique te plaît?

Unit 3 A few impersonal verbs

3-3   1. Il y a un chat dans la cuisine. 2. Il n'y a pas de serviettes sur la table. 3. Est-ce qu'il y a (Y a-t-il) un ordinateur dans la salle de classe? 4. Combien d'universités est-ce qu'il y a (y a-t-il) en France? 5. Est-ce qu'il y a (Y a-t-il) des toilettes à cet étage? 6. Il y a des nuages dans le ciel. 7. Est-ce qu'il y a (Y a-t-il) un bureau des objets trouvés ici? 8. Il y a une parabole sur le toit. 9. Il n'y a pas d'argent dans mon portefeuille. 10. Il n'y a pas de liberté d'expression dans ce pays.

3-5   1. il y a cinq semaines 2. il y a quatre heures 3. il y a deux siècles 4. il y a une décennie 5. il y a longtemps

3-6   1. Il faut être poli. 2. Il ne faut pas faire ça. 3. Il faut étudier la pédagogie pour devenir professeur. 4. Il faut avoir de la patience. 5. Il vaut mieux partir. 6. Il vaut mieux dire la vérité.

3-7   1. vrai 2. vrai 3. faux 4. faux 5. vrai 6. vrai 7. faux 8. faux

3-8   En Provence, il fait presque toujours beau. Il ne pleut que très rarement et il ne neige presque jamais. Mais il fait souvent du vent. On appelle ce vent fort qui souffle du nord « le Mistral ». Dans cette région, il y a beaucoup d'oliviers et des champs de lavande un peu partout. En juin, juillet et août, il fait très chaud. En septembre, octobre et novembre, il fait frais. En décembre, janvier et février, il fait assez froid. Et en mars, avril et mai, il fait doux. Les Provençaux sont tous bien bronzés car il fait (du) soleil la plupart du temps.
Quand il est midi, beaucoup de commerçants ferment leurs boutiques pour aller déjeuner. Lorsqu'ils reviennent, il est deux heures de l'après-midi.
En été, il y a beaucoup de touristes en Provence. Quand ils vont à la plage, ils mettent de la crème solaire parce qu'ils savent qu'il faut protéger la peau contre les coups de soleil. Il vaut mieux être prudent.

Unit 4 Reflexive verbs

4-1   1. Je m'amuse toujours. 2. Elles ne s'amusent pas. 3. Comment vous appelez-vous? 4. Comment t'appelles-tu? 5. Je m'appelle Romain. 6. Comment s'appelle-t-il? 7. Il s'appelle Jean. 8. Le TGV ne s'arrête pas souvent. 9. Je me couche tard. 10. Vous vous dépêchez. 11. Ils se déshabillent le soir. 12. Est-ce que vous vous disputez souvent avec vos parents? 13. Je m'ennuie. 14. Il ne se fâche jamais. 15. Nous nous habillons. 16. Il s'inquiète pour leur fils. 17. Est-ce que vous vous levez tôt? 18. À quelle heure est-ce que tu te lèves en général? 19. Damien se marie avec ma fille le mois prochain. 20. Ils se moquent du professeur. 21. Qu'est-ce qui se passe? 22. L'histoire se passe au Canada. 23. Je me peigne. 24. Elles se promènent tous les jours. 25. Est-ce que vous vous rappelez? 26. Je ne me rappelle plus. 27. Où se trouve la gare, s'il vous plaît? 28. Quand est-ce que tu te reposes? 29. Je me réveille quand le réveil sonne. 30. Vous vous trompez.

4-2   1. Elles s'attendent au pire. 2. Elle se baigne une fois par semaine. 3. Ils se comportent mal. 4. Je me débrouille en français. 5. Elle ne se détend pas. 6. Je m'excuse. 7. Nous nous fiançons cet été. 8. On s'habitue à tout. 9. Est-ce que tu t'intéresses à la politique? 10. Il se spécialise en sciences politiques.

4-3   1. Ils ne s'aperçoivent jamais de leurs erreurs. 2. Je m'assieds (Je m'assois). 3. Nous nous asseyons (Nous nous assoyons). 4. Est-ce qu'ils s'asseyent (Est-ce qu'ils s'assoient)? 5. Elles ne s'en vont pas. 6. Est-ce que tu t'en vas? 7. Nous nous endormons. 8. Je ne m'endors pas. 9. Il se met à pleurer. 10. Ils se plaignent tout le temps. 11. Je ne me sens pas bien aujourd'hui. 12. Nous nous sentons en sécurité. 13. Tu te conduis bien. 14. Je ne me souviens pas de cet homme. 15. Il ne se souvient de rien. 16. Est-ce que tu te souviens de moi? 17. Ils se souviennent encore de leur enfance. 18. Ma grand-mère se souvient toujours de mon anniversaire. 19. Les Chinois se servent de baguettes pour manger. 20. Ils ne se taisent jamais.

4-4   1. Est-ce que tu te brosses souvent les dents? 2. Je me lave les cheveux. 3. Elle se rase les jambes. 4. Vous vous brossez les cheveux. 5. Nous nous lavons les mains. 6. Ils ne s'essuient pas les pieds. 7. Vous vous coupez les ongles.

4-5   1. Je voudrais me présenter. 2. Tu dois te dépêcher. 3. Nous allons nous habiller. 4. Elle ne veut pas se coucher tard. 5. Est-ce que vous aimez vous lever tôt? 6. Nous venons de nous marier. 7. Je ne peux pas me rappeler (me souvenir). 8. Je veux me baigner. 9. Tu vas te débrouiller.

4-7   *Possible answers:* 1. En été, le soleil se couche à neuf heures du soir. 2. Je me lave les mains cinq fois par jour. 3. Je ne m'ennuie jamais. (Je m'ennuie quand je regarde un film ennuyeux.) 4. Je ne me trompe jamais. (Oui, je me trompe quelquefois.) 5. Mes parents s'appellent Émilie et François. 6. Les chutes du Niagara se trouvent au Canada et aux États-Unis. 7. Je me plains quand j'ai trop de travail.

4-8   1. se moquent de 2. nous ennuyons 3. se dépêche 4. s'arrête 5. me reposer 6. vous asseoir

4-9   1. s'inquiètent 2. se couchent, s'endorment 3. me lève 4. me rappelle 5. me souviens 6. se plaignent

4-10   Je m'appelle Anne et j'ai vingt ans. Tous les matins, je me réveille à sept heures, mais je ne me lève pas tout de suite. Je reste au lit pendant trente minutes. Puis, je me brosse les dents et je me douche. Je me maquille et m'habille. Ensuite, je prends le petit déjeuner. Après, je vais au travail. Quand il est tard, je me dépêche car je ne veux pas être en retard. À midi, je mange un sandwich au jambon et un morceau de tarte aux pommes. L'après-midi, je me promène ou je me repose. À dix-sept heures, je rentre à la maison. Le soir, je m'assieds devant la télévision et je me détends.

Je m'inquiète rarement et je ne m'ennuie jamais. Quelquefois, je sors en boîte avec mes amis et je m'amuse. À minuit, je me déshabille et je me couche. En général, je m'endors vite.

4-11   1. nous arrêtons 2. arrêtons 3. cachent 4. se cachent 5. me réveille 6. réveille 7. tuent 8. se tuent 9. t'inquiètes 10. inquiètes

4-12   1. amusent 2. s'amusent 3. s'appelle 4. appelle 5. rappelle 6. me rappelle 7. attendez 8. vous attendez 9. se conduit 10. conduit 11. couche 12. se couche 13. demande 14. me demande 15. s'excuse 16. excuse 17. mettons 18. nous mettons 19. se passe 20. passe 21. me promène 22. promène 23. se trompe 24. trompe 25. trouvent 26. se trouvent 27. se trouve

4-13   1. Ils se comprennent. 2. Nous nous aimons. 3. Est-ce que vous vous voyez souvent? 4. Elles se détestent. 5. Vous vous aidez. 6. Ils s'embrassent. 7. Elles ne se parlent plus. 8. Est-ce que vous vous connaissez depuis longtemps? 9. Ma fille et moi, nous nous téléphonons tous les deux jours. 10. Nous nous disons « bonjour ».

4-14   1. Les portes du magasin s'ouvrent à neuf heures. 2. Le mot « adresse » s'écrit avec un seul « d ». 3. Ce costume se lave à la main. 4. Ça ne se fait pas en France. 5. « Visiter quelqu'un » ne se dit pas. 6. La pièce se joue à la Comédie-Française. 7. Cette expression s'emploie souvent. 8. La tour Eiffel se voit de loin. 9. Comment se dit « singe » en anglais? 10. Le français ne s'apprend pas en un jour.

4-15   1. vrai 2. vrai 3. faux 4. faux 5. faux 6. vrai 7. vrai 8. vrai

Unit 5 The *passé composé*

5-1   1. J'ai oublié. 2. Elle a travaillé. 3. Nous n'avons pas écouté. 4. Ils ont pleuré. 5. Combien d'argent as-tu dépensé? 6. Je n'ai pas demandé. 7. Il a acheté une couverture. 8. Elles ont joué aux cartes. 9. Vous avez apporté des pâtisseries. 10. Elle a perdu le contrôle de sa voiture. 11. Ils ont étudié. 12. J'ai entendu le bruit. 13. Nous avons essayé. 14. Je n'ai pas attendu. 15. Avez-vous (Est-ce que vous avez) répondu? 16. As-tu fini? —Oui, j'ai fini. 17. Elle a obéi à son père. 18. Nous n'avons pas réussi. 19. Elles ont applaudi. 20. Elle a longtemps réfléchi.

5-2   1. J'ai bu un verre d'eau. 2. Elle n'a pas eu le temps. 3. Il a couru. 4. Nous avons cru cette histoire. 5. Elle a dû rire. 6. Qu'est-ce que tu as dit? 7. Nous n'avons rien compris. 8. Avez-vous (Est-ce que vous avez) bien dormi? 9. Je n'ai pas écrit le poème. 10. Avez-vous déjà été au Danemark? 11. As-tu (Est-ce que tu as) reçu mon cadeau? 12. Qu'est-ce que tu as fait? 13. Il a fait une faute. 14. Est-ce que vous avez lu (Avez-vous lu) le journal? 15. Où a-t-elle (Où est-ce qu'elle a) mis la calculatrice? 16. Le sommelier a ouvert la bouteille. 17. As-tu (Est-ce que tu as) vu le spectacle? 18. Il a plu. 19. La représentation m'a beaucoup plu. 20. J'ai pris l'ascenseur.

5-3   1. Quand as-tu (Quand est-ce que tu as) su la vérité? 2. Mon papa a connu ma maman dans une soirée. 3. Il a pu aller à l'université. 4. Je n'ai pas pu le faire. 5. Ils ont voulu se lever. 6. Elle n'a pas voulu dire son nom.

5-4   1. vendu 2. mises 3. lus 4. montrées 5. fermé 6. reçu, envoyées 7. souffert 8. cru, racontées 9. bue 10. vue, plu

5-5   1. Où est-ce que tu us (Où es-tu) allé(e)? 2. Il est venu seul. 3. Qu'est-ce qu'elle est devenue? 4. Vous êtes revenue. 5. Quand est-ce qu'elles sont arrivées? 6. Nous sommes partis à midi. 7. Qui est entré? 8. Est-ce que tu es (Es-tu) sortie hier soir? 9. Ils sont descendus du train à Lyon. 10. Elles sont montées au deuxième étage. 11. Où es-tu née? 12. Ma grand-mère est morte l'année dernière. 13. Combien de temps es-tu restée en France? 14. Elle est retournée dans son pays. 15. Je suis tombée dans le piège.

5-6   1. sont allés 2. est parti 3. est morte 4. sont sortis 5. sont descendus

5-7   1. est-(elle) rentrée 2. as rentré 3. est retournée 4. a retourné 5. avons monté 6. sont montés 7. avons descendu 8. sont descendus 9. avez sorti 10. est sorti 11. a sorti 12. sont passés 13. Nous sommes passés 14. (J') ai passé 15. as passé 16. Avez-(vous) passé 17. a passé

5-8   1. Nous nous sommes bien amusés. 2. Quand est-ce que vous vous êtes couché? 3. À quelle heure est-ce que tu t'es (t'es-tu) réveillée? 4. Elle s'est dépêchée. 5. Mon patron s'est fâché. 6. Est-ce que tu t'es ennuyée? 7. Elles se sont promenées. 8.(a) Je ne me suis pas rappelée. (b) Je ne me suis pas souvenue. 9. La pendule (L'horloge) s'est arrêtée. 10. Sa femme s'est trompée. 11. Elle s'est excusée. 12. Elles se sont perdues. 13. Nous nous sommes détendus. 14. Les enfants se sont tus. 15. Ils se sont fiancés. 16. Elle s'est assise. 17. Elles s'en sont allées. 18. Le bébé s'est endormi. 19. Je me suis cassé la jambe. 20. Qu'est-ce qui s'est passé?

5-9   1. brossée, brossé 2. serré 3. s'est demandé 4. rendu 5. trompée 6. écrit 7. plainte, cassé 8. plu, mariés

5-10   1. est allée 2. sont venus 3. n'ai pas pu 4. avez fait 5. ai suivi 6. ai été 7. ont fait 8. ai dû 9. a eu 10. a fallu 11. ont reçu 12. as voulu 13. a découvert 14. ont conduit 15. avons vu

5-11   1. sorties 2. venus 3. morts 4. tombés 5. née 6. bu 7. pleuré, plu 8. plu 9. été

5-12   1. est tombée 2. a deviné, est devenue 3. (j') ai reçu 4. As-(tu) fini? —(J') ai fini 5. n'ai pas compris, a dit 6. ai montré, a ri 7. Es-(tu) monté(e) 8. avez dû 9. a ouvert, a vu 10. a mis, est partie 11. Avez-(vous bien) dormi? 12. n'ai pas pris, (j') ai perdu

5-13   1. J'ai reçu le message hier après-midi. (*precise moment*) 2. Nous avons vécu en Irlande entre 2002 et 2004. (*limited time*) 3. L'autre jour, elle a déménagé. (*precise moment*) 4. Il a eu un accident la semaine dernière. (*precise moment*) 5. Je suis allé(e) au cinéma hier soir. (*precise moment*) 6. J'ai fait un cauchemar la nuit dernière. (*precise moment*) 7. Son fils a passé un examen avant-hier. (*precise moment*) 8. La première fois qu'elle est venue en Europe, elle est restée cinq jours. (*one time action*) 9. Ils sont partis il y a trois ans. (*precise moment*) 10. Nous avons visité le musée trois fois l'année dernière. (*specified number of times*) 11. Quand il m'a vu(e), il a ri. (*specific moment*) 12. La Belle au bois dormant a dormi pendant cent ans. (*limited time*)

5-14   1. Est-ce qu'il a plu le week-end dernier? (*precise moment*) 2. Tout à coup (soudain), le temps a changé. (*sudden change*) 3. Nous avons vendu notre maison le mois dernier. (*precise moment*) 4. Tout de suite, je me suis senti(e) à l'aise. (*sudden occurrence*) 5. Il a pris la souris et a cliqué sur le lien. (*successive actions*) 6. Dimanche dernier, nous avons vu un film policier. (*precise moment*) 7. Elle est morte dans un accident de voiture. (*one time action*) 8. Les pompiers sont venus tout de suite. (*sudden occurrence*) 9. Nous avons appris la nouvelle ce matin. (*precise moment*) 10. Elle s'est mariée en juin. (*precise moment*) 11. Hier, je me suis levé(e) à cinq heures. (*precise moment*) 12. D'abord, elle a couru chez le médecin et ensuite, elle est allée à la pharmacie. (*successive actions*)

5-15   *Possible answers:* 1. Je suis né(e) le deux juin 1986 à San Francisco en Californie. 2. L'été dernier, je suis allé(e) en Inde. 3. Hier soir, j'ai travaillé. 4. Le week-end dernier, je suis sorti(e) avec mon copain (ma copine). 5. Dimanche soir, je suis rentré(e) à la maison à minuit. 6. J'ai pris du café au lait. 7. Hier à midi, j'ai mangé de la soupe. 8. Non, je ne me suis pas ennuyé(e) samedi soir, je me suis amusé(e). 9. Non, je n'ai pas appris le français l'année dernière. 10. Aujourd'hui, j'ai mis un tee-shirt et un short.

5-17   1. took 2. ran 3. had to 4. disappeared 5. had a good time. 6. Did it rain 7. Did you like 8. were (fell) silent 9. could not 10. had to 11. got (received) 12. took

5-18   1. faux 2. vrai 3. vrai 4. vrai 5. faux 6. faux 7. vrai 8. faux

5-19   Je suis partie pour la France le 1er septembre, et je suis arrivée à Marseille le lendemain à quatre heures de l'après-midi. Ma famille d'accueil est venue me chercher à l'aéroport. Je leur ai offert des cadeaux, et j'ai reçu un bouquet de fleurs. Lorsque nous sommes arrivés à la maison de M. et Mme Rivière, je suis immédiatement montée dans ma chambre pour me changer. J'ai mis ma jolie robe rose et je suis descendue pour dîner. Nous avons passé trois heures à table et les Rivière m'ont posé beaucoup de questions. Mme

Rivière a servi du foie gras comme hors-d'œuvre, des escargots comme entrée et des coquilles Saint-Jacques comme plat principal. Après la salade, nous avons mangé du fromage et comme dessert, nous avons pris du yaourt. Et bien sûr, nous avons bu du vin pour accompagner notre repas.

Mes cours ont commencé le quinze octobre. Ce jour-là, chaque étudiant a dû passer un test d'orientation. Au Jour de l'An, mes parents m'ont rendu visite, et nous sommes allés en Italie et en Autriche. Partout, nous avons vu des paysages et des œuvres d'art extraordinaires. Nous avons même pris le TGV. En juillet, je suis retournée aux États-Unis avec beaucoup de bons souvenirs. Je dois dire que mon séjour en France m'a beaucoup plu.

Unit 6 The imperfect tense

6-2   1. travaillais 2. jouait 3. perdait 4. remerciions 5. partageais, étais 6. commençait 7. fallait 8. mentait, rougissait 9. faisions 10. dormaient 11. riiez 12. croyions, allait 13. pleuvait 14. pleurait 15. avais 16. allais 17. neigeait 18. s'appelaient 19. prenais 20. nous levions

6-3   1. Ma grand-mère allait à l'église tous les dimanches. 2. Ils se levaient de bonne heure tous le matins. 3. Elle sortait fréquemment. 4. Quand j'étais petit(e), je regardais des dessins animés tout le temps. 5. Tu jouais de la guitare tous les jours. 6. Nous mangions ensemble de temps en temps. 7. À l'époque, mes parents et moi vivions à Rome. 8. Vous oubliiez toujours vos lunettes. 9. Je le voyais rarement. 10. Maintenant, je pèse soixante-cinq kilos, avant, je pesais cinquante-cinq kilos. 11. Chaque fois qu'il avait un examen, il dormait mal. 12. Quand elle était enfant, elle aimait beaucoup la glace.

6-4   1. Ils voyageaient beaucoup. 2. Où habitiez-vous? 3. Tu lisais beaucoup de bandes dessinées. 4. Mon ami me téléphonait tous les soirs. 5. Je me couchais tôt. 6. Elle buvait un verre de lait tous les matins. 7. Nous nous voyions souvent. 8. Ils se plaignaient de tout.

6-5   1. Chaque fois que le professeur entrait, tous les élèves se levaient. 2. Il m'aidait toujours. 3. Quand nous habitions (vivions) en France, nous buvions du vin au déjeuner et au dîner. 4. Quand j'étais étudiant(e), je mangeais au resto-U chaque jour. 5. Ma maman me rendait visite une fois par mois. 6. Chaque fois, elle apportait de l'argent, des cadeaux et des friandises. 7. Je ne manquais jamais la classe. 8. Mes colocataires et moi, nous étudiions à la bibliothèque tous les après-midi. 9. Le soir, nous sortions ensemble et nous nous amusions.

6-6   1. La voiture ne marchait pas. 2. Je cherchais la télécommande. 3. Elle se demandait où vous étiez. 4. Tout le monde s'amusait. 5. Je pensais à toi tout le temps. 6. Il pleuvait des cordes. 7. Le bébé pleurait. 8. Disaient-elles (Est-ce qu'elles disaient) la vérité? 9. Qu'est-ce qu'elle faisait? (Que faisait-elle?) 10. Vous travailliez dur. 11. Je plaisantais. 12. Il écoutait la radio pendant que sa femme s'habillait.

6-7   1. Je nettoyais la maison quand le facteur est arrivé. 2. Ils jouaient au football quand il a commencé à pleuvoir. 3. Andrée allait au cinéma quand elle a rencontré ses amis. 4. Nous dormions quand quelqu'un a frappé à la porte. 5. Tu écrivais une lettre quand le téléphone a sonné. 6. Je conduisais les enfants à l'école quand la voiture est tombée en panne. 7. Qu'est-ce que vous disiez quand je suis entré(e) dans la chambre?

6-8   1. Elle avait les yeux verts et les cheveux bruns. 2. Le marié portait un smoking. 3. La mariée était belle. 4. Quel âge avais-tu à l'époque? 5. Comment s'appelait ton voisin? 6. Quel temps faisait-il? 7. Il faisait (du) soleil. 8. Il mesurait 1 m 90 et pesait cent kilos. 9. Les hors-d'œuvre étaient délicieux. 10. Le paysage était magnifique.

6-9   1. Elle adorait les enfants. 2. J'espérais être célèbre un jour. 3. Il ne s'attendait pas à cela. 4. Ils avaient peur. 5. Elle ne voulait pas partir. 6. Est-ce que tu avais (Avais-tu) froid? 7. Robert avait de la fièvre. 8. Est-ce que vous connaissiez (Connaissiez-vous) cette personne? 9. Est-ce qu'il croyait (Croyait-il) cette histoire? 10. Sophie détestait le rouge, elle préférait le violet. 11. Ils se sentaient coupables. 12. J'étais déçu(e). 13. Est-ce qu'ils étaient (Étaient-ils) de bonne humeur? 14. Je croyais que tu n'aimais pas ça. 15. Elles ne savaient pas qu'il était malade.

6-10   1. Quelle heure était-il quand tu es rentré(e)? 2. Il était trois heures. 3. Il était midi quand nous avons déjeuné. 4. Il était cinq heures moins le quart quand elle a téléphoné. 5. Quel jour était-ce? —C'était jeudi. 6. C'était le premier janvier. 7. Il était trop tard.

6-11   1. Si seulement j'avais plus de temps! 2. Si on allait au cinéma ce soir? 3. J'allais lui offrir un cadeau mais j'ai changé d'avis. 4. Elle allait acheter un appareil photo, mais elle n'avait pas assez d'argent. 5. Nous allions faire la lessive mais la machine à laver était cassée. 6. Qu'est-ce que tu allais dire? 7. Ils croyaient que la grève allait s'arrêter. 8. Je savais que ça allait être difficile. 9. Nous venions de déménager. 10. Ils venaient d'arriver quand je les ai vus. 11. Elle était en train de faire la vaisselle. 12. Ils étaient sur le point de perdre patience.

6-12   Quand j'étais petite, ma grand-mère venait toujours nous rendre visite à Noël. C'était un long voyage pour elle, car nous vivions aux États-Unis, et elle venait de France. Donc, son arrivée était un grand événement pour moi, et je l'attendais toujours avec beaucoup de joie. Chaque année, ma mamie me gâtait avec beaucoup de cadeaux, et il y avait toujours du chocolat et une nouvelle poupée. Quand j'étais plus âgée, elle m'apportait des CD avec des chansons françaises que j'adorais, et elle continuait à m'offrir du chocolat. Pendant son séjour, elle cuisinait des plats magnifiques et ses gâteaux étaient un délice. Elle faisait toujours une bûche de Noël pour nous, et nous fêtions un Noël français en Amérique.

6-13   1. a neigé 2. neigeait 3. faisait, faisait 4. a fait 5. sommes partis 6. partions 7. jouais 8. ai joué 9. travaillait 10. a travaillé 11. ont déménagé 12. déménageaient 13. se mariaient 14. se sont mariés 15. est venue, est descendue 16. venait, descendait

6-14   1. Chaque hiver, nous faisions du ski. 2. Nous avons fait du ski la semaine dernière. 3. Il est allé au marché aux puces dimanche dernier. 4. Il allait au marché aux puces tous les dimanches. 5. Quand j'étais enfant, je faisais toujours le même rêve. 6. J'ai fait un mauvais rêve cette nuit. 7. Je travaillais toujours de huit heures du matin à cinq heures de l'après-midi. 8. Hier, j'ai travaillé de huit heures du matin à cinq heures de l'après-midi. 9. Nous attendions l'autobus. 10. Nous avons attendu l'autobus pendant une heure. 11. L'année dernière, ils ont dîné au restaurant plusieurs fois. 12. Je rangeais ma chambre pendant qu'il dormait.

6-15   1. Je n'ai jamais aimé le beurre de cacahuètes. 2. Je n'aimais pas le beurre de cacahuètes quand j'étais enfant. 3. Ma fille ne jouait jamais avec des poupées quand elle était petite. 4. J'ai toujours rêvé de faire une croisière. 5. Quand j'étais jeune, je rêvais toujours de faire une croisière. 6. Mon fils a eu dix-sept ans mercredi dernier. 7. Elle avait dix-huit ans quand elle est arrivée à l'université. 8. Connaissais-tu cette femme? 9. Où as-tu connu ta femme? 10. Il ne savait pas faire la cuisine (cuisiner). 11. Il a su que c'était une erreur. 12. Je croyais que j'allais mourir. 13. Un instant, j'ai cru que j'allais mourir. 14. Elle avait mal à la tête. 15. Soudain, elle a eu mal à la tête.

6-16   1. dormais, est rentré 2. (j') habitais, (j') allais 3. était, vivait 4. a vécu 5. ont offert 6. (j') étais, (je) pensais, (n') était 7. avez pensé 8. jouions 9. a duré 10. (je) descendais, (j') ai entendu 11. est né, a terminé 12. ont lu, ont pris, se sont couchés

6-17   C'était dimanche après-midi et il pleuvait. Tout était calme dans la ville et il n'y avait personne dans les rues. Tout à coup, deux gangsters sont arrivés à motocyclette. Ils portaient des masques et l'un d'entre eux tenait un pistolet à la main droite. Ils se sont retournés pour voir si quelqu'un les suivait. Ils n'ont pas vu l'homme qui les observait de sa fenêtre. Les deux voleurs sont entrés dans la banque, ont ouvert le coffre-fort, ont pris l'argent et les bijoux et ont tout mis dans un grand sac. Pendant ce temps, le témoin a téléphoné à la police qui est arrivée immédiatement. Quand les braqueurs sont sortis du bâtiment, les policiers qui les attendaient les ont arrêtés et emmenés en prison.

6-18   1. (m') a fait 2. (j') étais 3. fonctionnait 4. voulais 5. étaient 6. (j') ai fait 7. (j') ai fini 8. suis parti 9. (j') ai pu 10. n'ai pas pu 11. pleuvait 12. suis resté 13. suis revenu 14. (j') ai visité 15. ai rencontré 16. s'est bien amusés 17. suis allé 18. venait 19. ai donc montré 20. l'ai laissée 21. attendait 22. (j') ai passé 23. n'ai rien fait 24. suis monté 25. suis resté 26. (j') allais 27. n'ai pas eu 28. (j') ai dû 29. venais 30. (j') ai reçu

6-19   Molière est né en 1622. En réalité, il s'appelait Jean-Baptiste Poquelin. Il était le fils d'un tapissier parisien qui travaillait pour le roi. De 1636 à 1642, Molière est allé à l'école à Paris, puis a étudié le droit à Orléans. Parce qu'il aimait beaucoup le théâtre, il a décidé de devenir acteur. En fait, il est devenu acteur, auteur et directeur d'une troupe de théâtre. Il a écrit des pièces dans lesquelles il se moque des faiblesses humaines et de la société de son temps. Malheureusement, il a dû aller en prison plusieurs fois car il avait beaucoup de dettes. Entre 1646 et 1658, Molière et sa troupe ont été en tournée en province. Il avait beaucoup de succès. En 1662, il s'est marié avec Armande Béjart, qui avait vingt ans de moins que lui. Parmi les comédies qu'il a écrites, *Tartuffe, Le Bourgeois Gentilhomme, l'Avare* et *Le Misanthrope* sont les mieux connues. Molière est mort en 1673, peu après avoir joué dans une représentation du *Malade imaginaire*.

Unit 7 The pluperfect tense

7-1   1. Ils étaient retournés 2. Nous étions venu(e)s 3. Elles avaient choisi 4. Vous aviez promis 5. J'avais ri 6. Nous avions beaucoup appris 7. Ils avaient été 8. La proposition était tombée 9. Il avait plu 10. Tu avais écrit 11. Il avait voulu 12. Ils s'étaient dépêchés

7-2   1. Robert cherchait la valise qu'il avait perdue. 2. Elle m'a finalement rendu l'argent que je lui avais prêté il y a longtemps. 3. Il a eu un accident parce qu'il avait bu. 4. Le professeur était déçu parce que les étudiants n'avaient pas fait leurs devoirs. 5. Quand ils avaient vendu leur maison, ils ont déménagé. 6. Lorsque Napoléon a décidé de quitter Moscou, l'hiver russe avait déjà commencé. 7. Elle avait vécu en Afrique avant de venir aux États-Unis. 8. Ils pensaient qu'il était mort à la guerre. 9. Elle était heureuse parce qu'elle avait reçu un prix. 10. Je ne savais pas où j'avais mis mon portefeuille.

7-3   1. Si seulement je l'avais écouté! 2. Si seulement ils n'avaient pas dit ça! 3. Si seulement il n'avait pas roulé si vite! 4. Si seulement nous avions suivi son conseil! 5. Si seulement tu étais arrivé(e) à l'heure! 6. Si seulement vous me l'aviez dit plus tôt!

7-4   1. Je n'avais pas eu de ses nouvelles depuis deux ans quand il a téléphoné. 2. Elles n'avaient pas nettoyé l'appartement depuis huit semaines quand le propriétaire est venu. 3. Il n'avait pas payé ses factures depuis trois mois quand il a reçu l'avertissement. 4. Elle n'était pas allée au travail depuis plusieurs jours quand son patron l'a renvoyée. 5. Je n'avais pas vu mes amis depuis longtemps quand je les ai rencontrés dans une soirée.

7-5   1. Quand elles avaient mangé, elles faisaient les boutiques. 2. Dès qu'il était parti, elle ouvrait les fenêtres. 3. Tous les samedis, après qu'il avait tondu la pelouse, ils sortaient ensemble. 4. Une fois que tu t'étais réveillé(e), tu pleurais toujours. 5. Tous les jours, quand il avait fini ses devoirs, il surfait sur le Net.

7-6   Les Madeleines. Stanislas, qui était roi de Pologne et duc de Normandie, avait l'habitude de passer l'été dans un château, en Lorraine, pour aller à la chasse.

   Il adorait les desserts. Ses cuisiniers essayaient d'inventer, chaque jour, quelque chose de nouveau. En 1755, une servante qui s'appelait Madeleine a proposé ce que sa mère lui avait montré, de petits gâteaux en forme de coquille, dorés à l'extérieur et moelleux à l'intérieur. Le roi a demandé comment s'appelaient les gâteaux qu'il avait mangés. Et puisqu'ils n'avaient pas de nom, on les a appelés « madeleines ». Au début du vingtième siècle, les madeleines sont devenues très célèbres parce que l'écrivain Marcel Proust les avait mentionnées dans son œuvre *À la recherche du temps perdu*.

7-7   Un voyage. J'avais toujours voulu visiter l'Europe, mais nous n'étions jamais allés à l'étranger. Notre fille avait déjà été en France plusieurs fois pendant que je rêvais toujours d'un tel voyage. Pour pouvoir passer nos vacances dans un pays étranger, j'avais commencé à travailler dans une librairie en ville, et Pierre, mon mari, avait arrêté de fumer pour faire des économies. Déjà avant notre mariage, il m'avait promis de faire beaucoup de voyages, car il savait que j'aime voyager.

   Finalement, le grand jour était arrivé. Pierre m'a dit qu'il avait reçu les billets d'avion, et que nous allions partir bientôt. Inutile de dire que j'étais très contente.

   Nous avons quitté les États-Unis le trois août et nous sommes arrivés à Monaco le lendemain matin. Mon mari est tout de suite allé au casino pour jouer. Je lui avais dit d'être prudent, mais il n'a pas voulu écouter. Malheureusement, il a perdu tout l'argent qu'il avait mis à la banque, et nous avons dû rentrer à la maison plus tôt que prévu. Puisque nous étions fauchés, nous avons vendu la maison que nous avions achetée il y a vingt ans, et nous avons loué un appartement dans un quartier où nous avions vécu auparavant. Si seulement nous n'avions pas fait ce voyage!

Unit 8 The *passé simple*

8-1   1. they waited 2. we lost 3. you found 4. they went 5. I looked for (searched) 6. you swam 7. he sang 8. they stayed 9. she married 10. I obeyed 11. you heard 12. they went down 13. we went 14. she sold

8-2   1. he was 2. he made 3. he saw 4. we came 5. we received 6. she wrote 7. it was necessary 8. he took 9. they said 10. he wanted 11. they put 12. she went 13. I drank 14. he lived 15. he had to 16. we had 17. he read 18. he ran

8-3   1. est né 2. a pris 3. s'est marié 4. est devenu 5. s'est rendu 6. a divorcé 7. a épousé 8. ont eu 9. a (immédiatement) reçu 10. a créé 11. a (aussi) fondé 12. a fait 13. a commencé 14. a gagné 15. a ouvert 16. est arrivée 17. a passé 18. a vu 19. a décidé 20. a fallu 21. ont perdu 22. a abdiqué 23. s'en est allé 24. est revenu 25. a été 26. s'est échappé 27. est retourné 28. a dû 29. est mort

8-4   The other day, at the bottom of a valley,
A snake bit Jean Fréron.
What do you think happened?
It was the snake that died.

Unit 9 The future tenses

9-1   1. Je demanderai. 2. Ils apporteront. 3. Écoutera-t-il? (Est-ce qu'il écoutera?) 4. Tu n'enseigneras pas. 5. Nous donnerons. 6. J'attendrai. 7. Est-ce que vous travaillerez? (Travaillerez-vous?) 8. Répondra-t-elle? (Est-ce qu'elle répondra?) 9. Tu perdras. 10. Il neigera. 11. Elles oublieront 12. Je ne me coucherai pas avant minuit.

13. Qu'est-ce qu'ils achèteront? 14. Je répéterai. 15. Nous essaierons. (Nous essayerons.) 16. Nous emploierons. 17. Tu te rappelleras. 18. Ils réussiront. 19. J'obéirai. 20. Tout le monde vieillira.

9-2   1. Je boirai de la bière. 2. Elle conduira prudemment. 3. Tu ne croiras pas cette histoire. 4. Vous ne direz rien. 5. Dormira-t-il bien? (Est-ce qu'il dormira bien?) 6. Nous écrirons une dissertation. 7. On lira des bandes dessinées. 8. Tout le monde prendra des photos. 9. Tu riras. 10. Ils ne comprendront jamais.

9-3   1. iront 2. prendrai 3. saura 4. devrons 5. ferai, voudras 6. verront 7. enverrez 8. viendras 9. serez 10. aurai 11. faudra 12. pourrai

9-5   1. Je m'assiérai. (Je m'assoirai.) 2. On verra. 3. J'irai à la boucherie. 4. Où ira-t-elle? (Où est-ce qu'elle ira?) 5. Aurons-nous assez d'argent? (Est-ce que nous aurons assez d'argent?) 6. Y aura-t-il une réunion (Est-ce qu'il y aura une réunion) ce soir? 7. Elle devra payer le dîner. 8. Elles seront heureuses. 9. Ça sera tout? (Est-ce que ça sera tout?) 10. Qu'est-ce que tu feras? (Que feras-tu?) 11. Vous vous souviendrez. 12. Il faudra se dépêcher. 13. Quel temps fera-t-il? —Il pleuvra. 14. Nous ne pourrons pas venir. 15. Ils recevront un coup de téléphone.

9-6   1. Demain après-midi, il y aura une fête. 2. Ce soir, j'enverrai une lettre à ma tante. 3. J'espère qu'il fera beau la semaine prochaine. 4. A l'avenir, il sera plus prudent. 5. Quand partiras-tu? (Quand est-ce que tu partiras?) 6. Je ne sais pas si j'irai à la réunion. 7. Auras-tu le temps (Est-ce que tu auras le temps) de le faire? 8. Il reviendra en juillet. 9. Je ne saurai jamais la réponse. 10. Pourras-tu (Est-ce que tu pourras) nous rejoindre? 11. Un jour, cette maison vaudra une fortune. 12. Il voudra voir votre passeport. 13. Ma mère m'achètera un ordinateur portable quand j'aurai quinze ans. 14. Elle téléphonera dès qu'elle pourra. 15. Désormais vous prendrez le métro. 16. S'il pleut, nous resterons à la maison. 17. Je partirai quand je voudrai. 18. Dans quelques semaines, cette usine fermera ses portes. 19. La grève ne durera que vingt-quatre heures. 20. Je serai de retour dans cinq minutes.

9-9   Tu vivras (habiteras) en Europe et tu voyageras beaucoup. Tu travailleras pour une entreprise française, et plus tard tu deviendras mannequin et vedette de cinéma. Tu joueras le rôle principal dans beaucoup de films et tu verras le monde entier. Tout le monde t'admirera. Tu pourras acheter beaucoup de choses parce que tu seras richissime. Quand tu auras trente ans, tu feras la connaissance de l'homme de tes rêves. Tu te marieras à Paris et tu passeras ta lune de miel à Tahiti où le soleil brillera tout le temps. Tu auras trois beaux enfants, un garçon et deux filles. Le garçon s'appellera Antoine et les filles s'appelleront Chantal et Denise. Ton mari t'aimera et tu adoreras ton mari. Vous ferez beaucoup de voyages ensemble. Tes enfants iront à l'université Harvard. Ils réussiront et ils deviendront riches et célèbres eux aussi. Tu seras très heureuse et tu vivras longtemps.

9-10   *Possible answers*: 1. L'été prochain, j'irai en Belgique. 2. Ce soir, je me coucherai à onze heures et quart. 3. Le week-end prochain, j'irai au Cirque du Soleil. 4. Oui, je pourrai sortir ce soir. 5. J'aurai probablement trois enfants. 6. Oui, je serai marié(e) dans dix ans 7. Selon la météo, il fera beau demain. 8. J'obtiendrai mon diplôme dans deux ans. 9. Non, je ne verrai pas mes parents la semaine prochaine. 10. Oui, j'enverrai des e-mails à mes amis cet après-midi.

9-11   1. Tu auras mal au cœur. 2. Il fera meilleur demain. 3. Elle finira ses études dans six ans. 4. Nous nous assiérons (assoirons) sur un banc. 5. Tu seras surpris. 6. Je me marierai en octobre prochain. 7. Il pleuvra. 8. Il pleurera. 9. Ils mourront. 10. Je courrai. 11. Il y aura un orage. 12. Vous verrez.

9-12   1. Voulez-vous me suivre? 2. Veux-tu m'aider? 3. Veux-tu me rendre un service? 4. Ce sont des choses qui arrivent. 5. La voiture ne veut pas démarrer. 6. Il ne veut pas le faire.

9-13   1. J'aurai acheté une voiture. 2. Elle sera allée chez le dentiste. 3. Nous nous serons couché(e)s. 4. Tu seras déjà parti(e). 5. Ils auront vu le film. 6. Je me serai amusé(e). 7. Vous aurez compris.

9-14   1. Après-demain, j'aurai terminé mon rapport. 2. D'ici la fin de l'année, nous aurons dépensé mille euros en médicaments. 3. En juillet, cette usine aura licencié cent ouvriers. 4. D'ici dix ans, ces oiseaux auront disparu. 5. J'espère qu'elle sera partie quand tu reviendras. 6. Est-ce que vous aurez écrit la recommandation ce soir?

9-16   1. Appelez-moi dès que vous aurez reçu ce message. 2. Ce sera votre tour quand j'aurai fini. 3. On saura plus lorsqu'il aura passé la radio. 4. Une fois que nous aurons récupéré nos valises, nous prendrons un taxi. 5. Tant que tu n'auras pas fait tes devoirs, tu ne pourras pas sortir. 6. Je t'écrirai après que nous serons arrivé(e)s.

9-17   1. Ce n'est pas possible. Elle se sera trompée. 2. Il revient. Il aura oublié quelque chose. 3. Je ne peux pas trouver mon stylo. Mon collègue l'aura pris. 4. Elle n'a pas encore téléphoné? Tu lui auras donné le mauvais numéro. 5. Ils n'ont pas faim? Ils auront déjà mangé.

Unit 10 The conditional

10-1   1. Nous mangerions. 2. Je n'achèterais pas ce tapis. 3. Tu demanderais. 4. J'essaierais. (J'essayerais.) 5. Ils travailleraient dur. 6. Je m'ennuierais. 7. Nous resterions. 8. Il amènerait ses petits-enfants. 9. Vous aideriez. 10. Il se rappellerait. 11. Vous réussiriez. 12. Elle obéirait. 13. Je rougirais. 14. Tu choisirais. 15. Elles perdraient. 16. Je ne répondrais pas.

10-2   1. Nous irions 2. Elle n'aurait pas 3. Il y aurait 4. Il serait 5. Je boirais 6. Courrais-tu (Est-ce que tu courrais) 7. Nous enverrions 8. Qu'est-ce que tu ferais 9. Il faudrait 10. Je mourrais 11. Il pleuvrait 12. Tu prendrais 13. Vous recevriez 14. Il saurait 15. Qui viendrait

10-3   1. Ce serait dommage. 2. Ça ne m'étonnerait pas. 3. Ça coûterait trop cher. 4. Il vaudrait mieux ne rien dire. 5. Il y aurait des émeutes. 6. Voilà mon numéro de téléphone au cas où tu aurais besoin de moi. 7. Au cas où vous changeriez d'avis, faites-le-moi savoir. 8. Qu'est-ce que vous voudriez? 9. Je voudrais un morceau de tarte aux fraises. 10. Voudriez-vous une place côté fenêtre ou côté couloir? 11. Elle voudrait bien parler couramment le français. 12. Auriez-vous une chambre pour deux personnes? 13. Sauriez-vous (Est-ce que vous sauriez) les coordonnées de M. Avenel? 14. Est-ce que nous pourrions (Pourrions-nous) voir la carte s'il vous plaît? 15. Est-ce que je pourrais avoir du riz à la place des frites? 16. Est-ce que je pourrais parler à Mme Duval? 17. Pourrais-tu fermer la fenêtre? 18. Pourriez-vous me dire où se trouve la station de métro la plus proche? 19. Ça devrait être interdit. 20. Je devrais aller chez le coiffeur.

10-4   1. Est-ce que je pourrais vous poser une question? 2. Pourriez-vous parler plus lentement s'il vous plaît? 3. Voudriez-vous me rendre un service? 4. Je voudrais avoir l'addition s'il vous plaît. 5. Pardon, Madame, auriez-vous la monnaie de cinquante euros? 6. Sauriez-vous où je peux acheter des fleurs?

10-5   1. Si j'avais beaucoup d'argent, je ferais le tour du monde. 2. Qu'est-ce que vous feriez si vous gagniez à la loterie? 3. Où irais-tu si tu avais un mois de congé? 4. Si j'étais malade, je resterais au lit. 5. Je serais heureux (heureuse) si tu venais à ma fête. 6. Si elle avait le temps, elle rangerait sa chambre. 7. Si j'étais toi, j'arrêterais de fumer. 8. Si nous allions en France, nous verrions beaucoup de belles cathédrales. 9. S'il voyait un chat noir, il ferait demi-tour. 10. S'ils avaient une parabole, ils recevraient cette émission.

10-7   *Possible answers:* 1. je me reposerais 2. je ne sortirais pas 3. je prendrais de l'aspirine 4. je voyagerais beaucoup 5. je mangerais bien 6. je ne pourrais pas comprendre les personnes francophones 7. je parlerais français avec eux 8. j'irais en Turquie 9. je mettrais un maillot de bain 10. je m'achèterais un bateau à voile *(sailboat)*

10-9   *Possible answers:* 1. Si j'étais fauché(e), j'emprunterais de l'argent à mes copains. 2. Si j'étais déprimé(e), je téléphonerais à mes amis. 3. Si ma voiture était en panne, je prendrais le métro. 4. Si je ne réussissais pas à l'examen, je serais triste. 5. Si j'avais mal aux dents, j'irais chez le dentiste. 6. Si je voyais mal, j'achèterais des lunettes. 7. Si j'avais froid, je mettrais un anorak.

10-10   1. Je ne pensais pas qu'il neigerait. 2. J'ai cru que ça ne marcherait pas. 3. Nous étions sûrs que vous seriez d'accord. 4. Il avait promis qu'il téléphonerait. 5. Ils ne pensaient pas que vous vous rappelleriez. 6. Elle ne savait pas si elle aurait le temps de le faire. 7. Il m'a demandé si je pourrais l'aider. 8. Je me demandais s'il y aurait un feu d'artifice.

10-11   Dans une conversation avec mon médecin (à la) fin (du mois de) décembre, j'avais mentionné que je voulais maigrir et rester en bonne santé cette année. Je me demandais si mes résolutions pour la nouvelle année se réaliseraient.

   « Qu'est-ce que je devrais faire? », j'avais demandé au docteur Martin. Il a répondu que s'il était à ma place, il se mettrait au régime. Il mangerait moins et il ferait plus d'exercice. Il ne boirait que du lait écrémé, du coca light et trois bouteilles d'eau par jour. Il éviterait les sucreries et les boissons alcoolisées. Au lieu de cela, il mangerait beaucoup de fruits et de légumes. Il ne prendrait pas la voiture mais le vélo pour se déplacer, sauf s'il pleuvait. Et il m'a dit qu'au lieu de regarder la télévision, il ferait de la marche, il nagerait et il jouerait au tennis tous les jours.

   Quand j'ai quitté le cabinet du médecin, j'étais déprimée. Je savais que je ne pourrais pas changer mes habitudes alimentaires. Je suivrais le conseil du docteur Martin si je n'étais pas si paresseuse.

10-12   1. Elle aimerait mieux bavarder avec ses amis que d'étudier. 2. Est-ce que tu n'aimerais pas mieux voyager? 3. Vous feriez mieux de suivre son conseil. 4. Elle ferait mieux de l'écouter. 5. Ils feraient mieux de partir. 6. Tu ferais mieux d'attendre.

10-13   1. seraient 2. il y aurait 3. irait mieux 4. gagneraient 5. feraient grève 6. serait

10-14   1. J'aurais été triste. 2. Elle aurait préféré vivre à la campagne. 3. Nous serions restés plus longtemps, mais nous avons dû partir. 4. Elles auraient ri. 5. Qui aurait cru qu'il démissionnerait? 6. Je me serais couché(e)

plus tôt. 7. À votre place, je n'aurais rien dit. 8. Vous seriez mort(e). 9. Il aurait eu peur. 10. Est-ce que tu serais venu(e)? 11. Elle aurait perdu. 12. Il aurait mieux valu attendre.

10-15 1. Est-ce que tu aurais vu mon sac à main par hasard? 2. Au cas où vous ne l'auriez pas remarqué, il neige. 3. Elle aurait dû venir plus tôt. 4. Tu aurais dû demander. 5. Vous auriez dû laisser un pourboire. 6. Nous aurions dû être plus prudent(e)s. 7. Vous n'auriez pas dû dépenser tant d'argent. 8. Ils auraient voulu (aimé) s'asseoir. 9. J'aurais voulu (aimé) savoir où elle est née. 10. Elle aurait voulu (aimé) devenir hôtesse de l'air. 11. Nous aurions pu avoir un accident. 12. Ça aurait pu arriver à n'importe qui.

10-17 1. Si j'avais su, je ne serais pas venu(e). 2. Elle aurait gagné plus d'argent si elle avait fait des heures supplémentaires. 3. Si le temps avait été beau (S'il avait fait beau) le week-end dernier, nous aurions fait du camping. 4. Si tu n'avais pas bu tant de vin, tu n'aurais pas eu mal à la tête. 5. S'il n'avait pas plu, je me serais baigné(e). 6. Si j'avais entendu mon réveil, je me serais réveillé(é) à l'heure. 7. Si elle avait lu *Internet pour les nuls*, elle aurait su surfer (naviguer) sur le Net.

10-18 1. Elle pensait qu'elle aurait fini son travail avant midi. 2. Nous savions que nous serions retournés avant eux. 3. Je ne savais pas si j'aurais pu le faire. 4. Ils croyaient que nous aurions été fâchés. 5. Je me demandais si j'aurais pu partir.

10-19 1. Il se serait noyé. 2. Elle aurait quitté son mari. 3. Ils auraient essayé d'enlever l'enfant. 4. Les cambrioleurs auraient pris tous les ordinateurs. 5. Il serait mort d'une crise cardiaque. 6. L'explosion aurait causé cinq morts. 7. Quarante millions de lecteurs auraient lu le roman *Le Da Vinci Code*. 8. La foudre aurait tué quatre personnes.

10-20 1. Si tu ne me dis pas la vérité, je me fâcherai. 2. Si nous nous dépêchons, nous arriverons à l'heure. 3. Si je le connaissais, je lui parlerais. 4. S'ils étaient allés au cocktail, ils se seraient amusés.

10-21 1. verrez 2. (j') irai 3. mettrais 4. travaillerais 5. feriez 6. me serais couché(e) 7. n'aurait pas épousé 8. ne l'aurais pas cru 9. seriez arrivé(e) 10. étais 11. aviez eu 12. sont

10-22 *Possible answers:* 1. paierai (payerai) mes dettes 2. (j') achèterais un avion 3. je ne serais pas sorti(e) de la maison 4. j'habitais sur la Côte d'Azur 5. j'avais soixante-cinq ans 6. je pouvais 7. tu m'avais invité(e) 8. (s') il avait fait chaud 9. vous aviez beaucoup d'argent 10. vous aviez eu beaucoup d'argent

10-23 1. a 2. avait 3. avait eu 4. aura 5. aurait

10-24 1. Chaque fois que je le voyais, il faisait semblant de ne pas me reconnaître. 2. Voulez-vous me suivre (s'il vous plaît)? 3. Voulez-vous me pardonner (s'il vous plaît)? 4. Je lui ai donné des conseils, mais elle n'a pas voulu écouter. 5. Je le lui ai dit plusieurs fois, mais il n'a pas voulu me croire. 6. Je lui ai demandé de me donner un coup de main, mais elle n'a pas voulu.

10-25 1. Est-ce que je pourrais vous poser une question? 2. Ça pourrait arriver. 3. Elles viendraient si elles pouvaient. 4. Nous serions heureux si vous pouviez travailler demain. 5. Je lui ai demandé s'il pourrait le faire. 6. Malheureusement, je n'ai pas pu te joindre hier. 7. Soyez prudent(e), l'animal pourrait devenir dangereux.

Unit 11 The subjunctive

11-1 1. a. travaille b. travailliez c. travaillent 2. a. réponde b. répondes c. répondions d. répondent 3. a. me lève b. nous levions c. se lèvent 4. a. emploies b. employiez c. emploient 5. a. partage b. partagions c. partagent 6. a. remercie b. remercies c. remerciions d. remerciiez 7. a. réussisse b. réussisse c. réussissions 8. a. me rappelle b. se rappelle c. vous rappeliez d. se rappellent 9. a. répète b. répète c. répétions 10. a. (j') essaie b. essayions c. essaient 11. a. prononces b. prononce c. prononcions

11-2 1. a. dorme b. dormiez c. dorment 2. a. boives b. buviez c. boivent 3. a. envoies b. envoyions c. envoyiez d. envoient 4. a. fasses b. fassions c. fassiez d. fassent 5. a. (j') aille b. alliez c. aillent 6. a. saches b. sachions 7. a. prenne b. preniez 8. a. voies b. voyiez c. voient 9. a. puisses b. puisse c. puissions 10. a. vienne b. venions c. veniez d. viennent 11. a. (j') ouvre b. ouvres c. ouvriez d. ouvrent 12. a. doives b. deviez c. doivent 13. a. connaisse b. connaissiez 14. a. écrives b. écrivions 15. a. dise b. disiez 16. a. veuilles b. vouliez c. veuillent 17. a. mette b. mettions c. mettent 18. pleuve 19. vaille 20. a. reçoives b. receviez 21. a. aies b. ait c. ayez 22. a. sois b. soit c. soyons 23. faille

11-3 1. a. (j') aie vu b. ayons vu c. aient vu 2. a. sois sorti(e) b. soit sorti c. soyez sorti(e)(s) d. soient sortis 3. a. (j') aie réussi b. aies réussi c. ait réussi d. ayons réussi e. aient réussi 4. a. me sois souvenu(e) b. se soit souvenue c. nous soyons souvenu(e)s 5. a. aies vendu b. ait vendu c. ayez vendu d. aient vendu 6. a. (j') aie trouvé b. aies trouvé c. ait trouvé d. ayez trouvé e. aient trouvé

11-4 1. comprennes 2. aies compris 3. puisse 4. ait pu 5. oubliiez 6. ayez oublié 7. doive 8. ait dû 9. soit 10. ait été 11. n'aies pas 12. n'aies pas eu

11-5 1. ait trouvé 2. soit arrivé 3. puisses 4. aies pu 5. partes 6. sois parti(e)

11-6 1. Je préfère que tu attendes. 2. J'aimerais mieux que tu partes maintenant. 3. Ils insistent pour que (Ils tiennent à ce que) j'aille à l'église avec eux. 4. Nous suggérons que vous preniez une retraite anticipée. 5. Elle a demandé que je prenne la décision. 6. Nous attendrons qu'il y ait moins de circulation sur l'autoroute. 7. Il souhaite que tu reçoives la lettre demain. 8. Il espère que tu recevras la lettre demain.

11-7 *Possible answers:* 1. la guerre sera bientôt finie 2. je réponde au téléphone 3. tout le monde se sente en sécurité 4. tu t'en ailles 5. je fasse mes devoirs 6. (qu') il me dise cela 7. les magasins soient fermés

11-8 1. Je voudrais être en France. 2. Je voudrais que tu sois là. 3. Ils voudraient avoir un enfant. 4. Ils voudraient que tu aies un enfant. 5. Nous voudrions savoir ce qui s'est passé. 6. Nous voudrions que tu saches ce qui s'est passé. 7. Elle voudrait que tu puisses venir. 8. Elle voudrait pouvoir venir. 9. Je voudrais boire du jus de pomme. 10. Vous avez besoin de payer les factures.

11-9 1. a. Je propose que tu viennes avec moi. b. Je te propose de venir avec moi. 2. a. Nous recommandons que vous visitiez ce parc d'attractions. b. Nous vous recommandons de visiter ce parc d'attractions. 3. a. Le médecin a permis qu'il sorte. b. Le médecin lui a permis de sortir. 4. a. J'ai demandé que ma sœur me conduise à l'aéroport. b. J'ai demandé à ma sœur de me conduire à l'aéroport. 5. a. Est-ce que tu as défendu qu'ils le fassent? b. Est-ce que tu leur as défendu de le faire?

11-10 1. Qu'est-ce que vous voulez que je dise? 2. Qu'est-ce que tu veux que je fasse? 3. Je veux que tu ailles à la boulangerie. 4. Il veulent qu'elle conduise. 5. Ma mère veut que nous allions au Japon cette année. 6. Mon père voudrait que je devienne informaticien(ne). 7. Il a besoin que tu sois son ami(e). 8. Je voudrais que vous teniez votre promesse. 9. Mes parents s'attendent à ce que j'obtienne mon diplôme le mois prochain. 10. Je ne m'attends pas à ce que ce soit facile. 11. Ils ne veulent pas que nous regardions des feuilletons. 12. Elle tient à ce que tu fasses la connaissance de ses parents.

11-11 Mon cher fils,

Comment vas-tu? J'espère que tu vas bien. Ton papa et moi voudrions que tu nous écrives plus souvent. Nous nous inquiétons pour toi et tu nous manques. Est-ce que tu aimerais mieux que nous te téléphonions une fois pas semaine? Nous voulons que tu saches que nous pensons souvent à toi et que nous sommes fiers de toi. Qu'est-ce que tu vas faire pendant les vacances de printemps? Nous suggérons que tu ailles en Suisse pour rendre visite à ton oncle Paul qui habite à Genève. Il souhaite que tu viennes le plus tôt possible, parce que vous ne vous êtes pas vus depuis longtemps. Il insiste pour que tu restes chez lui au moins deux semaines. Papa paiera le vol, mais il demande que tu réussisses d'abord à tes examens. Nous savons que tu travailles dur parce que ton père s'attend à ce que tu sois chirurgien un jour. Fais attention à toi!

Je t'embrasse,
Maman

11-12 1. C'est dommage que tu n'aies pas son adresse. 2. Je suis content(e) qu'il soit sain et sauf. 3. Il est déçu qu'elle ne puisse pas sortir. 4. J'ai peur que tu (ne) prennes froid. 5. Nous sommes désolés que tu doives attendre. 6. Ils craignent que ce pays (ne) perde son identité. 7. Il est inquiet que vous n'acceptiez pas l'invitation. 8. Es-tu fâché(e) que notre équipe ait perdu le match? 9. Nous sommes surpris que cela ne soit pas arrivé plus tôt. 10. Il est triste qu'elle n'ait rien dit. 11. Je regrette que tes lapins soient morts. 12. Ils sont heureux que vous ayez trouvé un emploi.

11-13 *Possible answers:* 1. vous soyez venu(e) si vite 2. nous manquions l'avion 3. notre équipe ait perdu 4. nous partions en vacances 5. cela soit arrivé 6. tout le monde (ne) s'en aille

11-14 1. d'avoir un bon salaire. 2. que vous ayez un bon salaire. 3. d'être vieux 4. que sa femme soit vieille. 5. d'être en retard 6. que l'avion ait du retard. 7. de manquer le train. 8. que vous (ne) manquiez le train. 9. de ne pas pouvoir dîner avec vous ce soir. 10. que vous ne puissiez pas dîner avec moi ce soir.

11-15 Ma chère fille,

Merci pour ta longue lettre. Je suis contente que tu sois bien arrivée à ton université en France, et que ta camarade de chambre Micheline soit sympathique. Je suis ravie que vous parliez français ensemble tout le temps. C'est dommage que je ne puisse pas te voir avant Pâques. Quand tu commenceras à suivre tes cours, tu seras surprise qu'il y ait peu de contact personnel entre les professeurs français et leurs étudiants. Mais tu t'y habitueras vite.

Je suis désolée que tu aies oublié ton (téléphone) portable, mais je te l'enverrai demain.

Veux-tu que je mette ton lecteur de CD aussi dans le colis? J'ai peur que tu ne reçoives pas le paquet la semaine prochaine à cause de la grève. Heureusement que tu es patiente.

Bisous,

Maman

11-16 1. Il faut absolument que j'aille chez le dentiste. 2. Il ne faut pas que tu partes. 3. Il vaut mieux qu'ils sachent la vérité. 4. Il est important que nous fassions attention. 5. Était-il nécessaire que vous me réveilliez au milieu de la nuit? 6. Il est essentiel que vous soyez poli(e). 7. Il est possible qu'il pleuve. 8. Il est probable que je suis (serai) en retard. 9. Il est préférable que tu apprennes le français. 10. Il est utile que vous étudiiez une langue étrangère. 11. Il est rare qu'il fasse si froid en avril. 12. Il est normal qu'elles fassent grève.

11-17 *Possible answers:* 1. nous protégions l'environnement 2. vous sortiez 3. tu prennes le taureau par les cornes 4. je sois franc(he) 5. (qu') il réussisse à le faire 6. (qu') elle prend la décision

11-19 1. boive 2. prenne 3. fasses 4. parte 5. aille 6. écrivions 7. ayez 8. soyez 9. mette

11-20 1. Il vaut mieux y aller. 2. Il vaut mieux que tu y ailles. 3. Il est essentiel de le faire. 4. Il est essentiel que vous le fassiez. 5. Il est inutile de se plaindre. 6. Il est inutile que vous vous plaigniez.

11-21 Chère Maman,

Je viens de recevoir ton courriel. Je suis désolé de ne pas avoir écrit plus tôt, mais il fallait que je finisse de réviser pour les examens finals. Il faut que tu comprennes que je suis très occupé en ce moment. Il ne faut pas que tu sois fâchée. Tu m'as toujours dit qu'il était important que j'obtienne de bonnes notes, n'est-ce pas? Il est probable que je ferai bien cette année car j'ai assisté à tous mes cours. Tu me demandes ce que je compte faire cet été. Il est peu probable que je vous rende visite. Il vaut mieux que je fasse des économies. Sinon, je ne pourrai jamais acheter un nouvel ordinateur. Il faut que j'y aille maintenant car j'ai une réunion dans cinq minutes et il est important que je sois à l'heure.

À la prochaine,

Martin

P.S. J'ai un grand service à te demander. Serait-il possible que tu dises à papa de m'envoyer de l'argent? Je viens de me rendre compte que je suis complètement fauché.

11-22 1. Je doute que ce soit vrai. 2. Es-tu sûr(e) qu'il ait une angine? 3. Il semble seulement qu'elle soit fâchée. 4. Il n'est pas certain qu'il ait dit cela. 5. Est-il vrai qu'elle soit amoureuse de David? 6. Il semble qu'il la connaisse. 7. Il me semble que je vous ai déjà vu quelque part. 8. Il est douteux qu'il ait changé d'avis.

11-23 1. Je ne suis pas convaincu(e) qu'il ait dit la vérité. 2. Il est certain que tout deviendra plus cher. 3. Il est évident qu'il est paresseux. 4. Nous savions que c'était loin. 5. Il paraît qu'il a beaucoup d'argent. 6. Il est douteux qu'elle puisse venir. 7. Est-il vrai qu'il ait la grippe? 8. Je ne doute pas qu'il le fera. 9. Il est vrai qu'elle comprend le chinois. 10. Je sais qu'elle est timide.

11-24 1. Elle n'est pas sûre de pouvoir nous rejoindre. 2. Es-tu sûr(e) de vouloir faire cela? 3. Es-tu sûr(e) qu'il veuille le faire? 4. Je doute de pouvoir y aller. 5. Je doute qu'il le sache. 6. Nous ne sommes pas certains d'arriver à l'heure.

11-25 1. avant qu'il (ne) soit trop tard 2. après que nous sommes rentrés 3. sans que je le sache 4. pour que nous puissions vous comprendre 5. à moins qu'il (ne) pleuve 6. bien qu'il fasse mauvais (bien que le temps soit mauvais) 7. jusqu'à ce qu'elle aille mieux 8. de peur que quelqu'un (ne) les prenne 9. après qu'ils sont partis 10. pourvu que tu réussisses à ton examen

11-26 *Possible answers:* 1. vous l'invitiez 2. (qu') elle soit malade 3. tout le monde puisse vous entendre 4. (qu') il fasse mauvais 5. vous arriviez au carrefour

11-27 1. Bien qu' 2. Pour qu' 3. à moins qu' 4. de peur qu' 5. pourvu que

11-28 *Possible answers:* 1. (d') être fauché(e) 2. (qu') il (ne) pleuve 3. sortir 4. reviennent 5. ses enfants aient de l'argent 6. gagner de l'argent

11-29 1. Ils ont déjeuné avant d'aller au centre commercial. 2. Ils ont déjeuné avant que leurs parents (n') aillent au centre commercial. 3. Il n'achète pas de vêtements à moins d'en avoir absolument besoin. 4. Il n'achète pas de vêtements à moins que sa femme le lui dise. 5. D'habitude, elles travaillent jusqu'à ce qu'elles soient très fatiguées. 6. Nous sommes heureux bien que nous ayons peu d'argent. 7. Je le ferai pourvu que je ne sois pas trop occupé(e). 8. Ils sont partis de bonne heure (tôt) de peur d'être en retard. 9. Tu auras un jouet pourvu que tu sois sage. 10. Tu peux rester dans la chambre à condition de ne pas faire de bruit

11-30 1. a perdu 2. puisse 3. connaisse 4. suis 5. saurai 6. faut 7. faille

11-31   1. Penses-tu qu'il fasse beau demain? 2. Je ne crois pas que l'espagnol soit plus facile que le français. 3. Il ne pense pas que nous puissions le faire. 4. Les scientifiques croient qu'il va y avoir un tremblement de terre. 5. Crois-tu que j'aie pris la bonne décision? 6. Ils ne pensent pas qu'il y ait des survivants.

11-32   1. faille 2. plaise 3. soient 4. as 5. fera 6. puisse 7. soit

11-33   Chère Mireille,

J'ai reçu ton message avant-hier. Il semble que tu sois très déprimée en ce moment à cause de la rupture avec ton fiancé. Je vais essayer de te remonter un peu le moral. Je suis surprise que Sébastien soit parti sans que tu le saches. Tu dis qu'il a trouvé une autre femme, mais je doute qu'elle ait ton charme et ton intelligence. De plus, je ne pense pas que ce jeune homme ait été le partenaire idéal pour toi. Vous vous êtes souvent disputés, et il me semble qu'il est assez égoïste. Ne sois pas triste qu'il t'ait quittée. Comme on dit, « un de perdu, dix de retrouvés ». Je crois qu'il vaut mieux être seul que mal accompagné.

Ne reste pas à la maison le week-end à moins que tu ne veuilles pas te marier. Tu trouveras quelqu'un de bien pourvu que tu sortes souvent. Parle avec beaucoup de personnes jusqu'à ce que tu fasses la connaissance de ton prince charmant. Il ne faut pas que tu aies peur d'une nouvelle relation, bien que tu sois encore sous le choc. Je veux que tu me promettes de suivre mon conseil.

Est-ce que tu as toujours l'intention d'aller en Afrique, la semaine prochaine? Tu verras, ça te changera les idées. Je voudrais que tu m'écrives un (petit) mot avant de partir.

Il faut que tu me dises la date et l'heure de ton retour, pour que je puisse venir te chercher à l'aéroport. J'ai hâte de te revoir. Bon voyage et bonne chance!

Bisous,

Anne

11-34   1. probable 2. possible 3. suis heureux (heureuse) 4. Heureusement 5. après que 6. avant que 7. semble 8. me semble 9. espère 10. veux (voudrais) 11. pensons (croyons) 12. Penses (Crois)

11-35   1. Nous aurions besoin de quelqu'un qui sache parler néerlandais. 2. Nous connaissons quelqu'un qui sait parler néerlandais. 3. Je cherche une maison qui convienne à mes parents. 4. Nous devons trouver quelqu'un qui soit expérimenté. 5. Il cherche un cadeau qui plaise à sa femme.

11-36   1. C'est la meilleure tarte que j'aie jamais mangée. 2. Vous êtes l'homme le plus sympathique qu'elle ait jamais rencontré. 3. C'est le dernier artisan qui sache le faire. 4. Je n'ai jamais vu personne qui soit si ambitieux. 5. Il n'y a que toi qui aies réussi. 6. Voilà les premiers sondages que nous ayons reçus. 7. C'est la seule solution qu'ils aient offerte. 8. Ce sont les dernières nouvelles que nous ayons. 9. Je ne connais personne qui fasse mieux la cuisine. 10. C'est le seul étage qui ait un balcon. 11. Il n'y a rien que vous puissiez faire pour améliorer la situation. 12. Il n'y a que Bertrand qui m'ait compris.

11-37   1. Quoi que tu fasses, fais-le bien. 2. Où que vous soyez dans le monde, nous vous trouverons. 3. Aussi incroyable que ça puisse paraître, tout le monde a survécu à l'accident d'avion. 4. Il faut aimer son travail, quel qu'il soit. 5. Quelles que soient les menaces, je ne partirai jamais! 6. Nous allons arrêter les assassins, quel que soit leur âge. 7. Qui que ce soit qui ait fait ça est un lâche. 8. Quelques erreurs que tu aies faites, essaie de les éviter à l'avenir. 9. Si intelligent(e) que tu sois, tu ne sais pas tout. 10. Aucune grammaire, si complète qu'elle soit, ne peut tout expliquer. 11. Je resterai à tes côtés, quoi qu'il arrive. 12. Il faut respecter les gens, quelles que soient leurs convictions.

11-38   Chère Françoise,

Ça fait longtemps que je n'ai pas eu de tes nouvelles. Où es-tu? Qu'est-ce que tu fais ces jours-ci? Est-ce que tu cherches toujours un manoir qui ne soit pas trop cher? Aujourd'hui, j'ai vu une maison que tu aimerais acheter, quel qu'en soit le prix. Malheureusement, elle n'est pas à vendre.

Hier soir, je suis allée au cinéma pour voir « À la folie, pas du tout » avec Audrey Tautou. C'est le meilleur thriller psychologique que j'aie jamais vu. Je ne connais aucune actrice qui sache jouer aussi bien qu'Audrey. Tous ceux qui la voient tombent amoureux d'elle.

Au travail, j'ai quelques clients exigeants en ce moment. Il n'y a rien qui soit plus difficile que de satisfaire tout le monde. Mais je fais des efforts. C'est la seule chose que je puisse faire. Je suis fière de mon travail, quoi qu'en dise mon patron.

En espérant que tu es en bonne santé, je te souhaite une excellente semaine, où que tu sois.

Bisous,

Anne

11-39   1. suives 2. parte 3. boive 4. soit, fasse 5. dise 6. rendes 7. restiez 8. suis, sois 9. écriras 10. prenne 11. doive 12. dois 13. apprenions 14. vit 15. vous taisiez 16. soyez 17. preniez 18. reçoive 19. soient 20. mette 21. souvienne 22. sachent 23. défendions 24. aies trouvé 25. faille, ait, agisse 26. ne soit pas arrivé 27. faut 28. lise 29. es venu 30. ne vouliez pas

1. écrives 2. puisse 3. pleuve 4. partiez 5. sommes arrivés 6. se fassent 7. revienne 8. est 9. sachiez 10. paraisse 11. appartienne 12. plaise 13. avez fait 14. faites 15. a 16. fait 17. vaille 18. faille 19. (c') est 20. avez 21. soit mort 22. est mort

11-41 1. passerez 2. rie 3. aperçoive 4. conduisions 5. s'en aille 6. vive 7. ayons 8. plaise 9. ait 10. ait vécu 11. veuille 12. puisse 13. aie 14. soit 15. ayons 16. aies prise 17. sache 18. soit sorti 19. fasse 20. aient comprise

11-42 1. Vive le roi! 2. Que tu le veuilles ou non, tu iras à l'université. 3. Autant que je sache, elle n'habite plus ici. 4. Qu'il vienne le plus tôt possible. 5. Que tous tes rêves se réalisent. 6. S'ils n'ont pas de pain, qu'ils mangent de la brioche! 7. Vive(nt) les vacances!

Unit 12 The infinitive

12-1 1. avoir aidé 2. t'amuser 3. y vivre 4. avoir vu 5. avoir trouvé 6. être 7. avoir obtenu 8. te rappeler (te souvenir) 9. être tombé 10. avoir défait

12-2 1. ne pas être 2. ne pas pouvoir 3. ne jamais mentir 4. ne plus manger 5. ne pas être allé(e)s 6. ne pas encore avoir écrit

12-3 1. petit déjeuner, déjeuner, dîner 2. devoirs 3. lever 4. sourire 5. pouvoir 6. goûter 7. souvenir 8. aller simple, aller-retour

12-4 1. Manger 2. Mentir 3. Construire 4. Pleurer 5. Rester 6. Trouver 7. Vouloir 8. Marcher 9. Rouler 10. Partir

12-5 1. Lire 2. Répondre 3. apprendre, faire 4. écouter, regarder 5. écrire 6. Rendre

12-7 1. avant de parler 2. sans dire au revoir 3. de peur de vous déranger 4. loin de partager 5. pour être 6. Au lieu de te plaindre 7. Pour pouvoir le faire 8. pour vivre, pour travailler 9. Après avoir fait la vaisselle 10. Avant de faire la vaisselle 11. Après avoir éteint la lumière 12. Après m'être levé(e)

12-8 *Possible answers:* 1. aller chez le coiffeur 2. pouvoir aller au Brésil 3. m'amuser 4. y aller 5. travailler pour gagner sa vie 6. être riche et en bonne santé que pauvre et malade 7. faire la sieste 8. utiliser leur calculatrice 9. nager 10. courir

12-9 1. J'adore faire la grasse matinée. 2. Nous ne pouvons pas le comprendre. 3. Ma fille compte se spécialiser en informatique. 4. Elle ne sait pas patiner. 5. Je ne sais pas quoi dire. 6. Nous n'aimons pas décevoir nos parents. 7. J'espère te revoir bientôt. 8. Les étudiants doivent écrire beaucoup de dissertations. 9. Qu'est-ce que vous allez faire? 10. Il va guérir. 11. Est-ce que vous devez vous lever tôt demain? 12. Je n'ose pas l'admettre. 13. Qu'est-ce que vous voudriez boire? 14. Il vaudra mieux attendre. 15. Il préfère payer en espèces.

12-10 1. Est-ce que je peux vous demander un service? 2. Est-ce que je pourrais emprunter votre parapluie? 3. On ne peut pas plaire à tout le monde. 4. Elle veut parler avec toi. 5. Les internautes vont connaître ce site Web. 6. Elle ne laisse pas ses enfants (ne permet pas à ses enfants de) regarder la télévision. 7. La petite fille a laissé tomber son ours en peluche. 8. Est-ce que tu as laissé tomber le cours? 9. J'ai entendu dire que vous avez écrit un livre. 10. As-tu déjà entendu parler de cet écrivain? —Oui, j'ai entendu parler de lui. 11. Elle n'a pas entendu le réveil sonner. 12. Vous n'êtes pas censé(e) télécharger cette musique. 13. Nous avons failli manquer l'avion. 14. J'ai failli me tromper. 15. À quoi bon continuer?

12-11 1. Il fait réparer sa voiture. 2. Ils font construire un château. 3. Il fera faire un costume. 4. Nous allons faire installer (l')Internet. 5. Nous venons de faire changer la serrure. 6. Elle a fait livrer des fleurs au domicile de sa mère. 7. Je dois faire renouveler mon passeport. 8. Le magicien a fait disparaître le lapin. 9. Il fait rire sa femme. 10. Ne me fais pas attendre.

12-12 1. Elles ont fait chanter leur patron. 2. Ils m'ont fait attendre (pendant) trois heures. 3. Je te ferai voir les photos. 4. Je vous le ferai savoir. 5. Nous avons fait venir le médecin. 6. Il a fait visiter Bordeaux à ses amis. 7. Je peux me faire comprendre en français. 8. Elle s'est fait couper les cheveux.

12-13 1. As-tu de quoi porter? 2. Il n'a pas de quoi payer le loyer. 3. J'espère que tu apporteras de quoi boire. 4. Il y aura de quoi faire pour tout le monde. 5. Vous trouverez de quoi manger dans le congélateur. 6. Les artistes viennent ici pour trouver de quoi peindre. 7. Il était si pauvre qu'il n'avait même pas de quoi s'acheter une chemise. 8. Elle gagne de quoi se nourrir.

12-14 *Possible answers:* 1. à le faire 2. à vous comprendre 3. à patiner 4. à ouvrir la porte 5. à avoir faim 6. à écrire votre curriculum vitae 7. à naviguer sur (l')Internet 8. des courses à faire

12-15 1. Aide-moi à me lever! 2. J'ai un grand service à te demander. 3. Tu n'as rien à craindre. 4. Est-ce que tu as quelque chose à faire en ce moment? 5. Ils ont du mal à marcher. 6. Il apprend à monter à vélo. 7. Il a commencé (Il s'est mis) à pleuvoir. 8. Je n'arrive pas à dormir. 9. Nous hésitons à poser cette question. 10. Je commence à comprendre. 11. Nous n'avons pas réussi à la convaincre. 12. Il faut s'habituer à vivre dans un monde dangereux. 13. Elles ont forcé les enfants à obéir. 14. Il nous a invité(e)s à prendre un verre. 15. J'ai passé mes vacances à ne rien faire.

12-16 *Possible answers:* 1. de le dire 2. de vous joindre par téléphone 3. de fermer la porte à clé 4. d'aller en Égypte 5. de travailler 6. de me reposer 7. de me marier

12-17 1. Elle a besoin de payer ses études. 2. Ils ont refusé de passer l'examen. 3. Il a décidé d'accepter le cadeau. 4. J'ai hâte de savoir plus de choses sur toi. 5. Nous n'avons pas l'habitude de travailler tous les jours. 6. J'ai essayé de vous avertir. 7. Je suis en train de traduire ces phrases. 8. Nous venons de recevoir le colis. 9. Je rêve de vivre à l'étranger. 10. Le serveuse a oublié d'apporter le plateau de fromage. 11. Il fait semblant d'être pauvre. 12. La vieille dame a peur de sortir. 13. Je n'ai pas le temps de me reposer. 14. J'ai envie de pleurer. 15. Tu n'as pas l'air de te rendre compte du danger. 16. Promets-moi d'être gentil avec les élèves. 17. Je vous conseille de faire attention. 18. Le médecin lui a défendu (interdit) de boire de l'alcool. 19. Il m'a dit de ne pas m'inquiéter. 20. Nous avons demandé au professeur d'être indulgent.

12-19 1. – 2. – 3. à 4. – 5. de 6. de 7. – 8. – 9. à 10. de 11. d' 12. à 13. – 14. – 15. de 16. de 17. à 18. – 19. à 20. – 21. à 22. de 23. – 24. à 25. à 26. de 27. – 28. à 29. de 30. à 31. –, – 32. de 33. à 34. de 35. de 36. d' 37. – 38. à 39. de 40. –, à

12-20 1. – 2. de 3. de 4. – 5. d', de 6. de 7. de 8. de 9. de 10. – 11. à 12. d' 13. de 14. de 15. de 16. de 17. à, d' 18. – 19. – 20. d' 21. de 22. à 23. à 24. de 25. de 26. à 27. – 28. – 29. – 30. –

12-21 *Possible answers:* 1. J'espère avoir un entretien d'embauche (*a job interview*). 2. Elle apprend à piloter un avion. 3. Je refuse de céder. 4. Il a du mal à parler. 5. Je veux m'asseoir. 6. Il faut travailler pour réussir. 7. Je ne peux pas le faire. 8. Je n'ai pas le temps de visiter l'exposition. 9. Je n'ai pas envie de rester. 10. Je dois faire le ménage. 11. Nous allons chercher du secours (*help*). 12. Je regrette de vous avoir fait de la peine. 13. Ils aiment faire des projets d'avenir. 14. J'hésite à changer de métier. 15. Il sait conduire. 16. J'ai décidé de dire « non ». 17. Elle aide la femme de ménage à laver les vitres. 18. Tu n'as pas besoin de t'inquiéter.

12-22 1. Nous étions obligés de le faire. 2. Je suis désolé(e) de vous déranger. 3. Il est triste d'avoir oublié le rendez-vous. 4. Je suis ravi(e) de faire votre connaissance. 5. Il est interdit (défendu) de stationner ici. 6. Il est utile de connaître une langue étrangère. 7. Il est facile d'apprendre le français. 8. Il est dangereux de conduire sans ceinture de sécurité.

12-23 1. Nous sommes prêt(e)s à partir. 2. Le taxi est lent à venir. 3. Elle est occupée à faire la lessive. 4. Je suis habitué(e) à le voir tous les jours. 5. Elle était la seule à savoir la réponse. 6. Tu es la première à me contacter. 7. Elles ne seront pas les dernières à me poser cette question. 8. Il est trop jeune pour se marier.

12-24 1. d' 2. d', à 3. à 4. d' 5. de 6. à 7. de 8. à 9. à, à 10. de 11. à 12. à 13. à 14. à 15. de 16. à 17. à 18. à 19. de 20. à 21. de 22. à 23. de, de 24. à 25. d'

12-25 1. de 2. de 3. d' 4. de 5. d' 6. de 7. de 8. de 9. d' 10. de

12-26 Aujourd'hui, j'ai envie de vous parler de mes projets pour l'avenir immédiat.

Après avoir obtenu mon diplôme, je compte me reposer un peu. Avant de commencer à travailler, je veux m'amuser. Pour être heureux dans la vie, il faut essayer de réaliser ses rêves. Au lieu de chercher un emploi, je préfère aller à l'étranger pendant un certain temps. J'espère voir beaucoup de pays. J'ai dit à mes amis de venir avec moi, mais ils pensaient qu'il valait mieux faire des études supérieures tout de suite. C'est dommage! Pendant qu'ils écriront leurs dissertations ennuyeuses, je passerai mon temps à lire de bons livres car j'ai l'intention d'apprendre quelque chose de nouveau chaque jour. Je pourrai écouter la radio sans être obligé de faire mes devoirs. Je n'aurai plus besoin de suivre des cours obligatoires et je n'aurai plus peur de rater un examen. Je serai libre de faire ce que je veux! Je ne verrai pas le temps passer. Mes amis vont pâlir d'envie quand ils m'entendront décrire mes aventures. Je suis sûr que je garderai toujours un bon souvenir de ces vacances.

Je vais vous laisser maintenant. Avant de prendre l'avion pour l'Asie, je dois encore faire mes valises.
Au revoir!
Sébastien

Unit 13 The imperative

13-1 1. Écoutez! 2. Ralentissez! 3. Attends! 4. Parle plus fort! 5. Parlez plus lentement s'il vous plaît! 6. Reste ici! 7. Paie la facture! 8. Achète des timbres! 9. Aidez les pauvres! 10. Répondez à la question! 11. Essaie ce manteau! 12. Continuez tout droit, puis tournez à gauche. 13. Mangeons chez MacDo! 14. Entrez! 15. Rentre bien! 16. Fermez la porte! 17. Ouvre la fenêtre! 18. Demandez au professeur! 19. Partons! 20. Viens ici! 21. Voyons! 22. Dors bien! 23. Bois ton lait! 24. Prends ton temps! 25. Prenez la deuxième rue à droite.

13-2 1. N'oublie pas! 2. Ne perdons pas notre temps! 3. Ne conduis pas si vite! 4. Ne travaille pas si dur! 5. Ne désobéis pas! 6. Ne voyageons plus! 7. N'exagérons rien! 8. Ne buvez pas cette eau! 9. Ne dites rien! 10. Ne pars pas! 11. Ne faites pas de bruit! 12. Ne riez pas!

13-3 1. Sois prudent(e)! 2. Soyez sage! 3. Soyons courageux! 4. N'aie pas peur! 5. Ayez du courage! 6. Aie confiance en moi! 7. Sache la vérité! 8. Sois fier (fière)! 9. Ne soyez pas en retard! 10. Ne soyons pas déçus! 11. Veuillez vous asseoir! (Asseyez-vous s'il vous plaît.) 12. Veuillez laisser un message après le bip.

13-4 1. n 2. d 3. h 4. e 5. b 6. g 7. c 8. f 9. k 10. m 11. j 12. a 13. l 14. i

13-5 *Possible answers:* 1. Trouve un travail! (Gagne de l'argent!) 2. Dors! 3. Sors avec tes amis! 4. Mets le chauffage! (*Turn the heating on!*) 5. Déshabille-toi! 6. Bois quelque chose! 7. Mange moins! (Fais de la gymnastique!) 8. Compte les moutons! 9. Reste au lit! 10. Va chez le pharmacien! (Prends de l'aspirine!) 11. Prends le train! 12. Cours!

13-6 1. Écoute-moi! 2. Fais-moi confiance! 3. Suivez-moi! 4. Espérons-le! 5. Demandez-lui! 6. Vas-y! 7. Aide-moi! 8. Téléphonez-leur! 9. Passe-moi le sel! 10. Achètes-en! 11. Faites-le! 12. Tiens-moi au courant! 13. Excuse-moi! 14. Attends-moi! 15. Regarde-la! 16. Essaye-le!

13-7 1. Donne-le-leur! 2. Mettez-les-y! 3. Donnez-lui-en! 4. Apportez-le-moi! 5. Montrez-la-leur! 6. Prête-m'en!

13-8 1. Ne me quitte pas! 2. Ne la croyez pas! 3. Ne nous dérangez pas! 4. Ne lui réponds pas! 5. Ne me faites pas rire! 6. Ne les écoute pas! 7. Ne me mens pas!

13-9 1. Ne les lui montre pas! 2. Ne la leur vendez pas! 3. Ne le lui offrons pas! 4. Ne m'en donne pas! 5. Ne la lui envoyons pas!

13-10 1. Asseyez-vous! 2. Dépêchons-nous! 3. Cachez-vous! 4. Réveille-toi! 5. Présentons-nous! 6. Va t'en! 7. Tais-toi! 8. Amusez-vous (bien)! 9. Mettez-vous à l'aise! 10. a. Rappelle-toi! b. Souviens-toi! 11. Détendez-vous! 12. Ne te plains pas! 13. Ne te moque pas de moi! 14. Ne vous endormez pas! 15. Ne t'inquiète pas! 16. Ne vous fâchez pas!

Unit 14 The present participle and the gerund

14-1 1. marchant 2. réfléchissant 3. attendant 4. voyageant 5. espérant 6. prononçant 7. venant 8. allant 9. croyant 10. ayant 11. étant 12. comprenant 13. faisant 14. riant 15. voyant 16. lisant 17. écrivant 18. craignant (ayant peur) 19. ne sachant pas 20. voulant

14-2 1. ayant entendu 2. étant venu(e)(s) 3. étant allé(e)(s) 4. ayant été 5. étant tombé(e)(s) 6. ayant perdu 7. ayant dormi 8. n'étant pas sorti(e)(s) 9. ayant choisi 10. n'ayant pas vu 11. ayant vécu 12. étant parti(e)(s)

14-3 1. Ne sachant (pas) quoi dire 2. Ayant faim 3. Étant fatigué(e) 4. Souhaitant passer le week-end dans votre région 5. Ne pouvant (pas) finir ses études 6. Ne voulant pas la déranger 7. Ayant la nationalité américaine 8. Voyant le feu rouge 9. Le métro étant en grève 10. Ayant manqué le bus 11. N'ayant pas reçu mon fax 12. Ayant vécu au Japon pendant dix ans 13. consommant peu d'essence 14. arrivant en sens inverse 15. L'avion arrivant de Madrid

14-4 1. Ouvrant lentement la porte, il est entré. 2. Il est descendu du train, oubliant sa valise. 3. Prenant son chapeau, il est sorti. 4. Ayant fini son discours, il s'est assis. 5. La bombe a explosé, tuant quatre-vingts personnes.

14-5 1. en voyageant 2. en marchandant 3. en utilisant 4. en buvant 5. en rangeant 6. en riant 7. en pleurant 8. en espérant 9. En vous remerciant 10. en claquant la porte 11. en écoutant cette chanson 12. En entrant dans la maison 13. En recevant le prix 14. en déjeunant 15. en téléphonant

14-6 1. Éteignez la lumière en sortant. 2. Il ne faut pas parler en mangeant. 3. C'est en visitant la France qu'on apprend le mieux à parler français. 4. Vous avez réussi en faisant un effort. 5. Je gagne ma vie en travaillant. 6. Il est tombé en descendant l'escalier. 7. Il s'est cassé la jambe en skiant. 8. Elle a trouvé cet emploi en lisant les petites annonces. 9. J'ai maigri en faisant du sport tous les jours. 10. De nos jours, on téléphone souvent en marchant et on prend ses repas en regardant la télévision.

14-7 *Possible answers:* 1. en écoutant la radio 2. en faisant du footing 3. en mangeant 4. en téléphonant 5. en dînant 6. en chantant

14-8 1. En allant au théâtre, Brice a rencontré un ami. 2. En lisant le journal, Mireille a découvert un article intéressant. 3. En regardant le journal télévisé, on se tient au courant de l'actualité. 4. En travaillant dur, nous réussirons. 5. En faisant du yoga, je me détends. 6. En s'entraînant tous les jours, les joueurs ont gagné le match. 7. En courant très vite, j'ai attrapé le bus. 8. En prenant la deuxième rue à droite, vous arriverez à la gare.

14-9   1. Il dort. 2. Qu'est-ce que vous faites? 3. Je meurs de peur. 4. Elle est en train de balayer la terrasse. 5. Nous regardions la télé quand il a téléphoné. 6. Il était en train de se raser quand la lumière s'est éteinte. 7. Elles le disent depuis longtemps. 8. Depuis combien de temps habitez-vous ici? 9. J'ai marché toute la matinée. 10. La police l'a arrêté car il avait dépassé la limitation de vitesse. 11. Il habitait à la Nouvelle-Orléans depuis quarante ans quand l'ouragan a détruit sa maison. 12. Elle fêtera son trentième anniversaire.

14-10   1. Entrez sans faire de bruit. 2. Ça va sans dire. 3. Téléphone-moi avant de partir. 4. J'adore faire du cheval. 5. Il n'aime pas prendre l'avion. 6. Avez-vous fini de peindre? 7. Je préfère rester ici. 8. Je l'ai vu traverser la rue. 9. Après être entré dans la maison, il a enlevé son manteau. 10. Après m'être habillé(e), je me suis peigné(e). 11. J'ai du mal à respirer. 12. Nous n'avons pas envie de jouer. 13. Il passe son temps à étudier. 14. Ce roman ne vaut pas la peine d'être lu. 15. Merci d'être venu(e)(s). 16. Elles sont assises au dernier rang.

Unit 15 The passive voice

15-1   1. Le cambrioleur est arrêté par la police. 2. L'Académie Française a été fondée par Richelieu. 3. Les otages ont été battus par les ravisseurs. 4. Le chien avait été écrasé par le tramway. 5. Les pantalons seront mis en solde par la vendeuse demain. 6. Il est important que le travail soit fait par les ouvriers.

15-2   1. Le vaccin contre la rage a été inventé par Louis Pasteur. 2. La vedette de cinéma est suivie par les photographes. 3. Une femme sur dix est battue par son mari. 4. Cinquante personnes ont été embauchées par la compagnie aérienne. 5. Ils ont été forcés de travailler. 6. En France, la peine de mort a été abolie (supprimée) en 1981. 7. Un jour, un remède contre le SIDA sera découvert. 8. La visite a été reportée plusieurs fois. 9. Thanksgiving est célébré le dernier jeudi en novembre. 10. Le cours vient d'être supprimé. 11. Heureusement, personne n'a été blessé dans l'accident. 12. Le distributeur de billets a été endommagé. 13. Vous êtes renvoyé(e). 14. Cela n'a jamais été fait. 15. Elle espère être invitée.

15-3   1. a. Gustave Eiffel a construit la tour Eiffel en 1889. b. La tour Eiffel a été construite par Gustave Eiffel en 1889. 2. a. L'Allemand Roentgen a découvert les rayons X. b. Les rayons X ont été découverts par l'Allemand Roentgen. 3. a. Rouget de Lisle a composé « La Marseillaise ». b. « La Marseillaise » a été composée par Rouget de Lisle. 4. a. Monet a peint le tableau « Impression, Soleil levant ». b. Le tableau « Impression, Soleil Levant », a été peint par Monet. 5. a. Lamartine a écrit le poème « Le Lac ». b. Le poème « Le Lac » a été écrit par Lamartine.

15-4   1. vrai 2. vrai 3. vrai 4. faux 5. vrai 6. vrai 7. faux 8. vrai 9. vrai 10. vrai

15-5   Lors des dernières émeutes, beaucoup de voitures ont été incendiées et de nombreuses vitrines ont été brisées par les émeutiers. Plusieurs magasins ont été pillés et des marchandises d'une valeur de plusieurs milliers d'euros ont été volées. Quand les CRS sont arrivés, une personne a été grièvement blessée par un cocktail Molotov. La victime a été transportée à l'hôpital où elle a été opérée tout de suite. Selon les médecins, elle serait dans un état critique. Quelques personnes ont été interpellées. Elles ont été condamnées à cinq mois de prison. Le jeune délinquant qui avait lancé le cocktail Molotov s'est enfui et n'a pas encore été retrouvé par la police. Aussitôt que le coupable sera attrapé, il sera arrêté et sanctionné. Le nombre précis des victimes sera connu dans les jours qui viennent.

15-6   1. Le voleur est déjà connu de la police. 2. Mon sac à dos a été volé par un voyou. 3. Notre secrétaire sera toujours appréciée de tout le monde. 4. Nous avons été punis par le professeur. 5. Cet homme est respecté (estimé) de tous. 6. Le président Kennedy était très admiré des Français.

15-7   1. Elle n'a pas été invitée. 2. Ils seront licenciés. 3. La date limite sera reportée (repoussée) d'une semaine. 4. La boutique vient d'être fermée. 5. Ce roman a été écrit par Balzac. 6. Le président va être élu par les Français. 7. Impossible 8. Impossible 9. Une récompense leur a été promise. 10. De nombreux vols on été annulés. 11. L'émission de télévision a été interrompue. 12. Elle a été agressée par un inconnu.

15-8   1. De nouvelles chutes de neige sont attendues dans la soirée. 2. Impossible 3. Impossible 4. Le chat a été écrasé par un autobus. 5. Impossible 6. L'avion a été détourné par des terroristes. 7. Les cartes de crédit ne sont pas acceptées dans ce restaurant. 8. La manifestation a été interdite. 9. Les paroles de cette chanson ont été écrites par le chanteur. 10. Trois personnes ont été prises en otage. 11. Le proviseur a été frappé par un élève. 12. Impossible

15-9   1. La police nous a demandé de partir. 2. On nous a demandé de partir. 3. On a répondu à la question. 4. Le professeur a répondu à la question. 5. On leur a promis un bon salaire 6. Le patron leur a promis un bon salaire. 7. On lui a permis de rester. 8. On nous a menti. 9. On se souviendra d'elle. 10. Est-ce qu'on vous a donné un avertissement? 11. On enseigne le chinois dans ces lycées. 12. On nous a conseillé de rester à la maison.

15-10 1. Ces voitures se vendent comme des petits pains. 2. Cela (Ça) ne se fait plus. 3. Le vin blanc se boit frais. 4. Le portugais se parle au Brésil. 5. Comment (est-ce que) ça s'écrit? 6. Ça s'écrit comme ça se prononce.

15-11 1. faux 2. vrai 3. faux 4. vrai 5. vrai 6. vrai 7. vrai 8. vrai (probablement!)

15-12 Jeanne d'Arc et la Guerre de Cent Ans. C'est le début du quinzième siècle. Une grande partie de la France est occupée par les Anglais. Est-ce que la France va devenir anglaise? Les Français attendent un miracle. C'est à ce moment-là que Jeanne d'Arc apparaît. Des voix lui avaient dit de sauver son pays. Elle quitte donc sa ville natale pour aller voir le roi Charles. Quelques paysans qui ont pitié d'elle lui offrent un cheval. Elle a beaucoup de mal à convaincre Charles de sa mission. Mais à la fin, on lui donne les soldats dont elle a besoin. Beaucoup de Français pensent qu'elle est envoyée par Dieu. La ville d'Orléans est libérée, et le roi couronné à Reims, grâce à Jeanne d'Arc. Après le sacre, Jeanne continue à se battre. Quand elle essaie de prendre Paris, elle est blessée. Ensuite, elle est trahie, faite prisonnière et accusée de sorcellerie. Elle est interrogée par des juges qui sont convaincus qu'elle est inspirée par le diable. À la fin du procès, elle est condamnée à mort. Elle n'a que dix-neuf ans lorsqu'elle est brûlée vive à Rouen en 1421. Aujourd'hui, Jeanne d'Arc est la Sainte Patronne de la France.